Disabling Barriers – Enabling Environments

Also published by
SAGE Publications
in association with
The Open University

Death, Dying and Bereavement

edited by Donna Dickenson and Malcolm Johnson

Health, Welfare and Practice: Reflecting on Roles and Relationships

edited by Jan Walmsley, Jill Reynolds, Pam Shakespeare and Ray Woolfe

All three books are Course Readers for the Open University Diploma in Health and Social Welfare.

Details of the Diploma and the related courses are available from The Information Officer, Department of Health and Social Welfare, The Open University, Walton Hall, Milton Keynes MK7 6AA, UK.

Disabling Barriers – Enabling Environments

edited by

John Swain, Vic Finkelstein, Sally French and Mike Oliver

in association
with The Open University

SAGE Publications
London • Thousand Oaks • New Delhi

First published 1993. Reprinted 1994, 1996, 1997

SAGE Publications Ltd
6 Bonhill Street
London EC2A 4PU

SAGE Publications Inc
2455 Teller Road
Thousand Oaks, California 91320

SAGE Publications India Pvt Ltd
32, M-Block Market
Greater Kailash – I
New Delhi 110 048

British Library Cataloguing in Publication Data

A catalogue record for this book is available from the British Library.

ISBN 0–8039 8824–9
ISBN 0–8039 8825–7 (pbk)

Library of Congress catalog card number 92–050881

Typeset by Type Study, Scarborough
Printed in Great Britain by The Cromwell Press Ltd,
Broughton Gifford, Melksham, Wiltshire

Contents

Acknowledgements

The editors and publishers wish to thank the following for permission to use copyright material.

Basil Blackwell Ltd for material from Sally French (1988) 'Experiences of disabled health and caring professionals', *Sociology of Health and Illness*, Vol. 10, No. 2, pp. 170–88;

Carfax Publishing Company for material from Jan Walmsley (1991) 'Talking to top people: some issues relating to the citizenship of people with learning difficulties', *Disability, Handicap & Society*, Vol. 6, No. 3, pp. 219–31; Mike Oliver (1989) 'Conductive education: if it wasn't so sad it would be funny', *Disability, Handicap & Society*, Vol. 4, No. 2, pp. 197–200; and Virginia Beardshaw (1989) 'Conductive education: a rejoinder', *Disability, Handicap & Society*, Vol. 4, No. 3, pp. 297–99;

Ken Davis for material from (1990) 'The crafting of good clients', *Coalition*, Sept., pp. 5–9;

Falmer Press Ltd for material from Mike Oliver (1989) 'Disability and dependency: a creation of industrial societies?' in *Disability and Dependency*, ed. L. Barton;

Institute for Public Policy Research for material from Mike Oliver and Colin Barnes (1991) 'Discrimination, disability and welfare: from needs to rights' in *Equal Rights for Disabled People*;

Jessica Kingsley Publishers for material from Vic Finkelstein (1991) 'Disability: an administrative challenge?' from *Social Work: Disabled People and Disabling Environments*, ed. Mike Oliver;

J. G. Kyle for material from Maggie Woolley (1987) 'Acquired hearing loss: acquired oppression' in *Adjustment to Acquired Hearing Loss*, Bristol: Centre for Deaf Studies, School of Education;

Philip Mason for material from Elizabeth Briggs 'Liz's Story' in *Project 81: One Step On*;

The Open University for Jenny Morris (1992) 'Housing, independent living and physically disabled people' and 'Prejudice'; Vic Finkelstein and Sally French (1992) 'Towards a psychology of disability'; Sally French (1992)

'Disability, impairment or something in between?'; and Vic Finkelstein (1992) 'The commonality of disability'

Research, Policy and Planning for material from Mike Oliver (1987) 'Redefining disability: some issues for research', *Research, Policy and Planning*, No. 5, pp. 9–13;

Royal National Institute for the Blind for material from Sally French (1991) 'What's so great about independence?' in *New Beacon*, Vol. 75, No. 886, pp. 153–6;

Therapy Weekly for material from Sally French (1991) 'Setting a record straight', *Therapy Weekly*, Vol. 18, No. 1, p. 4.

Every effort has been made to trace all the copyright holders, but if any have been inadvertently overlooked the publishers will be pleased to make the necessary arrangement at the first opportunity.

Notes on contributors

Paul Abberley is a senior lecturer in sociology at Bristol Polytechnic. He has contributed a number of papers to the growing literature in disability studies and is currently carrying out research into the ideology and practice of occupational therapy and its relationship to clients' wishes and needs. He is a member of the Avon Coalition of Disabled people.

Colin Barnes is well known as a disabled person active in disability organisations, notably the Integration Alliance (an organisation promoting inclusive education). He studied special educational needs at a teacher training college in Huddersfield and currently teaches in the Department of Social Policy and Sociology at Leeds University. He is also a researcher for the British Council of Organisations of Disabled People.

Virginia Beardshaw is Director of the Kings' Fund London Initiative. She is also Chair of the Bloomsbury Community Health Council and writes regularly on community care and health service issues.

Liz Briggs was a resident of a Cheshire Home before becoming a founder member of the Hampshire Centre for Independent Living. She is also a member of the Hampshire Coalition of Disabled People and Muscle Power (a group of adults with neuro-muscular impairments).

Mairian Corker, who is herself deaf, worked for the Deaf Children Society for some years and has a particular interest in the education of hearing impaired children and adults. She is known for her writing on deaf issues and has contributed to several Open University courses in this area.

Ken Davis is a leading figure in the emancipation activities of disabled people in Derbyshire where he was a founder member of both the Derbyshire Coalition and the Derbyshire Centre for Integrated Living. His work and writing is also widely recognised in national and international organisations of disabled people.

Vic Finkelstein is a former senior clinical psychologist in the health service. He has been associated with the Open University courses in disability studies since they were first presented in 1975, and is now Senior Lecturer in the Department of Health and Social Welfare. He has been involved in a number of organisations of disabled people, and was the first chairperson of the British Council of Organisations of Disabled People.

Sally French is a disabled person currently working as a lecturer in the

Department of Health and Social Welfare at The Open University. She is a qualified physiotherapist and also has higher degrees in psychology and sociology. She has taught psychology, sociology and disability studies to health workers for a number of years, and is an active researcher and writer in this field.

John Harrison recently retired from the National Health Service after 26 years as a consultant physician in Birmingham, during which disability became his special interest. Since 1984 he has been among a group of doctors working for the Royal College of Physicians of London, with the aim of promoting appropriate medical involvement in disability and rehabilitation.

Frances Hasler is currently Director of the Greater London Association of Disabled People (GLAD). Previously she worked in the National Health Service before joining the Spinal Injuries Association for five years as the Welfare Development Officer. She then worked for the Islington Association of Disabled People as Organiser for four and a half years. She has written on welfare and disability.

David Hevey has become well known following his contribution to several photographic exhibitions concerned with disability. He studied Fine Art Painting at Brighton Polytechnic before deciding to become an issue-based photographer working with disability representation. His clients have included the Trades Union movement, local authorities, the United Nations and the disability movement.

Marisa Lawton worked as a social worker in Prudhoe Hospital before becoming the Co-ordinator of a leisure project for disabled people financed by the voluntary sector. After two years with the project she has joined a social work team working with children in the community.

Joy Lenny is currently studying psychology and counselling at Roehampton Institute of Higher Education. She is a trained counsellor and previously worked for the Spinal Injuries Association.

Jenny Morris is a disabled feminist and freelance writer/researcher. She taught housing policy and sociology for six years before giving up the struggle against disablism within her workplace. She now puts her energies into research and writing which gives a voice to disabled people.

Elspeth Morrison is the editor of *Disability Arts in London* (DAIL) magazine. She is Chair of the Graeae Theatre Company, Britain's oldest professional company of disabled performers, and has written extensively on theatre and film representation and disability. She is also a well-known performer on the disability arts cabaret circuit.

Mike Oliver is Professor in Disability Studies at the University of Greenwich. He has written extensively on issues related to social work and disability, having previously lectured in social work at the University of Kent and worked as a development officer for Kent Social Services. He is active in the disability movement and is a former member of the Management Committee of the Spinal Injuries Association.

Gillian Parker is an assistant director and senior research fellow at the Social Policy Research Unit, University of York. Her research career has spanned many fields including education, primary health care and consumer credit and debit. Over the past 10 years, however, she has been involved in empirical research almost exclusively in the fields of disability and informal care.

Alan Roulstone is a postgraduate research student in the Department of Health and Social Welfare at the Open University researching employment experiences of disabled people using new technology. He has previous research experience in the field of the social aspects of technological change and has lectured in sociology and employment studies at Staffordshire Polytechnic.

Louise Silburn is a Keele University graduate in English and sociology. Following a period working for the Spastics Society in Manchester she moved to Derbyshire where she helped to set up and manage the Derbyshire Centre for Integrated Living. After three years she has taken the philosophy of Integrated Living to North Derbyshire Health Authority. She now runs a service for brain injured people in Sheffield for the AMI Health Care Group.

Ossie Stuart is currently an ethnic relations researcher at St Antony's College, Oxford University. Prior to taking up this post in 1989 he completed a Doctoral thesis on social protest movements in colonial Zimbabwe. He has also been closely involved with organisations concerned with issues important to disabled people.

John Swain contributed to the production of the Open University course, *The Handicapped Person in the Community*, as a course team member. He has written extensively, particularly on issues concerning learning difficulty, and is currently a lecturer at the University of Northumbria at Newcastle. He has completed a research project on the participation in decision-making of young people with special education needs.

Jan Walmsley is a course manager in the Department of Health and Social Welfare at The Open University. She has worked on three Open University courses in the field of learning disabilities and is currently undertaking research with people with learning disabilities which will, she hopes, contribute to a re-evaluation of their contribution to society.

Maggie Woolley is Director of the arts development agency Shape London. She is a graduate of Glasgow University (Department of Film, Theatre and Television) and has previously worked as a drama producer with the BBC Television programme 'See Hear!' before returning to the arts.

Gerry Zarb is a senior research fellow at the Policy Studies Institute. He has worked on several research projects on disability issues and consumer perspectives on health and social services, and is the author of the first major study on ageing and disability in the UK.

Introduction

Disabling Barriers – Enabling Environments recognises that any radical change in the prospects for a better quality of life for disabled people has been coming in the past 10 years from one direction: disabled people have taken the initiative. They have done so with the support of some non-disabled people, as is evident from various papers in this collection, who have supported disabled people's active participation in, and control over, their own lives.

This 'thrust of change' is clearly reflected in this Reader which aims to:

- increase knowledge about the more active role that disabled people are playing in the community and how this can be supported
- develop a greater understanding of the experiences and situation of disabled people from their own perspective
- further the involvement of disabled people in controlling their own lives through the development of an understanding of citizenship and empowerment.

The majority of the papers selected for this Reader are written by disabled people, and all directly focus on the control by disabled people of the services, policy and decision-making which shapes and determines their quality of life. We believe that this Reader makes a significant contribution to the growing literature by disabled people as they begin to write their own history, create their own images in literature and art, and develop their own theories of 'disability' which reflect their experiences and vested interests. It is, then, part of a long tradition of literature emanating from the experiences of marginalised groups, including black people and women, as they have pursued social and political change.

At this point we need to address a question which seems to arise in all substantial contributions to the field of disability: which 'disabilities' and 'disabled people' is the book about? While we can say that most of the examples drawn on in the papers in this volume concentrate on people with physical or sensory impairments, as editors we reject the assumptions behind this question. The categorisations asked for emanate from the very perspectives that are questioned in this book – that is, categorisations of people based on conceptions of disability as an individual or medical problem. Our focus is on, not categories of people, but rather their experiences of social barriers to full participative citizenship.

Finally we would like to make explicit the main assumptions underlying the compiling of this Reader.

- The title, *Disabling Barriers – Enabling Environments*, sets the scene at its most basic for the debates within the chapters of this book. From the viewpoint of disabled people, 'disability' is imposed on them by 'disabling barriers' and the independence they seek is in 'enabling environments': the barriers can best be understood from the viewpoint of disabled people and changing environments through barrier removal should be controlled by disabled people.
- Disability is not a condition of the individual. The experiences of disabled people are of social restrictions in the world around them, not of being a person with a 'disabling condition'. This is not to deny that individuals experience 'disability'; rather it is to assert that the individual's experience of 'disability' is created in interactions with a physical and social world designed for non-disabled living.
- From the viewpoint of disabled people, the focus becomes the barriers faced in a society geared by and for able-bodied people; barriers which exclude disabled people from full active citizenship. These barriers can permeate every aspect of the physical and social environment: attitudes, institutions, language and culture, organisation and delivery of support services, and the power relations and structures of which society is constituted.
- This definition of 'disability' builds on and furthers the growing orientation which has been developed in the writings emanating from active groups of disabled people in this country, particularly from the early 1970s. Arguments over definitions are often reduced to supposedly technical purposes, but they are in effect part of the struggle to establish and legitimise one way of thinking over another.
- The crucial factor in 'enabling environments' is the control by disabled people of their own lives and their participation in the community. The transformation of power relations is fundamental to overcoming disabling barriers and establishing enabling environments. This involves the establishment of equal opportunities and support for the emancipation of oppressed groups within society.

Section 1: Perspectives from the editors

Section 1 is a selection of papers by the editors. These papers show the growth of the new social approach, not as an alternative model to be set alongside other academic analyses, but as a way of understanding that has grown out of the lived experience of injustice and growing collective identity of disabled people.

The papers here provide a detailed exposition of the orientation taken in the Reader. Section 1 sets the scene by providing the reader with a kind of conceptual map and compass with which to explore subsequent sections of the Reader. It also makes explicit the perspectives of the editors. Finally, it seems appropriate to note that three of the editors are themselves disabled people and have contributed to the growing collective voice of disabled people in defining their own needs and taking control of the decision-making which determines their lives.

The first four papers address models and definitions of disability, approaching the issues from different directions. Vic Finkelstein's paper (1.1) argues that disabled people, through their shared experiences of social and physical barriers, have become a distinctive minority social group in modern societies. This is one of the conclusions of the social model of disability. Sally French (1.2) contributes to the debates by drawing on direct experiences of disability. She argues that discussions within the social model should be intensified and broadened to ensure that experiences of all disabled people are encompassed, recognised and confronted. The following paper, by Vic Finkelstein and Sally French (1.3), questions psychological perspectives which focus solely on individual adjustment and functioning. Such perspectives have more to do with gatekeeping of resources and service provision than contributing to the attainment of full citizenship and integrated living. In the fourth paper, Vic Finkelstein (1.4) presents some of the main issues in constructing a social model of disability. He documents the anger of disabled people and the growth of their collective response to the denial of their rights to full participative citizenship.

The following two papers raise a recurring theme in discussions of the meaning of disability, that is the concept of 'dependency'. Sally French's paper (1.5) tackles the issues at the level of direct experience and argues that the over-emphasis on independence is counter-productive and contributes to the maintenance of social restrictions faced by disabled people. Mike Oliver (1.6) takes a broader historical and sociological perspective to question the whole notion of 'dependency' and its role in defining the meaning of disability. In particular he examines the influence of social policy responses to disability and argues that they create rather than reduce dependency.

In the final paper (1.7), Mike Oliver turns his critical eye on to research in the field of disability and examines its failure to address or contribute to changing conceptions of disability.

Section 2: In our own image

The central feature of 'disabling barriers' is the lack of say that disabled people have in their lives and in society. Barriers are faced by disabled people in a physical and social environment which is created by and for able-bodied people. Disabling images, themselves created and controlled by able-bodied people, are essentially founded on concepts of dependency and associated categories defined by professionals as gatekeepers of services and support.

Images of disability, defined by the collective democratic voice of disabled people, have been constructed in direct opposition to those of dependency and individual tragedy. The essential heart of such images is the active involvement of disabled people in controlling the decision-making processes which shape their lives. This, then, is the prime focus of the papers in this section: the creation of images of disability and, in particular, the power they reflect and entail for disabled people.

The section opens with two personal accounts of the images of disability. The first, by Sally French (2.1), focuses on the pressures that disabled people face to deny their experiences and their reality of disability, and to conform to the prejudices and images imposed by others. Maggie Woolley (2.2) speaks of the growth of self-confidence and self-affirmation of identity that disabled people experience in the community and culture of disabled people, in this particular instance in the Deaf community.

The next group of papers shifts the focus from the experience of individuals to the analysis of barriers faced by disabled people in realising full participative citizenship. Jenny Morris (2.3) provides a broader-based examination of the social construction of both gender roles and disability and the interrelationship between the two from a feminist perspective. Ossie Stuart (2.4) argues that the multiple discrimination faced by black disabled people is not only a unique social experience but a challenge within the community of disabled people to rethink its attitudes on race and discrimination.

The next two papers take up a key theme in discussions of images of disabled people – that is, concepts of 'normal' and 'abnormal'. Jenny Morris (2.5) tackles this in an exploration of prejudice and disabled people's experiences of non-disabled people's reactions to difference. She seeks to challenge assumptions about normality through the celebration of difference generated from the experiences of disabled people. Paul Abberley's paper (2.6) presents a much broader social and historical analysis to show how accounts of abnormality within dominant theoretical perspectives have sustained and furthered the material disadvantage faced by disabled people. He advocates accounts of abnormality which address the economic dimension of disablement and the failure of society to meet the needs of disabled people as they define them. The final papers in this section (2.7 and 2.8) concentrate on the personal and public images of disability and the creation of stereotypes in the portrayal of disabled people by non-disabled people in advertising and the media generally. Disabled people, it is argued, are surrounded by images which do not reflect their experiences of disabling environments.

Section 3: Controlling lifestyles

The disabling barriers analysed in Section 3 are those which deny equal opportunities, deny rights and find their ultimate realisation in the segregation of disabled people from the community. 'Enabling' is again crucially dependent on the control of disabled people in their day-to-day lives in the community and the papers in this section are essentially concerned with the integration and participation of disabled people within the community.

As in the previous section we begin with a personal account. The first paper (3.1) describes the anxieties and triumphs of Liz Briggs, a disabled woman, as we follow her move from residential accommodation into her own home.

The first requirement of disabled people in participating as equal citizens within the community is a home which is suited to them, together with control over the necessary help they require to live independently. This is what Jenny Morris (3.2) addresses: the policies, access and support required by disabled people for integrated living.

The following three papers focus on education. Mairian Corker (3.3) identifies the key barriers to the true integration of deaf pupils within mainstream schools as the separation of special education policy from mainstream education policy. Policy-making decisions, she argues, are in the hands of non-disabled people and thus provide no basis for equal access to education for all. Reporting on a piece of qualitative research, John Swain (3.4) looks at the idea that disabled people could have a greater say in educational decision-making within schools. This paper essentially concerns the possibility that such active involvement of young disabled people in their own interests could provide a basis for the development of confidence and identity as disabled adults who join the struggle for broader social change. The next paper (3.5), comprising an article and a rejoinder, addresses the topic of conductive education. It presents two radically different views. Mike Oliver argues that conductive education is an oppressive system which attempts to engineer conformity to able-bodied 'normality'. Virginia Beardshaw, on the other hand, argues that the approaches used in Britain are, by contrast, oppressive by virtue of being ineffective.

Colin Barnes's paper (3.6) is taken from a study of day-centre provision for young disabled adults. He argues that higher levels of participation and control by those who use the day centres could only be realised through 'radical reformulation of internal policies that clarify the social and rehabili-tative function of the centres'.

Marisa Lawton (3.7) describes a project aimed at the developing opportuni-ties in 'leisure choice' for disabled people. The paper documents the small but significant steps taken in shifting the control and responsibility for the work of the project to those who are actually going to take up these choices.

Finally in this section, Gerry Zarb (3.8) writes about the experiences and issues of concern to one of the largest sectors of the disabled community: older disabled people who are noticing the effects of ageing.

Section 4: In charge of support and help

The fourth section turns to the help and support provided for and by disabled people. Disabling barriers here are those faced by disabled people within the service-providers' models (such as the medical model) for understanding, planning and evaluating services, and the understanding of disability in which these are grounded. The paper by Ken Davis (4.1) presents a radical critique of disability professionals and the whole professionalised system of help and support. The 'partnership' advocated here is that with non-disabled supporters of disabled people, to enable disabled people to participate in and control the policies and decision-making which shape and determine their lives.

The following paper (4.2), by Sally French, extends the dimensions of the debate about help and support. She provides valuable details of the experiences of disabled people in employment, and the paper counters simplistic notions of the relationship between disabled people and professionals, being about disabled professionals. As Sally French argues, disabled professionals 'might well undermine traditional professional values and beliefs'.

The remaining articles in this section have been selected to provide a critique of the theory and practice of professional support and as pointers to the creation of enabling environments. The next two papers tackle the still dominant medical model of disability. The first (4.3) is by a medical doctor, John Harrison, who argues that medicine and disability are inextricably linked and proceeds to consider some of the criticisms of medical approaches. He suggests that there are grounds for optimism and that medical professionals are beginning to recognise the views of disabled people. Louise Silburn's paper (4.4) takes this further by documenting some of the changes that are required of workers if they are to effectively support disabled people in participating in and controlling decision-making processes.

Sally French (4.5) looks first at the whole intervention process as inherent within and determined by a recording system. She shows how innovations which at first sight might appear to contribute to the effectiveness of services can reduce creative thinking and even reinforce the powerlessness of disabled people. Joy Lenny (4.6) argues on a positive note by advocating the use of person-centred counselling in creating enabling environments. Alan Roulstone (4.7) draws on his research to look at the potential of new technology to enable barrier-free employment environments. In the final paper Gillian Parker (4.8) discusses problems in caring relationships and identifies signs of more optimistic approaches to conflicts of interest in the provision of 'care'.

Section 5: Creating a society fit for all

Section 5 contains papers in which analysis is undertaken at the broadest, societal, level.

To create environments is to create full democratic participation in shaping society. The papers here explore the different strategies to be found within the disability movement, particularly the demand for civil rights legislation. So the Reader concludes by focusing on the democratic voice and struggle of disabled people for emancipation and equality in creating a physical and social environment fit for all.

The first two papers take the debate from 'needs' to 'rights'. Jan Walmsley (5.1) discusses the citizenship of people with learning difficulties, examining the barriers to exercising citizenship rights and outlining ways forward to the establishment of full participative citizenship for all. One possibility for action she mentions is the specific focus of the paper by Mike Oliver and Colin Barnes (5.2) – that is, anti-discrimination legislation. They explain why disabled people are demanding legal protection which would: empower them in their struggle for equal rights and against discrimination; provide a basis for enforcing service delivery; and establish mechanisms for professional accountability.

The final two papers concentrate on one of the major themes within this Reader: the dramatic development of the disability movement in Britain since the early 1980s. Frances Hasler (5.3) documents the increasing confidence of disabled people in constructing a political movement, developing their counter-arguments to dominant 'personal tragedy' thinking, and pressing for the development of services which are responsive to their self-defined needs. Finally, Ken Davis (5.4) provides a valuable history of the development of the disability movement in Britain. Disabled people are, indeed, engaged in writing their own history and creating their own future.

Disabling Barriers – Enabling Environments is the Course Reader for the Open University Course *K665 The Disabling Society*.

SECTION 1: PERSPECTIVES FROM THE EDITORS

1.1

The commonality of disability

Vic Finkelstein

Introduction

How a disabled person sees her or himself may not only affect the way problems that they face are identified but also influence the way help offered by others is accepted or rejected. Seeing oneself as suffering because of an impaired body or function could lead to demands for assistance to become as 'normal' as possible. On the other hand, if discrimination is seen as causing the difficulties then help aimed at providing equal opportunities could be the preferred option. How disabled people identify themselves, then, can be very important in developing intervention strategies for services as well as helping them to help themselves. The question is, what is this identity?

The growth of new organisations of disabled people during the past two decades has been compared to the development of the black and feminist movements for civil rights (especially in the USA) (see Oliver, 1984; Abberley, 1986; Driedger, 1989; Morris, 1991). However, in focusing on civil rights as a common feature of race, gender and disability discrimination it may be forgotten that each form of discrimination also has its own unique characteristics.

If, for example, an operation was introduced which transformed black people into white or women into men then discrimination could no longer be based upon skin colour or gender. However, in the first place such an operation would be universally rejected by these groups. Second, in the case of race, other features such as culture would replace skin colour as the new focus for discrimination;[1] or in the case of gender, success would lead to human extinction. Regarding race and gender, therefore, physical intervention like surgery on individuals could never be a route to the end of

This paper is based upon the ideas developed in V. Finkelstein (1990) '"We" are not disabled, "you" are', in S. Gregory and G. Hartley (eds) *Constructing Deafness*, Pinter, London/The Open University, Milton Keynes.

discrimination against these groups. This argument does not seem to apply equally well to the removal of discrimination against people who have an impairment of body or function.

First, very many disabled people would welcome physical interventions which *guarantee* elimination of an impairment. This is surely demonstrated by the continuing attraction of rehabilitation programmes to return function; support for research into modifying multiple sclerosis, epilepsy or spinal injury, etc.; the frequency of corrective surgery (such as removal of cataracts) and use of equipment to approximate normal behaviour (such as hearing and walking aids). Even disability organisations sceptical about experiments to make disabled people 'normal' do not campaign against the prospect of eliminating impairment. Parent agitation for 'conductive education',[2] which aims at developing normal behaviour in children who have an impairment (cerebral palsy), has no parallel amongst other groups struggling against discrimination. It is inconceivable, for example, to imagine a similar approach being supported by black parents to make their children white or parents and the government supporting systems to make their daughters into boys. Second, interventions which eliminate impairment not only remove the focus of the discrimination but cannot be replaced with another way of identifying the *same* group for continuing discrimination (as racial prejudice can shift from ethnic to cultural, religious or geographic origin).

A negative reality, negative attitudes

If people with significant hearing, visual, motor or learning impairments are disabled during their day-to-day encounter with a social and physical world designed for able-bodied living then their shared experience could lead to a common identity. This suggests that people with hearing impairments, for example, may have more in common with other disability groups than with other language-oppressed groups. This is not to deny that all oppressed groups share some common features. However, I believe disabled people's difficulties are best understood by looking at the link between body impairment and discrimination against people who have these impairments.

The reason why few individuals would willingly identify themselves as disabled until recently is not immediately obvious. Perhaps this has to do with the general confusion of disability as a synonym for physical impairment (with negative associations) and as a term for those who suffer discrimination. The universal instinct of disabled people to separate their experience of discrimination (which should be opposed) from the experience of living with a body impairment (which has to be managed) may explain the general reservation about identifying oneself with a term which confuses both states.

However, it may seem a mystery why, if most people who have bodily impairments, such as spinal injury or cerebral palsy, object to the label 'disabled', it has been so difficult to stop the use of the term or find an accepted alternative. The term, 'person with a disability', for example, not only still refers to disability but cannot be distinguished from the label 'person with an impairment'. Replacing one label with another while the day-to-day reality of disability remains unchanged seems to be an exercise in changing fashions, even adding more confusion to the relationship between impairment and disability.

All this suggests that there might be good reasons why many people remain opposed to the term 'disabled'. If despite all efforts attitudes are persistently negative, then we need to question the assumption that ignorance or misunderstanding leads to negative attitudes. On the contrary, perhaps there is some sense in negative attitudes towards disabled people because this reflects the actual negative status of disabled people in society.

Regardless of what disabled people like to think about themselves, then, as long as their unfavourable situation continues people will be likely to see disability in a negative light. One set of facts immediately stands out when we look at the situation of disabled people. Government statistics (see, for example, Office of Population Censuses and Surveys, 1988), independent research projects (Barnes, 1991) and personal experiences,[3] show that on nearly every indicator of participation in mainstream life disabled people come out extremely badly; for example on employment statistics, income levels, suitable housing and access to public transport, buildings, information (newspapers, radio and television) and leisure facilities. Being disabled, then, has clear negative implications.

The marginalisation of disabled people

If we look at history it should be possible to identify a process which led to the isolation of people with physical and mental impairments from their communities and created their present negative status.

Contemporary literature over the centuries shows that although people with physical and mental impairments have always had a low status in society they have, nevertheless, also lived in periods when they are publicly visible in their communities (as is still the case in many third world countries). The 'cripple' begging in the street or the deaf person working in some menial job were still members of a community. The public disappearance of cripples was a lengthy process which involved increasing acceptance of 'normality' as a criterion for social integration.

A case in point is the way that signing as a means of communication for deaf people was suppressed. That this may have been suddenly opposed may be historically true (see Ladd, 1991), but how are we to explain this change in attitude? In other words, despite their wishes what conditions led to the disablement of people who use signing as their means of communication? I believe that the meaning of disability is determined by the way our society is organised.[4] In this respect the decision to oppress sign language would not only be socially determined but also the meaning of deafness to the general public. If the social situation of deaf people is disabling (because auditory methods dominate all communication) then deafness will be considered as a disability regardless of what deaf people want. The only way to change this interpretation would be to remove the barriers to non-auditory communication.

One view, first raised in Finkelstein (1980), is that the predominant factor contributing to the disablement of different groups is the way in which people can participate in the creation of social wealth. For example, at a time when small-scale manufacture was carried out in the individual home, or when transport was individualised with the horse and cart, or when products were exchanged in small stalls in the market-place, then there might have been some scope for these activities to be carried out by people of different shapes and sizes. Being deaf or having a club foot and working a hand loom at home could be a viable means of livelihood.

However, the invention of the steam engine led to the introduction of more efficient machinery than, say, the home-based hand loom. But the new machinery of the industrial revolution had to be worked not by a specific individual but by an unknown 'average' person who might be hired off the street (that is, the 'hands'). People who deviated from this 'norm' were likely to become unemployed as more and more machinery was introduced into the productive processes. Operating increasingly sophisticated machinery also meant that potential workers had to be able to follow instructions designed for 'normal' workers (that is, oral and sometimes complicated written instructions).

Under these conditions it seems clear that the increasing dominance of large-scale manufacture created conditions which progressively raised the importance of 'normality' as well as the importance of designing machinery, buildings and transport systems to places of employment for normal people. Being normal, then, became a dominant criterion for employment in industrial societies and this would have encouraged the suppression of non-normal behaviour, such as the use of signing for communication, or the exclusion of those who could not see or walk.

Where this led to certain groups of people being marginalised from productive life, then they would have had no alternative except to beg and rely on charity.

Managing the marginalised

Undoubtedly this led to large numbers of beggars and made a policy for their removal a necessity. Once the process of removing these unemployed from the community was well under way (into alms houses and later into large institutions), then there must have been pressure to provide food and shelter *only* for those who were regarded as unable to work because of impairment.

From this perspective it became necessary to separate the unemployed into two categories: the infirm and the indolent (thieves, vagabonds, the so-called lazy, etc.). This need for classification would have enabled diagnostic experts (doctors) to secure a special role in relation to the infirm. I believe that doctors taking on this administrative task marked the beginning of classifying and interpreting disability in medical terms. Once disabled people are defined as unemployable it seems logical for the medical experts to concentrate attention on ways of making them 'normal', or as normal as possible. If disabled people could be rehabilitated and work machinery designed for normal people then they might cease being dependent upon charity and state handouts. This approach would have encouraged the growth of different professional interventions and the provision of specialist aids for different disability groups. To facilitate this, clearer classification would be needed to separate people who are mentally ill, blind, deaf, or have learning difficulties, etc. By the middle of the twentieth century all disabled people were being routinely classified and registered by many different agencies according to medically defined categories.

Once treatments (such as physiotherapy), special services (such as pro-vision of hearing aids) and specific benefits (such as mobility allowance) multiplied, the need to sharpen boundaries between categories of 'disability' became increasingly important and in the 1970s and 1980s there was a rapid increase in disability scales and measures. Disabled people, of course, played very little part in this process (although some organisations campaigning for financial benefits, such as the Disablement Income Group, needed to provide their own categories of people who would be eligible for the benefits that they were seeking).

Defying the label, denying the reality?

Regardless of personal wishes, therefore, being labelled as disabled is a fact of life for all disabled people in the contemporary world. As long a there is no possibility of gaining access to services or social and welfare benefits without surrendering to the label 'disabled' there will be no possibility of maintaining that an individual or group is not disabled. The use of equipment such as wheelchairs, or forms of communication such as braille and signing, not used by 'normal' people, only confirms the user as a disabled person.

In these circumstances, if being called disabled is thought to inhibit employment prospects and a better social status, there could be an incentive to distance possession of the particular condition from those thought to be lower down the scale. This, it is falsely believed, frees the individual, or group, to consider themselves as only a variation in the pattern of normality while the others, lower down the scale, can be regarded as really disabled. For example, people with spinal injuries may see themselves as normal (restricted only by barriers which limit wheelchair mobility – that is, they are mobility oppressed) whilst those with learning difficulties are regarded as 'really' disabled. Similarly, people with hearing impairments may think of themselves as normal (restricted only by barriers to British Sign Language as a form of communication – that is, they are language-oppressed) whilst those with a spinal injury are regarded as 'really' disabled!

Assumed levels of employability separate disabled people into different levels of dependency, and this, in turn, can lead to different types of services and provisions. At the bottom, those regarded as hopelessly unemployable are offered places in residential homes where they can have total care, whereas those who can work may have access to special equipment and adaptations funded by the state. Ranking disabled people according to degree of employability provides another context for disabled people to constantly fear that they may become associated with those that they see as less employable and more dependent. By trying to distance themselves from groups that they perceive as more disabled than themselves they can hope to maintain their claim to economic independence and an acceptable status within the community.

Subjective and objective factors in the lives of disabled people, then, constantly interact and encourage them to distance themselves from each other, denying that they are disabled while defining others with this label. When one group of people with a particular form of impairment (such as hearing impairment) see themselves as fitting into the normal range (for example their language is oppressed but they are not disabled) while at the same time they view people who have different impairments as disabled, they are attributing medical labels to others in exactly the same way that they reject such labels for themselves!

Reclaiming control: self-empowerment

I believe that despite the preference of people with physical or mental impairments not to see themselves as disabled current approaches to services present the general public with a powerful image of disabled people as a unified, dependent population. These approaches can be regarded as the outcome of the administrative role given to medical practitioners in the care of disabled people. The growth of specialist professions and their publicly visible role as gate-keepers to medical, social and welfare services provides an effective reinforcement to the view that disability is a medical problem. The fact that being 'normal' is still very important for employment, promotion, and gaining an independent livelihood, means that the role of medicine in the lives of disabled people remains extremely significant.

Publicity for rehabilitation aimed at normalising disabled people's be-haviour or appearance (such as surgery to enable children with cerebral palsy to walk, or electronic implants to enable hearing in people with auditory impairments) confirm the public's attachment to the medical interpretation of disabled people's needs. The medical approach towards disabled people has been much discussed and criticized (see, for example, Oliver, 1981; Brisenden, 1986; British Psychological Society, 1989; Abberley, 1991) but it still dominates current legislation and provides the main criteria for defining categories of people who shall have access to services and benefits. The overriding political feature of interventions administered by medical practitioners is that it brings all disability groups together under a single medical interpretation of the cause behind their marginalised position in society (the medical model of disability).

Criticism of the medical model has led to changes, and there are increasing signs that services are moving away from medical control provided by the health service to social and welfare interventions provided in community services. The problem is, however, that this shift does not necessarily result in disabled people having greater control over their lives. On the contrary, community-based service providers generally have a wider perspective than their medical colleagues in identifying areas of disabled people's lives for their professional assessments and interventions. This may leave very little for disabled people to do without feeling that an expert is waiting in the background to intervene. The community worker is there to provide expert assessments and advice on nearly everything, from the architecture of the home, the whole range of equipment that all people need for modern living, to advice and counselling for intimate personal and sexual problems.

In this respect experts are often encouraged to see the lives of disabled people in terms of problems to be solved and their role as providing solutions. Nationally, then, the existence of large and expensive social and welfare services provides ample evidence that a characteristic of all disabled groups is that they face a series of problems which they cannot solve on their own and which the state has had to administer through the provision of specialised services. From this point of view disabled people are socially dysfunctional (in Miller and Gwynne's words they are 'socially dead'; Miller and Gwynne, 1972; see also Finkelstein, 1991). This could be called the administrative model of service intervention. In the first instance the medical profession was given this role when they were unable to 'cure' an individual's impairment. The shift towards community-based services is transferring the duty to other professionals without, however, changing the basic approach to intervening in the lives of disabled people.

It is this administrative approach to disability that draws different groups of disabled people together in the assessment forms for problem-solving and service provision. From this point of view disabled people can be identified as a distinct social group (with several disability sub-groups). Modern disability movements which bring together groups of disabled people and encourage a common identity not only reflect the growth of a united front against medical and administrative dominance but also represent an historical leap in redefining disability in positive terms. Those who enact helping interventions need to recognise that the changing meaning of disability provides a new context for the construction of services with disabled people on a quite different, dynamic understanding of disability.

Notes

1 See paper 2.4, by O. Stuart, in this Reader, where this interpretation is first applied to the discrimination faced by disabled people from ethnic minorities.

2 For a discussion on this approach see paper 3.5, by M. Oliver, in this Reader, and the rejoinder by V. Beardshaw. See also Finkelstein (1990).

3 The journals of local disability associations regularly contain personal accounts of difficulties in managing to negotiate the immediate environment, for example on inadequate access to local public transport.

4 Oliver has written extensively on this issue; see, for example, Oliver (1983).

References

Abberley, P. (1986) 'The concept of oppression and the development of a social theory of disability', *Disability, Handicap and Society*, Vol. 2, No. 1, pp. 5–19.

Abberley, P. (1991) 'Handicapped by Numbers: a Critique of the OPCS Disability Surveys', paper presented at the second of a series of disability research seminars. Policy Studies Institute, London, 2 March.

Barnes, C. (1991) *Disabled People in Britain and Discrimination: a Case for Anti-Discrimination Legislation*, Hurst, London.

Brisenden, S. (1986) 'Independent living and the medical model of disability', *Disability, Handicap and Society*, Vol. 1, No. 2, pp. 173–8.

British Psychological Society (1989) *Psychology and Disability in the National Health Service*, British Psychological Society, Leicester.

Driedger, D. (1989) *The Last Civil Rights Movement: Disabled Peoples' International*, Hurst, London.

Finkelstein, V. (1980) *Attitudes and Disability: Issues for Discussions*, World Rehabilitation Fund, New York.

Finkelstein, V. (1990) 'A tale of two cities', *Therapy Weekly*, 22 March, pp. 6–7.

Finkelstein, V. (1991) 'Disability: an administrative challenge? (The health and welfare heritage)', in Oliver, M. (ed.) *Social Work: Disabled People and Disabling Environments*, Jessica Kingsley, London.

Ladd, P. (1991) 'Language oppression and hearing impairment', in *Disability – Identity, Sexuality and Relationships*, The Open University, Milton Keynes.

Miller, E.J. and Gwynne, G.V. (1972) *A Life Apart*, Tavistock, London.

Morris, J. (1991) *Pride Against Prejudice: Transforming Attitudes to Disability*, The Women's Press, London.

Office of Population Censuses and Surveys (1988) Report 1: *The Prevalence of Disability Among Adults*; Report 2: *The Financial Circumstances of Disabled Adults Living in Private Households*; Report 4: *Disabled Adults: Services, Transport and Employment*, HMSO, London.

Oliver, M. (1981) 'Disability, adjustment and family life: some theoretical considerations', in Brechin, A., Liddiard, P. and Swain, J. (eds) *Handicap in a Social World*, Hodder and Stoughton, Sevenoaks/The Open University, Milton Keynes.

Oliver, M. (1983) *Social Work with Disabled People*, Macmillan, London.

Oliver, M. (1984) *The Politics of Disablement: a Socio-Political Approach*, Macmillan, London.

1.2

Disability, impairment or something in between?

Sally French

Oliver (1983) defines impairment as 'individual limitation' and disability as 'socially imposed restriction'. Finkelstein (1981) illustrates, in a rather amusing article, that if the physical and social world were adapted for wheelchair-users their disabilities would disappear and able-bodied people would become disabled. According to this model, blindness is an impairment but lack of access to written information is a disability – a socially determined state of affairs which could be solved by more extensive braille production, more money to pay for 'readers' and the greater use of taped material. Similarly, not being able to walk is an impairment but lack of mobility is a disability, a situation which is socially created and could be solved by the greater provision of electric wheelchairs, wider doorways and more ramps and lifts. This constitutes a social model of disability, where disability is viewed as a problem located within society rather than within individuals who happen to have impairments. Thus the way to reduce disability is to adjust the social and physical environment to ensure that the needs and rights of people with impairments are met, rather than attempting to change disabled people to fit the existing environment.

While I agree with the basic tenets of this model and consider it to be the most important way forward for disabled people, I believe that some of the most profound problems experienced by people with certain impairments are difficult, if not impossible, to solve by social manipulation. Viewing a mobility problem as caused by the presence of steps rather than by the inability to walk, or regarding the inability to access information as due to the lack of sign language rather than to a hearing impairment, is easy to comprehend. Examples such as these are frequently put forward when the social model of disability is being explained. However, various profound social problems that I encounter as a visually impaired person, which impinge upon my life far more than indecipherable notices or the lack of bleeper crossings, are more difficult to regard as entirely socially produced or amenable to social action. Such problems include my inability to recognise people, being nearly blinded when the sun comes out, and not being able to read non-verbal cues or emit them correctly.

On occasions I have made an effort to find social solutions to some of these problems. On moving to my present house 10 years ago, I informed several of my new neighbours that, because of my inability to recognise them, I would doubtless pass them by in the street without greeting them. One neighbour who had previously seen me striding confidently down the road, refused to believe me on the grounds that I looked fully sighted, but the others said they understood and would talk to me if our paths crossed. For the first couple of weeks it worked and I was surprised how often we met, but after that their greetings rapidly decreased and then ceased altogether. Why this happened I am not sure, but I suspect that my lack of recognition strained the interaction and limited the social reward they received from the encounter. For my part, my inability to see them approaching meant that I was inevitably jolted abruptly from my thoughts when they did speak, which as well as feeling unpleasant, affected the normality of my response. This, in turn, may well have deterred them from talking to me again. All in all, my attempt to manipulate the social environment was not a success, and although my situation does give rise to social isolation, I do not feel inclined to repeat the experiment. The difficulty I have described is not entirely due to my impairment, for it involves other people's responses, but neither is it easily modified by social or environmental manipulation; it occupies a middle ground.

Some people might argue that all that is required to resolve this type of situation is the education of the general public regarding visual disability, with a view to changing their attitudes – the social constructionist model of disability. Visual impairment is often far from obvious, however, and therefore, for this to be successful, every single person would need to be informed. Oliver's (1987) rejection of this model in favour of the social creation model of disability, also points out that disability awareness strategies have not been successful in bringing about change in people's attitudes or in the situation of disabled people. Similarly Finkelstein (1990) states that campaigns to change public attitudes towards disability have been 'remarkably unsuccessful'.

The difficulty of reading non-verbal cues pervades many aspects of the lives of people with visual impairments. One situation where it surfaced most markedly for me was in my role as a lecturer, when I was confronted with a large group of students. Again, I did my best to minimise the problem by telling them, quite openly, that I could not see sufficiently to respond to their non-verbal signs, and urging them to speak up and tell me if anything was amiss, or if they wanted to make any comments or ask questions. The students were always totally co-operative and the lectures went well enough, but in this situation I was socially distanced from the students, not really knowing how they felt and not being able to adjust my performance accordingly. If a student asked a question I was aware of not knowing where to look, which adversely affected the interaction, from my perspective at least.

It is true that to some extent non-verbal communication can be replaced by verbal communication, but in reality the subtleties of non-verbal communication are difficult (perhaps impossible) to replace; a student may look bored, or interested, but is unlikely to verbalise such feelings. One social solution to these difficulties would be for me to give up teaching large groups of students altogether, or to have a sighted colleague with me all the time; all in all, however, the lectures were successful, the students were satisfied, I was sufficiently familiar with the situation to cope with it, and in many ways the problem, though far from trivial, was insufficiently serious to warrant any drastic action. Again, the situation I have described is not concerned solely with visual impairment, for it involves social interaction, but neither is it born of social oppression.

When discussing these issues with disabled people who adhere strictly to the definition of disability as 'socially imposed restriction', I am either politely reminded that I am talking about 'impairment' not 'disability', or that the problems I describe have nothing to do with lack of sight but do indeed lie 'out there' in the physical and social environment; my lack of perception of this is put down to my prolonged socialisation as a disabled person. Being told that my definitions are wrong, that I have not quite grasped what disability is, tends to close the discussion prematurely; my experiences are compartmentalised, with someone else being the judge of which are and which are not worthy of consideration. This gives rise to feelings of estrangement and alienation. Morris (1991) states: 'We can insist that society disables us by its prejudice and by its failure to meet the needs created by disability, but to deny the personal experience of disability is, in the end, to collude in our oppression.'

Regarding disability solely in terms of 'socially imposed restriction' also means that many people who define themselves as disabled, through symptoms such as pain and vertigo, are not regarded as such by other disabled people, a situation which many regard as oppressive (Morris, 1991). In reality a large proportion of disabled people do experience symptoms such as pain, for example those with arthritis and spinal-cord injury. It is, of course, vital that able-bodied people grasp the fact that disabled people do not necessarily experience such symptoms and can be extremely fit and healthy – indeed routinely to link disability with illness and disease has been very damaging – but should this change of perception be achieved by denying the disabling effects of symptoms or by focusing on specific problems which disabled people experience while ignoring others which may, for them, be more disabling? Does it make sense to separate experiences which so clearly interact, and is it not for people with impairments to decide whether or not the problems they experience amount to disabilities?

Even when a social remedy to a problem is found and put into practice, how often does it truly eliminate disability? I am sure that on many occasions it can. If a paraplegic person is given full access to all facilities in her place of work, for example, she may well experience no disability in that situation, according to the type of work she is doing. However, giving adapted computers, taped materials and large print books to visually impaired people does not have the same effect. It may enable them to do a job which otherwise they could not do, but it will not transform them into sighted people: their working speeds will still be slower than average, they will not be able to scan print and the act of reading and writing will still take more effort. For those who lose their sight in adulthood, becoming a proficient braille reader is extraordinarily difficult, and braille is in any case a less efficient medium than print as it cannot be scanned, making reading speeds slower. In addition those who have always used braille may be no more able or willing to work from tapes or with readers than sighted people. This is not to imply that many of the barriers they face are socially produced, but to argue that sophisticated equipment and alternative working methods are unlikely to eliminate these barriers – indeed they may well exacerbate them by removing human help.

By using examples such as braille production to explain the social model of disability, harmful misconceptions can be generated, and the self-damaging strategies that visually impaired people are often compelled to use in order to succeed at work – for example working very long hours – are denied. Visually impaired people are not, of course, unique in experiencing problems which relatively simple societal and physical adjustment cannot solve. Lones (1991), talking of physically disabled students, states that 'shortage of time is a constant problem', and Leaney (1986) points out that interpreters do not eliminate the problems of communication experienced by deaf people.

Other more profound societal changes, for example paying disabled employees the same amount as able-bodied employees for less work if their working speeds are slow, would more successfully reduce disability, but enormous attitudinal changes within society, and within disabled people themselves, would need to take place before this could be put into practice without causing even worse problems in terms of resentment, guilt and lowering of self-esteem. As disabled people we have had to minimise the difficulties we encounter and use self-damaging strategies, such as working twice as hard, to gain a foothold in the able-bodied world. With attitudes as they are at present I would not stress to a prospective employer the problems I may have at work – indeed even to write about them feels dangerous, especially as the issue of non-verbal communication is so often over-emphasised and used against visually impaired people. But to have other disabled people deny that such problems exist or matter, or to relegate them to a non-disability category, is alienating.

Putting into practice a social solution to eliminate disability can take considerable time and effort which the disabled person may not consider profitable, especially if the severity of her impairment fluctuates or is progressive. Thus a person with a hearing impairment who can hear speech under certain environmental conditions, may not feel that learning sign language and lip-reading is worthwhile even though her disability is considerable. I cannot see to read out of doors, have difficulty getting around on sunny days and can only see to tend my garden at dusk. In theory I could learn braille, get used to working with readers, train with a guide dog and attend courses for blind gardeners, but in practice, because I can see to do these things, albeit partially and only some of the time, I am not motivated to learn new strategies; in fact sight is such a primary sense in human beings that teaching people with minimal sight to be blind, even when blindness is imminent or present part of the time, has never been successful. There are other social solutions, of course, which would not involve learning anything new, such as employing a gardener and a human guide to assist me on sunny days; but as I enjoy gardening and often prefer to be alone, these solutions feel more disabling than the disability arising from the impairment, although that is by no means trivial. If the impairment were to worsen, the balance might well tip in favour of employing a gardener, or making the necessary effort to acquire the equipment and skills needed to garden without sight, but at present the personal costs of doing so are too great.

Having said all this I am prepared to believe that most of the problems I experience are, in theory, amenable to social solutions, which no doubt would be put into practice if the majority of the population had my particular visual impairments; indeed this type of situation has been a topic of some fascination to a number of science-fiction writers. Perhaps if everyone had my type of visual impairment we would devise ways and means of recognising each other in the street; perhaps we would put large sums of money into research in ophthalmology and optical equipment, or organise the world so that lack of sight did not matter. Or, as we would all be fully aware of each other's situation, perhaps we would consider it unnecessary to do any of these things. But we are not all visually impaired and, of the small proportion of people who are, my particular set of difficulties is only shared by some. How helpful or practical, then, are ideas of social and physical adjustment when we look beyond the simple examples of adapted buildings, braille production and large-print books? Even if it were possible to transform the world to eliminate the disabilities of a small minority of people, would there not be a danger of disabling the rest of the population, including many of those with similar impairments?

I know this is a dangerous line of argument and one which may attract those bent on resisting environmental and social change. My own belief is that with careful thought, informed by a knowledge of each other's impairments and disabilities, as well as the needs and rights of able-bodied people, it is usually possible to find practical ways of reducing disability without disabling others. But is it always possible? How, for example, do we resolve the conflict between visually impaired people who need public buildings, such as supermarkets and health clubs, to be brightly lit, and those who need the lighting to be dim, or those who need yellow stripes on steps and those who need them to be black or white? Perhaps I am simply lacking in imagination but I have yet to find even a specialised setting for visually impaired people where issues such as these have been resolved. The practice usually adopted is the one that suits the majority, which may make the environment less suitable for the minority than a 'normal' one – a situation I faced recently when working in a college for visually impaired students.

In terms of establishing a disability movement, with some hope of improving the lives of disabled people through political action, it is understandable why disability should be defined solely in terms of social creation. Scotch (1988) points out that 'disability' as a unifying concept is by no means obvious, and believes that a prerequisite for collective action may be 'a redefinition of disability as that imposed by the physical and social environment', and that a prerequisite for social action may be 'the social construction and promulgation of an inclusive definition of disability'. Disabilities are still largely defined in society as problems located within unfortunate individuals, an approach which has done considerable harm to disabled people and which has failed to improve their lives either socially or financially.

Unifying disabled people is problematic, however, because they are geographically dispersed and socially and culturally dissimilar; in addition they are one of the most powerless groups in society and may themselves have negative attitudes about disability and towards people with dissimilar impairments to their own, leading to considerable distancing between them. Lack of accessible housing and transport and the poverty experienced by many disabled people make it more difficult for them to meet, and their impairments are so disparate that a shared social identity is by no means obvious or easy to achieve. These divisions are emphasised and fostered by the state, which provides varying provisions and benefits to people according to their impairments. Viewed in this light any emphasis on difference is politically dangerous. Thus, in order to form a strong social movement, it would appear necessary for people with disparate impairments and their organisations to join forces and to present a clear, unambiguous social definition of disability aimed at removing disabling social and physical barriers. In the 1960s organisations which crossed impairment boundaries were formed and the trend has continued, with large organisations, such as the British Council of Organisations of Disabled People, being formed in the 1980s.

It can thus be asked, with some justification, why we should bother to expend time and effort thinking about aspects of disability which, it would appear, cannot be solved by social or environmental manipulation. What is the point of dwelling on problems to which no solution can be found, especially when this may provide people bent on resisting social change with intellectual arguments which can be distorted and used against disabled people? In my view it is important for the following reasons.

(1) The differing experiences of people with a variety of impairments must be taken seriously or some of those people will be alienated from the disability movement. This will weaken the movement both in terms of its membership and the richness of its knowledge. I believe that a definition of disability which excludes the experiences of a large number of people who define themselves as disabled serves to estrange such people from the disability movement.
(2) If we are not prepared to discuss all aspects of disability there will be no possibility of finding creative ways of reducing it. It is certainly true that many problems experienced by disabled people are similar whatever the impairment, for example finding work and gaining access to a good education, but is it sufficient to concentrate on these broad issues whilst ignoring the specific problems disabled people face, especially those with no apparent social solution?
(3) Even if nothing can be done to alleviate a disability it may be very

important to the person concerned that others should know of its existence. The disability in question may be a very central aspect of the person's life and one she wants to share. Women in particular appear to gain a great deal of social and psychological support and satisfaction from sharing experiences and confiding in each other, without necessarily seeking a solution to their problems. Morris (1991), a disabled feminist, states:

> Like other political movements, the disability movement both in Britain and throughout the world, has tended to be dominated by men as both theoreticians and holders of important organisational posts. Both the movement and the development of a theory of disability has been the poorer for this as there has been an accompanying tendency to avoid confronting the personal experience of disability.

Another reason for wanting people, including other disabled people, to understand our disabilities, is that they so often give rise to highly ambiguous situations which are likely to lead to damaging misunderstandings and embarrassment. This is particularly so with disabilities which are relatively hidden. How obvious is it, for example, that a visually impaired person who can see to read small print will use a white stick to cross the road, that she will recognise people indoors but not out of doors, or that on some days her sight will be better than on others? Understanding the disabilities experienced by people with different impairments helps us to adjust the social and physical world to accommodate them; this is all to the good, but may not be the main reason why disabled people discuss their disabilities. On closer reflection, my main purpose in alerting my neighbours and students to the difficulty of recognising them and responding to their non-verbal language was not to challenge them to produce creative solutions, or even to adjust their behaviour, but simply to reduce the likelihood of them labelling me a 'snob' or a 'crank'! If disabilities without apparent solutions are labelled 'impairments' and dismissed, there is no opportunity to accomplish this sort of task.

(4) Although attempts to change people's attitudes to disability have not been particularly successful overall, this does not mean that the attitudes of some people, including disabled people themselves, cannot be modified by an understanding of the complex experiences of people with impairments. My recent contact with various organisations of disabled people has demonstrated vividly that even those disabling facets of visual impairment which are easy and inexpensive to reduce – for example by offering large print or through careful orientation to a new environment – are not addressed, let alone the more complex issues of ensuring equal access to the learning process, group discussion and social interaction. This situation is worsened by a distinct coyness within these groups about discussing issues of impairment and 'difference'. The aim of the disability movement is to change the way society operates so that disabled people are accommodated on equal terms, but our credibility is undermined, among the membership at least, if we cannot respond to each other's needs and rights. This lack of accommodation to the more subtle aspects of disability excludes many

disabled people as effectively as a flight of steps excludes those who use wheelchairs.

Conclusion

It is no doubt the case that activists who have worked tirelessly within the disability movement for many years have found it necessary to present disability in a straightforward, uncomplicated manner in order to convince a very sceptical world that disability can be reduced or eliminated by changing society, rather than attempting to change disabled people themselves; and that disabled people, whatever their impairments, share many problems and should be regarded as one unified disadvantaged group. Any talk of difference, therefore, might threaten to weaken this united front. Similarly, dwelling on examples which fail to fit the social model of disability comfortably might provide ammunition for those with the power to oppose and prevent progress. On the other hand, to present people with complex arguments may have a very positive outcome: a glance at the psychological literature on attitude change and persuasion clearly indicates that the presentation of a complex argument is more effective than a one-sided argument in bringing about attitude change in intelligent, well-educated people, especially when they are opposed to the position advocated (Harvey and Smith, 1977; Pennington, 1986).

Whilst I agree wholeheartedly that the social model of disability represents the most important way forward for disabled people, and I understand the forces which have shaped the definition of disability to that of social oppression, I also believe that the time has now come to broaden and intensify our examination of disability and to develop and deepen our knowledge, to the benefit of all who define themselves as disabled.

References

Finkelstein, V. (1981) 'To deny or not to deny disability', in Brechin, A., Liddiard, P. and Swain, J. (eds) *Handicap in a Social World*, Hodder and Stoughton, Sevenoaks/The Open University, Milton Keynes.

Finkelstein, V. (1990) ' "We" are not disabled, "you" are', in Gregory, S. and Hartley, G. (eds) *Constructing Deafness*, Pinter, London/The Open University, Milton Keynes.

Harvey, J.H. and Smith, W.P. (1977) *Social Psychology: an Attributional Approach*, C.V. Mosby, St Louis.

Leaney, A. (1986) 'Deaf students in ordinary colleges', *Educare*, Vol. 26, November, pp. 20–1.

Lones, J. (1991) 'Higher education: the changing needs of students with physical disabilities', *Educare*, Vol. 39, March, pp. 3–6.

Morris, J. (1991) *Pride Against Prejudice: Transforming Attitudes to Disability*, The Women's Press, London.

Oliver, M. (1983) *Social Work with Disabled People*, Macmillan, London.

Oliver, M. (1987) 'Re-defining disability: a challenge to research', *Research, Policy and Planning*, Vol. 5, No. 1, pp. 9–13.

Pennington, D.C. (1986) *Essential Social Psychology*, Edward Arnold, London.

Scotch, R.K. (1988) 'Disability as a basis for a social movement: advocacy and the politics of definition', *Journal of Social Issues*, Vol. 44, No. 1, pp. 159–72.

1.3

Towards a psychology of disability

Vic Finkelstein and Sally French

Introduction

A psychology of disability could cover many aspects of the disability experience. For example, following an accident and loss of sight a newly disabled person could appear rather depressed. Previous employment might be regarded as impossible and financial independence thought of as unrealistic. Of course, more positive experiences could be just as possible. The newly disabled person might have a more confident self-image and feel emotionally secure following the rapid attainment of skills for independent living and an early return to work with the support of a responsible employer. However, the range of psychological responses to disability not only raises questions about identifying and classifying the psychological characteristics of 'being disabled' but also questions whether they are all concerned with the same aspect of 'disability'.

In the above example, is the depression an aspect of having a 'disability' rather than the outcome of uncertainty about the future? Could the prejudice of others be better explained in terms of general psychological reactions to difference rather than responses to 'disability'? In other words, is a psychology of disability to be concerned with the impact of mobility, visual, auditory or other 'impairments' on an individual, or should the psychology focus on the way that people with mobility, visual, auditory and other impairments make sense of the 'disabling' social and physical environment?

If confusion is to be avoided it seems necessary to clearly establish what concept of disability is under discussion before presenting any proposed interpretation of psychological reactions to this particular state. Sadly, comments about the psychology of disability very rarely begin with a clarification of this issue.

Even the British Psychological Society's report, *Psychology and Physical Disability in the National Health Service*, gets into a muddle. The report provides no definition of disability other than the World Health Organisation's (WHO) definitions of 'impairment', 'disability' and 'handicap' which, with no evidence, it claims are: 'commonly accepted uses of the above terms' (British Psychological Society, 1989). In contrast, Barnes (1991), for example, suggests that the very different definitions provided by organisations of disabled people 'are becoming widely recognised by the majority of organisations of and organisations for disabled people, an increasing number of professionals, as well as some sections of the general public'.

Although the report notes that the WHO definitions are not accepted by all disabled people and therefore 'they are not the definitions of terms adopted by the report' it fails to clarify its own definitions. This leaves a confusing picture about its view of disability. On the one hand, it tries to distance itself from the 'individual' or 'medical model' of disability by criticising this in a variety of ways. On the other hand, the report analyses the issues and makes recommendations under headings in precisely the same way as the medical model.

A few examples will suffice. The report opens with an early criticism of the medical model where it states.

> The focus on the individual with a disability ignores the extent that society favours able-bodied people and excludes people with disabilities from, for example, buildings, committees and employment opportunities. Some have argued that the social handicaps should be the subject of change rather than fitting the person to an arbitrarily defined norm set by able-bodied people.
>
> (British Psychological Society, 1989, p. 4)

Despite this, one of the main recommendations for service providers is that they should 'Appreciate the individuality of the problems experienced by people with disabilities and the development of the range of services and their delivery to meet individual needs'. This is precisely the same approach to services as the medical model.

The report goes on to discuss five psychological perspectives on disability:

1 disability as crisis
2 theories of stress and coping
3 representations of health, illness and disability
4 beliefs about the causes of illness or injury
5 beliefs about personal control.

However, the personal model of disability provides the framework for all these perspectives. This is clearly demonstrated in the paragraph under the heading 'Applications' at the end of the discussion on each perspective where perspective 1 refers to bolstering 'a *person* with a disability's coping'; perspective 2 to helping 'the *person* achieve a sense of mastery' as a coping strategy 'for different health problems'; perspective 3 talks about understanding 'how *each person* with a disability conceptualizes his/her problems'; perspective 4 refers to 'enabling a *person* to have clear understanding of why they have a physical condition'; and perspective 5 talks about assessing 'the impact of the many problems of disability on *their personal* sense of control' (emphasis added).

Apart from shaping all the perspectives within the individual model of disability it is also clear that the perspectives are all generated by problems. Again, this is precisely the criticism that the report raises about the medical model, for example, on p. 3 it criticises the medical model as follows: 'The focus of disability is exclusively negative. It does not highlight the abilities and requirements that people with disabilities have in common with everyone else.'

The confusion between *psychological aspects of impairment* and the *psychology of being disabled* perhaps finds its clearest expression under the heading 'Psychological assessment and intervention in physical disability'. It is here that the discussion adopts an uncompromising medical perspective on disability. For example, in the section 'Chronic diseases not affecting the central nervous system' we are told that this applies to 'three main types of disorder'. In the subsection below these are identified in medical diagnostic terms (as osteoarthritis, rheumatoid arthritis and ischaemic heart disease) and then in a subsequent subsection as 'three main types of disability'. Under one of the subsections (p. 33) the discussion is concerned with 'The psychological aspects of the . . . main types of disability' and in a subsection under the main heading 'Congenital and developmental disorders' (p. 36) this becomes 'The psychological effects of impairment'. In other words, the discussion adopts the medical model by starting the discussion on psychological interventions with medical categories, labelling these as disorders and then alleging that these cause disability (sometimes referred to as impairment).

In order to avoid confusion and to provide a more fruitful way of looking at the psychological aspects of impairment and disability we have adopted the following definitions in this discussion:

> *Impairment* is the lack of part of or all of a limb, or having a defective limb, organ or mechanism of the body.

> *Disability* is the loss or limitation of opportunities that prevents people who have impairments from taking part in the normal life of the community on an equal level with others due to physical and social barriers.

These definitions are based on the ones proposed by the former British organisation, the Union of the Physically Impaired Against Segregation, and the international disability association, Disabled Peoples' International.

Psychological aspects of impairment

There are many ways in which an impairment might have psychological implications for the person concerned. It must be said, however, that the ways in which a person responds to and copes with his or her impairment can never be divorced from the individual's personality, social situation and personal biography.

The direct effects of impairment

Few would argue that a severe head injury, or a disease such as Huntington's chorea or Alzheimer's disease, will give rise to various changes of mood and behaviour, as well as altered intellectual and social functioning. A person having such an impairment may, for example, become aggressive, depressed, anxious or confused. These psychological states are directly related to the impairment, although treatment approaches such as behaviour modification, or learning new strategies for coping with diminishing abilities, may also help (Davison and Neale, 1987). Environmental changes such as improving the quality of institutions may also have a positive effect on the mood of, for example, a brain-injured person. Clearly there is often an interaction between physiological and social factors which both contribute to the individual's mood and behaviour.

Symptoms of illness

Many disabled people are extremely fit and healthy, but for others their impairments are associated with illness. Illness can be defined as the subjective feeling of being unwell and may include symptoms of pain, breathlessness, tiredness, nausea and vertigo.

Diseases such as arthritis are often associated with considerable pain. Pain, particularly when prolonged, has the potential to cause anxiety and depression. This can give rise to a vicious circle as both states of mind tend to heighten the perception of pain (Bond, 1984). Prolonged pain, even if not particularly severe, tends to take the joy out of life; Peck (1982) states that 'the whole range of activities which previously seemed exciting begin to seem dull and uninteresting'. This lack of activity means that time hangs heavily and depression and anxiety are intensified. The whole situation is frequently made worse by lack of sleep. Pain is very intrusive and people experiencing it will find it very difficult to concentrate on anything properly or cope with physical or social demands; they will probably mix with other people less and have little to talk about, or talk only about their pain. In time their company can become less rewarding to others, who may withdraw. This can lead to a cycle of resentment and guilt as well as feelings of anger and irritability on the part of both the people in pain and their families.

Fatigue too can be associated with various impairments and may also have psychological implications. People with multiple sclerosis, for example, may tire easily, giving rise to depression and lack of concentration. Fatigue may also adversely affect the individual's social and sexual relationships, work, education, hobbies and pastimes. Similarly, breathlessness, associated with diseases such as asthma and cystic fibrosis, may arouse fear and panic. The psychological manifestations may be eliminated by reducing the symptoms of illness, for example by applying drug therapy, surgery, physiotherapy, or other interventions such as behaviour modification, relaxation, counselling and hypnotherapy.

Cognitive functioning – making sense of the world

People with particular impairments construe the world very differently from able-bodied people or people with dissimilar impairments. People who are deaf, for example, are very dependent on their vision, and for those born deaf their unique language and culture will affect the way in which they think and learn. Similarly people with cerebral palsy may have altered perceptual experiences. Visually impaired people too have a qualitatively different experience of the world, where subtle sounds and changes of texture, which other people ignore, become vitally important to their understanding of the world and their orientation in space. John Hull, a university lecturer who went blind in his 40s (Hull, 1991), gives a vivid account of how the sound of rain can build for him a detailed picture of his surroundings. He describes how a blind person 'is simply someone to whom the specialist function of sight is now devolved upon the whole body', and how he has taken up residence 'in another world'.

At certain times in the lives of disabled people it may be important for others to appreciate, at least in part, that disabled people experience and construe the world differently from their able-bodied peers. This may be particularly important during childhood so that disabled children can be helped to understand the world on their own terms, learning from their own abilities and experiences. For example, people interacting with visually impaired children may need to learn how to describe things to them and which experiences are important to them. Similarly, those interacting with deaf children may need to learn sign language or become unusually sensitive to visual stimuli in order to communicate effectively. Lewis (1987) provides detailed information on the development of children with a wide range of impairments, as well as interventions which may be used to enhance development and minimise detrimental effects.

Unfortunately, what often happens is that able-bodied people expect disabled people to be 'normal'. Thus deaf people have been deprived of their language and made to learn lip-reading, at great psychological cost. Conversely, before the Second World War children with 'low vision' who attended the so-called 'sight-saving schools', were prevented from using their sight to the extent of being forced to wear harnesses that prevented them from leaning forward to read or write (Corley *et al.*, 1989), and those in schools for blind children had paper bags put over their heads to stop them from looking at braille (Chapman, 1978). Children with limited sight automatically tend to use their vision to the full, and it is now known that preventing them from doing so has an adverse effect on their later visual functioning.

A delicate balance should be struck. It is very common, when considering the cognitive functioning of disabled people and their coping strategies, to assume that the problems lie within themselves and that the social and physical world is fixed. It may be appropriate to teach and encourage disabled people to develop specific strategies to cope with the particular situation they are in, but in reality environmental manipulation, both social and physical, is often all that is needed to make a radical change to the disabled person's situation. For example, the skill and concentration demanded of visually impaired people, as they move about in the environment, would be greatly reduced if pavements were free of obstacles.

Loss

The person who acquires a substantial impairment moves from the role of able-bodied person to disabled person, often very abruptly. It has been suggested that this can give rise to psychological reactions similar to those experienced in bereavement. The notion that disability is inevitably associated with grief and mourning has, however, been challenged by Oliver (1983); it is not unusual for disabled people to report that their lives have changed for the better following disablement, or that their lives remain much the same as they were before (Morris, 1989; Lonsdale, 1990).

Many people who acquire a disability suddenly, however, do report that the experience is profoundly disturbing and distressing. John Hull (1991) states that he grieved for four and a half years over his lost sight. His main areas of distress included the inability to see and relate fully to his children, feelings of isolation (although he was not alone), his greater dependency on others and his inability to initiate social contact; all of these are losses which cannot be fully regained. Maggie in Jo Campling's (1981) book had similar feelings. She recalls: 'I felt I had little to offer anyone and rather than face rejection, I avoided people. Grieving over the lively gregarious woman I had once been.' The disabled person may have lost abilities and attributes which cannot be replaced, such as physical beauty, ease of movement, the ability to look at magnificent scenery or to hear music. They may need to acquire a new body-image, adjust to life at a slower pace and allow others to help with intimate bodily functions. With impairments such as cystic fibrosis and muscular dystrophy, their very lives are threatened and are likely to be short. Whether or not any of this will have a negative psychological impact on the individual will, however, depend on his or her personality and the type of lifestyle which is valued. To lose a finger may be a disaster to the professional pianist but may hardly matter at all to the academic.

Psychological aspects of disability

Disabled people may feel negative and depressed about their situation because they have absorbed negative attitudes about disability both before and after becoming disabled, and much of the depression and anxiety they feel may be the result of social factors such as other people's attitudes, poor access, non-existent job prospects and poverty. In addition, people who acquire substantial impairments frequently experience serious problems with their relationships; Burnstein (1985) mentions that marriages often break down under the stress of multiple sclerosis, especially if they were under strain beforehand. The disabled person may need to develop a new self-image and body-image, cope with being more dependent on others and change direction in occupation and leisure activities.

Physical and social barriers continually impact on the lives of people with significant impairments; the visually impaired person who cannot read print and the deaf person who cannot hear speech, for example, are deprived of information and face barriers to communication. Lack of accessible buildings and a hostile physical and social environment inhibit access to employment, education, leisure and sufficient income to lead a full and interesting life. Indeed these social and physical barriers have the potential to affect adversely and retard every aspect of the disabled person's development – social, emotional, sexual and intellectual – at every stage of his or her life. Further barriers are created by the negative or misguided attitudes and behaviour of others, and their lack of knowledge about disability and impairment. Disabled people have a minority status where few understand or respond appropriately to their situation. If disabled people are denied access to normal social activities they will not only have different experiences from those of their able-bodied peers, but they will interpret, perceive, think, feel and talk about the world differently.

Disabled people, being part of society, frequently think of themselves in the same way as able-bodied people think of them and behave as others expect them to in their role as disabled people – the self-fulfilling prophecy. It is hardly surprising, therefore, that limitations imposed on disabled people by these barriers sometimes lead to depression, passivity, anxiety and hopelessness, which in turn may lead able-bodied people to regard them as unmotivated and poorly adjusted. It is very important that these barriers are seen as providing the context for personal mood states and psychological reactions, rather than seeing these states as psychological reactions to impairment.

With the growth of new (social) approaches to disability, there is a need to develop fresh insights into the way disabled people, and others, make sense of, cope with, manage and overcome disabling social and physical barriers. Some disabled people avoid the barriers only to become isolated and withdrawn; others attempt to accommodate themselves to the restrictions in their lives; while others fight for barrier removal – leading some to become strong and self-confident and others to become anxious, exhausted, cynical and depressed. Why is it that some disabled people confront the barriers they face, while others prefer to 'get by'? What effect would assertiveness training and counselling have, and how far have disabled people understood their own disadvantaged situation? It is questions like these which must be asked if we really want to understand the psychology of disability.

Conclusion

We question what might be appropriately termed psychological aspects of impairment and disability: what common features might be shared between them; in what situations could differentiating between responses to impairment and disability be important; and what psychological responses would need to be incorporated in a general psychology of disability? We have suggested that both impairment and disabling physical and social barriers can impact on individuals to create psychological differences and psychological reactions. There is a dynamic relationship between impairment and disability which we believe provides the starting-point for the construction of a new approach to the psychology of disability.

References

Barnes, C. (1991) *Disabled People in Britain and Discrimination*, Hurst, London.

Bond, M.R. (1984) *Pain: its Nature, Analysis and Treatment*, 2nd edn, Churchill Livingstone, London.

British Psychological Society (1989) *Psychology and Physical Disability in the National Health Service*, Report of the Professional Affairs Board of the British Psychological Society, Leicester.

Burnstein, A. (1985) *Multiple Sclerosis: a Personal Exploration*, Souvenir Press, London.

Campling, J. (1981) *Images of Ourselves: Women with Disabilities Talking*, Routledge and Kegan Paul, London.

Chapman, E.K. (1978) *Visually Handicapped Children and Young People*, Routledge and Kegan Paul, London.

Corley, G., Robinson, D. and Lockett, S. (1989) *Partially Sighted Children*, NFER-Nelson, Windsor.

Davison, G.C. and Neale, J.M. (1987) *Abnormal Psychology*, 5th edn, John Wiley, New York.

Hull, J. (1991) *Touching the Rock: An Experience of Blindness*, Arrow Books, London.

Lewis, V. (1987) *Development and Handicap*, Basil Blackwell, Oxford.

Lonsdale, S. (1990) *Women and Disability*, Macmillan, London.

Morris, J. (1989) *Able Lives*, The Women's Press, London.

Oliver, M. (1983) *Social Work with Disabled People*, Macmillan, London.

Peck, C. (1982) *Controlling Chronic Pain*, Fontana, London.

1.4

Disability: a social challenge or an administrative responsibility?

Vic Finkelstein

The meaning of segregation

Incarceration in residential homes has been practised long enough for it to be accepted as a perfectly legitimate way of 'caring' for 'the disabled'. Indeed the founders and supporters of such institutions have been showered with numerous awards from civic and voluntary authorities. Names of individuals have become household words for helping the 'unfortunate disabled' and they are acclaimed in public by every sector of the media (see, for example, Russell, 1980). There is a singular lack of awareness that there may be something profoundly undemocratic about able-bodied people supporting the systematic removal of disabled people from their communities, that it is only able-bodied people who write glowingly about each other for having done this to disabled people and that it is able-bodied people who give themselves awards for this contribution to the isolation of disabled people from the mainstream of life.

On the other side there is ample evidence in the writings of disabled people that they have always regarded residential institutions with considerable misgivings and only as a last resort.[1] When they have found themselves in a 'home' they have not only complained about being there but felt acutely aggrieved by the lack of control over their own lives in the day-to-day running of the institution. Residential homes, therefore, have been an active site for the struggle for citizenship rights.

A conflict between residents and the management committee at the Le Court Cheshire Home resulted in the residents inviting Miller and Gwynne (1972) to carry out a research project on the nature and running of the home. The hope was that this would provide evidence to support their right to manage their own lives. After visiting several residential homes Miller and Gwynne maintained that 'by the very fact of committing people to institutions

This paper is a revised and edited version of V. Finkelstein (1991) 'Disability: an administrative challenge? (The health and welfare heritage)', in Oliver, M. (ed.) *Social Work: Disabled People and Disabling Environments*, Jessica Kingsley, London.

of this type, society is defining them as, in effect, *socially dead*, then the essential task to be carried out is to help the inmates make their transition from social death to physical death' (1972, p. 89; my emphasis). In their words, once a disabled person had entered an institution 'society has effectively washed its hands of the inmates as significant social beings'.

In identifying *society* as defining disabled people as socially dead Miller and Gwynne had put their finger on the key social construction of disability. In this model as long as there is no medical 'cure' disabled people are inherently socially dead and permanently dependent upon others for their 'care' in the community or in an institution.

Rethinking assumptions

By the time the Cheshire Home residents (including Paul Hunt and Peter Wade) had managed to move out of the institution they were convinced that residential homes were an important symptom of public acceptance that disability means social death. They saw, therefore, organised campaigns to provide secure community-based alternatives as an essential component of regaining the citizenship rights of disabled people.

An organisation which attracted much attention was the Disablement Income Group (DIG); although it expressed wide concern for social rights it focused its activities on the single issue of a 'disability income' (see Editorial, 1981, for a criticism of DIG; see also Pagel, 1988; Oliver, 1990). The campaigning needs of DIG, however, provided an important forum for discussion at the grassroots level and there followed a period of vigorous debate about the potential of a disability allowance to facilitate integration. Concern about who was to receive any national disability income raised questions about the definition and meaning of disability.

DIG presented the 'disability allowance' as a way of *compensating* for disability. But this demand, far from challenging the view that disability results in an inability to function socially, tends to reinforce this assumption. Making pleas for compensation raises no questions about the social construction of disability as a form of social death (that is, to be denied full citizenship rights to live independently in one's own home, to attend mainstream education, be gainfully employed, have access to public leisure facilities, etc.). On the contrary, it encourages the dependency of disabled people on special provisions and the goodwill of able-bodied people for financial resources to facilitate their inclusion into society.

Paul Hunt saw DIG's approach as failing to analyse why disabled people had so little control over their lives – the same issue that had agitated the residents at Le Court. He suggested that a new, comprehensive, strategy towards disability issues was needed. He wanted an approach which would not focus on single-issue campaigns but which would combine all the concerns of disabled people within a unified philosophy (or theory) of disability. This, he felt, could provide a better foundation for developing a comprehensive support system in the community under the control of disabled people.

He pursued this idea by publishing a letter in a national newspaper inviting like-minded disabled people to contact him for discussions.[2] The outcome was the formation of the Union of the Physically Impaired Against Segregation (UPIAS). In my view, the UPIAS policy document marked a turning-point in understanding the meaning of disability. This was because for the first time in this country an organisation controlled by disabled people published the view that segregated facilities were a symptom of oppression. In saying 'since the means for integration now undoubtedly exists, our confinement to segregated facilities is increasingly oppressive and dehumanising' the document recognised that the inability to participate in mainstream community life (that is, Miller and Gwynne's social death) was the result of social and physical barriers, and that the central concern was barrier removal and the restoration of citizenship rights (Union of the Physically Impaired Against Segregation, 1976a). From this point of view the model of disability inherent in their philosophy could be called a 'social barriers model of disability'.

The administrative model

Ideas from UPIAS only attracted the most active disabled people at first, but the view that disability is socially created steadily percolated into the disabled community. Following a debate with the Disability Alliance UPIAS published a new document expanding its policy statement and presented for the first time a clearly articulated social definition of disability.[3] On this understanding it also argued that the problems faced by disabled people could only be effectively addressed when they were directly involved in decision-making to remove the barriers that they faced.

It maintained that while all those active in disability issues seem to agree that disabled people are, as a group, relatively impoverished, poorly housed, educated and serviced by public utilities compared to their peers (that is, they are non-beings),[4] they do not agree about how this originates. On the one side, this social deprivation is seen to be the result of personal inadequacy and on the other it is thought due to social and environmental barriers. The former encourages campaigns for state handouts (or relief) and extra (or special) services to compensate for the alleged permanent inadequacy (disability). The latter view leads to searches for new ways to engage disabled people more actively in their own affairs to change or eliminate the barriers (which are seen as disabling).

From the UPIAS point of view it is the organisation of society for able-bodied living that leads to discrimination against disabled people. For those who do not adopt this interpretation, but who wish to help, there are two intervention choices: either 'cure' the individual condition allegedly resulting in the deprivation or provide a system of 'care'. Both forms of

MODELS OF DISABILITY   SERVICE-PROVISION MODELS

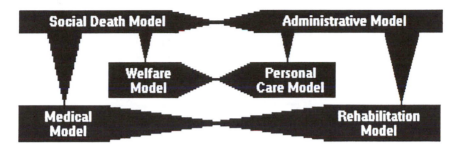

Figure 1

intervention assume that the problems of individual disabled people originate in their deviation from essential personal and social standards of *normality*. Because the underlying assumption is that disabled people are dysfunctional both approaches, too, assume that helping interventions are introduced and *administered* to disabled people by able-bodied people.

In my view administrative approaches dominate all forms of helping services for disabled people in the UK, whether these are provided by statutory agencies or voluntary charities, or demanded by pressure-group organisations. The cure and care forms of intervention are administered within the rehabilitation and personal-care services respectively. In this structure the medical model provides the framework for rehabilitation interventions and a welfare model of disability guides personal-care services.

The relationship between different models of disability and associated intervention approaches can be illustrated as in Figure 1.

The medical interpretation of disability, of course, is widely experienced as dominating service-provision models for disabled people. A consequence of this is that in day-to-day interactions the medical model appears to lend the only meaning to the experience of 'disability'. The spontaneous way of reducing this power, therefore, seems to require replacing it with a social model. In my view, however, the medical interpretation of disability does not provide the outstanding principles which govern the dominant understanding and servicing of disability. It is, rather, one of the subsets of the overarching 'social death' model of disability. Reducing the power of medicine in controlling the lives of disabled people while leaving the administrative approach to services intact, therefore, can only lead to the growing power of personal-care approaches. In recent times we have already seen evidence of this in the growing concern about the needs of carers and the call for trained and professional service-providers to administer more care in the community, while at the same time assumptions about the intrinsic dependency of disabled people remain unchallenged, if not actually reinforced (see, for example, White Paper, 1989).

In the early 1970s the struggle for greater control over their lives provided

MODELS OF DISABILITY   SERVICE-PROVISION MODELS

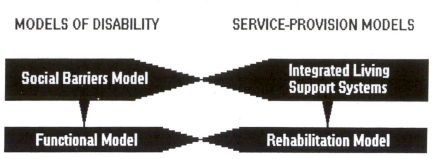

Figure 2

disabled people with the experience to challenge prevailing views about disability. Not only was there agreement about the need to cultivate a new social theory of disability as a counterbalance to the existing models, but it was argued that this should guide the development of future support services which they would control. However the new model is defined,[5] consensus is emerging that this should involve interpreting disability as the result of social and attitudinal barriers constructed by a world built for able-bodied living. This, I believe, can be called a 'social barriers' model of disability. Logically this view leads to service approaches which focus on barrier removal.

The relationship between a barrier model of disability and related service-provision approaches would also need to provide more acceptable boundaries between impairment and disability and their appropriate interventions, perhaps as in Figure 2.

In this scheme disabled people can exercise control over the support systems they use by structuring the medical 'functional model' and its associated 'rehabilitation model' below the 'social barriers' and 'integrated living support systems models' respectively.[6]

Towards integration

It is clear that new ways of interpreting disability arose directly out of disabled people's experiences when trying to influence the attitudes of service-providers about the control and delivery of support systems. However, the slow rate of change in the services led many disabled people to search for personal solutions which could establish the viability of living in their own homes under their own control. Amongst the most significant of the early projects started by disabled people was the Grove Road scheme set up by Ken Davis and Maggie Hines (Davis, 1981). Both had experienced living in a residential hostel and they were determined to set up their own home despite consistent advice from professional workers that this was not a possibility. They began by negotiating a site on which to build accommodation consisting of a number of accessible ground-floor flats with apartments for helpers on the first floor. The scheme involved subsidised rents for the able-bodied helpers and full management in the hands of all the residents in the building. This meant sharing decision-making between helpers and disabled people.

An important aspect of the scheme was the careful planning needed to organise the allocation of help that had to be built into the project. Basing their calculations upon professional advice and their experience of 'care' in the hostel, Ken Davis and Maggie Hines estimated the amount of paid time needed to facilitate security in their own home. This turned out to be a gross over-estimate and, in their view, illustrated both the limitations of professional expertise and the passivity generated by residence in institutions where all care and management is provided by able-bodied staff. The project was a tremendous confidence-booster and a practical challenge to informed opinion about what services were appropriate for disabled people.

These messages spread rapidly through the disability grapevine, feeding the growing consensus that disability is manufactured by attitudinal and environmental barriers rather than functional limitations in the individual. Ideas about practical ways of enhancing the control of disabled people over their own lives were shared between individuals and organisations working in many areas, such as the Association of Disabled Professionals (ADP) and the Association of Blind and Partially Sighted Teachers and Students (ABAPSTAS), who were promoting integrated education, and the Spinal Injuries Association (SIA), who were encouraging greater self-management in daily life. This led to a more robust public profile of organisations controlled by disabled people and an expansion of self-help philosophy.

The growth in power and influence of these organisations highlighted the lack of knowledge among disabled people about achievements that were possible in the community. It became increasingly clear that limited information was itself an important barrier hindering the development of new services planned, developed, set up and run by disabled people (Davis and Woodward, 1981). Ken Davis took the initiative and helped create a service run by disabled people to pass on information and advice. Disability Information and Advice Line (DIAL) local groups spread rapidly throughout the country and were very frequently managed and staffed by disabled people. DIAL not only contributed to the breakdown in the knowledge monopoly held by professional disability experts but also gave disabled people a deeper sense of the increased choices possible for those wanting to live independently in their own homes in the community.

New organisations were created to bring different disability groups together. Most of these 'coalitions of disabled people' not only presented themselves as the democratic voice of disabled people at the local level but also as a vehicle for setting up new integrated (or independent) living services under their control. The coalitions have also been joined by a rapid growth in arts groups. These have shifted their attention from the traditional focus of providing leisure activities for isolated disabled people and promoting access to able-bodied arts to the development and celebration of a disability culture (Finkelstein, 1987). The positive self-image emerging from these organis-ations directly contradicts the presentation of disabled people as inherently dependent on charity and functionally passive. The British Council of Organisations of Disabled People (BCODP) was founded in 1981 as the national body uniting all organisations controlled by disabled people. A common feature of all these groups is that disability is not seen as a personal problem but as the social consequence of a disabling society. The focus is on removing the barriers which prevent the equal opportunities of disabled citizens.

The past five years have consolidated the ideas developed during the earlier period of struggles against segregation, mainly against residential institutions but also in support of mainstream education and employment. This has taken the form of struggles to implement practical projects in which disabled people could be directly involved. The organisations controlled by disabled people provided space for confidence-building and the development of new skills. These experiences in turn paved the way for testing managerial and professional abilities in setting up and running community-based services – the Centres for Integrated Living (CILs). These are also often called Centres for Independent Living, but should not be confused with independent living centres run by able-bodied professionals.

Supported integration

A great deal of energy has been expended in trying to influence professional (local authority social services) and voluntary charities so that disabled people will no longer be regarded as incapable of functioning in the community without care. This has not been very successful. As a result some disabled people have gone on to try to start their own services. These are generally based upon the Centre for Independent Living services that were started in the USA. These were introduced as a means of involving disabled people directly in community-based services and were first adapted to the UK situation by Ken Davis (1983) in Derbyshire.

CILs function in a number of ways, challenging disability stereotypes, providing examples of more relevant services concerned with advice, housing adaptations and ways of managing independence in the home. The CILs are also a focal point for disabled people to marshal their citizenship rights in campaigning for an accessible public environment, suitable housing, mass transport system, educational facilities, leisure opportunities and employment prospects. The fact that the centres and services they provide have been devised and delivered by disabled people also presents a positive and vigorous public image contradicting the general depiction of disabled people as a burden on the state and the attention of charity.

The emphasis is on changing the real world, removing real barriers to equality of opportunity, and not just modifying attitudes and changing the practice of service-providers while maintaining dependency upon able-bodied people to 'administer' the solutions. From this point of view disabled people increasingly see themselves as oppressed, denied citizenship rights and disempowered. An important component of the changes wanted, therefore, is a 'Charter of Rights' and civil rights legislation which will facilitate more power in their own hands. Barrier removal is seen as involving not only the provision of ramps, information in braille and on tape, signing on television, etc., to enable access to able-bodied facilities, but also the right to develop a unique disabled people's perspective on the world and the opportunity to contribute to its future shape.

The modern challenge is to provide alternatives to current practice so that workers and disabled people can share expertise in barrier identification and removal, both at the personal level (for the individual setting their own goals) and at the social level, where public facilities need to be made truly public (and not just for able-bodied citizens).

Shifting attention from the individual to the disabling barriers involves seeing disability as a consequence of the totality of the individual's relationships and provides an opportunity for sharing an objective discussion about the perspectives between the helper and disabled person. I feel sure that there is no other more effective way of identifying and assessing the issues in disability than with and through disabled people. This approach, too, should help to identify boundaries between appropriate models of disability and service approaches. Where an individual, for example, has recently sustained a permanent impairment medical interventions involving rehabilitation to establish new skills in body management may well be appropriate.

However, the medical model and the rehabilitation service approach need to be planned in the context of the social (barriers) model.[7] In effect this means that the goals, extent, duration and nature of medical interventions should be guided by an analysis of the social and personal barriers to be overcome, rather than by any functional limitations of the individual. Such an analysis, of course, cannot be provided only by the professional helper without failing to re-establish administrative control over a disabled 'client'.

The 'barriers model' of disability and 'integrated living support systems model' logically align disability-related services with other government sections concerned with social and physical barriers which impact on the lives of able-bodied people. This would suggest that the Department of the Environment rather than Health and Welfare should be the main 'home' for organizing disability-related services in the community. This would enhance the role of disciplines such as engineering and architecture in the lives of disabled people. From this point of view, it seems perfectly appropriate for housing and adaptations officers working in local authorities for disabled people to be trained in the schools of architecture (or perhaps engineering).

Social workers are experienced in working with vulnerable and oppressed sectors of the community and would clearly have a significant role in assisting disabled people to attain and maintain their citizenship rights. Assistance with skills in managing personal support staff and liaising with CILs are other areas where the expertise of social workers could be very relevant. However, I believe that their main contribution could be as advocates in support and working with disabled people to identify and help to remove social and physical barriers in the local environment.

To summarise: a social barriers model of disability suggests at least the following fundamental changes:

1 The base for disability-related services should be shifted from health and welfare to environment-based services.

2 Disability-related services should be reformulated so that they are no longer service-led but provided as a resource with clear access rights for disabled people.

3 Disability-related services should be restructured so that the integrated living support systems (CILs) provide the necessary central focus and guidance for all services used by disabled people, including medical, educational, housing and transport services.

4 The education and training of all service-providers should be redirected so that there are more fitting criteria for determining appropriate intervention (service) models, especially in relation to medical rehabilitation approaches, and the education and training of community-based service-providers should be improved so that their analytical and organisational skills are better focused on barrier identification and removal with less emphasis on functional assessment.

5 Civil rights legislation should be enacted to provide a framework for guiding the development of community-based support systems for disabled people living in their own homes and to ensure equal opportunities in employment and equal access to education and medical services, housing, leisure, the environment and information.

The adoption of a programme promoting aims along these lines will, I am sure, win the approval of disabled people who have pioneered a totally new perception of themselves and the services that they need. It will also bring to an end the long process which led to the view that to be disabled means to be unable to function independently in mainstream society.

Notes

1 See especially copies of *Cheshire Smile* published in the late 1960s and early 1970s for a sample of critical writing from disabled residents.

2 The letter was published in the *Guardian* on 20 September 1972, and subsequently in many of the 'disability' journals.

3 For example 'impairment [is defined] as lacking part of or all of a limb, or having a defective limb, organ or mechanism of the body; disability [is defined] as the disadvantage or restriction of activity caused by a contemporary social organisation which takes no or little account of people who have physical impairments and thus excludes them from participation in the mainstream of social activities. Physical disability is therefore a particular form of social oppression' (Union of the Physically Impaired Against Segregation, 1976b).

4 See, for example, the latest Office of Population Censuses and Surveys (OPCS) findings.

5 The Disabled Peoples' International (DPI) definitions, for example, refer to 'disability' and 'handicap' (in British terms 'impairment' and 'disability' respectively) as follows: 'Whereas disability has too long been viewed as a problem of the individual and not the relationship

between an individual and his/her environment, it is necessary to distinguish between: (a) disability is the functional limitation within the individual caused by physical, mental or sensory impairment, and (b) handicap is the loss or limitation of opportunities to take part in the normal life of the community on an equal level with others due to physical and social barriers' (DPI Constitution).

6 Functional models not only service medical interventions with rehabilitation goals but also all approaches which assume that poverty amongst disabled people directly results from individual disability. The Disablement Income Group, the Disability Alliance and the Office for Population Censuses and Surveys have assumed just such an individualistic functional (or medical) model. Their concern is to clarify eligibility for the allocation of financial benefits to compensate for disability and determine the administration of resources.

7 The Disabled Peoples' International does not go this far, but is concerned with drawing boundaries between rehabilitation and community-based services: 'Whereas rehabilitation is a process aimed at enabling a person to reach optimum physical, mental and/or social functioning level in order to provide that person with the tools to direct his/her own life, independent living and community services are not, and should not be, part of that process' (DPI Constitution).

References

Davis, K. (1981) 'Grove Road', *Disability Challenge*, No. 1, May, Union of the Physically Impaired Against Segregation, London.

Davis, K. (1983) *Consumer Participation in Service Design, Delivery and Control*, Derbyshire Coalition of Disabled People.

Davis, K. and Woodward, J. (1981) 'Dial UK: development of the National Association of Disablement and Advice Services', in Brechin, A., Liddiard, P. and Swain, J. (eds) *Handicap in a Social World*, Hodder and Stoughton, Sevenoaks/The Open University, Milton Keynes.

Editorial (1981) *Disability Challenge*, No. 1, May, Union of the Physically Impaired Against Segregation, London.

Finkelstein, V. (1987) 'Disabled people and our cultural development', paper presented to the London Disability Arts Forum conference.

Miller, E.J. and Gwynne, G.V. (1972) *A Life Apart*, Tavistock, London.

Oliver, M. (1990) *The Politics of Disablement*, Macmillan, London.

Pagel, M. (1988) *On Our Own Behalf*, Greater Manchester Coalition of Disabled People.

Russell, W. (1980) *New Lives for Old: the Story of Cheshire Homes*, Victor Gollancz, London.

Union of the Physically Impaired Against Segregation (1976a) *Policy Statement*, UPIAS, London.

Union of the Physically Impaired Against Segregation (1976b) *Fundamental Principles of Disability*, UPIAS, London.

White Paper (1989) *Caring for People: Community Care in the Next Decade and Beyond*, Cm 849, HMSO, London.

1.5

What's so great about independence?

Sally French

> They think you've got to do everything absolutely independently of anyone else. Why? There is no sensible reason for it.
>
> (Blind physiotherapist; quoted in French, 1989)

Independence is generally considered to be something disabled people desire above all else. In many ways this is true, for if a person is excessively dependent on others then he or she must fit in with their schedules and plans, with a subsequent loss of freedom and autonomy. In addition, it is all too easy for the relationship between the helper and the person being helped to develop into an unequal one, with the helper having undue power and the disabled person being compelled to constantly express gratitude, or at best never to complain. However, I believe that the notion of independence can be taken too far, restricting the lives of disabled people rather than enriching them.

I started thinking along these lines years ago when, as a 16-year-old school-leaver, I worked as an assistant housemother in a residential school for multiply disabled children. There was George who was made to struggle for 15 minutes every evening to get his socks off, which he eventually achieved by rubbing his ankles together. There was Peter who took 20 minutes every morning to get one arm into his shirt sleeve, and Simon who took even longer to get his arm out. The older, more experienced staff said that the children valued every bit of independence they could achieve (though it certainly did not show) and the physios talked endlessly of joint range and muscle strength as if that was all that mattered.

Is it right to insist on this kind of independence? Corbett (1989) thinks not. She states:

> The basics of self-help, which are second nature to the able bodied, might be an intolerable chore to some people with disabilities. Why should they bother with them? A narrow focus upon basic skills impedes the quality of life and inhibits self-expression.

I was recently studying part-time at a polytechnic, and was very satisfied with the willingness and helpfulness of the librarian. How my heart sank when she announced with pride one day that a special computer was to be installed

This paper was first published in *The New Beacon* 1991, Vol. 75, No. 886, pp. 153–6 (the Royal National Institute for the Blind).

to enable me, and several other partially sighted students, to find our own references. She was appalled by the lack of provision made for us in the library and was determined that we should get our rights whatever the cost. She sincerely believed that our main mission in life was to be as independent as possible.

The thought of this machine filled me with foreboding. If it were to be installed, chances are it would not suit me, as people's problems, even within the same disability pigeon-hole, differ so much. Worse still, if I were able to use the computer, I would almost certainly take longer than the librarian, and having located the references on the screen I would still need her assistance to pick them from the shelves! Despite the inconvenience this machine would almost certainly cause, I would be expected to use it, for to shun such an expensive item, purchased especially with me in mind, would seem thoroughly ungrateful! The introduction of this aid would, at best, enable me to cope inefficiently with half a task, while at the same time disallowing me from asking for help. Even if special equipment is appropriate, it is all too often located in an inconvenient or inaccessible place – like the photocopier that enlarged which was located in a different building to the one I was studying in.

Disabilities tend to make us slow, they are inconvenient enough without making matters worse in a futile attempt to be independent. I lacked the courage to voice these 'negative' views – it is difficult when people are obviously so well-meaning. But happily the computer, for whatever reason, never materialised.

Some people may by now be commiserating with the librarian, feeling that perhaps she was overburdened and eager to get me off her hands. This was not the impression I received, however, and I do not believe it to be so. Like many well-meaning people she assumed that I wanted to be independent and that any help she could provide would inevitably be second-rate. Like many people she grossly undervalued the help she was providing and was so sure of what was best for me that she did not think to ask.

Others may be feeling that it is unreasonable for disabled people to ask for help with tasks they can achieve unaided. However, the writers Shearer (1981) and Sutherland (1981) believe that to insist on independence is a form of oppression. It individualises disability rather than viewing it in social terms. Another writer, Oliver (1981), believes that individualising disability has a depoliticising effect which is politically convenient. The onus is very firmly placed on disabled people to cope and adapt in a society adapted to the needs of non-disabled people. Thus the status quo is maintained. Brechin and Liddiard (1981) state: 'Clinical work has traditionally occurred on the basis of individual referral, and assessment procedures have evolved around the assumption that in the individual lies the problem and the solution.'

Corbett (1989) describes how people with learning difficulties can regress if independence is forced upon them. Sutherland (1981) quotes a disabled person as saying:

> I've known a few people who, as adults, have refused to walk even though they could because it's just not worth the effort. And people have often got angry with

them, often. They've been labelled lazy and all sorts of things. They're definitely considered odd if they choose to be in a wheelchair, in the same way as you're considered odd if you don't struggle to do something that you can actually do even though it takes you six hours.

If Peter and Simon had been relieved of their 'self-help' chores, think how much time they would have had for more interesting pursuits. Similarly, if librarians continue to help me find my references I will have more time to read them – a particularly important point as my reading speed is slow. Striving for independence in terms of basic practicalities when, for that person, there are better things to do can seriously reduce independence by restricting the disabled person's freedom of thought and action. As Corbett (1989) says:

> Real independence is nothing to do with cooking, cleaning and dressing oneself. If you ask me what is my experience of being independent, I would not automatically think about self-help skills but of being able to use my imagination to create fantasy, of enjoying music and drama, of relishing sensual pleasures and absorbing the natural life around me.

Closely associated with the pressure to be independent is the pressure to appear 'normal'. This can give rise to enormous inefficiency and stress, yet many disabled people are well into adulthood before they manage to abandon such attempts – see Campling (1981) and French (1987). In his book *Disabled We Stand*, Sutherland (1981) talks at length of this and believes that:

> We are subjected to continual pressure to conform to a 'normal' image. This is one of the major reasons for the manufacture of elaborate prosthetic limbs and hands, which are often poor substitutes for the purely functional devices such as wooden legs or metal hooks which they replace.

Technological aids are a mixed blessing. I am writing this article on a word-processor which enlarges the print on the screen. It is a marvellous machine and I would not want to be without it. Yet aids can become a burden too, because other people have such faith in technology that they believe the disabled person is managing perfectly well and requires no assistance. A partially sighted physiotherapist explained: 'The more visual aids there are, the more they think you can do the job. Frankly, I don't think they can turn me into a sighted person . . . They can make us less efficient because no one is helping' (French, 1989).

In an article on 'the disabled student in 2001', Heinz Wolff (1986) proposes that technology can never replace the quality of interpersonal relationships. Instead, it can isolate the disabled individual, and firmly locate the problem of disability within the individual, thereby inhibiting societal change. On various occasions when, as a student, I have struggled to read something on the blackboard with a small personal telescope, lecturers have enthusiastically remarked, 'You're doing really well with that little gadget' – a conclusion reached more through wishful thinking than knowledge (French, 1988a). Sutherland (1981) believes that this type of response is very convenient to non-disabled people because it means that they do not have to help or adapt.

We are all dependent on each other to some degree, yet any limitations disabled people have are labelled and regarded as qualitatively different.

When looking for work, in particular, these problems become a major issue: they are focused on a great deal and the task of the disabled person is to persuade the sceptical interviewers that she can cope – that she will not need help. Once in the job, however, it soon becomes apparent that everyone has their share of limitations, sometimes far outstripping those of the disabled person. The crucial difference is that able-bodied people's problems are regarded as normal and acceptable, and thus they can ask assistance of each other without feeling guilty or inferior. Disabled people can ask for help too as long they steer clear of any problems directly associated with disability. In my previous role as a polytechnic lecturer, I would not hesitate to ask a colleague to help me plan a course, but I would not feel able to ask him to read aloud my marking, even though I could return the favour in other ways.

Thus disabled people are often expected to cope with their limitations in a way not expected of other people. Even if colleagues are prepared to assist with disability-related difficulties there are problems. Because disabled people have been conditioned to 'manage' and 'overcome' their disability, to be 'independent', to be 'normal' and to play the 'disabled' role, the real problems and the best solutions are often hidden from view. These pressures make accepting help difficult – nowhere in the socialisation of disabled people have they been encouraged to do so. Yet giving and receiving help can greatly enrich human experience, as a blind social worker I interviewed explained: 'I'm able to say to my clients "I'll help you but there are certain ways in which you are going to have to help me", and the client doesn't feel totally taken over or totally worthless' (French, 1988b).

Though not wishing to deny the importance of basic independence – especially when living in a society which places such store by it – I believe the notion has been pushed too far. Narrowly defined, independence can give rise to inefficiency, stress and isolation, as well as wasting precious time. Striving for independence and normality can lead to frustration and low self-esteem, for as Corbett (1989) points out: 'The realities of our limitations are parameters which most of us evade.' An over-emphasis on physical independence can rob disabled people of true independence by restricting their freedom of thought and action.

Perhaps the client who demands a wheelchair even though he can walk, or the one who refuses to struggle with domestic chores even though he can do them, given the time, are not so unreasonable and incomprehensible after all.

References

Brechin, A. and Liddiard, P. (1981) *Look At It This Way – New Perspectives in Rehabilitation*, The Open University Press, Milton Keynes.

Campling, J. (1981) *Images of Ourselves – Women with Disabilities Talking*, Routledge and Kegan Paul, London.

Corbett, J. (1989) 'The quality of life in the "independence" curriculum', *Disability, Handicap and Society*, Vol. 4, No. 2, pp. 145–63.

French, S.A. (1987) 'Disability – do professionals help or hinder?' *Therapy Weekly*, Vol. 17, No. 35, p. 4.

French, S.A. (1988a) 'In sight – the value of aids for partially sighted people', *Times Educational Supplement*, 3 March, p. 37.

French, S.A. (1988b) 'Experiences of disabled health and caring professionals', *Sociology of Health and Illness*, Vol. 10, No. 2, pp. 170–88.

French, S.A. (1989) Ongoing PhD research.

Oliver, M. (1981) 'The individual model of disability', in *Rehabilitation: Supplementary Readings*, compiled by V. Finkelstein. The Open University Press, Milton Keynes.

Shearer, A. (1981) *Disability – Whose Handicap?* Basil Blackwell, Oxford.

Sutherland, A.T. (1981) *Disabled We Stand*, Souvenir Press, London.

Wolff, H. (1986) 'The disabled student in 2001 – deserted or liberated by new technology?' *Educare*, Vol. 24, pp. 3–8.

1.6

Disability and dependency: a creation of industrial societies?

Mike Oliver

The social construction of the disability problem

The category disability is not fixed and absolute, but can be, and indeed has been, defined in a variety of different ways throughout history, within particular societies and in any given social context. The fact that definitions of disability are relative rather than absolute has led some sociologists in particular to conclude that disability can only be properly understood as a social construction (Albrecht and Levy, 1981, p. 14).

But this process of social construction is not dependent solely on individual meanings or the activities of powerful groups and vested interests, for the category disability is itself produced in part by policy responses to it. Thus, to take an extreme position:

> Fundamentally, disability is defined by public policy. In other words, disability is whatever policy says it is . . . The fact that disability is basically determined by public policy, moreover, seems to demonstrate the need for careful investigations of definitions that are embedded in existing policies.
>
> (Hahn, 1985, p. 294)

While not denying that policy definitions play an important role in the social construction of disability, it is clear that these definitions are themselves socially constructed. And further, it is ideology which has influenced this social construction to the point where disability has become a problem of individual disadvantage to be remedied through the development of appropriate social policies (Borsay, 1986; Oliver, 1986).

Social policy analysis has been slow to recognise the role of ideology in the development of social policies (George and Wilding, 1972) although in recent years it has been given a much more central focus (see Wilding, 1982; Manning, 1985). However, disability policy has not been subjected to any rigorous analysis of its ideological underpinnings in the same way that many other social problems have been deconstructed and even reconstructed.

This paper is an edited version of M. Oliver (1989) 'Disability and dependency: a creation of industrial societies?' in L. Barton (ed.) *Disability and Dependency*, Falmer Press, London.

'Although little conscious attention has been devoted to the problem, the recognition that public policy contains some unspoken assumptions about the level of physical or other abilities required to sustain a person's life seems almost inescapable' (Hahn, 1985, p. 296).

There are a number of reasons why these unspoken assumptions or ideologies have not received much attention. Historically, disability policies have not developed in their own right, and so:

> What is coming to be called disability policy is in fact an aggregate of a variety of policies, each with quite different origins and purposes, reflecting a historical situation in which concern for disability has been intertwined with efforts to establish policy in much broader issue areas.
>
> (Erlanger and Roth, 1985, p. 320)

But this is no longer true in many industrial countries which have begun to develop policies specifically in respect of disabled people. Hence the explanation for the current failure to examine these hidden assumptions or ideologies underpinning even these specific policy initiatives must lie elsewhere. Part of the answer is undoubtedly that these ideologies are so deeply embedded in social consciousness generally that they become 'facts'; they are naturalised. Thus everyone knows that disability is a personal tragedy for individuals so 'afflicted'; hence ideology becomes common sense. And this common sense is reinforced both by 'aesthetic' and 'existential' anxiety:

> widespread aversion toward disabled individuals may be the product of both an 'aesthetic' anxiety, which narcissistically rejects marked deviations from 'normal' physical appearances, and of an 'existential' anxiety, which may find an implicit or projected danger of dehabilitating disability even more terrifying than the inevitability of death.
>
> (Hahn, 1986, p. 125)

The central idea underpinning the social construction of disability as a particular kind of social problem has been that of dependency, and in this paper I shall suggest that the creation of dependency amongst disabled people is an inevitable consequence of the social policies that prevail in all modern industrial societies.

The idea of dependency

Before considering the ways in which dependency is created, it is necessary to define what is meant by the term. In common-sense usage, dependency implies the inability to do things for oneself and consequently the reliance upon others to carry out some or all of the tasks of everyday life. Conversely, independence suggests that the individual needs no assistance whatever from anyone else and this fits nicely with the current ideological climate which stresses competitive individualism. In reality, of course, no one in a modern industrial society is completely independent for we live in a state of mutual interdependence. The dependence of disabled people, therefore, is not a feature which marks them out as different in kind from the rest of the population but as different in degree.

There is obviously a link between this common-sense usage of the term dependency and the way it is used in discussions of social policy, but these more technical discussions see at least two dimensions to the term. The first of these concerns the ways in which welfare states have created whole groups or classes of people who become dependent upon the state for education, health care, financial support, and indeed any other provision the state is prepared to offer. The second focuses on the inability of individuals or groups to provide their own self-care because of their functional limitations or impairments. Both of these dimensions of dependency have figured large in current attempts to restructure welfare states by reducing the size and scope of state benefits and services and by shifting existing provision away from institutions and into the community.

An economic basis for the creation of dependency

Work is central to industrial societies not simply because it produces the goods to sustain life but also because it creates particular forms of social relations. Thus anyone unable to work, for whatever reason, is likely to experience difficulties both in acquiring the necessities to sustain life physically, and also in establishing a set of satisfactory social relationships. Disabled people have not always been excluded from working but the arrival of industrial society has created particular problems: 'The speed of factory work, the enforced discipline, the time-keeping and production norms – all these were a highly unfavourable change from the slower, more self-determined methods of work into which many handicapped people have been integrated' (Ryan and Thomas, 1980, p. 101).

The onset of industrial society did not simply change ways of working, but also had a profound effect on social relations, with the creation of the industrial proletariat and the gradual erosion of existing communities. Industrialisation had profound consequences for disabled people, therefore, both in that they were less able to participate in the work process and also because many previously acceptable social roles, such as beggar or 'village idiot', were disappearing.

The new mechanism for controlling economically unproductive people was the workhouse or the asylum, and over the years a whole range of specialised institutions grew up to contain this group.

The point about this brief historical detour is that the issues are still the same; disabled people are likely to face exclusion from the workforce because of their perceived inabilities, and hence dependency is still being created. And even where attempts are made to influence the work system, they do not have the desired effect:

> Progams focusing on labor supply will always be a major part of any comprehensive approach to disability. But these efforts alone tend to segregate disabled people

from society rather than integrate them into it. The alternative, or more properly the supplement, to these programs is a focus on the demand side of the market, making people more employable and more a part of general social life by changing the social organisation of work and of other aspects of everyday life, through removal of architectural barriers, nondiscrimination and affirmative action programs, main-streaming in the schools, and so on. Until recently, there has been almost no concern with these possibilities.

(Erlanger and Roth, 1985, p. 339)

It could, of course, be argued that government policy aimed at providing aids to employment and the adaptation of workplaces uses precisely this approach, but it does nothing of the kind. These initiatives are all geared towards the supply side of labour, at making individual disabled people more economically productive and hence more acceptable to employers. There are no government incentives to create barrier-free work environments, nor can Ford claim a grant if it wants to make its assembly line usable by all the potential workforce. Neither can other manufacturers wishing to design machinery or tools that are usable by everyone, regardless of their functional abilities, seek government assistance. There are virtually no attempts in modern industrial societies that are targeted at the social organisations of work, at the demand side of labour. And given the size of the reserve pool of labour that currently exists in most industrial societies, it is unlikely that such targeting will occur in the foreseeable future.

Given this historical and current situation it is hardly surprising that one commentator can write of disabled people and other groups: 'Their condition or situation makes them economically unproductive and hence economically and socially dependent' (Illsley, 1981, p. 328). This is only partly true, however, for despite the high rates of unemployment in the industrialised world, the majority of those of working age do have a job, and hence are economically productive. In addition, day centres, adult training centres and sheltered workshops make a considerable economic contribution by carrying out jobs that cannot easily be mechanised, at wage rates that make third world workers look expensive. But more importantly, this takes a narrow view of the economy and fails to recognise the importance of consumption. At present the benefits paid to disabled people amount to some three billion pounds a year (Disability Alliance, 1987), most of which 'will almost invariably be spent to the full' (George and Wilding, 1984). The numbers of firms now producing aids and equipment for disabled people and the seriousness with which motor manufacturers now take disabled motorists are testament to the important and productive role that disabled people play in the economy.

A political basis for the creation of dependency

Policies enacted through the legislative process also have the effect of creating dependency, and the current restructuring of the British welfare state is legitimated by the desire to reduce our 'culture of dependency'. In the case of disability, both the National Assistance Act 1948 and the Chronically Sick and Disabled Persons Act 1970 aimed to provide services for disabled people and in so doing reinforced 'the notion that people who happen to have disabilities are people who are "helpless", unable to choose for themselves the aids to opportunity they need' (Shearer, 1981, p. 82).

More recently, the Disabled Persons (Services, Consultations and Representation) Act 1986, born out of both a recognition of the inadequacies of previous legislation and a wish to involve disabled people more in shaping their own destinies, is underpinned by the desire to improve the services for this dependent group. It offers disabled people the right to be assessed, consulted and represented. However, it is noticeably silent on how these rights can be achieved in the face of recalcitrant local authorities, just as previous legislation was silent on how services could be obtained. In fact, this Act is yet a further extension of the professional and administrative approaches to the problems of disability, rather than an acknowledgement of disability as a human rights issue.

Yet in the aftermath of the Second World War, the Disabled Persons (Employment) Act 1944 recognised that disabled people had a right to work. This legislation was not uninfluenced by the shortage of labour at the time or the collective guilt at seeing ex-service men who had been disabled while fighting for their country; but economic and social climates change, and these rights have never been enforced. Unsuccessful attempts to acknowledge the human rights issue involved have, through the passage of anti-discrimination legislation, surfaced in recent years, but Parliament in its wisdom has never allowed the issue to receive legislative acknowledgement (Oliver, 1985). Thus the legislative framework remains locked into a professional and administrative approach to service provision.

A further way in which dependency is, at least, reinforced is through the manner in which the discourse with regard to disability and social policy is conducted. From the patronising way politicians discuss disability in Parliament, through the failure of social policy analysts to examine critically the concept of disability (Oliver, 1986), to the failure of policy-makers to consult with disabled people, this dependency is reinforced. Nor, indeed, when attention is turned to community care does the discourse alter, for community care implies 'looking after people' (Audit Commission, 1986). The nature of this discourse has recently been criticised thus:

> the need to be 'looked after' may well adequately describe the way potentially physically disabled candidates for 'community care' are perceived by people who are not disabled. This viewpoint has a long history, and a correspondingly successful application in practice – which has led to large numbers of us becoming passive recipients of a wide range of professional and other interventions. But, however good passivity and the creation of dependency may be for the careers of service providers, it is bad news for disabled people and the public purse.
> (British Council of Organisations of Disabled People, 1987, paragraph 3.2)

A professional basis for the creation of dependency

There are a number of ways in which dependency is created through the delivery of professionalised services. The kinds of services that are available – notably residential and day-care facilities with their institutionalised regimes, their failure to involve disabled people meaningfully in the running of such facilities, the transportation of users in specialised transport and the rigidity of the routine activities which take place therein – all serve to institutionalise disabled people and create dependency. While in recent years some attempts have been made to address this problem of dependency creation in these facilities, it is still unfortunately true that power and control continue to remain with professional staff. Many community services are delivered in similar ways and reinforce dependency: disabled people are offered little choice about aids and equipment, times at which professionals can attend to help with matters like toileting, dressing or preparing a meal are restricted, and the limited range of tasks that professionals can perform are further limited because of professional boundaries, employer requirements or trade union practices.

The professional–client relationship can itself also be dependency creating, and indeed the very language used suggests that power is unequally distributed within this relationship. Recent attempts to address this problem through changing the terminology from 'client' to 'user' or 'consumer', acknowledge that the problem exists but do little to change the structures within which these power relations are located. Economic structures determine the roles of professionals as gate-keepers of scarce resources, legal structures determine their controlling functions as administrators of services, career structures determine their decisions about whose side they are actually on and cognitive structures determine their practice with individual disabled people who need help – otherwise, why would they be employed to help them? This is not just another attack on overburdened professionals for they are as much trapped in dependency-creating relationships as are their clients. However, all is not as it seems, for in a fundamental sense it is professionals who are dependent upon disabled people. They are dependent on them for their jobs, their salaries, their subsidised transport, their quality of life, and so on.

Thus if disabled people and professionals are trapped in these dependency-creating relationships, is there a way out of the trap? A false start has already been made through the promotion of the goal of independence which figures largely in the interventions of most professionals and the articulated aims of most disabled people. It has been a false start, however, because in advancing the idea of independence, professionals and disabled people have not been talking about the same thing. Professionals tend to define independence in terms of self-care activities such as washing, dressing, toileting, cooking and eating without assistance. Disabled people, however, define independence differently, seeing it as the ability to be in control of and make decisions about one's life, rather than doing things alone or without help. Hence it is 'a mind process not contingent upon a normal body' (Huemann, quoted in Crewe and Zola, 1983).

If disabled people and professionals are ever going to engage in dependency-reducing rather than dependency-creating relationships, then the following advice from a disabled sociologist must be taken into account:

> We must expand the notion of independence from physical achievements to sociopsychologic decision-making. Independent living must include not only the quality of physical tasks we can do but the quality of life we can lead. Our notion of human integrity must take into account the notion of taking risks. Rehabilitation personnel must change the model of service from doing something to someone to planning and creating services with someone. In short, we must free ourselves from some of the culture-bound and time-limited standards and philosophy that currently exist.
>
> (Zola, 1982, p. 396)

The creation of the dependent individual

A recent study of a small group of young disabled people attending a further education college found that: 'Many of the students arrive in college with very negative self-image and poor self-esteem. Often they appear to have been conditioned into accepting a devalued social role as sick, pitiful, a burden of charity' (Hutchinson and Tennyson, 1986, p. 33). Precisely how and why these disabled young people came to see themselves in this way now needs to be addressed.

All of the young people studied came to the college from special schools, and there is no doubt that the medical hegemony in special education has hardly been challenged by recent legislative changes (Warnock, 1978; Education Act 1981). In practice, medical need still predominates over educational need; disabled children still have operations (necessary and unnecessary) at times which fit in with the schedules of surgeons and hospitals rather than educational programmes, children are still taken out from classes for doctors' appointments or physiotherapy and the school nurse is still a more influential figure than are the teachers. If children are brought up to believe, through experiencing a range of medical and paramedical interventions, that they are ill, we cannot be surprised if they passively accept the sick role.

But it is not only the intrusion of medicine into education which creates dependency through an acceptance of the sick role. They also see themselves as pitiful because they are socialised into accepting disability as a tragedy personal to them. This occurs because teachers, like other professionals, also hold to this view of disability, curriculum materials portray disabled people (if they appear at all) as pathetic victims or arch villains, and their education takes place in a context in which any understanding of the history and politics of disability is absent.

However, it is not just the educational environment which creates this dependency: the social environment also plays a significant role in shaping the view that some disabled people hold of themselves as burdens of charity.

To begin with, many of the traditional voluntary organisations for disabled people are quite shameless in the way they reinforce this charitable image through their fund-raising campaigns. The prime objective is to maximise income, regardless of the image presented. The unfortunate thing about this is that many of these organisations are not even aware of the way in which this approach creates dependency, and even if they are, then an instrumental, 'ends justifies means' philosophy is used.

But it is not only voluntary organisations who beg on behalf of disabled people; some professionals are even employed by government agencies so to do. For example, disablement resettlement officers (DROs) employed by the Department of Employment, instead of ensuring that employers are carrying out their legal duties under the Disabled Persons (Employment) Act, are given the task of persuading employers to give jobs to disabled people.

Finally, many disabled people are forced into the position of passive recipients of unwanted gifts or inappropriate services, for to refuse such 'generosity' would be to confirm the 'fact' that disabled people have not come to terms with their disability and have a 'chip on their shoulder'. Examples of unwanted or unsuitable gifts are the wheelchairs designed by Lord Snowdon which turned out to be unusable by anyone who is paralysed; and examples of inappropriate services are the special vehicles, usually with the name of the donor written large all over the side, which are often used to transport disabled people. These are particularly used to carry disabled people to and from segregated facilities such as special schools, day centres and residential homes.

The restructuring of the welfare state: the elimination of dependency

Since the mid-1970s there has been a world economic recession, one result of which has been to call into question both the nature and future of welfare states in the industrial world. This questioning has usually been raised within the language of crisis, of which there are at least three dimensions: (a) a crisis in the welfare state in that it was not meeting social needs; (b) a crisis of the welfare state in that it was creating needs that it could not meet; and (c) a crisis by the welfare state in that the rising cost of welfare was creating a crisis of capitalism itself. Further, 'the crisis definition is now being used as an ideological basis for reducing social expenditure, changing redistributive patterns in disfavour of the marginal groups and reducing government responsibility in social policy' (Oyen, 1986, p. 6).

While both the precise nature of this crisis and the ideological response to it differs from industrial country to industrial country, all have had broadly similar experiences. In Britain, the left have broadly subscribed to the view that there is a crisis in the welfare state and that the solution is to increase public expenditure on it. The right, on the other hand, have subscribed to the view that there is a crisis of the welfare state and, if not properly managed and controlled, it could indeed become a crisis of the capitalist state. As the right have held political power for most of this period, it is their view of the nature of the crisis which has shaped the process of restructuring the welfare state. A major underpinning of the ideological basis for this restructuring has been the issue of dependency. Reductions in expenditure, changes in redistribution and the gradual withdrawal of the state from people's lives have all been legitimated on the grounds of the need to reduce dependency.

There is little doubt, with regard to disabled people, that their experiences of the welfare state coincide with both the 'crisis in' and 'crisis of' dimensions. In other words, they have not received all the services they need and in many cases those services that they have received have created or reinforced their dependency. So, it has to be said that future policy options stemming from either (or both) of these dimensions are unlikely to succeed in reducing dependency, whether it be physical or social. Simply increasing public expenditure will only serve to lock disabled people further into the dependency-creating relationships I have already described, and reductions and redistributions will condemn disabled people to isolation and loneliness in the community or institutionalisation in residential care. This raises the issue of what, if anything, can ease this crisis as far as disabled people are concerned.

There are a number of things which can be done to tackle the political and professional bases for dependency creation among disabled people. So far, the political right have been making the running and their main strategy has been to resolve the 'crisis of' the welfare state by tackling the problems of dependency creation through the privatisation of state services. There are also a number of strategies that could be adopted by the left to tackle the 'crisis in' the welfare state and these will be discussed. These strategies are the introduction of anti-discrimination legislation, freedom of information and the proper financial and other support of organisations controlled and run by disabled people themselves.

It is, perhaps, ironic that the model for providing privatised services is that of the supermarket; the argument being that packages of care can be purchased just as customers purchase products from supermarket shelves. Many disabled people find shopping in supermarkets difficult, if not impossible, because of physical access, difficulties in reaching shelves and the fact that products and packaging are tailored to the needs of the modern nuclear family and not to the needs of individuals. In short, supermarkets offer a limited range of products which suit the needs of particular groups in society and if not in these groups, then the consumer is not 'king', as the rhetoric would have it. Thus, for many disabled people, the supermarket model of provision is unlikely to offer anything substantially different from the provision of state services; that is to say, little choice over what is provided and little control over how it is provided.

What the supermarket is alleged to offer, but clearly does not, is choice and control. The key issue for the future as far as the left is concerned is whether the 'crisis in' the welfare state can be resolved by offering users of services choice and control. I want to suggest that, by the modification and adaptation of first principles, it can:

> The challenge that faces us is not the choice between universalist and selective services. The real challenge resides in the question: what particular infrastructure of universalist services is needed in order to provide a framework of values and opportunity bases within and around which can be developed acceptable selective services provided as social rights, on criteria of needs of specific categories, groups and territorial areas and not dependent upon individual tests of means?
>
> (Titmuss, 1968, p. 122)

To update the language somewhat, it should be possible to allow for choice and control in service provision within a universalist infrastructure, if consumers have social rights to these services and if there are mechanisms whereby the needs of groups and communities, whether local or interest communities, can be articulated by these groups themselves.

It has become clear that if disabled people are to have social rights to services, then the legislative framework must do more than simply list these services (Chronically Sick and Disabled Persons Act) or provide professional and administrative approaches to their provision (Disabled Persons (Services, Consultation and Representation) Act). This inevitably implies the necessity for anti-discrimination legislation which would not only provide public affirmation of the unacceptability of discrimination against disabled people, but also, if properly drafted, a framework for the enforcement of service delivery and a mechanism for professional accountability.

By itself it would not be enough, of course, as the experience in the areas of race and gender demonstrate. Therefore an essential adjunct would be legislation facilitating complete freedom of information which goes beyond current attempts to provide access to information held on computers and local authority files. The locked medical cabinets would need to be opened and the unofficial documents that are kept as ways of avoiding information disclosure would (as with current practices which require information to be provided to parents under the statementing regulations of the Education Act 1981) need to be made available.

Finally, a mechanism whereby the needs of groups and communities can be articulated needs to be developed. This can only be accomplished through the adequate funding and resourcing of organisations controlled and run by disabled people, which have been going from strength to strength throughout the world in the 1980s. Significantly, there is some evidence that these organisations of disabled people find it easier to flourish in the under-developed rather than the industrial world. This is due, in part, to the resistance to change of bureaucratic and professional structures in the industrial world but also to the existence of a large and powerful sector of traditional organisations for the disabled who remain locked into dependency-creating service provision and attitudes, and who, consequently, have vested interests in maintaining the status quo.

None of these developments by themselves, or an incremental approach to them, are likely to prove successful. Anti-discrimination legislation without freedom of information and a supportive network of disabled people will simply mean that the lawyers will get rich; freedom of information by itself will mean that individual disabled people will be subjected to professional mystification and sleight of hand; and support for the disabled people's movement without a framework which guarantees basic human rights will leave the movement politically emasculated. But an integrated programme, as suggested above, could provide a means of addressing the problems of dependency creation at both political and professional levels, and hence go some way to resolving the 'crises' both in, and of, the welfare state, at least as far as disabled people are concerned.

Conclusions

An inevitable consequence of living in industrial society is that we all live in a condition of mutual dependency. However, the dichotomy of dependence/independence has been a significant influence on both the way disabled people are perceived in general and on the development of social policies geared towards them in particular. Dependency is created by a variety of economic, political, professional and other forces, and recent changes in the structure of the welfare state have been legitimated on the grounds of the need to reduce this dependency. Policies based upon the 'crisis in' the welfare state thesis are unlikely to succeed in reducing dependency, though they may temporarily resolve the crisis of capitalism created by public expenditure on the welfare state.

Ultimately, only attempts to tackle the 'crisis of' the welfare state are likely to be successful, for the creation of an infrastructure of state services which facilitate user choice and control is the only way in which dependency can be permanently removed. While this will be more costly for the capitalist economy in the short term, it may not only prevent such a crisis of capitalism from occurring, but will also create a much happier environment for us all to live in a state of mutual interdependence.

References

Albrecht, G. and Levy, J. (1981) 'Constructing disabilities as social problems', in Albrecht, G. (ed.) *Cross National Rehabilitation Policies: a Sociological Perspective*, Sage, London.

Audit Commission (1986) *Making a Reality of Community Care*, HMSO, London.

Borsay, A. (1986) 'Personal trouble or public issue? Towards a model of policy for people with physical and mental disabilities', *Disability, Handicap and Society*, Vol. 1, No. 2, pp. 179–96.

British Council of Organisations of Disabled People (1987) *Comment on the Report of the Audit Commission*, BCODP, London.

Crewe, N. and Zola, I. (1983) *Independent Living for Physically Disabled People*, Jossey-Bass, London.

Disability Alliance (1987) *Poverty and Disability: Breaking the Link*, London Disability Alliance.

Erlanger, H. and Roth, W. (1985) 'Disability policy: the parts and the whole', *American Behavioural Scientist*, Vol. 28, No. 3, pp. 319–46.

George, V. and Wilding, P. (1972) *Ideology and Social Welfare*, Routledge and Kegan Paul, London.

George, V. and Wilding, P. (1984) *The Impact of Social Policy*, Routledge and Kegan Paul, London.

Hahn, H. (1985) 'Disability policy and the problem of discrimination', *American Behavioural Scientist*, Vol. 28, No. 3, pp. 293–318.

Hahn, H. (1986) 'Public support for rehabilitation programs: the analysis of US disability policy', *Disability, Handicap and Society*, Vol. 1, No. 2.

Hutchinson, D. and Tennyson, C. (1986) *Transition to Adulthood*, Further Education Unit, London.

Illsley, R. (1981) 'Problems of dependency groups: the care of the elderly, the handicapped and the chronically ill', *Social Science and Medicine*, Vol. 15a, No. 3 (Part II).

Manning, N. (ed.) (1985) *Social Problems and Welfare Ideology*, Gower, Aldershot.

Oliver, M. (1985) 'Discrimination, disability and social policy', in Brenton, M. and Jones, C. (eds) *The Year Book of Social Policy in Britain 1984–5*, Routledge and Kegan Paul, London.

Oliver, M. (1986) 'Disability and social policy: some theoretical issues', *Disability, Handicap and Society*, Vol. 1, No. 1, pp. 5–18.

Oyen, E. (ed.) (1986) *Comparing Welfare States and Their Futures*, Gower, Aldershot.

Ryan, J. and Thomas, F. (1980) *The Politics of Mental Handicap*, Penguin, Harmondsworth.

Shearer, A. (1981) *Disability: Whose Handicap?* Blackwell, Oxford.

Titmuss, R. (1968) *Commitment to Welfare*, Allen and Unwin, London.

Warnock Report (1978) *Special Educational Needs: Report of the Committee of Enquiry into the Education of Children and Young People*, HMSO, London.

Wilding, P. (1982) *Professional Power and Social Welfare*, Routledge and Kegan Paul, London.

Zola, I. (1982) 'Social and cultural disincentives to independent living', *Archives of Physical Medicine and Rehabilitation*, Vol. 63.

1.7

Re-defining disability: a challenge to research

Mike Oliver

Introduction

In recent years definitions of disability have undergone a number of changes and modifications. Starting from the work of Harris (1971) and her national survey of disabled people, a threefold distinction of impairment, disability and handicap was proposed. Following various discussions and refinements, a more sophisticated scheme advanced by Wood (1981) was accepted as the basis for classifying illness, disease and disability by the World Health Organisation.

However, these definitions have not received universal acceptance, particularly amongst disabled people and their organisations. A major criticism is that they have been based upon able-bodied assumptions of disability and, as a consequence, they do not accord with the personal realities of disabled people (Oliver, 1983). This 'lack of fit' between able-bodied and disabled people's definitions is more than just a semantic quibble for it has important implications both for the provision of services and the ability to control one's life.

However, the debate is not just about services but also about the politics of control; who should be in charge of the rehabilitation process, disabled people or the professionals? And should disabled people receive the services the professionals think they need or those that they themselves choose?

A major dimension of this debate has centred on the issue of where the problems of disability are located. Able-bodied professionals have tended to see these problems as stemming from the functional limitations of the impaired individual, whereas disabled people have argued that they stem from the failure of physical and social environments to take account of the needs of particular individuals or groups. Is the problem of access to buildings caused by people being unable to walk or by the widespread social practice of having steps into buildings? Elsewhere (Oliver, 1983) these different needs have been characterised as individual and social models of disability. However, this debate has not taken place in a neutral way but against a

This paper is an edited version of M. Oliver (1987) 'Re-defining disability: some issues for research', *Research, Policy and Planning*, No. 5, pp. 9–13.

cultural and political backdrop of discrimination against disabled people and the struggle by some disabled people against this discrimination. Thus the neutral terms, 'individual', and 'social' models, could easily be replaced by the more emotionally laden ones of 'personal tragedy theory' as opposed to 'social oppression theory'.

The importance of definitions

If disability is seen as a tragedy, then disabled people will be treated as if they are the victims of some tragic happening and circumstances. This treatment will occur not just in everyday interaction but will also be translated into social policies which will attempt to compensate these victims for the tragedy that has happened to them.

Alternatively, it logically follows that if disability is defined as social oppression, then disabled people will be seen as collective victims of an uncaring or unknowing society rather than as individual victims of circumstances. Such a view will be translated into social policies geared towards alleviating oppression rather than compensating individuals. It almost goes without saying that at this point in time, the individual and tragic view of disability dominates both social interactions and social policies.

Official definitions

In the late 1950s and early 1960s there was an upswing in the economy and a growing concern to provide more services for disabled people. But clearly no government was going to commit itself to a whole range of services without some clear idea of what the financial consequences of such a commitment might be. Thus, after some pilot work, the Office of Population Censuses and Surveys (OPCS) conducted a national survey in the late 1960s, which was published in 1971 (Harris, 1971).

Critical to this survey was the definition of disability underpinning it, and the survey adopted a threefold classification along the following lines:

> *Impairment*: 'lacking all or part of a limb, or having a defective limb, organ or mechanism of the body'.
> *Disability*: 'the loss or reduction of functional ability'.
> *Handicap*: 'the disadvantage or restriction of activity caused by disability'.

Criticisms of research based on official definitions

Finkelstein (1980) argues that all approaches to disability up to now have focused on the impairment of individuals as the ultimate cause of disability.

He is critical of the narrow focus that research has adopted up to now but he suggests that an alternative approach is emerging.

> The predominant focus of attitudes, help, research and so on has, as a natural expression of one side of the disability relationship, been towards the disabled person. Nearly all references concerned with attitudes towards disability use the disabled person as the point of focus. The emergent approach is to focus on the behaviour, roles, perceptions, attitudes, etc., of the helpers as representatives of a socially determined relationship.

This emergent approach has developed largely as a consequence of disabled people organising to articulate their own definitions of disability.

This leads to a second general criticism of research on disability, in that it has failed to involve disabled people except as passive subjects. Davis (1986) makes this point:

> Much of the work which has already been done on definitions has been carried out by people who do not themselves experience the daily problems of disability. This has drastically affected the solutions, and in turn has often served to perpetrate discrimination against us, as well as wasting resources on an enormous scale.'

The issue of research actually discriminating against disabled people is a general criticism that needs to be made. There are two aspects of this: first, much research on disability has utilised theoretical models so divorced from the everyday experience of disabled people that 'they have felt victimised by professionals who write articles about the reactions to disability that are based more upon theory than fact' (Trieschmann, 1980). A second aspect concerns the fact that much research on disability has contributed little or nothing to improving the quality of life of disabled people, though it might have substantially improved the career prospects of the researchers. As a consequence of this situation, more and more disabled people are refusing to participate in research design, controlled and published by able-bodied researchers who are either unaware or lack an understanding of the research issues involved in the social causation of disability and who fail to involve disabled people in the research process.

Criticisms of research in the personal social services

With regard to specific criticisms of research in the personal social services, as I have already indicated, most of this was of the conceptual framework developed by Harris (1971) and built on by ICIDH (Wood, 1981). The problem with this is that these schemes, while acknowledging there are social dimensions to disability, do not see disability as arising from social causes – ultimately their rationale rests upon the impaired individual, with disability and handicap arising as a direct consequence of individual impairments. As a result of this fundamental flaw, Disabled Peoples' International has opposed the ICIDH scheme since its inception in 1981.

Much of the work that researchers do in the personal social services consists of either counting heads to contribute to the statutory obligations of local authorities to keep a register of disabled people or simply to provide a reliable data base to plan services. There are a number of reasons why researchers should stop this sterile business of head-counting. First, at the level of epistemology, if disability is really socially caused, then research should aim to identify those social causes with a view to eradication rather than further contributing to the individualisation of disability. It is also a waste of resources. If disability is socially caused, then changes in social organisation (which occur all the time) may increase or decrease the numbers of disabled people in society at any particular point in time.

Even if we are prepared to leave questions of epistemology aside and take a pragmatic approach, the counting of numbers of disabled people is still a waste of time and resources. A major reason for this is that no accurate and reliable data have ever been produced (and I would argue that for epistemological reasons it cannot be). Let us take the Harris (1971) survey as an example, for it broadly estimated that there were three million disabled people in Britain. Townsend (1979), in another survey carried out at the same time but published later, came up with an estimate of ten million. When local authority registers were compared to the local estimates made by Harris, it was found that local authorities were only able to identify one-third of the disabled people who, according to Harris, should have been there (Warren *et al.*, 1978).

This failure to come up with reliable figures is serious, not just for the credibility of researchers, but for the development of policy and the planning of services. Again, to give another example, on the basis of the Harris survey, the government introduced the Attendance Allowance for severely disabled people, safe in the knowledge that only 25,000 people in the country would qualify. By the end of the first year 75,000 people had successfully claimed it and in 1986 there were 580,000 recipients. That either means that there has been more than a twenty-fold increase in severely disabled people in the past 15 years or that the original research was wildly inaccurate.

Head-counts cannot, therefore, produce reliable data for planning and policy purposes and, in addition, they contribute to the further oppression of disabled people.

Towards a better understanding

Given these developments and the criticisms that can be made of much current research on disability, the question of what research in general, and able-bodied researchers in particular, can actually do, now needs to be considered. Before doing this, however, clarification of some of the issues concerning definitions perhaps needs further discussion. This I shall do by suggesting a scheme which proposes that disability can be defined in three ways: as an individual problem, as a social construction and as a social creation.

Initially, disability was seen as an individual problem and its meaning was non-problematic. Earlier I referred to this as the 'personal tragedy theory' of disability, underpinned by the assumption that becoming disabled is a tragic event and it is the disabled individual who has to adapt himself or herself to society. However, both in research and social policy terms this definition has proved inadequate in both understanding and providing an adequate solution to the problems of disability.

This failure has given rise to a social constructionist view of disability, what Borsay (1986) refers to as an interpretive account. This approach recognises the importance of defining the problem correctly in the first place and acknowledges that disability has a social dimension. However, it has tended to see the process of construction as important and has focused largely on attitudes, with the implications that if the attitudes of the able-bodied are to change then the problems of disability will be resolved. Unfortunately, there is ample evidence that awareness training does not work; for example, racism awareness training aimed at the attitudes of white people (Gurnah, 1984; Sivanandan, 1986). Indeed, in the area of disability policies aimed at changing employers' attitudes have not worked either (Oliver, 1985).

Both the individual and social constructionist approaches have proved inadequate and, following the criticisms discussed earlier, have led to disabled people defining disability as a social creation: not as merely an individual or attitudinal problem, but as a problem created by the institutions, organisations and processes that constitute society in its totality. Borsay (1986) refers to this as a structural account of disability. Clearly, if disability is a structural or socially created problem, then attempts to resolve it need a wider range of political strategies (Oliver, 1984) and professional interventions (Oliver, 1983) than can be considered here. However, the urgent task for research, and indeed researchers, is to create an epistemology and methodology which takes as its starting-point the central idea that disability is socially created. This need not be as difficult as it sounds, for in the social sciences there is a tradition of being able to critically examine some of the individualistic notions underpinning a whole range of social problems.

With regard to methodology, there have been one or two attempts to develop strategies which shift the focus away from the impaired individual and on to disabling environments, whether they are physical or social. Notably, Wolfensberger and his Programme Analysis of Service Systems (PASS), (Wolfensberger and Glenn, 1975) with regard to people with mental handicaps, and Finlay's (1978) attempt to measure 'housing disability' in Rochdale are examples of ways in which some of the issues in disability can be researched without resorting to methodologies focused on individuals or head-counts. The crucial point to be made is that these developments can only be facilitated by establishing a partnership between researchers and disabled people, for neither can do it alone. Disabled people do not (as yet) have the knowledge or skill to develop an appropriate research epistemology and methodology, and researchers do not (and cannot ever have) sufficient knowledge or experience of disability in order to ground their researches on an adequate experiential base.

What can researchers actually do?

The first task of research is to attempt to operationalise the concept of disability based upon the notion that disability is a social creation. This implies a fundamental break with current research practice based upon measuring individual needs and counting heads.

That is not to imply that measuring may not be necessary in working with the conceptual framework of disability as a social creation. It is what is measured and counted that becomes the crucial issue. Again, without being prescriptive, a number of important issues can be addressed; for example, how far is your own organisation involved in the creation of disability in terms of (a) its physical access, (b) its presentation of information and (c) the kinds of services provided? It is worth emphasising that none of these questions can be addressed without fully involving disabled people and their organisations. Such questions can be operationalised using quantitative methods – and might it not be a better aim for researchers to construct indications of disabling environments rather than continue to count the numbers of disabled people? Indeed, how much more interesting would it be to construct a 'disability index' for each local authority, for example, so that Brent could be compared with Camden or Kent, to see which local authorities had the most and which had the least disabling policies.

What has so far been argued is that the targets for research activity have to change, not the way it is undertaken. There is one area, however, that does imply a fundamental break from the positivist tradition. Research on disability can no longer be carried out in isolation from disabled people themselves. Strategies have to be devised to ensure that research on disability provides an accurate and fruitful account and this can only be done by ensuring that the experience of disability is fed into the project by disabled people themselves, and at all stages: planning, design, fieldwork, analysis and report writing. Having said this, it should be clear that no ideal design blueprint for research on disability can be provided in advance, for satisfactory research can only be constructed by researchers and disabled people participating in the joint enterprise.

Having attempted to specify some of the things researchers could actually do, it is only fair to recognise some of the constraints that researchers in the personal social services work under. First, such researchers are not autonomous and often are simply handed down projects from above. Second, many personal social services organisations have certain functional requirements to be fulfilled: planning cycles; budgeting; ordering aids and equipment and so on; and researchers may be required to provide the necessary information. Third, the general issue of the need to estimate numbers and the specific issue of the Chronically Sick and Disabled Persons' Register hangs over most attempts to undertake research and gather information in the personal social services about disability.

These constraints will not disappear overnight but what needs to be recognised is that the issue of institutionalised disablism can be addressed within this organisational context in exactly the same way as issues of institutionalised racism and sexism have been addressed, namely through equal opportunities policies.

Conclusion

In this paper I have argued that most social research has failed to acknowledge or even be aware of recent attempts by disabled people to reformulate and devise more appropriate definitions of disability. Hence this research has failed to incorporate important issues into its epistemology and methodology resulting in severe criticisms of its findings, usefulness and relevance, and hence has contributed to the oppression of disabled people. This paper has therefore been an attempt to raise awareness among researchers of what these issues actually are and to provide a tentative pointer to some of the directions into which research must go. Failure to address these issues will not only further contribute to the irrelevance of much research but continue to place disabled people in the role of victims and add to their feelings of exploitation. The only way ahead is for disabled people and researchers to work together in constructing a more appropriate research enterprise, the failure of researchers to acknowledge this will inevitably mean that disabled people will construct their own research enterprise without them.

References

Borsay, A. (1986) *Disabled People in the Community*, Bedford Square Press, London.

Davis, K. (1986) *Developing Our Own Definitions: Draft for Discussion*, British Council of Organisations of Disabled People, London.

Finkelstein, V. (1980) *Attitudes and Disabled People*, World Rehabilitation Fund, New York.

Finlay, W. (1978) *Housing and Disability: a Report on the Housing Needs of Physically Handicapped People in Rochdale*, Rochdale Voluntary Action.

Gurnah, A. (1984) 'The politics of racism awareness training', *Critical Social Policy*. No. 11, pp. 6–20.

Harris, A. (1971) *Handicapped and Impaired in Great Britain*, HMSO, London.

Oliver, M. (1983) *Social Work with Disabled People*, Macmillan, London.

Oliver, M. (1984) 'The politics of disability', *Critical Social Policy*, No. 11, pp. 21–32.

Oliver, M. (1985) 'Discrimination, disability and social policy', in *The Year Book of Social Policy 1984–5*, Routledge and Kegan Paul, London.

Sivanandan, A. (1986) 'Racism awareness training', *New Society*.

Townsend, P. (1979) *Poverty in the United Kingdom*, Penguin, Harmondsworth.

Trieschmann, R.B. (1980) *Spinal Cord Injuries*, Pergamon Press, Oxford.

Warren, M., Knight, R. and Warren, E. (1978) *Changing Capabilities and Needs of People with Handicaps*, Health Services Research Unit, University of Kent.

Wolfensberger, W. and Glenn, L. (1975) *Programme Analysis of Service Systems*, National Institute on Mental Retardation, Toronto.

Wood, P. (1981) *International Classification of Impairments, Disabilities and Handicaps*, WHO, Geneva.

SECTION 2:
IN OUR OWN IMAGE

2.1

'Can you see the rainbow?'
The roots of denial

Sally French

Childhood

Some of my earliest memories are of anxious relatives trying to get me to see things. I did not understand why it was so important that I should do so, but was acutely aware of their intense anxiety if I could not. It was aesthetic things like rainbows that bothered them most. They would position me with great precision, tilting my head to precisely the right angle, and then point to the sky saying 'Look, there it is; look, there, there ... THERE!' As far as I was concerned there was nothing there, but if I said as much their anxiety grew even more intense; they would rearrange my position and the whole scenario would be repeated.

In the end, despite a near total lack of colour vision and a complete indifference to the rainbow's whereabouts, I would say I could see it. In that way I was able to release the mounting tension and escape to pursue more interesting tasks. It did not take long to learn that in order to avert episodes such as these and to protect the feelings of the people around me, I had to deny my disability.

The adults would also get very perturbed if ever I looked 'abnormal'. Being told to open my eyes and straighten my face, when all I was doing was trying to see, made me feel ugly and separate. Having adults pretend that I could see more than I could, and having to acquiesce in the pretence, was a theme throughout my childhood.

Adults who were not emotionally involved with the issue of whether or not I could see also led me along the path of denial. This was achieved by their tendency to disbelieve me and interpret my behaviour as 'playing up' when I told them I could not see. Basically they were confused and unable to cope with the ambiguities of partial sight and were not prepared to take instruction on the matter from a mere child. One example of this occurred in the tiny country primary school that I attended. On warm, sunny days we had our lessons outdoors where, because of the strong sunlight, I could not see to read, write or draw. It was only when the two teachers realised I was having similar difficulties eating my dinner that they began to doubt their interpretation that I was a malingerer. On several occasions I was told off by opticians when I failed to discriminate between the different lenses they placed before my eyes. I am not sure whether they really disbelieved me or whether their professional pride was hurt when nothing they could offer seemed to help; whatever it was I rapidly learned to say 'better' or 'worse', even though all the lenses looked the same.

It was also very difficult to tell the adults, when they had scraped together the money and found the time to take me to the pantomime or wherever, that it was a frustrating and boring experience. I had a strong sense of spoiling other people's fun, just as a sober person among a group of drunken friends may have. As a child, explaining my situation without appearing disagreeable, sullen and rude was so problematic that I usually denied my disability and suffered in silence. All of this taught me from a very early age that, while the adults were working themselves up about whether or not I could see rainbows, my own anxieties must never be shared.

These anxieties were numerous and centred on getting lost, being slow, not managing and, above all, looking stupid and displaying fear. I tried very hard to be 'normal', to be anonymous and to merge with the crowd. Beaches were a nightmare; finding my way back from the sea to specific people in the absence of landmarks was almost impossible, yet giving in to panic was too shameful to contemplate. Anticipation of difficulties could cause even greater anguish than the difficulties themselves and was sufficient to ruin whole days. The prospect of outings with lots of sighted children to unfamiliar places, was enough to make me physically ill, and with a bewildering mix of remorse and relief, I would stay at home.

Brownie meetings were worrying if any degree of independent movement was allowed; in the summer when we left the confines and safety of our hut to play on the nearby common, the other children would immediately disperse, leaving me alone among the trees, feeling stupid and frightened and wondering what to do next. The adults were always adamant that I should join in, that I should not miss out on the fun, but how much they or the other children noticed my difficulties I do not know; I was never teased or blamed for them, they were simply never discussed, at least not with me. This lack of communication gave me a powerful unspoken message that my disability must be denied.

By denying the reality of my disability I protected myself from the anxiety, disapproval, frustration and disappointment of the adults in my life. Like most children I wanted their acceptance, approval and warmth, and quickly learned that this could best be gained by colluding with their perceptions of my situation. I denied my disability in response to their denial, which was often motivated by a benign attempt to integrate me in a world which they perceived as fixed. My denial of disability was thus not a psychopathological reaction, but a sensible and rational response to the peculiar situation I was in.

Special school

Attending special school at the age of nine was, in many ways, a great relief. Despite the crocodile walks, the bells, the long separations from home, the regimentation and the physical punishment, it was an enormous joy to be with other partially sighted children and to be in an environment where limited sight was simply not an issue. I discovered that many other children shared my world and, despite the harshness of institutional life, I felt relaxed, made lots of friends, became more confident and thrived socially. For the first time in my life I was a standard product and it felt very good. The sighted adults who looked after us were few in number with purely custodial roles, and although they seemed to be in a permanent state of anger, provided we stayed out of trouble we were basically ignored. We lived peer-orientated, confined and unchallenging lives where lack of sight rarely as much as entered our heads.

Although the reality of our disabilities was not openly denied in this situation, the only thing guaranteed to really enthuse the staff was the slightest glimmer of hope that our sight could be improved. Contact lenses were an innovation at this time, and children who had previously been virtually ignored were nurtured, encouraged and congratulated, as they learned to cope with them, and were told how good they looked without their glasses on. After I had been at the school for about a year, I was selected as one of the guinea-pigs for the experimental 'telescopic lenses' which were designed, at least in part, to preserve our postures (with which there was obsessive concern) by enabling us to read and write from a greater distance. For most of us they did not work.

I remember being photographed wearing the lenses by an American man whom I perceived to be very important. First of all he made me knit while wearing them, with the knitting held right down on my lap. This was easy as I could in any case knit without looking. He was unduly excited and enthusiastic and told me how much the lenses were helping. I knew he was wrong. Then he asked me to read, but this changed his mood completely; he became tense, and before taking the photograph he pushed the book, which was a couple of inches from my face, quite roughly to my knees. Although I knew he had cheated and that what he had done was wrong, I still felt culpable for his displeasure and aware that I had failed an important test.

We were forced to use equipment like the telescopic lenses even though it did not help, and sometimes actually made things worse; the behaviour of the adults clearly conveyed the message, 'You are not acceptable as you are'. If we dared to reject the equipment we were reminded of the cost, and asked to reflect on the clever and dedicated people who were tirelessly working for the benefit of ungrateful creatures like ourselves. No heed was ever taken of our own suggestions; my requests to try tinted lenses were always ignored and it was not until I left school that I discovered how helpful they would be.

The only other times that lack of sight became an issue for us at the school were during the rare and clumsy attempts to integrate us with able-bodied children. The worst possible activity, netball, was usually chosen for this.

These occasions were invariably embarrassing and humiliating for all concerned and could lead to desperate manoeuvres on the part of the adults to deny the reality of our situation – namely that we had insufficient sight to compete. I am reminded of one netball match, with the score around 20/nil, during which we overheard the games mistress of the opposing team anxiously insisting that they let us get some goals. It was a mortifying experience to see the ball fall through the net while they stood idly by. Very occasionally local Brownies would join us for activities in our extensive grounds. We would be paired off with them for a treasure hunt through the woods, searching for milk-bottle tops – the speed at which they found them was really quite amazing. They seemed to know about us, though, and would be very kind and point the 'treasure' out, and even let us pick it up ourselves sometimes, but relying on their bounty spoiled the fun and we wished we could just talk to them or play a different game.

Whether the choice of these highly visual activities was a deliberate denial of our disabilities or simply a lack of imagination on the part of the adults, I do not know. Certainly we played such games successfully among ourselves, and as we were never seen in any other context, perhaps it was the latter. It was only on rare occasions such as these that our lack of sight (which had all but been forgotten) and the artificiality of our world became apparent.

As well as denying the reality of their disabilities, disabled children are frequently forced to deny painful feelings associated with their experiences because their parents and other adults simply cannot cope with them. I am reminded of a friend who, at the age of six or seven, was repeatedly promised expensive toys and new dresses provided she did not cry when taken back to school; we knew exactly how we must behave. Protecting the feelings of the adults we cared about became an arduous responsibility which we exercised with care.

Bravery and stoicism were demanded by the institution too; any outward expression of sadness was not merely ridiculed and scorned, it was simply not allowed. Any hint of dejection led to stern reminders that, unlike most children, we were highly privileged to be living in such a splendid house with such fantastic grounds – an honour which was clearly not our due. There was no one to turn to for comfort or support, and any tears which were shed were, of necessity, silent and private. In contrast to this, the institution, normally so indifferent to life outside its gates, was peculiarly concerned about our parents' states of mind. Our letters were meticulously censored to remove any trace of despondency and the initial letter of each term had a compulsory first sentence: 'I have settled down at school and am well and happy.' Not only were we compelled to deny our disabilities, but also the painful feelings associated with the lifestyles forced upon us because we were disabled.

Such was our isolation at this school that issues of how to behave in the 'normal' world were rarely addressed, but at the next special school I attended, which offered a grammar school education and had an entirely different ethos, much attention was paid to this. The headmaster, a strong, resolute pioneer in the education of partially sighted children appeared to have a genuine belief not only that we were as good as everyone else, but that we were almost certainly better, and he spent his life tirelessly battling with people who did not share his view.

He liked us to regard ourselves as sighted and steered us away from any connection with blindness; for example, although we were free to go out by ourselves to the nearby town and beyond, the use of white canes was never suggested although many of us use them now. He delighted in people who broke new, visually challenging ground, like acceptance at art school or reading degrees in mathematics, and 'blind' occupations, like physiotherapy, were rarely encouraged. In many ways his attitudes and behaviour were refreshing, yet he placed the onus to achieve and succeed entirely on ourselves; there was never any suggestion that the world could adapt, or that our needs could or should be accommodated. The underlying message was always the same: 'Be superhuman and deny your disability.'

Adulthood

In adulthood, most of these pressures to deny disability persist, though they become more subtle and harder to perceive. If disabled adults manage to gain control of their lives, which for many is very difficult, these pressures may be easier to resist. This is because situations which pose difficulties, create anxieties or cause boredom can be avoided, or alternatively adequate assistance can be sought; many of the situations I was placed in as a child I now avoid. As adults we are less vulnerable and less dependent on other people, we can more easily comprehend our situation, and our adult status makes the open expression of other people's disapproval, frustration and disbelief less likely. In addition, disabled adults arouse less emotion and misplaced optimism than disabled children, which serves to dilute the insatiable drive of many professionals to cure or 'improve' us. Having said this, many of the problems experienced by disabled adults are similar to those experienced by disabled children.

Disabled adults frequently provoke anxiety and embarrassment in others simply by their presence. Although they become very skilful at dealing with this, it is often achieved at great cost to themselves by denying their disabilities and needs. It is not unusual for disabled people to endure boredom or distress to safeguard the feelings of others. They may, for example, sit through lectures without hearing or seeing rather than embarrass the lecturer, or endure being carried rather than demanding an accessible venue. In situations such as these reassuring phrases, such as 'I'm all right' or 'Don't worry about me' become almost automatic.

One of the reasons we react in this way, rather than being assertive about our disabilities, is to avoid the disapproval, rejection and adverse labelling of others, just as we did when we were children. Our reactions are viewed as resulting from our impairments rather than from the ways we have been treated. Thus being 'up front' about disability and the needs which emanate from it can easily lead us to be labelled 'awkward', 'selfish' or 'warped'. Such labelling is very difficult to endure without becoming guilty, anxious and depressed; it eats away at our confidence, undermining our courage and leading us to deny our disabilities.

Disbelief remains a common response of able-bodied people when we attempt to convey the reality of our disabilities. If, for example, I try to explain my difficulty in coping with new environments, the usual response is, 'Don't worry we all get lost' or 'It looks as if you're doing fine to me'. Or when I try to convey the feelings of isolation associated with not recognising people or not knowing what is going on around me, the usual response is 'You will in time' or 'It took me ages too'. This type of response renders disabled people 'just like everyone else'. For those of us disabled from birth or early childhood, where there is no experience of 'normality' with which to compare our situation, knowing how different we really are is problematic and it is easy to become confused and to have our confidence undermined when others insist we are just the same.

An example of denial through disbelief occurred when I was studying a statistics component as part of a course in psychology. I could see absolutely nothing of what was going on in the lectures and yet my frequent and articulate requests for help were met with the response that all students panic about statistics and that everything would work out fine in the end. As it happens it did, but only after spending many hours with a private tutor. As people are generally not too concerned about how we 'got there', our successes serve to reinforce the erroneous assumption that we really are 'just like everyone else'. When I finally passed the examination, the lecturer concerned informed me, in a jocular and patronising way, that my worries had clearly been unfounded! When people deny our disabilities they deny who we really are.

This tendency to disbelieve is exacerbated by the ambiguous nature of impairments such as partial sight. It is very hard for people to grasp that although I appear to manage 'normally' in many situations, I need considerable help in others. The knowledge of other people's perceptions of me is sufficiently powerful to alter my behaviour in ways which are detrimental to myself; for example, the knowledge that fellow passengers have seen me use a white cane to cross the road, can be enough to deter me from reading a book on the train. A more common strategy among people with limited sight is to manage roads unaided, thereby risking life and limb to avoid being labelled as frauds.

A further reaction, often associated with the belief that we are really no different, is that because our problems are no greater than anyone else's we do not deserve any special treatment or consideration. People who react in this way view us as whingeing and ungrateful complainers whenever we assert ourselves, explain our disabilities, ask that our needs be met or demand our rights. My most recent and overt experience of this reaction occurred during a visit to Whitehall to discuss the lack of transport for disabled people. Every time I mentioned a problem which disabled people encounter, such as not being able to use the underground system or the buses, I was told in no uncertain terms that many other people have transport problems too; what about old people, poor people, people who live in remote areas? What was so special about disabled people, and was not a lot being done for them anyway? I was the only disabled person present in this meeting and my confidence was undermined sufficiently to affect the quality of my argument. Reactions such as this can easily give rise to feelings of insecurity and doubt; it is, of course, the case that many people do have problems, but disabled people are among them and cannot afford to remain passive or to be passed by.

College

At the age of 19, after working for two years, I started my physiotherapy training at a special segregated college for blind and partially sighted students. For the first time in my life my disability was, at least in part, defined as blindness. Although about half the students were partially sighted, one of the criteria for entry to the college was the ability to read and write braille (which I had never used before) and to type proficiently, as, regardless of the clarity of their handwriting, the partially sighted students were not permitted to write their essays or examinations by hand, and the blind students were not permitted to write theirs in braille. No visual teaching methods were used in the college and, for those of us with sight, it was no easy matter learning subjects like anatomy, physiology and biomechanics without the use of diagrams.

The institution seemed unable to accept or respond to the fact that our impairments varied in severity and gave rise to different types of disability. We were taught to use special equipment which we did not need and were encouraged to 'feel' rather than 'peer' because feeling, it was thought, was aesthetically more pleasing, especially when dealing with the poor, unsuspecting public. There was great concern about the way we looked in our professional roles; white canes were not allowed inside the hospitals where we practised clinically, even by totally blind students, and guide dogs were completely banned. It appeared that the blind students were expected to be superhuman whereas the partially sighted students were expected to be blind. Any attempt to defy or challenge these rules was very firmly quashed so, in the interests of 'getting through', we outwardly denied the reality of our disabilities and complied.

Employment

Deciding whether or not to deny disability probably comes most clearly to the fore in adult life when we attempt to gain employment. Until very recently it was not uncommon to be told very bluntly that, in order to be accepted, the job must be done in exactly the same way as everyone else. In many ways this was easier to deal with than the situation now, where 'equal opportunity' policies have simultaneously raised expectations and pushed negative attitudes underground, and where, in reality, little has changed. Although I have no way of proving it, I am convinced that the denial of my disability has been absolutely fundamental to my success in gaining the type of employment I have had. I have never completely denied it (it is not hidden enough for that) but rather, in response to the interviewers' sceptical and probing questions, I have minimised the difficulties I face and portrayed myself in a way which would swell my headmaster's pride.

Curiously, once in the job, people have sometimes decided that certain tasks, which I can perform quite adequately, are beyond me, while at the same time refusing to relieve me of those I cannot do. At one college where I worked it was considered impossible for me to cope with taking the minutes of meetings, but my request to be relieved of invigilating large numbers of students, on the grounds that I could not see them, was not acceded to; once again the nature of my disability was being defined by other people. On the rare occasions I have been given 'special' equipment or consideration at work it has been regarded as a charitable act or donation for which I should be grateful and beholden. This behaviour signals two distinct messages: first that I have failed to be 'normal' (and have therefore failed), and, second that I must ask for nothing more.

In these more enlightened days of 'equal opportunities', we are frequently asked and expected to educate others at work about our disabilities, 'We know nothing about it, you must teach us' is the frequent cry. In some ways this is a positive development but, on the other hand, it puts great pressure on us because few formal structures have been developed in which this educative process can take place. In the absence of proactive equal opportunity policies, we are rarely taken seriously and what we say is usually forgotten or ignored. Educating others in this way can also mean that we talk of little else but disability, which, as well as becoming boring to ourselves, can lead us to be labelled adversely or viewed solely in terms of problems. Challenging disabling attitudes and structures, especially as a lone disabled person, can become frustrating and exhausting, and in reality it is often easier and (dare I say) more functional, in the short term at least, to cope with inadequate conditions rather than fight to improve them. We must beware of tokenistic gestures which do little but put pressure on us.

Conclusion

The reasons I have denied the reality of my disability can be summarised as follows:

1 To avoid other people's anxiety and distress.
2 To avoid other people's disappointment and frustration.
3 To avoid other people's disbelief.
4 To avoid other people's disapproval.
5 To live up to other people's ideas of 'normality'.
6 To avoid spoiling other people's fun.
7 To collude with other people's pretences.

I believe that from earliest childhood denial of disability is totally rational given the situations we find ourselves in, and that to regard it as a psychopathological reaction is a serious mistake. We deny our disabilities for social, economic and emotional survival and we do so at considerable cost to our sense of self and our identities; it is not something we do because of flaws in our individual psyches. For those of us disabled from birth or early childhood, denial of disability has deeply penetrating and entangled roots; we need support and encouragement to make our needs known, but this will only be achieved within the context of genuine structural and attitudinal change.

In this paper I have drawn upon my life experiences and personal reactions to elucidate the pressures placed upon disabled people to deny the reality of their experience of disability. This approach is limited inasmuch as personal experiences and responses can never be divorced from the personality and biography of the person they concern. In addition these pressures will vary according to the individual's impairment. But with these limitations in mind, I am confident that most disabled people will identify with what I have described and that only the examples are, strictly speaking, mine.

2.2

Acquired hearing loss: acquired oppression

Maggie Woolley

The experience of loss is central to the experience of the newly deafened adult and yet the opportunity to fully express initial fear, anger, distress and grief is rarely fully realised. A continuing sense of loss, therefore, remains as a barrier to adjustment, and the deafened person is impeded in 'giving up the tragedy' of deafness. Whilst still a hearing person the deafened person learned to have able-bodied attitudes towards disability which deaf and disabled movements now identify as key disabling factors in their oppression. But the newly deafened person continues to function from these oppressive attitudes and sees them daily reinforced by society now that she also has a disability. Initial strategies involve denying disability, pretending to hear and avoidance of situations in which the disability will be exposed. The deafened person looks to medicine to provide a cure for problems which are seen as stemming from faults in the ear. When the cure is not forthcoming, the deafened person experiences a further loss – that of hope. Rehabilitation medicine in the form of hearing aids, lip-reading, hearing therapy and other therapies offer help with mechanical aspects of communication and relating to the sound environment, but the professional–patient relationship is characterised by dependency on the part of the patient and control on the part of the professional in terms of priorities, the definitions of 'problems' and the provision of 'solutions'. The fundamental experience of loss and tragedy remains and the deafened person still struggles with despair, powerlessness, loss of self-confidence and positive self-image. The deafened person blames her deafness and hates being deaf, with self-contempt therefore, lurking at the periphery of her consciousness. Society in turn blames the victim of deafness.

Have we anything to learn from the past 10 years, in which the movements of disabled people and the Deaf community have rejected medical models of who they are; located disabling factors in the attitudes and power structures of society; created new identities based on proud self-definitions and celebration of their difference, and tried to build confidence so that they can intervene more effectively in creating new and more appropriate services which are under their direction? Does adjustment to acquired hearing loss

This paper was first published in J.G. Kyle (ed.) (1987) *Adjustment to Acquired Hearing Loss*, Bristol: Centre for Deaf Studies, School of Education.

also involve adjustment to, or rather liberation from, oppression which is social, psychological and political? Does an agenda for the future require a liberation movement of deafened people?

I was diagnosed as deaf at the age of 18 in 1967. Twelve years later I finally sat down and cried about it. I've never enjoyed such a jolly good cry in my life. It was marvellous. My whole body shook and I seemed to be going down deep inside me trying to get rid of every ounce of pain in great sobs and tears. I must emphasise that this happened in a counselling session where I was quite free to express such emotion without being thought mad or without upsetting anyone else or without anyone leaping forth to stop me crying. After some time I stopped, blew my nose, calmed down, giggled for a bit and then felt very happy. The world seemed to be a great place to be in and I was glad to be so powerfully alive. I was finally dealing with feelings of loss in the most natural way known to human beings. I was physically expressing grief, fear, anger and a whole range of emotion that had been locked inside me for 12 years. I was dealing with loss in a totally safe environment.

I am not a psychiatrist. I'm not well read in the psychology of loss and bereavement, but I do know that a key word is that of loss. My own experience and that of other deafened people I know tells me that an understanding of loss is essential to anyone around the newly deafened person and especially to the professional. Family and friends may be too upset by the deafened person's loss to cope with the physical expressions of grief I have described above but professional counsellors may be better equipped to provide the necessary safe environment. If loss can be fully expressed then the necessary grieving period can be relatively short and the deafened person can more rapidly adjust to the changes in her life. She can meet them as a much stronger and more confident person than if she were still suppressing the initial trauma.

We acquire a hearing loss we didn't ask for and most certainly didn't deserve. It may be the result of an accident, disease or even human error or cruelty (I am thinking here of deafness caused by medical error or deafness by noise levels in industry or acts of war). A deafened person may have to deal with feelings of injustice and powerlessness which relate to the way in which she was deafened. She may even have the right to take her deafness into a court of law.

In my case, I inherited a form of deafness which is always acquired rather than present at birth. I could hardly turn round and blame my parents for falling in love and creating me. As a hearing child I enjoyed a very happy childhood with a deafened father and hearing mother. I don't remember any family relationship problems which stemmed from my father's disability. We all knew how to talk so that he would understand and he was always included in everything we did. We automatically helped him to understand other people and thought nothing of it. Indeed, as a very young child I discovered that I was the only person who had a deaf father and I was so proud of the fact. It made my father, and more importantly me, a very special person. I had a daddy who couldn't hear a thing but who could read lips. My father never talked about losing his hearing. To me he had always been deaf. As I grew older I realised that his deafness meant it was harder for him to get work or to get the jobs he deserved and we were all angry about that in my family. But on the whole his deafness was no big deal. He was just a man that we all loved a lot.

So whilst I had a wonderful understanding of the deafened person's communication needs, I didn't really know what it felt like to be deafened. After I was diagnosed as deaf, I assumed that my father and I would be able to talk about it and that he would be someone I could share my feelings with. But when I told him, he said that the news had broken his heart. I felt that I had broken my parents' hearts. There was no way I could show them how distressed I was about being deaf. I had to help them feel that there was no cause for worry. I was just the same happy daughter they had always had. So I talked to my parents about everything else except being deaf. Family and friends were also upset. My teachers at drama college were upset. It was as if I had to help others with their distress rather than expect help with mine. After all, it was my deafness that was causing the upset. Everyone in the world was upset except my ear, nose and throat (ENT) specialist! As the only person I could talk to without breaking people's hearts, he became the only person I did talk to – for 10 minutes twice a year!

All this happened 20 years ago, but even today this experience is common to most people in Britain who lose their hearing. In my work with a television programme for the deaf and hard of hearing I receive letters every week from deafened people who tell me things about their experience that they have never told anyone else, including their own husbands and wives. Poets talk of 'worlds of silence' when they write about the deafened, but this kind of trapped silence seems to me to be the most tragic of all. So we seem to acquire a tragedy far greater than a hearing loss itself.

On one occasion I rehearsed a question for my ENT specialist and plucked up the courage to say: 'I'm worried about what deafness is doing to me. It's not the fact that I can't hear, but what this is doing to my life.' He looked up and said: 'Oh you mustn't worry; that will only make things worse. Eventually you will come to terms with it.' His response made it clear that he regarded the worries of the deafened patient as not his concern at all. One cannot blame him for dismissing my distress in such a way. Indeed, what he said turned out to be the most influential thing that anyone had said to me up to that time. After I left him, I walked about in the Glasgow rain for hours. I was so angry and my mind chattered over and over. 'I can't come to terms with living like this. I can't come to terms with a world in which I hardly know what anyone is saying. I can't come to terms with being left out of everything. I can't come to terms with this weight of hopelessness and being expected to deal with these problems all alone. The day I come to terms with it will be the day life isn't worth living. If my family and I as a child knew what it took to relate to a deafened person, then the rest of the world can. It isn't that I have to come to terms with this disability but that the very terms themselves have to be changed. The terms on which I am disabled have to be changed.' I am now 38 years old and I still have not changed my mind about this.

I suggest that despite all the loss and pain of acquiring something they didn't ask for, deafened people have a strength hidden within them that holds far more appropriate analyses of their disability and solutions than any person in the medical profession they are likely to encounter. And deafened people have this knowledge without knowing any more about the insides of the ear than they do about life on Mars. But there is no one around who can really listen to them. Even lip-reading teachers and hearing therapists are functioning from established and rigid solutions which require the deaf person and not the rest of the world to do most of the adjusting; which require the deaf person to adjust to hearing people's rules in a society which is constructed without much thought for the deaf. The deafened person is also at a disadvantage with her knowledge because of communication barriers and her own loss of self-confidence. She is new to deafness and there seem to be so many people around who claim to know so much more than she does. They are articulate and can use a wide range of very sophisticated language and are able to mystify her with their expertise. All the deafened people I know went home from encounters with professionals to look words up in dictionaries and read up about deafness in medical books. So here we are at this stage in our loss, feeling as though everyone knows more about deafness than we do. Not only that, but everyone who can hear seems to know more about everything than we do. We have become so dependent on professionals and other hearing people.

Now we are really learning what disability is about for those who have been disabled or deaf for all their lives. As hearing able-bodied people we learned how to see disabled and deaf people as dependent and pretty useless members of society. As deafened people we have carried this prejudice towards disabled people into our own deafness. We are also experiencing feelings of powerlessness, and how we are made to be dependent. So those attitudes are being reinforced every day.

We want 'the hearing person I once was' back again, because she had control of her life. We think that all this is happening because we can't hear; because of some tiny fault in our ears. But we aren't faulty people. If we could get our hearing back, then 'all the problems would go away'. So we shop around for cures for a bit until finally giving up, except perhaps to monitor cochlea implant experiments. All this happens not because of the fault in our ears or because we can't hear, but because society does not value the deafened person, and because we who were once hearing, like the rest, also learned not to value the deafened person. We are oppressed from without by a society which does not value us and therefore does not give priority to our needs, and we are oppressed from within because we have internalised those same attitudes towards ourselves. Read any book on deafened people and the lack of self-confidence and the poor self-image of the deafened person is discussed. But, without exception, all see this as being a product of the inability to hear, of faults in the ears, and not of a society which does not value us. We are stuck with these pathological models and medical definitions of who we are, when in reality we are not sick people. We are people who are socially, psychologically and politically oppressed.

When I was 23 I was in a restaurant with three hearing people and unable to follow their conversation. I looked across to the people at the next table. They were laughing and very happy. They were also very deaf. I could see this because they were using sign language. Hey! I thought. People like that could go out and buy meals, chat to the waiter and get him to understand them even though they didn't speak. People like that could do all this without a hearing person to help them or without being terrified that they would lip-read things wrongly. People like that could go out for a meal and enjoy themselves and have no problems understanding each other. And they didn't even care if people like me stared at them because they were different. People like that could be happy. People like that were deaf. So was I. I could be happy being deaf.

Born deaf people in the Deaf community weren't upset that I was deaf. They welcomed me. I made so many friends. I learned sign language and with interpreters could go to conferences, meetings and ultimately stand on a platform myself. They gave me back my confidence. I went back to teaching and eventually I went into my original chosen profession as an actress and television presenter. Deaf people gave me not only their world but access to the whole world. Born with far greater odds against them than I was, they gave me a completely new insight into being deaf which no other person had been able to give me before. I learned that their oppression was different from mine. It wasn't that they had lost their hearing but that their linguistic rights were being denied. With sign language banned in deaf education since 1880 and actively suppressed throughout the Western world, deaf people had known the most inhumane cruelty through being deprived from an early age of the only language which could help them acquire spoken languages. I, on the other hand, had spoken English as my native language. My problem was one of access to spoken English. Their language of signs gave me access to spoken English, but more than that their analysis and ideology helped me to see that deaf people were not alone. We share fundamentals of oppression with the deaf and many other oppressed groups in the world.

Why had I never been told about sign language or deaf people? Talking with my father later, I discovered that my grandfather who was deafened at 18 learned sign language and had many deaf and hearing friends who used Sign and finger-spelling to ease his lip-reading. As a young hearing child, my father and his family also used Sign. But when my father became deaf after my grandfather's death, he was told by the Ewings in Manchester not to mix with the deaf or use sign language or he would lose his speech. It is of interest here that these changes in attitudes towards the deafened closely follow the changes in attitudes towards the deaf. We were denied the help of Sign during exactly the periods that sign language was being denied to the deaf. My father and his family were told the very same lies about sign language that parents of deaf children have been told for a century.

With a new ability to make friends not only in the Deaf community but in the hearing world, I then began to meet people who were disabled. Once again I was welcomed, and I had to learn a lot about my own wrong attitudes to them as disabled people. Through them, I began to understand so much about hearing people's attitudes to me. If I could think such silly things about the disabled, then how easy it was for hearing people to have such nonsense in their heads about me. What a great world it would be if everyone including those in the corridors of power could understand deaf and disabled people as they are on their own terms.

Disabled people were rejecting medical definitions and medical models of who they were in much the same way as deaf people were doing. They were disabled not by the faults in their bodies but by society. By the 1980s, it was possible to see a deaf movement and a disabled movement which were both national and international. Disabled and deaf people began to lobby parliament in great numbers as successive anti-discrimination bills failed. Deaf people throughout the world were campaigning for their linguistic rights. Disabled and deaf people began to fight for positions in voluntary organisations and in local authority services. We still have a long way to go in having fully equal opportunities but we know we can only be strong individually if we are strong together.

Among these disabled people and among deaf people, there is a feature that can be found in all liberation movements – pride. They are proud to be disabled. They are proud of their culture and language as Deaf people. They are proud to be who they are. They began with self-definition and a search for identity which related not to impairment but to who they were as people. Can we be proud of being deafened people? Ultimately the problem is not that we are oppressed but what that oppression does to us. We have to be very aware of what it does to us as human beings before we can emerge as intelligent and valuable members of the human race. We can only do that together.

I don't know whether we need or can have a movement of deafened people. Perhaps we will achieve change for ourselves in the deaf and disabled movements. Quite a few deafened people are identifying themselves as deaf or disabled in this way. But our own experience and particular needs must not be lost in these campaigns. Five years ago I discovered that my young daughter will also acquire the family deafness. Thousands of people are still losing their hearing today. They need a positive identity and the ability to deal with loss and to meet oppression which perhaps only we can encourage.

Finally, I have drawn on personal experience here, which lays me open to accusations that my experience has been different from most and is therefore inadmissible as evidence for acquired hearing loss as acquired oppression. I would reply that the true experience of every person who acquires a hearing loss is a valid and important experience. Our experience is always unique and yet when we begin to talk openly about it, we find that others begin to rejoice in those parts of our experience which have also been their own. My experience is no more invalid than the experience of any deafened person. From the celebration of our difference and shared experience, great movements and a better world can evolve. There is no good reason why my deafened daughter should suffer as we have done. There is no good reason why any of us should deserve anything less than total respect.

2.3
Gender and disability

Jenny Morris

Introduction

Disability research and theory either treats gender as invisible or separates the issue out into a focus on the experience of disabled women. Thus, research often assumes the experience of disabled men to be representative of the disabled experience in general, and, when gender is introduced into the discussion, it is commonly in terms of disabled women experiencing a 'double disadvantage'. However, if we give full recognition to the importance of gender, the experience of both disabled men and disabled women will be more closely represented and explained.

In recent years there has been a highlighting of the particular experience of disabled women and of the need for disabled women to assert their interests as both women and disabled people. This has tended to be recognised more in the USA (see Deegan and Brooks, 1985; Fine and Asch, 1988) than in Britain (although see Morris, 1989; Lonsdale, 1990). However, there is now an increasing challenge by disabled feminists in Britain to the way in which mainstream feminist research and theorising has failed to address the concerns of disabled women (see Morris, 1991; Begum, 1992). At the same time, disabled women have started to confront the way in which both disability research and disability politics have also generally failed to address their concerns.

This paper builds on the foundations laid down by this important work but it is not intended to focus on disabled women. Rather the focus is on gender and how this social construct has an important part to play in the lives of both disabled men and disabled women.

Gender and disability as social constructs

Gender and disability are both social constructs predicated upon physical characteristics. In each case the physical characteristic has implications for the individual's life chances, but the experience takes place within a social context which largely determines the consequences of being male, female or having a physical impairment.

The work of feminist academics, from Margaret Meade to Ann Oakley, Simone de Beauvoir to Germaine Greer, has firmly established the distinction between sex and gender. It is now commonly accepted that the qualities that we think of as 'naturally' masculine or feminine are in fact socially determined, and so too is the sexual division of labour within both the family and the workplace.

The experience of physical impairment is similarly socially constructed, as indeed is its incidence, which varies across societies and also within societies according to class, race, gender, occupation and geographical location. An individual's experience of a particular impairment must be placed within its social context. For instance, the actual course of a condition such as multiple sclerosis will be influenced by socio-economic factors, and the experience of associated impairments, for example loss of mobility or sight, will depend on factors such as an individual's economic resources and available services, all of which interact with other social constructs (class, race and gender in particular).

Our society thinks of certain characteristics as 'naturally' a consequence of disability, primarily poverty, loneliness, stigma. However, as Mike Oliver (1990) and others have pointed out, the experience of disability is culturally variable, and in Western society is largely determined by the way in which economic development, and the ideology which accompanied it, set disabled people at the margins of social and economic activities and institutions.

The individualisation of disability treats impairment as a personal tragedy, failing to place the experience in its social context. This ideology also categorises disabled people's behaviour in terms of individual psychological problems. Susan Hannaford's research on institutional establishments for physically disabled people found, for example, that a wish to leave the institution was categorised as troublesome and inappropriate, and explained either in terms of a feature of the disability, such as 'multiple sclerosis euphoria' or in terms of a failure to accept disability (Hannaford, 1985). Miller and Gwynne's research, which must be one of the most oppressive pieces of work ever published, presented the disabled people in their study of institutions as having psychological problems which were an inevitable part of physical disability (Miller and Gwynne, 1972).

The assumption that physical characteristics are associated with negative psychological characteristics is, of course, a familiar one to women, and feminist research and analysis has done much to place such an assumption applied to women in its sociological context. To take just one example, Joan Busfield (1983) has argued that the higher level of mental illness recorded among women than among men is a function of the way in which the term 'mental illness' is socially defined rather than an indication of women's greater emotional volatility or irrationality. Her analysis suggests that the differential rates of mental illness to be found between men and women are not even a product of the greater tension and stress to be found in women's lives; rather, they 'are primarily a reflection of psychiatry's differential involvement with the problems and difficulties of men and women and, thereby, of the way in which the category "mental illness" has been constituted'. She goes on to say that 'the only generalisations we can make from patient statistics and symptom reports concern the nature of psychiatric thought and practice; they do not themselves provide a basis for generalisations about the characteristics of men and women or their social situation' (p. 107).

Elaine Showalter's (1987) historical analysis illustrates how cultural ideas about what constitutes appropriate feminine behaviour have structured the definition and treatment of insanity in women. As such her work is also a powerful illustration of how explanations of the phenomenon of mental illness among women are more likely to be found through studying the society which categorises and treats them. The parallels with the experience of impairment are clear. It is not disabled people who have defined the experience, neither have they had control over either medical treatment or the social consequences of impairment. Thus if disability is to be made sense of, it is the non-disabled society and its institutions which should be the subject of study.

Much work remains to be done to challenge assumptions about disabled people which lie at the heart of the academic community. Certainly, following Busfield's approach, we can see how Miller and Gwynne's research tells us more about the psychology of the researchers and the way that the non-disabled society reacts to disability than it does about the lives of the disabled people who were supposedly the subject of the research (see Morris, 1991, pp. 130–3).

Masculinity, femininity and disability

Analysis of the relationship between masculinity and disability as social constructs tells us something of the way that the non-disabled society defines physical impairment. To be a disabled man is to fail to measure up to the general culture's definition of masculinity as strength, physical ability and autonomy. Status and authority, also key components of masculinity, are similarly associated with an absence of disability. A person who is revered cannot be disabled, for this would be to detract, to take away, from his appeal. The clearest illustration of this was the American president Franklin D. Roosevelt. Roosevelt was completely paralysed from the waist down, yet this was hidden from the American and international public. In particular he was never seen in a wheelchair, for this was, and is, the ultimate symbol of dependency and lack of autonomy (Gallagher, 1985).

This association of disability with dependency and lack of autonomy has in fact been used by film-makers in recent years to explore an experience of vulnerability for men. Two films released in 1990, *My Left Foot* and *Born on the Fourth of July*, both used a wheelchair as a metaphor for exploring how awful it is for a man to be dependent, in the emotional as much as in the physical sense. The exercise was dependent on the stereotype that to be a man in a wheelchair is to be impotent, unable to be a (hetero-) sexual being, and therefore not a 'complete' man. As such they tell us little about the actual experience of being a disabled man, but a lot about the non-disabled society's definitions of both masculinity and disability.

This is also the case if we look at the relationship between femininity and disability as social constructs. As part of a research project carried out in 1986, some American college students were asked to write down whatever came to mind when they heard the phrase 'disabled woman'. Many students left their paper blank, having been unable to think of anything when they heard the term. Of those who did write something the majority wrote words signifying passivity, weakness or dependency. They wrote 'almost lifeless', 'pity', 'lonely', 'crippled', 'wheelchair', 'grey', 'old' and 'sorry' (*Disability Rag*, January/February 1987, p. 11). When the 145 students were asked to list what came to mind when they heard the word 'woman', they wrote down terms associated with heterosexuality and heterosexual relationships, work and motherhood. These terms were almost entirely missing from the associations with the words 'disabled woman'.

Again, this exercise tells us much about the non-disabled society's definitions of femininity and disability, indicating at least some element of incompatibility between the two social constructs. However, the relationship between femininity and disability is possibly more complex than that between masculinity and disability; a key part of being a woman in our society is dependency and passivity, yet this, too, is a key part of the social experience of physical impairment. As Fine and Asch (1985) point out, being a man and being disabled are two incongruous roles – in the sense that being a man in our society is to be strong, assertive and independent. In contrast, there is a partial congruity between the two roles of being a woman and being disabled, in that both are associated with weakness, passivity and dependency (see Fine and Asch, 1985, p. 11). Disabled women therefore receive conflicting messages from the non-disabled society: they are considered to be unable to fulfil the role of homemaker, wife and mother, neither can they conform to the stereotype of femininity as it applies to physical appearance; yet, at the same time, the passivity and dependency which lies at the heart of disability as a social construct is certainly compatible with what it means to be a woman in our society.

This partial congruity between the two roles of being a woman and being disabled has significant consequences for disabled women in terms of the unequal power relationship that characterises their social experience. For example, it may be particularly difficult for disabled women to assert their needs in the context of their dealings with the medical profession, or to obtain access to housing and support services necessary for independent living. Furthermore, dependency and passivity place disabled women in a very vulnerable position in terms of an abuse of power by non-disabled people, for they are not only constrained to behave in a dependent and passive way by the stereotype applied to them but they may also be practically dependent on an abuser. Thus the young girl who experiences 'public stripping' whenever she comes into contact with the medical profession is rendered powerless by her experience of disability and gender, *and* by the fact that she is dependent on her abusers for a service. A disabled woman who has been raped by someone who provides personal assistance to her has had her lack of power as a woman confirmed by her dependency as a disabled person. Moreover, the experience of dependency, especially when accompanied by an abuse of power by those on whom she is dependent, creates low self-esteem, reconfirming the stereotype by which a disabled woman is constrained. As a woman who was raped by an ambulance attendant said: 'My life was worth nothing – that's what it all meant to me' (Morris, 1991, p. 185).

It is important to recognise therefore that although gender and disability operate as structures of oppression for both disabled men and disabled women, this happens in different ways, primarily because of the way in which dependence/independence are key parts of the social meanings of what it is to be a woman or a man. The fact that dependence is a key part of the social construction of gender for women *and* of the social construction of disability means that women's powerlessness is confirmed by disability. In contrast, a man who is disabled will experience a conflict between the two roles and may attempt to use masculinity as a way of resisting the disabled role. This is not to say, however, that disabled men do not experience masculinity as an oppressive social construct, for, as the example discussed below illustrates, the consequences of the failure to measure up to what is socially defined as being a man can be devastating.

The 'double disadvantage' trap

Feminist research and theorising has often been driven by a sense of outrage at the consequences of women's powerlessness in relation to men. Whether it is domestic violence, rape, unequal pay or sex-role stereotyping in children's books, such research refuses to see women as passive victims and the motivating anger is an important part of an empowerment process. The focus has very much been on men and social institutions as the problem.

However, there is a tendency among non-disabled academics, when writing or researching on disabled women, to focus on the way in which such women experience a 'double disadvantage' as a consequence of their gender and their disability. The attention shifts away from non-disabled people and social institutions as being the problem and on to disabled women as passive victims of oppression.

Such an emphasis also ignores the way in which gender as a social construct affects disabled men. Yet, for example, James Haig's experience of disability was quite clearly dominated by the social construct of masculinity. A tetraplegic as the result of a motor-bike accident, he felt that his life was not worth living. The *Guardian* journalist Polly Toynbee wrote about him: 'He tried writing but football had been his great interest before the accident and he found he could not adapt. He was told he could never have any kind of job . . . He looked down at his immobilised and wasted arms and legs. "Suicide is the sensible answer for someone like me."' Both work and leisure activities for a man like James Haig were linked with physical ability, and both these areas of his life were characterised by the social meanings of masculinity. Once his physical ability to do these 'male' activities was removed, he was status-less, role-less and this was articulated by his wish to die.

Just as feminist research on, say, domestic violence was fuelled by a sense of outrage that women were trapped within violent relationships by the consequences of their social, economic and political powerlessness, so disability research must be motivated by anger at the structures of oppression created by gender and disability. It is outrageous that these structures of oppression caused a young man to think that if he couldn't play football then life wasn't worth living.

Leaving out gender

While a concern with gender and disability has generally meant a focus entirely on the experience of disabled women, much research on disability actually leaves out the issue of gender altogether, assuming that men represent the general experience. Integral to this type of approach is also an assumption that gender is not an issue for men.

One example of this type of research is *Walking into Darkness: the Experience of Spinal Cord Injury* (Oliver et al., 1988). This was a study of 77 men who had all passed through one particular spinal injury unit and the research intended to analyse the personal and social consequences of spinal cord injury. Accordingly, the interviews covered areas such as family and personal relationships, work and leisure activities as well as financial consequences of injury and experience of the medical and social services professions.

The authors justify their exclusion of spinal cord injured women from the study by the limitations of their sampling frame (which used the records of one particular consultant, most of whose patients were men) and comment that research on the experience of women is clearly needed. Throughout, the study treats the male experience as the general but, perhaps more significantly, it also fails to consider the issue of gender for men. Thus, not only is the research inadequate in that it fails to recognise that the work experiences, financial consequences, family relationships, and so on, described are *particular* to men but also there is no consideration of how gender as a social construct gives particular meaning to these areas of experience for the men in the study.

For example, the presentation of men's experience of returning, or not returning, to work following injury fails to address the particular meaning of work for men, how this is crucial to their role as provider, and the extent to which work is tied up with status as a man in our society. Neither does the analysis of family and personal relationships place the experience in the context of the sexual division of labour within households, the social construction of sexuality, or the expectations placed on men in personal relationships. All these factors have major implications for men's experience of disability. Nasa Begum (1992) has illustrated how gender roles, self-image and sexuality are crucial to understanding the experiences of disabled women; this is also the case for understanding the experiences of disabled men.

In *Walking into Darkness*, as in other studies, an attempt to present the male experience as the general experience has meant that gender cannot be recognised as an issue. The consequence is an incomplete analysis of men's experience of disability, as well as a total exclusion of women's experience.

Far from being a 'diversion' from mainstream concerns, a focus on gender is a necessary part of understanding the experience of disability. It is difficult to justify a presentation of men's experience of disability as the general experience and women's as the particular, when the majority of disabled people are women. The Office of Population Censuses and Surveys (OPCS) survey, published in 1988, found that there were 3,656,000 disabled women compared with 2,544,000 disabled men. This is only partly due to women's greater longevity, for prevalence rates of disability are higher for women of all ages except below the age of 20. The difference in the prevalence rates increases with age. Thus, while 9 per cent of all working-age women are disabled, compared with 8 per cent of working-age men, 63 per cent of women over 74 are disabled compared with 53 per cent of men in this age group.

The nature of impairment varies according to gender, with conditions such as arthritis being more prevalent among disabled women than among disabled men. These different patterns have major implications for the nature of health and social services required, as they do for rehabilitation services, acute and long-term health care, and so on. It is difficult to see how policy-making, service-planning or service delivery can be appropriate, adequate or efficient without taking into account the relationship between gender and disability.

Patterns of employment, income, housing tenure and conditions, and so on, vary according to gender within the non-disabled population, and there are similar variations within the disabled population (some of which are exacerbated by the relationship between gender and disability). Such factors are the material context of disability and are very important influences on the experience. To take just one example, a disabled person's housing opportunities are influenced by both disability and gender. Disability itself commonly creates a specific housing need because of the way that the housing market has generally produced housing suitable for fit, young people with no impairments. At the same time, disability brings a high risk of reduced earning power and poverty, thereby placing disabled people at an additional disadvantage within the housing market and making them more reliant on social housing. Disability, therefore, is an important influence on housing opportunities. However, there is also much evidence of the way that gender influences housing opportunities (see Morris and Winn, 1990, Chapter 4), showing in particular that women are placed at a disadvantage in the owner-occupied sector. It would therefore be impossible to analyse adequately disabled people's housing experience without incorporating the ways in which disability and gender interact. Both factors will have a significant influence on whether a disabled person achieves a housing situation which is an enabling one or a disabling one.

Conclusion

Research which only concerns the experience of disabled men cannot tell us much about the general experience of disability; rather, it is research on a *particular* experience of disability. Furthermore, the issue of gender as a social construct is as important for men as it is for women. This is because the interrelationship between gender and disability is a key factor in determining not only the life chances of disabled men and disabled women but also the social meaning of disability. We may want to identify the way that women experience particular disadvantages and powerlessness as a result of the structures of oppression associated with both gender and disability, but we should not lose sight of the fact that disabled men can also experience gender as an oppressive social construct.

References

Begum, N. (1992) 'Disabled women and the feminist agenda', *Feminist Review*, No. 40, pp. 70–84.

Busfield, J. (1983) 'Gender, mental illness and psychiatry', in Evans, M. and Ungerson, C. (eds) *Sexual Divisions, Patterns and Processes*, Tavistock, London.

Deegan, M.J. and Brooks, N.A. (eds) (1985) *Women and Disability: the Double Handicap*, Transaction Books, Oxford.

Fine, M. and Asch, A. (1985) 'Disabled women: sexism without the pedestal', in Deegan, M.J. and Brooks, N.A. (eds) *Women and Disability: the Double Handicap*, Transaction Books, Oxford.

Fine, M. and Asch, A. (1988) *Women with Disabilities: Essays in Psychology, Culture and Politics*, Temple University Press, Philadelphia.

Gallagher, H. (1985) *F.D.R.'s Greatest Deception*, Dodd, Mead, New York.

Hannaford, S. (1985) *Living Outside Inside*, Canterbury Press, Berkeley, California.

Lonsdale. S. (1990) *Women and Disability*, Macmillan, London.

Miller, E.J. and Gwynne, G.V. (1972) *A Life Apart*, Tavistock, London.

Morris, J. (ed.) (1989) *Able Lives: Women's Experience of Paralysis*, The Women's Press, London.

Morris, J. (1991) *Pride Against Prejudice: Transforming Attitudes to Disability*, The Women's Press, London.

Morris, J. and Winn, M. (1990) *Housing and Social Inequality*, Hilary Shipman, London.

Oliver, M. (1990) *The Politics of Disablement*, Macmillan, London.

Oliver, M., Zarb, G., Moore, M., Silver, J. and Salisbury, V. (1988) *Walking into Darkness: the Experience of Spinal Cord Injury*, Macmillan, London.

Showalter, E. (1987) *The Female Malady: Women, Madness and English Culture 1830–1980*, Virago, London.

2.4
Double oppression: an appropriate starting-point?

Ossie Stuart

There is a temptation to represent the experience of disabled people within ethnic minority communities as a 'double oppression'. It is assumed that these people have to contend with the disabling experience of impairment and that they must do so within a social environment which in Britain is discriminatory and bigoted against ethnic minority communities (Confederation of Indian Organizations, 1987).

This interpretation seems to be widely accepted in the debate about black disablement (Oliver, 1990).[1] It is my view that the assumptions behind the phrase 'double oppression' make this an inadequate starting-point. There has been minimal research to define clearly what is meant by this or any other concept of the black disabled experience (Atkin and Rollins, 1991). As a consequence, the phrase 'double oppression' is rather empty; rhetoric has replaced clear thinking.

The nature of racism in Britain today means that it is not enough to challenge oppressive models of disability. What is required by black disabled people is a wider interpretation, one which includes their experience as British citizens. The starting-point for this should be an acceptance that black disabled people have been marginalised.

The predominant concept of disability – which I shall call the norm – is that it is regarded as a personal tragedy needing medical attention (Oliver, 1990). This idea is vigorously challenged by the disability movement. Likewise, anti-racist writers challenge what has become the norm within the philosophy of 'the new racism'. Until very recently, racism has been understood as a form of discrimination based upon skin colour or genetic make-up. In this understanding, the right of access to housing, education and employment depends upon these physical attributes. Racism involves the deliberate exclusion of individuals from these resources because of their colour.

New racism has replaced this rather straightforward form of prejudice and substituted a more sophisticated one. The idea is a response to the steady erosion of racist bigotry and practices that has been dominant. Rather than focusing upon skin colour, new racism attempts to use culture as the marker of difference. The idea of an exclusive 'English' cultural identity has become critical to those who argue that resources should still be allocated upon racist criteria. However, for new racism skin colour is no longer the determining factor. The question that has taken its place is whether one can subscribe to being 'English'.

Therefore the frontier of racism has shifted from skin colour to culture. The question ceases to be 'what colour are you?' Instead, it becomes 'can a black person of a different culture really be part of this society?' The consequence of this question is to emphasise a new racist ideology. For new racism the promotion of an 'English culture' becomes critical. This may be exemplified by, say, the 'English rose' or Yorkshire pudding. It may also include emphasis upon language and Britain's imperial history. Its effect is to exclude. New racism has not abandoned prejudice based upon skin colour, but widened this and made the culture aspect dominant.

So, marginalisation is the characteristic experience of both black and disabled people within this society. The frequency of disabilist language is an indication of the degree to which disabled people are left on the outside in our society. By way of comparison, immigration policy – the state's way of including or excluding others from this country – makes new racism more acceptable to wider society. Immigration determines who may and who may not belong to the national community. By definition immigration policy includes reasons for segregation and banishment.

Both the disability movement and anti-racist writers have sought to present a different image of this society to the one generally described. In my view black disabled people cannot fully associate with either of the interpretations of their situation which are provided by the disability movement and anti-racists. It is here that a complete feeling of estrangement can arise.

Simultaneous oppression: the way forward

So, I reject the belief that black disabled people experience a kind of double oppression. The oppression black disabled people endure is, in my opinion, unique. I suggest that for these people racism involves a process of simultaneous oppression in their day-to-day experience. It is also an experience which divides black disabled people from their black able-bodied peers.

However, there is a dearth of research and limited social and political awareness of this situation (Atkin and Rollins, 1991). Because of this it is necessary to construct a distinct and separate black disabled identity. The purpose of such a process would be to clearly define this group, but not only for its own sake. It would also help us to obtain a better understanding of how the development of particular identities in Britain today includes or excludes people from mainstream life.

I am not demanding a special place for black disabled people in a hierarchy of oppression. On the contrary, racist practices have a wider impact. The experience of black disabled people can provide greater insight into its wider practice. Equally the experience of other groups can help to inform that of black disabled people. One such group is black women. Their debates about the question of oppression do provide a clue to the direction that black disabled people ought to take.

At the beginning of the 1980s black radical feminist writers began to assert strongly that their experience of oppression differs in substance and intensity from that understood by their white peers. Carby (1982) makes this point clearly.

> The experience of black women does not enter the parameters of parallelism [the attempts to parallel race and gender divisions]. The fact that black women are subject to *simultaneous* oppression [her emphasis] of patriarchy, class and 'race' is the prime reason for not employing parallels that render their position and experience not only marginal but invisible.

Simultaneous oppression, which I unashamedly borrow from Carby, is the key to understanding the experience of black disabled people. It is a form of oppression which separates them from all other groups.

I have identified three areas where I consider that black disabled people experience a distinct form of oppression. These are, first, limited or no individuality and identity; second, resource discrimination; finally, isolation within black communities and the family. Each is influenced by the ideas of new racism. In sum they isolate black disabled people and place them at the margins of the ethnic minority and disabled populations.

A marginal and invisible fraternity

The image of English culture propagated at the centre is characterised by the 'English rose', 'roast beef' and the myth of a 'glorious' imperial history. I do concede that if disability is portrayed at all, the image chosen is based upon the concepts of personal tragedy. The ideas propagated by new racism are more culturally familiar to white disabled people than to disabled people from any other ethnic groups. Disabled people of New Commonwealth descent, as well as black people in general, are the outsiders; they are regarded as different from the norm in a way rarely experienced by their white disabled peers.

Unlike white disabled people, black disabled people are not fully incorporated into this society. Instead, they are continually judged as outsiders or aliens (Gamble, 1974; Levitas, 1986). I suggest that it is this critical distinction which informs the feelings of marginalisation that black disabled people may have.

Despite a greater awareness of colour discrimination, organisations of disabled people have failed to attract disabled people from within the ethnic minority communities in any numbers. It should never be suggested that the disability movement has in the past deliberately fostered racial discrimination. Nevertheless, despite the absence of meaningful data on black disabled people, their absence from positions of influence in the movement is marked.

It should not be forgotten that this situation is no different to that of English society in general.

Until recently the absence of black disabled people had not been regarded as an issue by the movement. Apart from obvious evidence of blatant race discrimination, nothing distinguishes black disabled people from their peers within the movement. The priority for all leading disabled people, it had been assumed, was to attack the medical model of disability.

Ethnic minority communities are in the main located in the poorest regions of Britain (Rex and Moore, 1967). A labour force survey (*Employment Gazette*, 1990) shows that (averaged over the years 1986–8) among young people aged between 16 and 24 economic activity rates were much lower in ethnic minority groups than in the white population. Among all women of working age, women of West Indian or Guyanese origin had the highest economic activity, women of Pakistani or Bangladeshi origin had the lowest. Self-employment was reported more frequently among employed members of the ethnic minority groups than the white community. In 1988, as in 1987, the rate of unemployment for the ethnic minority groups was 60 per cent above that for the white population (*Employment Gazette*, 1990).

This is particularly relevant when questioning the absence of statistics of poor health and impairment within the ethnic minority groups. Yet to explain poor health and disability without reference to the social and economic disposition of this section of Britain's population is a serious error, if not implicit racism (Atkin and Rollins, 1991). I would argue that until relevant data show otherwise it can be inferred that poor health and impairment is a common experience within ethnic minority groups.

Nevertheless, in the absence of data, researchers (Goel *et al.*, 1981; Rocheron, 1988) have projected a cultural image of disability and ill health on to the ethnic minority population. For example, black health problems have been explained as a deviation from the norm; the norm, of course, is Western eating habits or lifestyle. 'Asian rickets' is a case in point. They have suggested that changes in diet and lifestyle would alleviate this condition. The social and economic situation of the observed community is given little consideration.

Those excluded from the dominant image of 'Englishness' are perceived as alien, and are judged accordingly against an assumed consistent, unchanging and homogeneous Western culture (Benson, 1991). In contrast, these 'experts' fail to emphasise the role that employment, housing conditions or levels of wealth may have in influencing health within the observed populations. These are factors more easily acceptable when applied to the white population.

Equal access to resources?

For black disabled people discrimination in access to resources is a significant site of oppression. Henderson and Karn demonstrate how the allocation of finite resources – in this case housing in Birmingham – can adversely affect Britain's ethnic minority groups (Henderson and Karn, 1987). Quite simply, because of the vulnerability of this section of the community they were obliged to accept the poorest quality state housing from local housing officials. Why was this the case? What does it tell us about the experience of black disabled people?

To address the first question, Henderson and Karn show that the presence of bigots at the gate – those controlling housing allocation to tenants – was not the critical factor when determining the causes of unequal provision. Rather, discrimination occurred through what they call 'social determinants of housing allocation'. This meant that housing officers, on a day-to-day basis, made decisions which were in accord with the norm in an environment of competing interest groups and scarce resources – in this case housing.

The result was that the classification of tenants was vital for Birmingham's housing officers to enable them to allocate housing. The norm upon which such decisions were made agreed with new racist assumptions. The result was that black tenants were frequently categorized as 'disreputable' or a 'problem'. Thus they regularly received poorer quality, inner-city, housing. Furthermore, as black families were more desperate for housing, they would accept lower quality accommodation. The coding used by the housing officers placed negative weight to race, thereby further stigmatising these families.

In answer to the second question, what does this tell us about access to resources and the experience of black disabled people? Like any other group of disabled people, black individuals are dependent on local and central authorities for the provision of finite and limited resources. However, the institutions that allocate these resources rely upon officers who, as in the Birmingham case, have to use their subjective judgement to discriminate between different claimants.

The databases of social discrimination to differentiate between claimants created by these officials will similarly be subjective (Evers *et al.*, 1989). The fieldwork of Evers *et al.* (1989) has identified the existence of ethnocentric opinions based on racist assumptions held by community health and social service practitioners. In other words, new racist assumptions appear to influence the decision-makers when they deal with black disabled people.

Whose identity? Whose defence?

I now want to address the final part of my argument, mainly that the identity of black disabled people is also informed by their separation from the wider ethnic minority community. Yet again, this experience can only be understood within the context of a particular form of racism which is now predominant in Britain today. I shall argue that the isolation of black disabled people is made more difficult by the strategies adopted by their black able-bodied peers to combat this climate of racism.

These responses to racism include the use of cultural forms to reinforce a sense of identity. Yet these forms are only relevant to the existing conditions. If those conditions change, the form the culture takes will also change (Hobsbawn and Ranger, 1983). Though it may borrow from former cultural forms – even be given the same label as past identities – identity can only be understood if directly related to the present (Hall, 1991). Quite simply, the adoption and exploitation of one particular image or cultural identity over another at a particular time is directly related to the prevailing social and economic environment (Gilroy and Lawrence, 1982).

To take a simplistic example: during the 1970s one of the most significant cultural forms to influence black British youth was Jamaican reggae, and its ideological component, Rastafarian culture. The attractiveness of this cultural form, as expressed by Bob Marley, was its political language, symbols and meanings relevant to the social movements for emancipation and equality that were taking place in Britain at that time (Hebdige, 1983). It mattered little that Bob Marley's music was expressing the experience of life in early 1970s' Jamaica. His message became a metaphor for life in the inner city for the urban young – black and white (Gilroy, 1987; Hall, 1991).

Yet this 'capture' of reggae is part of a complex process of adoption and transformation which is still taking place in Britain. Black cultural identity adopts and changes external ideas and these then acquire a life of their own (Benjamin, 1984). This identity may at times be expressed in powerful cultural forms. It is, however, grounded in the harsh reality of racism and poverty which is the experience of the majority of this society's ethnic minority population.

I question whether black disabled people can benefit or actively participate in the reconstruction and assertion of a black identity in the face of new racism. For example, 'to be of worth' is one of the main empowering symbols within any community or family. Yet high unemployment and the marginal position that ethnic minority communities occupy in Britain has meant that the expected roles of worth within the family – employment, the ability to clothe and feed offspring, and so on – are denied. New roles have had to be constructed to empower individuals.

Self-employment, for example, has played a key part in providing male employment and self-esteem. For Afro-Caribbean women and South Asian women their roles are likewise shaped in the labour force. The wider acceptance of new racism in British society has forced ethnic minority populations to adopt certain patterns of employment. These patterns have coalesced around manual labour or retail ownership. However, this form of employment does provide the local community with esteem (Shaw, 1989). Just as important, these forms of employment have provided the building-blocks from which the construction of an ethnic minority identity has taken place.

In contrast, the inability of black disabled people to gain employment in the limited opportunities open to the black population and their inability to contribute resources to the family render them powerless within black communities. Furthermore, it should not be forgotten that ethnic minority groups can be just as prejudiced towards disabled people as their white neighbours are. In sum, the inability to attain accepted roles within black communities and the force of disablist prejudice are the social barriers which confirm and compound the isolation of black disabled people within ethnic minority communities.

It is not my intention to provide an excuse for bigots to blame the unique position of black disabled people on a supposed pathology within black families. The development of black identity is, in the main, a response to the prevailing conditions in society. However, like other constructions, the image of disability is absent. At best, the rehabilitation of the black identity has gone hand in hand with a lack of criticism of the tragedy view of disabled individuals. Black disabled people have no distinctive image and are isolated within their own communities.

Conclusion

It is not my intention to provide a complete outline of the black disabled experience. What I want to do is drag the debate out of the rhetorical pit into which the discussion of this experience appears to have fallen. As a consequence, I have tried to identify the basis of modern racism in Britain today. With this in mind, I argue that new racism has confined black communities to the margins of this society. Unlike other sections of society in a similar situation, black people are systematically portrayed as outsiders and interlopers.

This analysis creates a clear separation between the relative experience of black and white disabled people. It also reinforces my belief that being a black disabled person is not a 'double' experience, but a single one grounded in British racism.

I suspect that many readers will interpret my call for the construction of a separate and distinct identity for black disabled people as a call for separatism. On the contrary, I think the marginal position of black people within their respective communities makes this a very futile option indeed. The persistence of the tragedy model of disability throughout this society means that the unity the disability movement has provided is vital. However, what I do call for is an acknowledgement that black people do indeed endure a specific experience as disabled people.

Note

1 Throughout this paper I will use the term 'black' to describe people of New Commonwealth origin in the UK and including people of Arabic, Vietnamese or Chinese origin.

References

Atkin, K. and Rollins, J. (1991) *Informal Care and Black Communities*, Social Policy Research Unit, York University.

Benjamin, P. (1984) 'The Afro-American musician: messenger of a unique sensibility in Western culture', in *Views on Black American Music*, Proceedings of the 12th and 13th Annual Black Musicians' Conference, University of Massachusetts at Amhurst, No. 2, 1984–5.

Benson, S. (1991) 'Asians have culture, West Indians have problems: discourses in race in and outside anthropology', paper given at St Antony's College, Oxford University.

Carby, H. (1982) 'Black feminism and the boundaries of sisterhood', in *The Empire Strikes Back: Race and Racism in 70s Britain*, Hutchinson, London.

Confederation of Indian Organizations (1987) *Double Bind: To Be Disabled and Asian*, Confederation of Indian Organizations, London.

Employment Gazette (1990) 'Ethnic origins and the labour market', March.

Evers, H., Badgers, F., Cameron, E. and Atkin, K. (1989) *Community Care Project: Working Papers*, Department of Social Medicine, University of Birmingham.

Gamble, A. (1974) *The Conservative Nation*, Routledge and Kegan Paul, London.

Gilroy, P. (1987) *'There Ain't No Black in the Union Jack': the Cultural Politics of Race and Nation*, Hutchinson, London.

Gilroy, P. and Lawrence, E. (1982) 'Two-tone Britain: black youth, white youth and the politics of anti-racism', in Bains, H. and Cohen, P. (eds) *Youth in Multi-Racist Britain*, Macmillan, London.

Goel, K.M., Sweet, E.M., Campbell, S., Attenburrow, A., Logan, R.W. and Arneil, G.C. (1981) 'Reduced prevalence of rickets in Asian children in Glasgow', *Lancet*, i, pp. 405–7.

Hall, S. (1991) 'The myth of an Afro-Caribbean identity', The Walter Rodney Memorial Lecture, Warwick University.

Hebdige, D. (1983) 'Ska tissue: the rise and fall of Two Tone', in Simon, D. and Davis, S. (eds) *Reggae International*, Thames and Hudson, London.

Henderson, J. and Karn, V. (1987) *Race, Class and State Housing: Inequality and the Allocation of Public Housing in Britain*, Gower, London.

Hobsbawn, E. and Ranger, T. (1983) *The Invention of Tradition*, Cambridge University Press.

Levitas, R. (1986) *The Ideology of the New Right*, Polity Press, Oxford.

Oliver, M. (1990) *The Politics of Disablement*, Macmillan, Basingstoke.

Rex, J. and Moore, R. (1967) *Race, Community and Conflict*, Routledge and Kegan Paul, London.

Rocheron, Y. (1988) 'The Asian mother and baby campaign: the construction of ethnic minorities' health needs', *Critical Social Policy*, Vol. 22, pp. 4–23.

Shaw, A. (1989) *A Pakistani Community in Britain*, Oxford University Press.

2.5
Prejudice

Jenny Morris

Since becoming disabled, I have on countless occasions been told by both strangers and acquaintances how 'wonderful' they think I am. I eventually realised that at the heart of such remarks lay the judgement that being disabled must be awful, indeed intolerable. It is very undermining to recognise that people look at me and see an experience which they would do everything to avoid for themselves.

How can we take pride in ourselves when disability provokes such negative feelings amongst non-disabled people? In answering this question disabled people have developed an understanding of the nature of prejudice and its effect on us.

Normality, difference and prejudice

Prejudice is associated with the recognition of difference. In theory 'normal' could be a value-free word to mean merely that which is common, and to be different from normal would not therefore necessarily provoke prejudice. In practice, the word is inherently tied up with ideas about what is right, what is desirable and what belongs.

Disabled people are not normal in the eyes of non-disabled people. Our physical and intellectual characteristics are not 'right' or 'admirable' and we do not 'belong'. Having given such a negative meaning to abnormality, the non-disabled world assumes that we wish to be normal, or to be treated as if we were. It is supposedly progressive and liberating to ignore our differences because these differences have such negative meanings for non-disabled people. But we *are* different. We reject the meanings that the non-disabled world attaches to disability but we do not reject the differences which are such an important part of our identities.

Prejudice lies at the heart of the segregation which many disabled people experience both as children and as adults – and has its most extreme expression in the mass slaughter of disabled people under the German Third Reich. Prejudice can, however, also take more subtle forms. Hidden

This paper is an edited version of a chapter that was originally published in J. Morris (1991) *Pride Against Prejudice: Transforming Attitudes to Disability*, The Women's Press, London.

assumptions form the bedrock to most of our interaction with the non-disabled world. It is often difficult for us to identify *why* someone's behaviour makes us angry, or feel undermined. Our anger and insecurity can thus seem unreasonable not just to others but also, sometimes, to ourselves.

From her interaction with non-disabled people, Pam Evans has identified a number of assumptions which are held about disabled people.

That we feel ugly, inadequate and ashamed of our disability.
That our lives are a burden to us, barely worth living.
That we crave to be 'normal' and 'whole'.
That whatever we choose to do or think, any work or pursuit we undertake, is done as 'therapy', with the sole intention of taking our mind off our condition.
That we don't have, and never have had, any real or significant experiences in the way that non-disabled people do.
That we can't ever really accept our condition, and if we appear to be leading a full and contented life, or are simply cheerful, we are 'just putting a good face on it'.
That we need 'taking out of ourselves' with diversions and rewards that only the normal world can provide.
That we desire to emulate and achieve normal behaviour and appearance in all things.
That we go about the daily necessities or pursue an interest because it is a 'challenge' through which we can 'prove' ourselves capable.
That we feel envy and resentment of the able-bodied.
That any emotion or distress we show can only be due to our disability and not to the same things that hurt and upset them.
That our disability has affected us psychologically, making us bitter and neurotic.
That it's quite amazing if we laugh, are cheerful and pleasant or show pleasure in other people's happiness.
That we are ashamed of our inabilities, our 'abnormalities', and loathe our wheelchairs, crutches or other aids.
That we never 'give up hope' of a cure.
That the inability to walk, to see or to hear are infinitely more dreadful than any other physical aspects of disability.
That words like 'walk' and 'dance' will upset us.
That when we affirm that we cannot, or do not wish to, do something, our judgement and preferences are overridden and contradicted as inferior to theirs.
That we are asexual or at best sexually inadequate.
That if we are not married or in a long-term relationship it is because no one wants us and not through our personal choice to remain single or live alone.
That any able-bodied person who married us must have done so for one of the following suspicious motives and never through love: desire to hide his/her own inadequacies in the disabled partner's obvious ones; an

altruistic and saintly desire to sacrifice their lives to our care; neurosis of some sort; or plain old-fashioned fortune-hunting.

That if we have a partner who is also disabled, we chose each other for no other reason and not for any other qualities we might possess. When we choose 'our own kind' in this way the able-bodied world feels relieved, until of course we wish to have children; then we're seen as irresponsible.

That if our marriage or relationship fails, it is entirely due to our disability and the difficult person this inevitably makes us, and never from the usual things that make any relationship fail.

That those of us whose disability is such that we require a carer to attend to our physical needs are helpless cabbages who don't *do* anything and have nothing to give, and who lead meaningless empty lives.

That if we are particularly gifted, successful or attractive before the onset of disability our fate is infinitely more 'tragic' than if we were none of these things.

That we should put up with any inconvenience, discomfort or indignity in order to participate in 'normal' activities and events. And this will somehow 'do us good'.

That our need and right to privacy isn't as important as theirs and that our lives need to be monitored in a way that deprives us of privacy and choice.

(Pam Evans, from an interview with the author)

We could also add the assumption that disabled people could not possibly be lesbians or gay, and that if we are this is because we cannot achieve a 'normal' heterosexual relationship rather than being an expression of our sexuality. Nasa Begum drew my attention to some of the assumptions imposed on black and ethnic minority disabled people. These include the assumptions that, as she put it, 'it is our ethnic culture which restricts our lives as disabled people' and that 'we should be grateful for the services we receive in Western societies, because we wouldn't be able to get them in our own countries'.

One of the biggest problems for disabled people is that all these undermining messages become part of our way of thinking about ourselves and/or our thinking about other disabled people. This is the internalisation of *their* values about *our* lives.

Although overt hostility is not a common experience for most disabled people, it is yet the iron fist in the velvet glove of the patronising and seemingly benevolent attitudes which we experience. This is clear from the experience of those of us who step out of the passive role which society accords to us. In these situations we often have to confront dislike, revulsion and fear.

The importance of physical difference

In an interview with the author, Molly McIntosh talked of other people's reactions to physical difference.

> I have horrible scars on my face. What I mean by that is that people react to them with horror. Forty years ago, when I was in my twenties, and also when I was a child,

I *so* hated the way that I looked. I tried not to think about it but every time I went out in the street I would be reminded about how I looked because of the way people reacted to me. As I walked down the street and someone was coming towards me, they would look and then drop their eyes or move their head, as if the horror was too much. But then they could never, ever resist looking again.

Molly McIntosh felt that her life was split in two. When she was at home she felt at ease with herself but when she set foot outside her front door she felt a deep sense of unease. Most of us experience this same sense of unease each time we interact with the non-disabled world, particularly in a public situation where we are dealing with strangers' reactions to us.

Going out in public so often takes courage. How many of us find that we can't dredge up the strength to do it day after day, week after week, year after year, a lifetime of rejection and revulsion? It is not only physical limitations that restrict us to our homes and those whom we know. It is the knowledge that each entry into the public world will be dominated by stares, by condescension, by pity and by hostility.

Some of us find that the only way we can survive in a non-disabled world is either not to recognise how much we are feared and hated, or to pretend that we don't know about it. Some of us feel that we can confront the stares and hostility head on. I talked to Anna Mathison, who lives within a black community in which she feels she belongs. She has the confidence to refuse to be intimidated by other people's reactions to her. 'If people stare, I shout "What are you staring at? You want to feel? You need glasses?" I feel I should challenge them because otherwise they think you're stupid and that they are entitled to stare.'

However, Anna remains all too aware that people look at her and think her life is not worth living. 'They just see the wheelchair and they think, you'd be better off dead. And that's a problem because it hurts. But if I shout at them it makes me strong.'

We receive so many messages from the non-disabled world that we are not wanted, that we are considered less than human. For those with restricted mobility or sensory impairments, the very physical environment tells us we don't belong. It tells us that we aren't wanted in the places that non-disabled people spend their lives – their homes, their schools and colleges, their workplaces, their leisure venues, The refusal to give British Sign Language the status of a language means that Deaf people are forced to use a language suited to people with different biological characteristics. The refusal to give Braille the same status as printed material shuts out people with a visual impairment. As Susan Hannaford writes, 'For no access read Apartheid' (Hannaford, 1985, p. 121).

Rachel Cartwright, who was born blind, talked to me about her experience of exclusion.

All through my childhood, I felt set apart from my brothers and sisters. I went to a different school and because it was a residential school I felt as if I wasn't part of my family a lot of the time. When my parents talked about our future, they always thought in different terms when it came to me. As a child and as an adult I've been very aware of being excluded by the way that most printed material is not available on tape or in braille, and that if it is it's only because a special effort has been made – for which I'm supposed to feel grateful.

Such exclusion give us a clear message about the attitude of non-disabled people towards us.

Our physical or intellectual differences make us less than human in the eyes of non-disabled people; we can be excluded from normal human activity because we are not normally human. A physically different body, or a body which behaves in a different way, means an incomplete body and this means that our very selves are similarly incomplete.

Non-disabled people feel that our difference gives them the right to invade our privacy and make judgements about our lives. Our physical characteristics evoke such strong feelings that people often have to express them in some way. At the same time they feel able to impose their feelings on us because we are not considered to be autonomous human beings.

Many of us have experienced the total stranger on the slight acquaintance coming up and asking us the most intimate things about our lives. Our physical difference makes our bodies public property. Clare Robson experienced this when – as a result of having multiple sclerosis – one side of her body started shaking and she had to use a stick to help her to walk. 'People would come up to me in the street and ask me what was wrong. If I told them, they would say "Oh, how awful, there's no cure for that, is there?"'

Looking at someone with a physical disability does not always have the effect of undermining the disabled person. There is a difference between staring and gazing. As one young woman put it,

> Now some people can look at me forever and I wouldn't care. Those are the people who seem to see, not just the *best* of me, but the *most* of me. They're not *staring*, they're *gazing*.
> A stare is kind of like a vampire bite – it sucks life out of you. A gaze is just the opposite – a love transfusion.
> (Disability Rights Education and Defense Fund, 1982, p. 50)

Wanting to be normal?

One of the most oppressive features of the prejudice which disabled people experience is the assumption that we want to be other than we are; that is, we want to be normal. Yet, as Pam Evans says, 'Do we only have value, even to ourselves, in direct relation to how closely we can imitate "normal" appearance, function, belief and behaviour?' We may have the same aspirations as non-disabled people (in terms of how we live our lives) but quite patently we are not just like them in that we have physical differences which distinguish us from the majority of the population. Nevertheless the pressures on us to aspire to be 'normal' are huge – 'friends and family all conspire from the kindest and highest of intentions to ensure we make the wrong choice', says Pam. 'Better to betray ourselves than them!'

I myself prefer to go shopping with my child because her presence at my side gives me, I mistakenly think, a passport into the world of normal people.

To assert that I am a mother is to distance myself from the abnormality of being disabled. Some of us take pride in 'looking normal except for sitting down'. Very few of us feel able to celebrate our physical difference, although more of us do as the disability movement grows stronger.

One of the most important features of our experience of prejudice is that we generally experience it as isolated individuals. Many of us spend most of our lives in the company of non-disabled people, whether in our families, with friends, in the workplace, at school, and so on. Most of the people we have dealings with, including our most intimate relationships, are not like us. It is therefore very difficult for us to recognise and challenge the values and judgements that are applied to us and our lives. Our ideas about disability and about ourselves are generally formed by those who are not disabled.

In this situation, the emergence of a disability culture is difficult but tremendously liberating. Such a culture enables us to recognise the pressure to pretend to be normal for the oppressive and impossible-to-achieve hurdle which it is. Most importantly, this culture challenges our own prejudices about ourselves, as well as those of the non-disabled culture. This is vital for, as Pam Evans says,

> Just as no feminist would think of trying to change discriminatory laws and conventions of society without *first* changing her own attitudes to her personal inheritance of conditioning, so no disabled person should see liberation from prejudice as solely a matter of changing others. The *real* liberation is essentially our own. For we are all accomplices to the prejudice in exact proportion to the values and norms of our society that we are prepared to endorse.

She goes on, 'We are *not* normal in the stunted terms the world chooses to define. But we are not obliged to adopt those definitions as standards to which we must aspire, or indeed, regard as something worth having in the first place.' Physical disability and illness are an important part of human experience. The non-disabled world may wish to try to ignore this and to react to physical difference by treating us as if we are not quite human, but we must recognise that our difference is both an essential part of human experience, and, given the chance, can create important and different ways of looking at things.

References

Hannaford, S. (1985) *Living Outside Inside*, Canterbury Press, California.
Disability Rights Education and Defense Fund (1982) *No More Stares*, DREDF, Berkeley, California.

2.6
Disabled people and 'normality'

Paul Abberley

In this paper, I examine three different kinds of approach to the notion that disabled people are not normal. The accounts of our abnormality that arise out of the theoretical perspectives of individual psychology and of non-materialist social psychology are rejected on the grounds of their incoherency, and their ideological nature is indicated. In contrast, a materialist account of our abnormality, which stresses the unmet needs of impaired people is advocated, and the need for detailed concrete explorations of how this discrimination operates identified.

Individual psychology

The dominant approaches in psychology in the first half of this century were summarised by Kammerer in 1940 as follows:

> Although there is agreement that personality maladjustment results from crippling, there are essentially two points of view as to how it actually occurs. The first seems to assume that the presence of any sort of crippling or physical handicap is sufficient in itself to occasion the development of personality disorder. The second viewpoint maintains that in cases of personality maladjustment, the crippled child has been subject to unwise family influences.
>
> (Kammerer, 1940, p. 47)

Allen and Pearson (1928) had concluded, on the basis of case studies, that:

> It is as essential to treat the relationships between the child and his parents and the attitude of the latter towards the disability at the time of its occurrence, in order that the personality may not be crippled as it is to treat the disease itself. Such a crippling of the personality is probably a more serious menace to the future happiness of the individual than a very marked physical disability.
>
> (Allen and Pearson, 1928, p. 235)

Whilst the Adlerian Rudolf Dreikurs argued in 1948 that:

> Not what the child has – in hereditary endowment and environment – but what he does with it, is all important. Courage and social interest, or the lack of them, determine whether a disability permits a good adjustment or leads to permanent failure.
>
> (Dreikurs, 1948, p. 53)

Since then individual psychology and its therapeutically oriented offshoots have continued in this vein, and debated the degree and nature of pathology supposed to follow, directly or indirectly, from impairment.

For example, Harper and Richman (1978) claim to identify greater degrees of behaviour inhibition that in control groups. Anderson and Clarke (1982) identify low self-esteem as characteristic of disabled adolescents, and Kasprzyk (1983) finds despondency in people who have had a spinal injury. These psychological pathologies are attributed to failure to come to terms with impairment (Lindowski and Dunn, 1974; Shindi, 1983).

Such research is systematised and operationalised as therapy through the application of bereavement theory, developed as a way of conceptualising normal and 'healthy' mourning of the loss of a loved one, to disablement:

> Patients must be allowed to come to terms, they must grieve and mourn for their lost limbs, lost abilities or lost looks and be helped to adjust to their lost body-image. Personally, I doubt if anyone who has not experienced the onset of irreversible disability can fully understand the horror of the situation.
>
> (Dickinson, 1977, p. 12)

A more theoretically sophisticated account of processes of 'recovery' from impairment, which argues that a new 'healthy but disabled' self can be constituted, again asserts the validity of the metaphor of death.

> The transformation of a patient to a healthy person again is a triumphant victory. Yet a death has occurred; and it is critical that this death is acknowledged. The body has undergone major alterations. It is not the same body. A new self has risen from the ashes of the old body.
>
> (Seymour, 1989, p. 122)

So convinced are such people that to be impaired is to 'die' that no amount of protestation to the contrary seems to make any difference. This should lead us to harbour severe doubts about the 'scientific' nature of such research, since it seems to already know the answer before it goes out to investigate.

The main deficiency of such approaches, however, is that they locate the 'problem of disability' in the individual and in the effectivity or otherwise of her/his adjustment to a set of beliefs, values and practices which are taken for granted.

In contrast to this, I wish to argue that *if* disabled people display psychological abnormalities, this is because they have been socialised into such traits as a result of the ways in which society meets, or fails to meet, our needs, and that the claim that such features are a consequence of impairment is itself an aspect of the oppression of disabled people since it misidentifies, and thus does nothing to overcome, the main source of psychological distress.

Disabled people do not need to deny the individual psychological costs they pay; rather, we need to identify them as a most directly experienced aspect of oppression, and dispute not the existence of psychological distress in disabled people but the kinds of causal account that are produced.

We may usefully draw an analogy here with the women's movement in which it soon became apparent that if the real extent and nature of sexual oppression were to be understood, and services appropriate to real needs

struggled for, feminist psychologies which recognised the individual consequences of collective oppresssion, and traced their causes beyond the
individual to the mechanisms of that oppression, would have to be
developed. Fanon makes a parallel point as regards racism, at the beginning
of *Black Skins, White Masks*, where he states: 'I am talking of millions of
people who have been skilfully injected with fear, inferiority complexes,
trepidation, servility, despair, abasement' (Fanon, 1968).

Individual psychological adjustment studies, then, fail to provide a useful
analysis because they do not locate the disabled person in a society which
contains a whole set of beliefs, practices, and so on, surrounding disability,
and fail to see the consequences of these practices as expressed in the
psychology of the individual disabled person. Rather, they present as an
individual property, following from the impact of impairment on the 'self',
what are in fact learnt behaviours.

Ideas about the abnormality of disabled people that arise out of research
based on adding together the particular psychological attributes of individual
disabled people are then systematically misleading, since they fail to include
'social forces, structural features of society, institutional factors and so on'
(Lukes, 1973, p. 122) in their explanations – in other words, because they
treat disability as if it were the same thing as impairment.

Social psychology

Social psychology, in apparent contrast, has focused on social attitudes
towards disabled people as the causal nexus, and is thus not open to this
criticism. For example, Bull and Rumsey (1988) argue that for visibly different
children negative social feedback results in low self-esteem. It is still the
disabled person's 'problem' that requires explanation, but the explanatory
structure is no longer bounded by the individual's psyche; rather, answers are
sought in the belief-system of the whole society. From the general identification of 'negative attitudes' (Chesler, 1965; Yuker, 1965), these attitudes are
documented in more detail (Wada and Brodwin, 1975; Seifert, 1979; Wright,
1983) and 'distancing scales' constructed (Tringo, 1970).

Paradoxically, this move beyond the individual to the social has resulted in
a much more pessimistic prognosis for disabled people. If the 'problem of
attitude' is not primarily located in the individual, but in the society, then no
amount of individual effort at 'adjustment' to impairment can solve it. Whilst
the quantitative researchers referred to above, following the innate cau-
tiousness of their method, make few explicit generalisations and predictions,
no such reticence characterises the qualitative studies of disabled people
produced by researchers of the interactionist school.

The best known interactionist accounts of disablement employ the concept
of 'stigma' and have their origin in the work of Erving Goffman (1963). Whilst
mechanisms, sometimes of 'passing', more often of 'coping', are described,

we are left with the impression that 'shameful difference' and its consequences are an immutable fact of social life, for physically impaired people: 'it
is possible that there are no exemptions for incapacity in such areas as
aesthetic norms' (Haber and Smith, 1971, p. 95).

In this tradition, the proceedings of a more recent conference (Ainsley *et al.*,
1986) seem to contain all the deficiencies of earlier work which employed the
concept. In her summing up Coleman reveals the ultimate poverty of a
perspective which poses questions only to deem them unanswerable. 'We
began this volume with two basic questions: what is stigma and why does
stigma remain? Because stigmas mirror culture and society, they are in
constant flux, and therefore the answers to these two questions continue to
elude social scientists' (Ainsley *et al.*, 1986, p. 211).

In answer to the question 'why does stigma persist?' the products of
interactionism shy away from the realities of social structures, preferring to
provide an 'answer' in terms of the spurious generalities of 'eternal verities'.

> The ultimate answers about why stigma persists may lie in an examination of why
> people fear differences, fear the future, fear the unknown, and therefore stigmatize
> that which is different and unknown. An equally important issue to investigate is how
> stigmatization may be linked to the fear of being different.
>
> (Ainsley *et al.*, 1986, p. 227)

Now, it is an extremely dubious proposition that people do, in general, fear
'differences', 'the future', 'the unknown', and that they 'therefore' stigmatise
people who represent these things. Rather, people fear and stigmatise fairly
specific things, people and conditions, even though they may admittedly
know very little about them. But because it operates only at the level of ideas,
without any attempt to specify why particular ideas are held in particular
societies at particular times, other than by reference to other ideas,
interactionist social psychology can only describe peoples' beliefs, not
explain them. Its accounts, however accurate at this level, remain stuck at this
preliminary stage of scientific enquiry.

Furthermore, as cogently argued by Finkelstein (1980), Goffman, in
borrowing the concept of stigma from ancient Greece, where it referred to 'a
bodily sign . . . cut or burned into the body and advertising that the bearer was
a slave' (Goffman, 1963, p. 19) *chooses* to interpret its meaning as one of
'blemish and ritual pollution' rather than of the power and inequality which
allowed one person to be a slaveholder and compelled another to be a slave.
It is telling that a theory unable to recognise the nature of power relationships
in today's society, should exhibit a similar incapacity in its assessment of
ancient history. Theories which ignore power conflicts and subscribe to a
consensus view, as interactionism does, have no choice but to see existing
inequalities as inevitable.

These kinds of account, which span the blurred borderland between social
psychology and sociology, in effect justify the 'abnormality' of disabled
people by claiming that it is inevitable. Any society, they argue, must
discriminate against impaired people to safeguard its own general social
health. Again, then, we find our 'abnormality' being explained ultimately in

terms of our impairment, which qualifies us for admission to an unavoidably disadvantaged category of people.

Material abnormality

For all its deficiencies, the 1988 Office of Population Censuses and Surveys (OPCS) survey of disability in Britain makes clear that an overwhelming feature of the disabled state is poverty (Abberley, 1991). It is this, the economic dimension of disablement, that the perspectives we have considered so far so conspicuously fail to address. Rather, by producing individual or social accounts of disabled individuals' pathology in society, any economic disadvantage is presented as a byproduct of incapacity or of prejudice. It would be equally reasonable, however, to say that rather than disabled people being generally poor and powerless because people are prejudiced against us, people are prejudiced against us because we are poor and powerless. Such accounts locate the 'abnormality' not in disabled people, but in the society which fails to meet our needs. This kind of definition is perhaps most concisely encapsulated in the UPIAS definition, where 'Disability is . . . caused by a contemporary social organisation which takes no or little account of people who have physical impairments' (Union of the Physically Impaired Against Segregation, 1976, p. 4).

In such a view, our abnormality results from the failure of society to meet our 'normal' needs as impaired people, which are different from those of some, but by no means all, of our fellow citizens. Our abnormality consists in us having, compared to the general population, a particular and large set of our human needs unprovided for, or met in inappropriate and disempowering ways. The most familiar of these are in the areas of physical access and transportation, but in almost any aspects of life an impaired person is likely to confront a disabling dimension. It is in this sense, of having an abnormal number of our normal needs unmet, that I think it right to speak of disabled people as not being normal. This abnormality is something we share with women, black, elderly, gay and lesbian people, in fact the majority of the population. To understand the specific nature of the abnormality experienced by disabled people we have not only to document a general failure to provide for needs. We must also investigate how legislation framed in terms of the 'normal' citizen systematically disadvantages us, creates and perpetuates our abnormality. By so doing we start to produce accounts of what needs changing if the oppression of disabled people is to be overcome, we start to develop a disabled perspective which we can progressively apply to all aspects of society. In doing so we are going beyond the consideration of the facts of disadvantage to uncovering the mechanisms through which it is produced and perpetuated.

For illustration and example, I will consider some recent legislation, and show how its failure to treat disabled people as having special, 'abnormal', requirements results in disadvantage.

An examination of the implications of the social security 'reforms' of April 1988 (National Association of Citizens Advice Bureaux, 1988; Turner and Kepley, 1988) indicates how regarding disabled people as 'normal' results in a substantial increase in disadvantage. Under the previous system of benefits, unemployed disabled people could claim social security at a higher rate, and were also eligible for a number of additional requirement payments (ARPs) to meet such needs as extra laundry expenses, special dietary requirements, extra heating, wear and tear on clothing, and so on, which were a consequence of specific disabilities. For all its deficiencies and inadequacies, this system in principle recognised that the needs of disabled people are often different from those of the 'normal' claimant.

Under the new Social Fund, the higher long-term benefit rate was abolished and the ARPs replaced by flat-rate premiums, which are not geared to specific needs but based on two categories of basic and severe disability. A system of transitional payments is in operation, which slows down the effects of these changes on current claimants.

Under the single payments system grants, involving certain rights to payment backed up by a right of appeal to an independent tribunal, disbursed some £350 million in 1986/7.

The Social Fund, limited in expenditure to £203 million in its first year, made discretionary loans, with no right to appeal decisions. The system involves an obligation to provide evidence of having sought help from charities, friends and relations, and even if this can be provided and the request deemed a reasonable one, no payment will be forthcoming if it involves the breach of cash limits.

Hardship is clearly caused to disabled people (40,000 on government estimates, up to half a million according to the Disablement Income Group) who are able to live in the community. With the withdrawal of ARPs some people will doubtless be forced back into residential care as the value of the fixed transitional payment is eroded by rising costs and inflation or as their condition leads to further special requirements.

For individuals hoping to make the move from institutional care to living in the community the situation is far more problematic than it was before. With no right to payment for essential items, and community care grants cash-limited and discretionary, both the initial move and its long-term viability are thrown into question.

Whilst other sections of the population are clearly severely affected by these government policies, disabled people experience these particular 'reforms' as an attack on their human right not to be incarcerated without trial and conviction, in so far as it renders it in some cases impossible to live outside institutions. The abolition of need-based ARPs, and the consequent treatment of disabled people as 'normal' welfare recipients, is by no means a desirable kind of 'normality'.

The field of housing provision is another area where the special needs of disabled people make it necessary to develop specialised knowledge and policies, to recognise that disabled people are done no service by being regarded as normal.

The vast majority of owner-occupied housing in Britain is unsuitable for people with major physical disabilities. The least satisfactory housing tends also to be that inhabited by sections of the population of which disabled people form a disproportionately large percentage, elderly people and people on low incomes.

Local authorities have always been the main providers of wheelchair and mobility adapted housing, and although the actual number of such dwellings decreased between the periods 1970/81 and 1982/6 due to an overall decline in their house-building programme, the percentage of wheelchair and mobility adapted housing increased in this period. As far as the main alternative source, housing associations, are concerned, an expansion in their activity in the 1980s was accompanied by a declining proportion of adapted housing, and a decline in actual numbers (see Table 1). On current performance, any contraction in local authority building programmes disproportionately disadvantages disabled people. Thus the decline in local authority housing budgets has a specific and disproportionately disadvantageous effect upon disabled people, which can only be obscured by regarding disabled people as 'normal'.

Table 1   *Provision of wheelchair and mobility adapted housing*

	1970–81		1982–6	
	Average no. built per year	No. built as % of total completions	Average no. built per year	No. built as % of total completions
Local authority				
wheelchair	483.2	0.5	281.4	1.3
mobility adapted	2364.3	2.6	1693.4	6.8
Housing association				
wheelchair	105.4	0.7	42.2	0.4
mobility adapted	587.2	4.0	138.0	1.2

Source: Department of the Environment housing construction statistics, cited in Morris, 1988.

Again, Fry's study of difficulties confronted by disabled people in voting in the 1987 general election (Fry, 1987) indicates a series of problems in the exercise of democratic rights which are to large degree *sui generis*, and can only be understood through specific knowledge of disability.

Finally, as regards the poll tax, it was on the grounds that disabled people should be treated as 'normal' citizens that the government rejected the Allen amendment in the House of Lords, which would have offered extra rebates to poor disabled people to cover the full cost of poll-tax payments wherever they may live.

Such concrete explorations of the effects of social policies and practices on disabled people indicate that any adequate understanding of the oppression of disabled people requires macro- as well as micro-level investigation. This is an area which is only susceptible to research via detailed investigation which, however it is carried out, certainly cannot be in terms of the 'normality' of disabled people, since its concerns must be to explicate the kinds and degrees of difference between the needs of impaired people and the general population, and with the multifarious features of 'normal' social life which prevent disabled people from being 'normal'.

Such investigations also serve to indicate that, rather than being an unchangeable feature of social life, the disablement of impaired people can be overcome, through legislation and practices which remove the impediments to fuller participation in social life.

References

Abberley, P. (1991) 'The significance of the OPCS disability surveys', in Oliver, M. (ed.) *Social Work: Disabled People and Disabling Environments*, Jessica Kingsley, London.

Ainsley, S., Becker, G. and Coleman, L. (1986) *The Dilemma of Difference: A Multidisciplinary View of Stigma*, Plenum Press, New York.

Allen, F.H. and Pearson, G.H.J. (1928) 'The emotional problems of the physically handicapped child', *British Journal of Medical Psychology*, Vol. 4, pp. 27–43.

Anderson, E.M. and Clarke, L. (1982) *Disability in Adolescence*, Methuen, London.

Bull, R. and Rumsey, N. (1988) *The Social Psychology of Facial Appearance*, Springer Verlag, New York.

Chesler, M. (1965) 'Ethnocentrism and attitudes towards the physically disabled', *Journal of Personality and Social Psychology*, Vol. 2, pp. 877–82.

Dickinson, M. (1977) 'Rehabilitating the traumatically disabled adult', *Social Work Today*, Vol. 8, No. 28, p. 12.

Dreikurs, R. (1948) 'The socio-psychological dynamics of physical disability: a review of the Adlerian concept', *Journal of Social Issues*, Vol. 4, No. 4, pp. 42–53.

Fanon, F. (1968) *Black Skins, White Masks*, Macgibbon and Kee, London.

Finkelstein, V. (1980) *Attitudes and Disabled People: Issues for Discussion*, World Rehabilitation Fund, New York.

Fry, E. (1987) *Disabled People and the 1987 General Election*, Spastics Society, London.

Goffman, E. (1963) *Stigma: Some Notes on the Management of Spoiled Identity*, Penguin, Harmondsworth.

Haber, L. and Smith, T. (1971) 'Disability and deviance', *American Sociological Review*, Vol. 36, pp. 78–95.

Harper, D. and Richman, L. (1978) 'Personality profiles of physically impaired adolescents', *Journal of Clinical Psychology*, Vol. 34, pp. 636–42.

Kammerer, R.C. (1940) 'An exploratory psychological study of crippled children', *Psychological Record*, Vol. 4, pp. 47–59.

Kasprzyk, D.M. (1983) 'Psychological factors associated with responses to hypertension or spinal cord injury: an investigation of coping with chronic illness or disability', *Dissertation Abstracts International*, Vol. 44, No. 4B, p. 1279.

Lindowski, D.C. and Dunn, M.A. (1974) 'Self-concept and acceptance of disability', *Rehabilitation Counselling Bulletin*, September, pp. 28–32.

Lukes, S. (1973) *Individualism*, Basil Blackwell, Oxford.

Morris, J. (1988) *Freedom to Lose: Housing Policy and People with Disabilities*, Shelter, London.

National Association of Citizens Advice Bureaux (1988) *Losers and Gainers: a Comparison of Benefits*, Yorkshire and Humberside Area Social Policy Group, Leeds Citizens Advice Bureau.

Seifert K.H. (1979) 'The attitudes of working people toward disabled persons', *International Journal of Rehabilitation Research*, Vol. 2, pp. 79–94.

Seymour, W. (1989) *Bodily Alterations*, Allen and Unwin, Sydney.

Shindi, J. (1983) 'Emotional adjustment of physically handicapped children: a comparison of children with congenital and acquired orthopaedic disabilities', *International Journal of Social Psychiatry*, Vol. 29, No. 4, pp. 292–8.

Tringo, L. (1970) 'The hierarchy of preference toward disability groups', *Journal of Special Education*, Vol. 4, No. 3, pp. 295–306.

Turner, J. and Kepley, A. (1988) *Shake-Up! A Guide to the New Social Security Benefits*, BBC, London.

Union of the Physically Impaired Against Segregation (1976) *Fundamental Principles of Disability*, UPIAS, London.

Wada, M.A. and Brodwin, M.G. (1975) 'Attitudes of society towards sexual functioning of male individuals with spinal cord injury', *Psychology*, Vol. 12, No. 4, pp. 18–22.

Wright, B. (1983) *Physical Disability: a Psychosocial Approach*, Harper and Row, New York.

Yuker, H. (1965) 'Attitudes as determinants of behavior', *Journal of Rehabilitation*, Vol. 31, pp. 15–16.

2.7

The tragedy principle: strategies for change in the representation of disabled people

David Hevey

In all forms of the media, disabled people have been represented as tragic. There has been little discussion, however, about what this 'tragedy' might be or mean. In this paper, I would like to explore the theory behind what I have called 'the tragedy principle' in the representation of disabled people. In the history of disability representation or 'arts and disability', we find a history of representation that was done in our name but not done by us. The beginning of a strategy for change would be to examine some key stereotypes of disability within that history of misrepresentation which are present today and which need to be challenged.

Mr Magoo, Long John Silver and Richard III are examples of disabled people as ignorant, destructive or warlike. Other examples include childlike (charity advertising), hyperdependent (the BBC television play *Keeping Tom Nice*) and flawed (Lenny, from Steinbeck's *Of Mice and Men*). All of these stereotypes (of which the above are a small sample) come about because disabled people have not had an input, let alone a controlling interest, in culture and representation done in our name. Furthermore, I would argue that the general history of disability representation is one of oppressive or 'negative' forms and that this has happened precisely because disabled people are excluded from the production of disability culture and excluded from the dominant 'disability' discourses.[1] We are excluded from most history but particularly, and perversely, from the history of 'disability representation'.

To say this, then, leaves us with the position that historical representation has been either absent or negative, and that disabled people want something positive. This 'position' has become a ritual, where the word is repeated as if that would change things. Where once disabled people would be represented in a state of sub-consciousness (that is, portrayed as unaware of themselves and their situation), we are now witnessing a small current coming into circulation of 'positive' images of the grinning disabled. This is an extremely superficial gain but it is nonetheless currently considered 'positive'.

So, what do I mean by disability representation? Does the gaze fall on the impaired body or on social barriers? I would argue that what we should mean by disability representation is the dynamic between the two. By this criterion, we can see that traditional disability representation is in fact *impairment representation*. Disability representation, like black representation and the representation of women before it, is seen as representation *on the body*. It is this which unites practically the entire discourse of disability representation, from Greek Theatre to James Bond villains to charity advertising to all the Richard IIIs, Ravens,[2] and so on. It is that disablement means impairment and impairment means flaw. This is the tragedy principle.

The basic rule of oppressive disability representation assumes the social non-worth of an impairment or the person with an impairment. This visual construction is incorporated within representation by characters who carry this invariably destructive 'flaw'. This can be seen in Shakespeare's *Richard III*. Richard's opening soliloquy (which is also the opening text of the entire play) must count as the clearest 'policy' statement of the tragedy principle in representation:

> Deform'd, unfinish'd, sent before my time
> Into this breathing world scarce half made up
> And that so lamely and unfashionable
> That dogs bark at me as I halt by them –
> Why, I, in this piping time of peace,
> Have no delight to pass away the time
> Unless to spy my shadow in the sun
> And descant on mine own deformity.

Before this, Richard has let us know that he is not happy with the non-warring state of affairs and is set to provide destruction. The reasoning then comes through his narration of having an impairment. Doom enters with impairment, and disability is not in society but on the body.

The aesthetic construction of a part or parts of the body as the site of all that is socially unacceptable, a flaw, began life within classical Greek theatre (Boal, 1989) and has continued today. The villain of the piece may begin a hero and even contain some hope (Lenny, from *Of Mice and Men*) then a flaw becomes apparent, and they then disembowel or impair themselves (or have it done to them) as an act of retribution.

The story of Richard III in particular sets up the basic rule of the tragedy principle within representation, which is that fate must be made physical *on the body*. For the character to know and demonstrate their doom, their body must physically manifest the flaw through an impairment. The testimony, the words and actions, of this doomed character will then reveal to the audience the 'natural' and inevitable decline of the disabled character. By their social destruction, the message is conveyed that the impairment represents the greatest fall for a person this side of death. The purpose of this device in art is that the audience may cathart their projected anxieties surrounding disablement and 'able-bodiedness'. The Oedipus fable, for example, begins with a non-disabled person whose transgressions are dealt with by the addition of an impairment. This is the conclusion. In tragic theatre, where the character enters already impaired, then doom enters the narrative that much earlier.

The tragedy principle, then, positions a flaw on the body related to the deepest possible social fall. Where impairment enters, the character is proven to be socially dead (Finkelstein, 1991). Whether in television, theatre, cinema, fine art or charity advertising, the tragedy principle uses the impairment as a metaphor and a symbol for a socially unacceptable person and it is this tragedy principle which is the bone-cage surrounding historical and current disability representation. It is this impairment-as-flaw that is 'negative' representation, and this form is intolerable.

What are the underpinnings of this form? These forms of disability representation naturalise the exclusion of disabled people from societies which are organised on an ability to gain employment and these representations are the target of non-disabled people for the ridding of their fears over their own 'able-bodied' decline, mortality or loss of power. It is important, however, in terms of creating radical and new forms of disability representation, to acknowledge that it is both the organisation of economic production *and* the projection of (non-disabled) negative desire, which contains disabled people within oppressive cultural representation.

The fall of the tragic character into either a real (that is, narrated) death or a (again, narrated) living death will aid the disavowal, the catharsis, of the non-disabled audiences' ever-present fear for the loss of their own 'able-bodiedness'. 'The Disabled' is a non-disabled construction, a representational framework no more real than a hologram but which has to contain two properties if it is to have any cathartic meaning for society. To repeat, these two 'able-bodied' cathartic needs are: (1) the ridding or disavowal of health, fitness and other physical/functional issues pertaining to the ability to work, and (2) the disavowal of the presence of death and mortality. This is how 'negative' representation serves 'able-bodied' people. Its positive active purpose is in supporting the 'able-bodied' management of these two fears.

Given the growing criticism of traditional representation and the confusion about what is an appropriate representation, what is to be done? If we are to move beyond this state of affairs, the cultural task for disabled artists and culture workers is threefold. First, how to shift disability representation off from the body and into the interface between people with impairments and socially disabling conditions. Second, how to create aesthetic forms which are seen to deal with this successfully (that is, which can be internalised by disabled people in struggle). Third, how can this shift be played out in the portrayal of disabled people in relationship to their impairment so that they no longer see themselves as able-bodied people who are flawed.

So, the history of the portrayal of disabled people is that disabled people are portrayed as flawed able-bodied people. Disabled people have never been recognised as having a distinct identity. So far so good. However, an analysis of the mechanics of historical and oppressive tragedy/impairment/ disability representation is not in itself sufficient to change those forms of representation. What is necessary in the first instance is a shift in the surrounding social relations and economic conditions. Finkelstein has written on the shift from 'phase two' to 'phase three' within the shaping of social disablement.[3] As an extremely broad overview, the shift from heavy manufacturing through the electronics and cybernetics revolution is creating the conditions for a different position for disabled people in society and this theoretical position is currently being borne out. We have had three Conservative governments that have been and still are committed to the rolling back of the 'nanny' state. One aspect of this has been the Care in the Community programme, which has seen the closure of many long-stay institutions and which has resulted in large numbers of disabled people re-entering the social arena, but still having to struggle for basic rights of access. Within this, the UK disability movement has grown.

A particular, and in representational terms crucial, development of this new activism (and one which links it to other movements based on class, gender, colour, and so on) is the de-biologising nature of the disability. That is to say, the issue of disability, like other issues pertaining to women and blacks and gays and lesbians, and so on, is shifting its view away from the body and on to society.

Although the disability movement has taken the initiative in articulating this shift, it is a shift which is affecting all sides of the disability issue. For example, and again as Finkelstein has pointed out, the dominant form of oppression of disabled people is shifting the medical 'cure or care' view to reveal the underlying administrative control. While this may mean that disabled people are shifting from institutions to ghettoes, it nevertheless heralds an age when disabled people are not to be cured as such. Despite liberal panic over this new agenda, it represents greater possibilities for the re-examination and re-presentation of disabled people. In this context at least, new definitions can be re-negotiated.

Since this shift is reflected within the social disability movement, it clearly creates conditions for its emulation within disability representation and the disability arts movement. Indeed, the shift from 'arts and disability' to 'disability arts' is proof of this movement. The disability arts movement is the first sign of a post-tragedy disability culture. To state this clearly, the disability movement is the articulation that: (1) impairment and disability are no longer synonyms, and (2) that they are no longer exclusively focused on the body. The disability arts movement is the only area which is dealing with the cultural vacuum which now exists given this shift.

However, as much as we have gained the initiative, there are still problems which face the disability arts movement and which need to be unravelled. One in particular is that we currently lack a theory, or theories, of an alternative process. The final part of this paper, I hope, begins one.

Part 1: Gazing where? Moving off the body. We need to define what we mean by 'disability representation'. Do we mean the representation of impairment, or do we mean the representation of social barriers, or do we mean the recording of the interface between the two? Artistic and cultural disabled-led practice which positions its gaze towards this interface begins to reflect the struggle.

Part 2: Changing the meaning of impairment. We need to reclaim, in the light of the shifts of disability-definition (from medical to community care interventions, from institution to care in the community, from arts and disability to disability arts), the cultural meaning of impairment. We need to undo the tragedy principle and the notion of impairment as flaw. This is clearly linked to Part 1, since what is being projected on to the person with an impairment by 'able-bodied' culture is in itself changing. However, the point of radical art and culture is to create a political poetic of the self and the group. We will be able to redefine our impairments away from flaws by making culture and art which shows the process of our transformations. The left has traditionally made a mistake within representation by positioning 'positive' images against 'negative' ones, picket lines against victims. However worthy this has been (and necessary in places), our purpose should be to create work which records the process of change, not just two 'negative' or 'positive' poles.

Part 3: The control of meaning. Our artworks and cultural works must tell both of the issue and of themselves. This is critical. We must not assume that any reading of any artwork is *in itself* permanent or natural. The best new image in the world can have its meaning altered by adding a different text in or around it.[4] In the final analysis, negativity or positivity within any given cultural form only exists within the *positioning* of the piece. It is not implicit in the surface of the work. Its meaning can be altered by its altered context. The success of our counter-culture is in our ability to position meaning.

Part 4: The act of showing must also be shown. Brecht in particular dealt with the relationship between real struggle and the metaphorical or symbolical illumination of struggle in art. In the Brechtian aesthetic, the real struggles of life and oppressed peoples cannot be shown, as it were, naturally. Naturalism as an aesthetic may work as a tool of catharsis – we may suffer with those we see suffering – but it does not illuminate methods for action after the catharsis. Therefore, what is needed is a critical relationship within the story-telling or story-showing *within and between* the form and the issue. The aesthetic form of presentation is itself part of the reinterpretation. This is to acknowledge that the representational forms themselves are conveyers of messages but are not innocent of the struggle. The point of new methods with new messages is that they convey the sense of a new order (or at least the decline of the old one). This links itself to the three previous parts because it displays a process which metaphorically or symbolically represents change.

Part 5: The success or failure of a new form. Again, radical drama theory, particularly that of the 1970s involving class politics and gay and lesbian politics (and, of course, both at once), dealt with the extremely critical issue of the relationship between producer and consumer. The success of new forms of disability representation can be judged in my estimation by their consumption by disabled people and their ability to mobilise disabled people into action. One of the main characteristics that has distinguished all radical art, from that of the Soviet revolution to the art of South Africa, from the art of our movement to the work of the AIDS practitioners in the United States, is its proximity to an active audience.

However, there is the problem of the romantic notion of pure art devoid of social responsibility. Some people engaging in the issue of disability representation have tried to affect the taste of non-disabled audiences and supporters, rather than engage in a political creativity within and about the disability struggle. Picasso said that taste was the enemy of creativity and, eventually, those disabled artists who pursue that path of affecting taste will find their work stagnating, since they are facilitating an outsider's vision of themselves. This is a mistake, though understandable, because we have a profound lack of role-models in this area. If people entering this issue align their aesthetics and texts to a field which operates between their sense of self and their relationship to the movement, the changes to both will create the base of their continued aesthetic change and growth.

Finally, the strategies for change can be found in an analysis of what has gone before and a cultural intervention in what is socially happening to disabled people. This dialectic is our terrain. Within this dynamic, we can affect and create cultural forms and an agenda which bring the non-disabled world to us, not we to it.

Notes

1 By the word 'discourse', I mean an exchange or flow of information within a given social form or context.

2 Graham Greene's anti-hero in *A Gun for Sale*.

3 For further discussion on this see, for example, Finkelstein (1980).

4 See, in particular, the representational theory of Victor Burgin, who has worked extensively on 'scripto-visual' reading and meaning of representation, for example Burgin (1982, 1986).

References

Boal, A. (1989) *Theatre of the Oppressed*, Pluto Press, London.
Burgin, V. (ed.) (1982) *Thinking Photography*, Macmillan, Basingstoke.
Burgin, V. (1986) *The End of Art Theory: Criticism and Post-Modernity*, Macmillan, Basingstoke.
Finkelstein, V. (1980) *Attitudes and Disabled People*, World Rehabilitation Fund, New York.
Finkelstein, V. (1991) 'Disability: an administrative challenge? (The health and welfare heritage)', in Oliver, M. (ed.) *Social Work: Disabled People and Disabling Environments*, Jessica Kingsley, London.

2.8

Broken arts and cultural repair: the role of culture in the empowerment of disabled people

Elspeth Morrison and Vic Finkelstein

Introduction

In every society human beings come together in groups and subgroups so that their social and physical environment can be modified to improve the quality of life (in food, shelter and leisure). How these different groups actively engage in shaping the world they live in, the artifacts they produce and the mannerisms observed in their use, the different interpretations they make of their lives and the way they present and convey these views to each other, all form the sum total of a society's culture. In all societies, then, we can locate evidence of the real experiences and aspirations of different social subgroups by the level and way their culture is expressed, especially in its concrete form in the arts.

However, from time to time different subgroups can become dominant within a larger social structure, and the culture of this subgroup is then likely to become the dominant culture in the greater society. When any dominant group asserts its power by imposing its culture on others, or diverts wealth to its chosen art forms, then the cultural expression of other groups in the arts will be suppressed. The output of these groups may fail to develop, or their culture may disintegrate or disappear. If culture and artistic developments are interpreted as integral aspects of the human social condition, a subgroup's lack of artistic development could be seen as the result of its failure to develop an active social life, or as a reflection of the dehumanisation and suppression of that group. The very limited opportunities for disabled people to take part in all forms of the arts as spectators, creators or participants raises questions about whether or not we are an oppressed and marginalised subgroup and what we might be trying to do about this.

This article was prepared from a paper written by Elspeth Morrison and Vic Finkelstein; the paper is now published in S. Lees (ed.) (1992) *Disability Arts and Culture Papers: Transcripts of a Disability Arts and Culture Seminar*, SHAPE, London.

It is arguable that while the most powerful groups in society have placed their cultural tastes at the top of a hierarchy of artistic forms, not all people will be equally devoted to these fashions and traditions. The lower status of their own customs could then well lead to a general loss of interest in the arts and this could gradually spread throughout society. This could be expressed in encouraging schoolchildren to think that careers in 'science' and 'maths' are for the brightest pupils while 'arts' and 'vocational training' are for others. In this context it seems understandable why those active in promoting empower-ment through self-help organisations might not see an equally important role for disability arts and culture in advancing the well-being of disabled people. Participating and enjoying disability arts could then be seen as only a side-show in the drama of struggle for change, something to provide relief from the tensions of boring or stressful committee meetings. In this paper we will argue that the presence or absence of disability culture, and involvement of disabled people in the arts, is an indication of the general state of their success in reflecting upon and managing their own affairs.

Cultural dependency

In our society cultural custody has, for the most part, passed into the hands of a small elite who acquire fame and fortune through support and funding from the most powerful sections of the community. Through its support the white upper middle and upper classes have come to dominate all arts and culture. Unsurprisingly then, in this climate, disabled artists may look for self-esteem and financial gain in the non-disabled dominated arts and media.

After all, when the little information that does exist about disabled artists is often patronising if not actually offensive, there will be a strong incentive to keep this side of one's life somewhat hidden. If disabled artists or musicians are recognised, living or dead, all too often their lives are seen in terms of their medical condition and their imagined ability to 'overcome' personal tragedy. Passivity and dependence are attributed to us, and our only *collective* identity is as 'the disabled' – as tragic *individuals* who, to a varying degree, are the recipients of care, unlikely to be creative without the stimulation and assistance of others often in an institutional setting such as the day centre or 'rehabilitation' unit.

It is very unusual for interpretations of their creative work to be analysed in relation to how (and if) the person's impairment informs their work. While we know that Stevie Wonder is blind, there seems to be a lack of interest in how this might influence and enhance his music. Could insight about the music of one disabled artist have some particular relevance to other disabled musicians? Isolation due to lack of information about other disabled artists could encourage an individual to develop their creativity no further than as a tool for assimilation into the dominant culture and access to their arts. They may, then, easily become culturally dependent on the dominant sections of society and miss the opportunity to experience the growth in self-confidence that can follow identification with others who see themselves as members of a distinctive social subgroup with a unique, but equal, identity to other groups.

Many disabled people feel that there cannot be any such thing as a 'disability culture'. Even among the more informed the idea that our shared experiences and perspectives might contribute to the birth of a culture can generate anxiety. There appear to be two general reasons for hostility towards the growth of a disability culture:

1 In Britain many people believe that 'culture' equals 'opera and art galleries' where the middle class go instead of watching football. Viewed this way, culture is seen as a possession of the elite and a pursuit of the rich. 'To be cultured', it is imagined, is to be rather like a pearl, understated, refined and in the best possible taste. It is often seen as having nothing to do with the 'real' world – that is, as a reflection of one's experiences and perceptions quite independent of those of the dominant group. Recognition of the importance of participation in the arts and culture of one's own group, as part of human development, is not something that is cultivated in the British character.

2 Many disabled people believe that encouraging a disability culture can only reinforce negative images of 'disability' – that is, they have not questioned the tragedy view of disability and when they think of a disability culture they assume that this must mean art forms which only present the negative side of disabled living. They ask: Why should I give credence to a life that has imposed barriers on me? What is there to celebrate and explore when my life is so grim?

Both these reactions miss the point. Discrimination against people on the grounds of 'non-normal' bodies or intellectual capacity places them outside the mainstream of social life. In order to participate meaningfully within the community members of this group must actively engage in the issues that confront them. In doing this they provide the material for their own cultural development that is self-determining and self-governing. This activity is an affirmation of existence despite insistent illustrations all around us which portray what we will never be! For example, a deaf person goes to the theatre and experiences a hearing writer being translated; or a wheelchair-user finds art gallery paintings endlessly drawn from the shoe-using artist's point of view. The struggle against disabling barriers, however, is an active and creative engagement. From this point of view the struggle to remove barriers could be regarded as the seed bed for human arts. For us, the only difference is that the barriers which we have to address are dissimilar to those faced by able-bodied people.

Pressure for change

Of course, not all disabled people accept that they are incapable of functioning independently and equally with others in society. The discussion among organised and informed disabled people has always focused on finding new ways to integrate into the mainstream community but on their own terms. Thus the day-to-day experiences of disabled people can be characterised as involving a unique tension which, at one level, involves the passive experience of being prevented from controlling one's own life, and at the other, actively struggling to overturn this situation. Both the absence, and recent emergence, of disability arts and culture might be thought of as a mirror reflecting the current status of this tension between passive and active roles.

As long as traditional media imagery, and so on, represents disabled people as tragic individuals, with no collective voice and with little access to each other, we can expect the activities of disabled people to go no further than personal complaint. At an early stage in coming together in associations, then, the first choice is almost always to make a combined plea to those in power for greater access to resources. If joint action is undertaken, these associations often settle into the familiar pattern of 'pressure-group' politics – that is, appealing to existing power structures to be relieved of their debilitating situation.

Arising out of the struggles of *individuals*, pressure-group politics encourages the development of an elite leadership who then negotiate with those who hold power. In pressure-group politics the struggle for civil rights is controlled by the active few, while the mass of disabled people remain in their traditional passive relationship to others. Only now the 'others' are not able-bodied benefactors but other disabled people. For this elite, negotiating for an improved quality of life, there is unlikely to be sensitivity about the absence of disability arts. This is because they are concerned with clarifying and presenting *their own* perspective of the issues and an inactive membership has little to express when it is in a passive relationship to others.

The cultural record

Pressure-group politics can be the natural first line of action when disabled people come together. However, organising a collective voice may perversely end up by only transferring the microphone to the voice of the elite. The presence or absence of a disability culture and the numbers of disabled people involved, frequency of performances and general social recognition for disability arts can provide important insights into the progress of disabled people moving from passivity to an active role in their own affairs.

If disabled political activists and disabled artists see little point in supporting each other we can be sure that progress towards equal rights has not yet moved beyond the efforts of individuals to escape their own personal restrictions. The disabled political activist is likely to be locked into pressure-group politics, escaping a passive disabled lifestyle by becoming the active spokesperson for others, who continue in their passive and dependent lives. Similarly, the disabled artist could be locked into expressing personal life events in the hope that fame will allow escape from the dependency role that society expects of its disabled citizens.

On the other side, the spontaneous growth of a disability culture, in the absence of support from organisations of disabled people, can be regarded as a symptom of ordinary disabled people losing interest in the issues that an elite leadership regards as a priority. A developing disability culture can not only increase insight into the progress of disabled people becoming active in the area of civil rights, but can provide important opportunities for individuals to gain confidence by forming a new and independent social identity. From this point of view the formation of a distinctive and vibrant disability culture is a vital component in the construction of an accessible route to empowerment.

Accountability

Many people are uncertain about accepting that disabled artists might also be accountable to a disabled constituency. Art involves personal creativity and some people may have difficulty in seeing the disabled artist as anything other than an independent and uncontrollable misfit. They may dismiss creative works with 'Well, that is only their view', or confuse personal dislike of an art form with the observation that the person is generally 'no good'. While the portrayal of disability issues in the arts arena should be viewed with the same critical eye as the presentation of issues in the political arena, we should also take care not to underestimate the role of the arts in assisting the processes of change.

While there is broad agreement among disabled people in the UK that the portrayal of the disability experience is generally both negative and inaccurate, it is participants in the arts who can breathe life into alternative images. This should mean that while we share a common understanding of disability we may express this in many different forms and in different arenas. Taking part in the arts should also be viewed as a tool for change as much as attending meetings about, say, orange badge provision.

Artistic effects

Gaining access to new ideas or creating challenging alternatives when passivity predominates among the disabled community can be hard work. Charity imagery, tales of tragedy or outstanding courage in the media, fairy tales and other children's books loaded with disabled villains can all combine to undermine a view of ourselves as valid human beings. If one of the creative activities of art is to present a mirror to society, what we generally see is a distorted reflection of ourselves. Disability arts, on the other hand, where, for example, sculpture is designed to be touched as well as seen, and songs are written about the world as we see it, can redress the balance and engage a lot of people in questioning assumptions that their exclusion from society is a fact of life.

The arts can have a liberating effect on people, encouraging them to change from being passive and dependent to being creative and active. We may not all want to be 'artists', producing and performing work, but arts events can provide another accessible route for looking at the world in relation to disabled people. Meeting together at a disability arts event can also provide rare opportunities for disabled people to exchange ideas. Having someone on stage communicating ideas and feelings that an isolated disabled person never suspected were shared by others can be a turning-point for many.

However, unless there is a flowering of cultural activity new artists will not be inspired to develop more sensitive presentations of our place in society and to inform future generations. One of the ways of understanding long-gone societies is to look at their cultural artifacts. If historians only uncover images of disability in charity advertising and stories of helplessness or courage, with no alternatives, what will that mean for a future population of disabled people? Evidence of pride in ourselves is also provided by the legacy we leave behind. Our cultural development will provide not only a record of an active journey, a passing view of ourselves as we are, but also a perspective on the world for future generations to build on and develop.

Cultural interventions

Arts should provide disabled people with ways of confirming their own identity and, as a secondary gain, inform, educate and attract the non-disabled world. Until recently the arts have placed too much emphasis on educating non-disabled people rather than providing a medium for communication with each other. What is needed is that disability arts (and the disability movement) does not simply imitate the view of the world that pleases white, middle-class males. The arts, and the new cultural development, can provide space for reflection on disability life from the rich variety of experiences of different groups of disabled people. Helping disabled people to ensure an integrated role for disability arts and culture in the nation's repertoire of cultural life can provide an opportunity to challenge narrow thinking, elitism and dependency on others. Introducing disabled people to the social role of artistic creativity and opening a debate about disability culture is a dynamic way of assisting disabled people to challenge their assumed dependency and place in mainstream society.

SECTION 3: CONTROLLING LIFESTYLES

3.1

Striving for independence

Liz Briggs

I had always lived at home with my family. Mum has rheumatoid arthritis and, as neither of us could manage the stairs, we shared the same room downstairs. I started at a nearby special school when I was 3. Mum looked after me at home.

When I was 16 I gained GSE grade one English and chose not to accept the only job suggested, packing boxes; instead I tried further education. The technical college was next door to the special school, and I was able to continue attending my old school and go to the A-level English lessons in the college.

At this time I was thinking of a career in writing. I had not thought about much else except that. Unlike many of my friends, I did not want to leave home. I used to be scared of the possibility that one day mum wouldn't be able to get me up. Even then, though, from time to time, things could be difficult.

A taste of residential care

All the way through school, my mum used to go away for a fortnight's rest during the summer and I would go and stay in one of the various holiday homes for disabled children.

Soon after I got my English A-level, mum learned that she had to go into hospital for quite a long time. Her only concern was where I should go while she was away. Mum did all the work of trying to find something. Being 18, I was too old for many children's homes and too young for adult residential homes. Fortunately I was able to go to a rehabilitation and assessment centre for two weeks. Whilst there I was introduced to the nearby Cheshire Home and went there for five weeks. I hated it. For the first time in my life I was made conscious of not being able to control my own situation. All I can remember

This paper is edited from material first published in E. Briggs, *Project 81: One Step On.*

was that everything was uncomfortable, especially getting up and going to bed. It wasn't like having mum around.

When mum came out of hospital I returned home. District nurses were made available to help mum look after me, though they were very unreliable. I began to realise that life like this could not last for ever and so I asked to go back to the Cheshire Home for a holiday. I cannot really remember why. Perhaps I just wanted to go back to find out why I hadn't got on with the place when everyone else had! Anyway, mum says I was restless when I returned from my second holiday there.

Next summer mum was told she would have to go back into hospital for a long time, and because I already knew the place, I agreed to go back to the Cheshire Home for this period. Something went wrong while mum was in hospital and I ended up being in the home for seven months. During this time I began to realise that perhaps I wasn't going to go home. Understandably there were lots of tears. Until then I had always thought that I could go home, but now I wasn't sure.

A diet of residential care

When my mum came out of hospital she was still in plaster and couldn't look after me. Because the home was planning to cut down its numbers I was asked to find somewhere else to live. I left in the following March, and went to a local authority home for six weeks. This place just did not have the necessary staff levels for my needs, as I was classed as requiring heavy care. Apart from having to get up and go to bed at certain times, I was fed up because nearly everyone else spent the day at the day centre making baskets and playing Bingo. I did not want to do this and didn't go. The building, the staff and the food were wonderful, but I wasn't allowed out of the front door on my own. I spent my days with a lovely old lady who stayed in bed because the staff didn't have enough time to get her up. Luckily I had friends living locally who came to visit me regularly and I went home every weekend, otherwise I would have gone mad.

I contacted my social worker and told her that I could not stay at this place and that she would have to find me a Cheshire Home. She came up with the placement centre at Heenan House, which was part of the St Joseph's Hospice for the Dying in Hackney. Dr Agerholme was in charge and she was quite willing to have me there. I moved in and was there for three months. I had a great time. There were lots of young people working there whose main ambition was to get me into a good home.

During my stay my mother and I went to see Dr Agerholme. She explained that I could stay at Heenan House until I could find somewhere suitable to live. Then she asked if I would consider returning home with someone living in to look after me. She explained what this would mean. I don't know why, but I felt it would not work in my situation. I know dad wouldn't particularly like a stranger living in. Also my mum had to share a bedroom with me and she didn't like watching someone else seeing to me. What was more, I was 21 years old now and I had discovered just how much freedom I could have away from home! I chose residential care and so it was that I came to Le Court in September 1977.

Le Court

Soon after arriving at Le Court I knew that this was the place for me. I was enjoying myself. I could not get over the fact that people were giving me the responsibility of telling them how to get me up, and that I could choose what time I went to bed! I quickly settled in and became increasingly involved in the life of the home. It was the policy that residents were expected to contribute to the life of the community.

As time passed, my feelings towards the home slowly changed. I wanted to do more for myself. I was going out of the home more often and people had begun to comment on this. I began to feel a little restricted. There was a growing unrest among the younger residents. Some of us resented the level of continual commitment to the home which was expected of us. Also, none of us wanted to spend the rest of our lives there, even though we did not know what else there could be. I think the arrival of a new resident, John Evans, had begun to focus our restlessness. He was quite determined not to stay in residential care.

During 1979 I went to Taylor House for a holiday. Taylor House is a very small hostel for disabled students. It is an enlarged ordinary house in an ordinary street. The four students and the staff work out the running of the household between them and share the responsibilities. I was so struck with the place that when I came back to Le Court I told John that he ought to go there for a visit.

Project 81

Soon after John came back from Taylor House several of us started meeting together more formally. That was the beginning of Project 81. The idea was that a group of us would move into a big house and have young people as 'staff' helping us. Just like Taylor House. For a long time I was not exactly sure what I wanted from Project 81. I just felt I ought to be doing something and so I stuck to it. We were looking for a big house in Southampton.

A year passed and then a big house in Oxford Street came along. A lot of personal things had been happening to me during that year. I was growing up very quickly. I did not really know what I wanted to do with my life most of the time. I was able to explore a lot of ideas and possibilities through Project 81, and it gave me something to concentrate on. I was now certain that I could not see myself in any type of residential home in the future.

I intended being one of the three people to live in Oxford Street, until I saw the place. I did not like the building, but the others were so enthusiastic about

it I thought there was something wrong with me. Also, as we discussed details, I found that our ideas of care were totally different. I felt that I needed to
have someone around me all the time, whereas the others did not, and I was
scared. I did not want to be isolated. I could see that if the others achieved
their work ambitions they would not be in the house all day, and I did not
want to be at home on my own.

Around this time I went to see my sister. On the visit I was looked after by
a Danish girl called Merete. We were talking about Project 81, and I had said
I was very undecided. I said that what I would really like was a little place of
my own with two people looking after me. Seeing at close quarters the ordinary domestic life of my sister put this in my mind. I realised that I fitted happily into that sort of setting. Merete suggested I try and do just that.

Ideas into reality

I wrote to my home social services and asked them what they would do if I
moved from residential care into a home of my own. They said I would
become the responsibility of the local county and they would not help me.
At the prompting of my friends I wrote back and asked them why not! They
sent a social worker to talk to me. She admitted later that she came thinking
this was just some hare-brained scheme, but left with the understanding that
it was a well-thought-out and well-planned idea.

My friends from Project 81, the head of home and the head of care at Le
Court worked together in order to present a convincing case. Our proposal
was based on the fact that living outside would possibly be cheaper and, if
they didn't agree to pay for me to do so, I would remain in the home as an
expense to them anyway. Soon after this I received a favourable response
and I began house-hunting and discussing the details of how to meet my
care needs.

The only real hiccup was that the local DHSS would not assess my
benefits until I had moved in, and social services were not prepared to fina-
lise the amount of their commitment until they knew the DHSS's! And so we
went around and around in circles, trying to get some idea of what money
would be available, but never succeeding. This was a worry to me because I
could not work out how much money I would have to live on.

House-hunting

I saw my new home in October 1981; it was about the seventh or eighth
place I had been to look at. The housing association submitted the project to
the housing corporation before Christmas and the project was quickly accepted. Then there was a long wait. £5,000 was needed for adaptations.
This was much more than we had expected and was largely due to the need

to raise the path to the front door, which involved relocating two man-hole covers.

Delays and frustration

Everything took an age. At first the cost was queried by the housing corporation. Eventually they agreed to go ahead, but already 1982 was well advanced. Then the building specifications had to go out to tender. The tender had to be accepted by the housing corporation and then the builders had a summer holiday! The builders said the work would take six weeks, so I planned to move in after this, at the end of July. When the time came around, however, the work had not even started!

In August, when the builders still had not started work, I decided to move in September, ready or not. I had already employed an attendant, Toril, who had come over from Norway at the end of July to help me during and after my move.

During this period I finalised the details of how my care needs would be met. I felt that I needed someone to be with me all day and all night. I did not want to be left on my own. My idea was to have my carers living in, as I did not like the idea of people popping in and out to see to me. I had some experience of this when I lived at home, having to wait hours for the district nurses. I prepared an around-the-clock chart detailing all my care requirements. It came to something like 60 hours and I decided that I could share it between two people. I costed this on the basis of staff receiving standard wages and being told on their contract that they would work 30 hours, to cover 24 hours a day.

A home at last

When I finally moved at the end of September, it was an enormous step in my life. Further, it was a huge step for the staff and everybody else associated with me, because this sort of thing had never been done before. On top of this there were practical pressures that made those early days very difficult. I did not go into a perfect situation. The building work was not complete – indeed, the kitchen was not finished until January, and we had to survive with only a gas primus stove. The conditions made everybody uptight, and it was very difficult to have a normal working atmosphere. What annoyed me most was the red tape. The kitchen was not done because the local authority could not produce the money until I was a tenant, and I was not a tenant until the builders had finished. And so it was not until January, four months after moving in, that I had a reasonable chance of settling down.

I could not get into a routine because there was nothing to get into a routine with! Besides the problem with the kitchen, there was no central heating, and my room and the bathroom were incomplete. For the first two weeks I was living in a double room with Toril. It was all so dreadful, but I don't really remember it now. More than anything else I think I was worried about what other people would say if I failed. A lot of people were waiting to see what happened to me. Everybody wanted me to succeed, and I was scared I would fail. I think they thought they were supporting me, by saying, 'You'll be OK!', but really it just increased my anxiety.

I hadn't anticipated so much pressure in my new life. I had not been prepared for the volume of decisions I had to make. Simple things, such as: sorting out looing routines; how to use the local launderette; finding out where all the allowances come from and how to get them; sorting out local tradespeople; sorting out dustbin collections, milk deliveries, a doctor, a chemist; and so on. But the worst thing was the incomplete building work. I was trying to start a new life on a building site!

In these early days I got overwhelmed very easily. Sometimes I thought that within a few months I would be back in Le Court, because I did not think I could continue. If I had not had the support of Project 81 members, the head of care at Le Court and other friends, I do not think I could have survived.

All sorts of things seemed to flood in, including the fact that I was not getting on with one of my attendants. She decided that she did not want to stay because she did not like the job. She felt that she did not have enough to do. I found it tiring to have somebody in the house whom I knew was not really enjoying what she was doing. Sometimes we annoyed each other. The long dark evenings, the unfinished building work, the awful autumn weather, and the fact that we could not get out made these interpersonal difficulties, for which I was not prepared, much worse. Precious moments of light relief came when a couple of friends would turn up out of the blue and say, 'Come to the Indian Restaurant'. That sort of thing was invaluable.

Since those early days I have grown considerably in confidence, on top of which all the furnishings and fittings are complete. This makes a very big difference! I look back now and wonder how I managed. Really, I moved into a building site and tried to make a life while work was in progress!

The neighbourhood

I like the area; it is friendly and peaceful. I think I could probably leave the front door open all night and nobody would walk in. It takes only 10 minutes to get to the shops in the wheelchair. It is good for me to get out and do the shopping; I enjoy that bit of fresh air every day, and it is something I have got to do because this is when I meet people.

My neighbours are friendly but I don't really know anybody intimately. I know a lot of people to say 'Hello' to, but that is about it. The guy across the road keeps me up to date with what is going on, and I have got to know his family quite well. There is always somebody there. We have told them about my alarm system, and they would do something if they heard it.

I don't feel that I have succeeded in mixing with the community as well as I would like to have done. I think that mixing is difficult because many houses are not accessible and so I cannot just 'drop in'. Also, we haven't got things in common – like kids. I go to night schools and force myself to mix, but I only tend to socialise with my present or former care assistants, former Le Court friends and a few other people.

In conclusion

I feel settled in my home. It seems as if I have been here a lot longer than a few years, and I do not think that I could ever fit into an institutional regime again. People say that I have changed as a person. I don't know. I think I have become a bit more positive. A home of my own has given me confidence. I expect people to regard this as my house and not to abuse my privacy.

I share my home with my dog Holly. I couldn't think of living here without her. She relies on me. I rely on everybody else, but she has to rely on me for her food and comfort. She also helps with the care assistants, giving them something to do when they are not dealing with me. She helps break the ice when I am interviewing. When I am out walking, people stop and talk to her. Instead of saying, 'What a nice chair', they say, 'What a nice dog'. She barks at anything in sight, but doesn't bark at night! She would probably lick an intruder to death.

As for advising someone else who might want to do the same thing as myself, I don't know what to say. You cannot write a book to tell people exactly how to do things because things change all the time. The idea of people coming and saying, 'I want to move out, what shall I do?', worries me. I would not know how to tell them what to do, because their disabilities might be completely different from mine, their attitudes different, their ideas different, their hopes different. All I can do is to share my experience with them and tell them how fulfilling I have found it all, and how I have grown as a person.

I have been living in the same bungalow now for 10 years, and it seems no easier now than it was 10 years ago to find staff. Three years ago I changed the staffing arrangements and now have one full-time live-in helper. During week-ends I have two part-time helpers and I also have a couple of part-time helpers from time to time. But I am managing and am still pleased to be living in my own home.

3.2
Housing, independent living and physically disabled people

Jenny Morris

Independent living forms part of the aims of the international civil rights move-ment of disabled people. The 1975 United Nations Declaration of Rights of Disabled Persons asserted the right of disabled people to be self-reliant, to live as they choose and to participate in the social, creative and recreational activi-ties of their communities. If we do not have appropriate housing and personal assistance, then such basic human rights are unachievable.

For many disabled people, unwanted dependence on others would disappear overnight if they lived in a physical environment which did not handicap them. Those who need personal assistance to enable them to live in their own homes have too often been consigned either to institutions or to enforced dependence on their families.

This paper summarises a survey of housing and support services carried out for Shelter in 1989 (see Morris, 1990).

The role of local authorities

The role of local authorities in meeting housing needs stems from disabled people's lack of economic power. Only 31 per cent of disabled adults under pensionable age are in paid employment and, for one-half of disabled adults under pensionable age, there are no earners in the family unit at all (Office of Population Censuses and Surveys, 1988a). Two-thirds of disabled people are over the age of 60 and poverty is correlated with being old.

Forty-five per cent of disabled adults are council or housing association tenants compared to 31 per cent of the general population (Office of Population Censuses and Surveys, 1988a, p. 12). This is partly because access into council housing is through housing need rather than ability to pay but also because local authorities are the main providers of wheelchair and mobility adapted accommodation, with very little provision made in the housing association, private, rented or owner-occupied sector.

Disabled people find it increasingly difficult to gain access to council

This paper is a summary of the research published in J. Morris (1990) *Our Homes, Our Rights: Housing, Independent Living and Physically Disabled People*, Shelter, London.

housing, and homelessness among physically disabled people increased by 92 per cent between 1980 and 1986 compared with 57 per cent among all types of household (Morris, 1988a, p. 6).

As homeowners, disabled people are more likely than other households to experience poor housing conditions. This is partly because of the association between old age and poor housing conditions, but it is primarily because of the association between poor housing conditions and low-income owners. As the English House Condition Survey put it, 'Poor housing [is] related, above all, to income' (Department of the Environment, 1988, p. 41).

The Prince of Wales Advisory Group on Disability has drawn attention to the problems faced by severely disabled adults below the age of 60. The Group's report *Living Options Lottery*, concluded, 'The reality of housing and care support options revealed . . . is alarming . . . few people obtain the flexible, dependable services essential for personal autonomy. The amount and kind of help a disabled person receives is determined less by need than by chance – a "living options" lottery' (Fiedler, 1988).

In the context of the new community care legislation, organisations of disabled people are increasing the pressure on central and local government to provide the necessary housing and support services required to enable disabled people to fully participate in society. Local authorities need comprehensive and coherent policies to meet both these demands and their minimum legal obligations.

The Shelter survey

A representative sample of 21 local authorities in England and Wales was taken and information gathered on knowledge, policies and services relating to disabled people. Analysis was carried out of the 1988/9 housing investment programme (HIP) statements for each authority. The number of 'significantly disabled' people in each area was calculated using the Office of Population Censuses and Surveys Disability Survey. This statistical analysis is published in the full research report (Morris, 1990).

The handful of local authorities who were identified as having policies which should be encouraged have been named, but this does not mean that these particular local authorities are doing everything right (indeed most of them recognise that they are not). It may also be that policies and practices have changed since the survey was carried out, for example because of a change in political control.

Housing departments

Housing strategies and housing policies

Only three housing departments had a written policy on meeting the housing needs of disabled people. In two cases these policies had been developed as a result of dialogue between the housing department and local disability organisations. The policies covered: new building programmes; adaptation of existing stock; modernisation programmes; allocation procedures; grants to private owners; staff training.

However, among the rest very few even mentioned such needs in their housing strategy. One local housing authority stated that there was 'a need for greater provision of special needs accommodation for the disabled and handicapped' yet there was no indication as to how such accommodation was to be provided. There was, for example, no indication that, either within its own construction programme of housing for single people or in its collaboration with a local housing association, any consideration was given to the housing needs of single disabled people.

Where housing departments were developing strategies on homelessness, there was no recognition that disabled people become homeless as well, and conversely, that some homeless households contain disabled people. Thus, where a council was developing hostel accommodation to cut down on the use of bed-and-breakfast placements there was no provision within that hostel accommodation for disabled people. Similarly, a number of housing departments were developing policies aimed at ethnic minority communities, yet only one recognised that disabled people would also be part of such communities.

No housing department had a policy on identifying vacant properties with adaptation potential. This is a crucial oversight as, with the reduction in new building programmes, it is often only by adapting existing property that any significant increase in the supply of housing for disabled people can be achieved. There was only one example of good practice in this area. Rochdale Metropolitan Borough Council appointed a housing officer who, working with the local disability organisation, developed a comprehensive policy for meeting the housing needs of disabled people. Rochdale has built all new housing to mobility standard since 1980, a significant number to wheelchair standard and has an expanding capital budget for adaptations to existing stock.

Awareness of housing needs

There was general lack of knowledge of the housing needs of disabled people. Information on numbers of elderly and disabled households and of the supply of suitable accommodation, together with adaptations carried out, is provided annually by local authorities to the Department of the Environment, yet the majority of housing departments stated that this information was not available. This paradox is explained by the fact that the figures are of no relevance to the operation of the housing department throughout the rest of the year. It must also mean, of course, that the figures provided by the local authority on their HIP returns are highly questionable.

Only three of the housing departments that provided information were able to state how many households on their waiting or transfer list required wheelchair or mobility adapted housing, and only two of these were able to break this information down by bedroom size.

Only four local authorities could state how many households had been housed into wheelchair or mobility adapted accommodation during the previous year, and five could say whether any such nominations had been made to housing associations. Again, this lack of information indicates a lack of concern about whether the housing needs of disabled people are being met.

Access to housing

Most housing departments failed to integrate disabled people into their allocation policies. When a disabled person applied for housing they would generally be referred for medical assessment. This practice is criticised by disability organisations for failing to take account of the practical difficulties of living in unsuitable housing and focusing instead on health problems.

One typical local authority produced *A Guide to the Waiting List*, which set out criteria for rehousing. No mention was made of disability. The booklet made clear that only households with children, who had no home of their own, or elderly people needing warden-assisted accommodation, had any chance of being rehoused. A disabled person living in physically unsuitable housing would therefore assume that there was no point in registering on the waiting list, unless they happened to fall into one of the categories mentioned.

Housing departments often exclude homeowners from being eligible for rehousing. The property of disabled owner-occupiers may be totally unsuitable for them. They may consequently be unable to leave hospital or institutional care, may be made dependent on others, or imprisoned within a physically unsuitable home. They may be unable to afford appropriate housing, or may live in an area where such housing does not exist in the private sector, and thus would look to the local housing authority to solve their housing problem. In most areas, the door would be slammed in their faces because of the housing department's assumption that owner-occupiers can meet their own housing needs.

An example of good practice in incorporating disabled people into an allocations policy was again provided by Rochdale Metropolitan Borough Council.

Knowledge of supply of dwellings

Five housing departments had information on the numbers of wheelchair and mobility properties in their stock, but only two of these could analyse them according to bedroom size. Only one knew how many such properties were provided by housing associations in their area. There was a similar lack of knowledge about the supply of adapted accommodation. Again, Rochdale Council was highlighted as an example of good practice.

A housing authority cannot develop a strategy to meet the needs of its disabled population without data on the expressed demand and the supply of dwellings within its own housing stock. Ideally, there should be more comprehensive information on housing need and the supply of dwellings across all tenures (particularly if local authorities are to take on more of an enabling role). Lack of such information leads to the common misapprehension that housing for disabled people should consist of one-bedroom properties, whereas the majority of the demand for housing from disabled people below the age of 60 is for two bedrooms and above (Morris, 1986, 1988b; Robinson, 1987).

Adaptation of existing dwellings

Only three authorities had a specific policy on adaptations to council dwellings. Local authority housing departments require a close working relationship with occupational therapists employed within the social services departments (SSDs), who advise on the technical aspects of adaptations. However, some housing departments, who had no specific policy on or budget for adaptations to existing council properties, clearly had very little knowledge of the work of occupational therapists.

The survey was carried out before the implementation of the new grant system for adaptations so could not assess its effectiveness (see Morris, 1991, for an assessment of the new system; Royal Association of Disability and Rehabilitation, 1992).

Wakefield Council had set up an Adaptations and Disability Unit, bringing together staff from social services, environmental health and housing departments. The unit deals with private and public sector residents, minor and major adaptations, as well as requests for equipment, and co-ordinates both the carrying out of the work and its financing.

Partnerships with the private sector

Housing authorities were not considering the needs of disabled people in their dealings with private developers and housing associations. They attempted to increase the supply of low-cost housing through, for example, shared-ownership schemes, but did not encourage developers or housing associations to build accessible housing. There are many aspects of the local authority's role as enabler – through the provision of land, planning permission and so on – which should make it possible to exert such influence on the private sector. Influence can also be exerted where the partnership is with a housing association, yet this did not seem to be happening.

Liaison between housing and social services departments

Only two housing departments had formal regular liaison arrangements with SSDs. There seemed little awareness of how the mainstream activities of the housing department are of relevance to social services' role in enabling independent living. For example, one district council's housing department was proud of its support for a resource centre, jointly funded with social services, which would 'enable the physically and mentally handicapped to learn life skills'. Yet the housing department had no strategy for providing the accommodation required to enable people to use 'life skills' by living independently.

Social services departments

SSDs had more knowledge of the number of disabled people in their area than had housing departments, and they were more likely to have specific policies on meeting their needs. However, the extent of the knowledge and of the policies was still surprisingly inadequate.

Residential care

Residential care is still considered as inevitable for many disabled people. Sometimes this is a solution of last resort, because of a lack of housing and support services. More often there is little awareness of either the potential for independent living or how its denial is a denial of a basic human right.

The majority of SSDs knew how many disabled people were in local authority institutions, but only two knew how many were in health-authority-run facilities, and five how many were in private and voluntary establishments. Only three SSDs said that they did not use residential facilities outside their area. The majority of SSDs are placing physically disabled people in residential accommodation outside their own community and have little knowledge about them. One local authority admitted that it was placing severely disabled children, including those under the age of 5, 100 miles away or more in residential care.

The role of social services departments in facilitating independent living

SSDs have two key roles to play in facilitating independent living: working with housing departments to ensure that appropriate accommodation is available; and ensuring that support services are available to disabled people in their own homes. Three SSDs had developed strategies for independent living and three others were in the process of developing such a policy.

Some SSDs had developed principles which motivated their service delivery to disabled people. However, with three exceptions, there was little evidence that disabled people and their organisations were properly consulted about the kind of service which they wanted.

Working with housing departments

There was little evidence of housing and social services departments working together to facilitate independent living. Most SSDs worked closely with health authorities through Joint Care Planning Teams but these often did not include representatives from the housing authority. When initial policy discussions are held it is rare for housing to be represented. This is either because SSDs and health authorities have failed to identify the role of housing officers, or because, when they have, housing departments have failed to respond.

Where a local authority had started to develop policies to meet the housing needs of disabled people, initiatives usually involved *either* the housing department *or* the social services department, rarely both. Housing departments commonly complained that SSDs were not playing their full part in offering technical advice on adaptations, or in providing personal assistance support within the home. In turn, SSDs often despaired of finding suitable accommodation for physically disabled people and complained that housing officers made unwarranted assumptions about the inability of disabled people to live independently. One SSD, for example, had great difficulty in persuading a district council housing department to offer accommodation to a single mother who had become disabled but who wished to leave hospital and look after her daughter.

Provision of support services

Only three SSDs had a strategy for helping disabled people to achieve independent living; three others were preparing one. The majority of authorities relied on *ad hoc* arrangements when providing personal assistance, mainly consisting of utilising the home care service. Only two authorities actually had a separate budgetary provision for personal care packages. One was a rural authority and funded 10 disabled clients' personal care needs. In contrast, an urban authority – with a much larger population – was considering funding two clients. Whether someone can live independently depends very much on where they live.

Two SSDs that are in the process of developing independent living strategies already provide some support. One employs 12 care assistants, whose services are provided free to physically disabled clients. One other authority has a joint budget with the health authority, funding a crossroads care attendant scheme and health care assistants.

Transition to independent living

For some disabled people their experience of dependence makes independence difficult to achieve. Someone who has been in residential care for a number of years may initially find independent living a frightening prospect. Younger disabled people are often denied the experiences which enable them to become adults independent of their parents.

Some SSDs recognised the need for transition to independent living services, although unfortunately it is more common to expect the disabled person to find all the motivation within themselves. Four SSDs either co-operated with the housing authority to provide interim accommodation or made provision out of their own capital budget.

Any such scheme must also plan for permanent accommodation and personal assistance; indeed it was the difficult experience of getting district councils within their area to house people who had tried out the transition project and wanted to live independently which prompted one SSD to address itself to the task of influencing local housing authorities.

Working with disabled people and their organisations

Most of the disability organisations represented on Joint Care Planning Teams were those run by non-disabled people *for* disabled people rather than organisations *of* disabled people.

Derbyshire County Council Social Services Department provides a good-practice example of involving disabled people. For some years the SSD has funded a Centre for Integrated Living (CIL), which is run by disabled people. Its role is to develop initiatives which would aid independent living. It also acts as an important source of information for disabled people, acting as an advocate where necessary. The local authority has continued to respond to new roles as they were identified, for example, by funding the CIL to maintain a register of adapted housing in the district.

Conclusion

The picture which emerges is a grim one for disabled people. They look to local authority housing and social services departments to help them achieve a basic human right. A lucky few live in parts of the country where their local authority will be able to respond with the housing and support services that they need. The majority will find that there is little knowledge of the needs of the physically disabled community, that there are no policies for meeting such needs and that housing and social services departments are failing to work together to help disabled people achieve the things which most non-disabled citizens take for granted.

Not only is there a failure to work together at local level, but central government also fails to provide the framework of legislation and subsidy that would enable housing and social services departments to address jointly the aspirations of disabled people. During the 1980s, legislation and public subsidies were directed at an increase in owner-occupation and an attack on council housing. Such policies have been directly against the interests of disabled people, whose economic position and need for housing with particular physical characteristics mean that the private sector has little to offer.

While government policy fails to link housing policy to other social policy areas, local government fails to integrate disabled people's housing needs into their mainstream activities and housing and social services departments fail to work together, disabled people will continue to be condemned to institutional care or imprisoned in housing which unnecessarily restricts their lives.

References

Department of the Environment (1988) *English House Condition Survey*, HMSO, London.

Fiedler, B. (1988) *Living Options Lottery: Housing and Support Services for People with Severe Physical Disabilities*, Prince of Wales Advisory Group on Disability, London.

Morris, J. (1986) 'Housing disabled people: providing for us all', *Housing*, November.

Morris, J. (1988a) *Freedom to Lose: Housing Policy and People with Disabilities*, Shelter, London.

Morris, J. (1988b) *Housing and Disabled People in Tower Hamlets*, Action for Disability, Tower Hamlets, London.

Morris, J. (1990) *Our Homes, Our Rights: Housing, Independent Living and Disabled People*, Shelter, London.

Morris, J. (1991) 'Adding injustice to disability', *Inside Housing*, 18 October.

Office of Population Censuses and Surveys (1988a) *Surveys of Disability in Great Britain, Report 1: The Prevalence of Disability Among Adults*, HMSO, London.

Office of Population Censuses and Surveys (1988b) *Surveys of Disability in Great Britain, Report 2: The Financial Circumstances of Disabled Adults Living in Private Households*, HMSO, London.

Robinson, I. (1987) *Re-Evaluating Housing for People with Disabilities in Hammersmith and Fulham*, Hammersmith and Fulham Special Needs Unit, London.

Royal Association of Disability and Rehabilitation (1992) *The Disabled Facilities Grant: Necessary and appropriate? Reasonable and practicable?*, RADAR, London.

3.3
Integration and deaf people: the policy and power of enabling environments

Mairian Corker

> Democracy of the shared classroom experience is the cradle of democracy in the outside world.
>
> (Warnock, 1988, p. 6)

Introduction

Integration is, put simply, the education of people with 'special needs' with those who do not have special needs, in mainstream schools and colleges. Deaf people, whether they be children, young people or adults, have always posed something of a challenge to generalised policies of integration, for reasons which will be laid out clearly below. This paper examines some of the features of present-day policies and practice with respect to educational integration, and argues that the framework of special education has created a 'dependency culture' (Corker, 1990) of deaf people, which has its roots in alienism. It is suggested that enabling educational environments can only be achieved by a re-examination of the way in which special education relates to mainstream education. It is argued that it is the present two-tier education system, as defined by policy and practice, which is the primary disabling factor and not deafness *per se*. The paper concludes with one view of how a workable integration practice might be achieved by going back to the drawing-board and examining the aims and objectives of educational integration.

An overview of policy and practice

It could be argued that integration is one of the few educational principles which has gained all-party political support. Yet an overview of practice suggests that different political philosophies mould very different approaches to educational integration. For example, we can observe an emerging conflict between the equal opportunities/human rights agenda of the centre-left as evidenced in the recent Labour Party policy document *Every Child a Special Child* (1991), and the assimilationist policies of the right which run throughout educational legislation since 1983 and are enshrined in the statute books.

The term 'assimilationist' is used here to mean approaches to education which do not recognise the value of individual differences in the structure of today's multicultural society. It is sometimes used interchangeably with the term 'integration', but is quite distinct from the ideal of integration. It could be argued that the emphasis on 'special needs', as defined by the Education Act 1981, is one example of assimilationist policies. This emphasis frequently serves to obscure the real differences between deafness and learning difficulties, for example, in the attempt to place all people with special needs under one legislative umbrella. The failure to prioritise needs realistically or to genuinely recognise people's individuality sometimes leads to competition for resources which badly damages the educational chances of some individuals.

The equal opportunities/human rights lobby believes that people with special needs have a right to participate fully at all levels of education on a par with their peers who do not have special needs. This view is based on the firm belief that people with special needs have many abilities which can make a valuable contribution to education. The difficulty with this philosophy, however, is that it can be taken to the extreme, as can be seen in some Local Education Authorities (LEAs) which have an all-out integration policy. Such policy appears to place political beliefs above the concept of needs when some individuals demonstrate that they cannot flourish educationally in an integrated environment. The Conservative view of the benefits of privately funded education (which, it should be said, includes education in many special schools), opposes such strategies.

Why do deaf people pose a challenge to integration?

The very nature of deafness and the subsequent difficulty in defining the term 'deaf', the way it manifests itself in disrupted communication, the history and structure of deaf education and the size of the deaf population, have traditionally given deafness a high profile within special education. Deaf education itself has been the subject of much dispute relating to the 'how' of education – that is, primarily, what method of communication do we use to educate deaf people? There has been little debate concerning the 'what' and the 'why' of deaf education. Yet the what, the why and the how are all of integral importance *in mainstream education*.

The campaigns of the deaf community, from within and linked to those of voluntary organisations such as the British Deaf Association, to be recognised as a separate linguistic cultural group have added impetus to the debate, but have posed problems both for the policy-makers and for deaf people themselves. This is because the recognition of sign language as the natural language of deaf people would mean that they would become aligned with members of other cultural minorities who are isolated from special needs legislation because their 'home language' is different from that which is the language of instruction used in schools (Section 1(2), Education Act 1981). For deaf people, this isolation may lead to lack of access to the legal machinery of statementing, which presently conveys at least some protection to those who are struggling with their education. (A statement of special educational needs is a document which outlines the special needs of an individual and lists what resources should be made available to meet those needs in the educational setting.) Yet for deaf people the isolation could well be more serious in integrated environments if such a policy change were to be effected which allowed this alignment.

The lack of fully bilingual teachers, the dominance of 'hearing culture' among the peer group, and the tendency for the home language of the vast majority of deaf people to be an inaccessible spoken language militate against full integration from birth. If such integration were the aim, it would immediately have enormous resource implications in an already impoverished education system. Yet integration could be achieved from the special-school base if policy did not discourage the placement of deaf people in such educational settings.

The disabling education system and the concept of alienism

It remains true, however, that the overall thrust of deaf education policy is towards making deaf people more invisible by encouraging the use of teaching practices which subtly tip the power balance between deaf and hearing people in favour of the latter. The education system, as viewed from the perspective of deaf people, is therefore seen to be disabling for a number of reasons:

1 Education law is open to multiple interpretations which translate to lack of consistency in approaches to educating deaf people.
2 Integration is viewed in physical terms; policy increasingly concentrates on people but neglects the true characteristics of people in favour of resources-led practice. This practice dictates that there is only so much money available and so meeting needs, and therefore needs themselves, must fit within financial constraints.
3 Educational policy frequently becomes confused with social policy, as can be seen, for example, in the way that educational integration can come to be viewed as a sometimes misguided way of caring rather than a means of achieving access to society through education.
4 Policy is not consistent at different stages of education; there is, for example, no clearly defined national policy for pre-school education (widely recognised as being the most crucial stage for deaf children), and further and adult continuing education appear to be viewed in terms of direct provision of training and qualifications (Department of Education

and Science, 1991) rather than as routes into training and qualifications from the policy perspective.

5 Integration in its widest sense is about how to fit special education into mainstream education rather than how to devise a single system of education which creates equal access to education for all – a common policy for education (Warnock, 1988). This concept of 'the best fit' becomes synonymous with the survival of the fittest. It assumes that mainstream education is receptive to special education in its present state when this is far from true. We only have to look at two key areas of education (the curriculum and teacher training), to see the reality of segregation within the integrated environment.

Policy remains in the hands of people who do not have disabilities and who are frequently so far on the other side of the experiential divide between people with and without disabilities that 'objective policies' – that is, those which ignore the experiential divide – simply serve to reinforce the notion of *dis*-ability rather than the values and abilities of those who are different. This is because objective policies are linked to fear of, or alienism towards, people with disabilities. Alienism is at the root of all forms of oppression derived from the exploitation of the weaker by the stronger (Southgate and White, 1989). It describes the process whereby oppression and prejudice come about and is therefore, like the term 'special needs', an attempt to bring together a number of behaviours such as sexism, racism, disablism and homophobia. Unlike the term 'special needs', however, the assumption that the underlying process is the same for all these behaviours is correct.

One manifestation of alienism is that deaf people are not seen by the various professions in education to have a professional view. This happens because alienistic attitudes towards deaf people by 'professionals' hinge upon the commonly held view that deaf people are not capable of contributing to professional life because of their 'limited experience'. Deaf people are therefore reduced to providing accounts of personal experience of deafness, which fall upon deaf minds supported by the old adage that experience is subjective and can therefore be dismissed. Alienism obstructs the progress of deaf people aiming to become professionals in education, because it is subsequently translated into policy.

Alienism can also be observed amongst people with disabilities. An interesting example of this can be seen in the way that people with different disabilities view educational integration. Some, notably those with physical disabilities, see integration as a human right (Reiser and Mason, 1990) and align themselves with the views of organisations such as the Centre for Studies in Integration in Education (CSIE). Others, including many deaf people, see integration as an 'erosion of identity' (Ladd, 1991) and deaf people as a distinct cultural group who have more in common with black cultures, for example, than with disabled culture. Finkelstein (1991) has argued that this has created a hierarchical view of disability, with groups higher up the hierarchy adopting alienistic attitudes to those seen to be lower down.

The ideological divisions evident among people with disabilities are exploited to the full by policy-makers. This may be one reason why sign language has come to be regarded as a special need in itself rather than being aligned with other home languages, which would exempt deaf children from the legislation of the Education Act 1981. This plays upon the naturally alienistic attitudes of hearing parents who desperately want their deaf children to speak because of parental fear of physical expression and the implications of having to express themselves in a predominantly physical mode in order to achieve basic communication. Policy props up parental wishes and desires, but does it acknowledge the effect on the deaf child? Does it adequately outline assessment procedures which will identify the needs of the deaf child?

Putting education in the context of the system

The point about the above argument is that alienistic attitudes can become the prevalent force at every stage of a deaf person's education. They begin, albeit unwittingly, in the home, but the way in which they are perpetuated by educational policy and practice shows widespread ignorance of systems theory (Corker, 1990). Systems theory is a way of understanding how human beings in groups work. It suggests that the individual cannot be seen in isolation from the other parts of the system, and that each part of the system is essential and related to every other part in order to attain a certain outcome. The constant interplay between the parts of the system determine how the system manages itself. It is recommended that the reader refers to Satir (1988, Chapter 10) for a user-friendly account of systems theory.

Identity and attitudes are acquired. They stem from the environment in which the individual lives and from the people with whom the individual forms relationships. These people in turn acquire *their* attitudes and identity from their own particular niche in the environment. The problem with alienistic attitudes is that if they are allowed to become the foundation of the system – the part of the system that everything else hinges upon – they are hard to shift. If the whole system of deaf education is based on underexpectation and the undervaluing of deaf people's abilities, then it becomes remarkably easy to make sure that the system does not allow them to develop these abilities.

Shifting alienistic attitudes would necessitate a complete restructuring of the education and social systems of which we are a part. This is what we must be prepared to do if we are to achieve the vision of educational integration that reflects the kinds of values that deaf people would wish to see perpetuated. Such a restructuring of the education system is something that Warnock (1988) points to as being long overdue, but she makes only fleeting references to the implications that this might have for special needs.

Beating the alienistic system

Towards a common language

We can now begin to examine how the experience of deaf people can be used to structure an integrated education system more realistically and also, more importantly, to identify ways in which this restructuring might be achieved. Deafness is unique among disabilities in that it is the clearest example we have of the way a different experience of the world can forge a completely different approach to life, which is expressed through a separate and unique language and culture. The sensory world is a very different world without audition, and sign language is possibly the only way of fully expressing the meaning that this world has, for it is a gestural–visual–spatial language.

We have seen how societies in which large numbers of deaf people co-exist with hearing people can become predominantly 'deaf' and bilingual in spoken and sign language (Groce, 1985), and also how some mixed families can become 'deaf' in an attempt to fully integrate a deaf child (Fletcher, 1987; Luterman, 1987). What we do not see, except in isolated cases such as that found in Leeds LEA, is an attempt to bring the enabling qualities of these environments into the education system. Most deaf people are still educated within a system which has at its base a language that is, at best, not fully accessible because it is based on hearing; at worst, it is a language which is completely alien and does not adequately describe deaf experience. Yet language is the tool of curriculum delivery, training and the expression of experience. How can equal opportunity of access to education be achieved when there is no common language?

Defining the qualities of enabling environments

Within education, enabling environments are those which allow full access to learning and free expression of knowledge, skills and understanding. The location of the environment is immaterial compared with the language environment, the breadth of knowledge of teaching staff and the peer group, and the fluency of communication. Integration in such circumstances is only enabling if communication is based on a classroom experience which is truly shared between all students and teachers, regardless of the source of that experience. It should be recognised that communication consists of production and reception of language. A curriculum which facilitates the shared experience will enable an integrated education for all who take part in it.

Educational integration therefore becomes a wider concept than social integration since it involves, among other things, how we use the knowledge given to us by the act of socialisation. Further, much emphasis is placed upon socialisation with a peer group, but the relationship between child and teacher is also of crucial importance (Gregory and Bishop, 1991). The above description gives credence to this, and therefore avoids the reality of integration for many deaf people, which is dependency on a third party. This is a move away from present LEA policy on support teaching, which dictates that educational support is provided by specialist teachers or, more rarely, interpreters. Within such policy, there are limited direct links between mainstream teachers and deaf pupils, and mixed ability, mixed age special units of small numbers of deaf students do not help social integration with both deaf and hearing peer groups. Frequently, the support teacher becomes the source of all forms of support as the boundaries between education and counselling are blurred. It is this that leads to the dependency culture predominant among deaf people in integrated education.

The importance of an integrated curriculum

Warnock (1978, p. 214) makes several references to special curricula for deaf children within mainstream education without recognising that a special curriculum is also a different curriculum. It is not possible to achieve equality of knowledge and learning with different curriculum materials and different aims and objectives for curriculum planning. The typical curriculum for deaf children and young people places so much emphasis on language and communication that it fails to acknowledge the importance of the accessibility and quality of the surrounding language environment or the depletion of general education that withdrawal into units for specialised tutoring in language and communication causes. Deaf people educated by such approaches may well leave school or college with a (limited) knowledge of language and communication, but what of their knowledge of science, mathematics, sociology, hearing people and sex, to name but a few examples?

In the real world, deaf people have different abilities to 'hear'; they also have different abilities to see, feel, touch, taste, smell and learn. Enhancement can be experienced in any one or more of these areas, and where enhancement happens it needs nourishment. For example, the national curriculum is labelled 'a curriculum for all', but is it? If the national curriculum were an experientially based, integrated curriculum it might be an accessible curriculum for all. If it were a requirement, for example, that all pupils need knowledge, skills and understanding in non-verbal communication (body language, facial expression, and so on) and how this influences overall communication strategies, attainment target 1 for the English curriculum (speaking and listening) might have a more integrated feel about it from a deaf perspective. If it were a requirement that all pupils need knowledge, skills and understanding of alienistic language and the power of language to challenge and to change experience, we might move more in the direction of a democratic society. If the national curriculum were about bringing difference into the open instead of separating the desirable from the undesirable and suppressing the latter, we might see more people who are confident in their identity and can integrate from the basis of knowledge and strength rather than one of weakness.

Integrated training

The divisions between special and mainstream education extend to a division between curriculum and curriculum delivery. We not only have different curricula, but also different teaching approaches. Most deaf people in education wither under the onslaught of methodologies, because specialist teacher training remains 'narrowly conceived' and focused on the how of deaf education much criticised by Warnock (1978, p. 215). Too many teachers of deaf people find themselves learning communication skills on the job – a slow process in the absence of total immersion in a deaf language environment – and their deaf pupils mirror their frustrations; too many teachers of deaf people do not have a knowledge of a specialist subject and persist in taking generalist primary school approaches into secondary and further education. Language modification is about simplification, not about explanation, which deprives deaf people of access to broad-based knowledge.

It is certainly important that teachers working with deaf people acquire a specialist theoretical knowledge of deaf language, deaf culture and deaf education, and most of these teachers acquire this *in addition to* experience in mainstream education working with hearing students. However, it is generally true that mainstream teachers do not have access to specialist knowledge beyond very generic special needs training. This could be seen to increase the gulf between special and mainstream education and lessen the chances of functional integration. Further, the lack of visible staff-room integration serves to reinforce alienistic attitudes because it can be taken as evidence that these attitudes have a firm base in reality.

Conclusion: the case for policy integration

Throughout this paper it has been argued that separating special education policy from mainstream education policy creates an artificial division between special and mainstream education. This division reinforces the concept of difference, but it further allows alienistic attitudes to gain a stranglehold, generating an 'us and them' approach to education. There is no conceivable way in which educational integration can occur within such a scenario.

This may be because we have lost sight of what education is about, or, at best, because we disagree on the aims and objectives of education. But in doing this, we are backtracking into the old dilemma identified by the American philosopher John Dewey (1966). He recognised the potential conflict between the ideal of education as an instrument and that of education as self-development. However, he also went a long way towards showing that this apparent conflict could be reconciled by isolating ways in which the two ideals were similar. Warnock's definitions of integration (1978, pp. 100–1), whilst clearly defining the difference between integration practices based on location (locational integration) and those based on the needs of the individual (social and functional integration), do not fully address the real issues of integration.

Educational policies are generally arrived at through painstaking research into past and present practices, yet policies which ultimately dictate the future are rarely radical enough to reflect all the detail and ramifications of this research. Once policies are on the statute books, there is reluctance to change them, or change is very slow and largely through non-statutory guidance. However, just as basic systems theory suggests that every system begins and ends with the individual and, therefore, that all systems are circular, there is good reason to believe that a common policy for education can only be arrived at by looking at the array of experiences of different individuals instead of others' perceptions of these experiences.

Experience is learning, but only when the reality of experience is acknowledged and valued. This has always been one of the basic ingredients of good adult education. Educational integration is ultimately based on an integration or sharing of experience, but requires integration at every level of the education system, including the policy level, and an awareness of the place of education in the wider system. It is not about the promotion of one particular kind of experience over another, for this only creates the kinds of divisions so obvious in the political and religious systems of today. We cannot reach an understanding of these divisions if we are constantly denied the alternative perspectives. So, if hearing people are told that deaf people are 'disabled' or 'sick' – a layperson's view which is widespread in the system surrounding the deaf individual – they can never begin to understand how they themselves may be disabling deaf people or can be the source of the infection.

References

Corker, M. (1990) *Deaf Perspectives on Psychology, Language and Communication*, National Association of Tertiary Education for Deaf People/SKILL (National Bureau for Students with Disabilities), London.

Department of Education and Science (1991) *Education and Training for the Twenty-First Century: Proposals for the Government's White Paper*, DES, London.

Dewey, J. (1966) *Democracy and Education*, Macmillan, New York.

Finkelstein, V. (1991) ' "We" are not disabled, "you" are', in Gregory, S. and Hartley, G. (eds) *Constructing Deafness*, Pinter, London/The Open University, Milton Keynes.

Fletcher, L. (1987) *Language for Ben*, Souvenir Press, London.

Gregory, S. and Bishop, J. (1991) 'The mainstreaming of primary age deaf children', in Gregory, S. and Hartley, G. (eds) *Constructing Deafness*, Pinter, London/The Open University, Milton Keynes.

Groce, N. E. (1985) *Everyone Here Spoke Sign Language*, Harvard University Press, Cambridge, Massachusetts.

Ladd, P. (1991) 'Making plans for Nigel: the erosion of identity by mainstreaming', in Montgomery, G. (ed.) *The Integration and Disintegration of the Deaf in Society*, Scottish Workshop Publications, Glasgow.

Luterman, D. (1987) *Deafness in the Family*, Little, Brown, Boston.

Reiser, R. and Mason, M. (eds) (1990) *Disability Equality in the Classroom: a Human Rights Issue*, Inner London Education Authority.

Satir, V. (1988) *The New Peoplemaking*, Science and Behaviour Books, Mountain View, California.

Southgate, J. and White, K. (1989) 'Alienism: the underlying root of racism, sexism and oppression', *Journal of the Institute for Self-Analysis*, Vol. 3, No. 1, pp. 35–8.

Warnock, M. (1978) *Special Educational Needs: Report of the Committee of Enquiry into the Education of Handicapped Children and Young People*, Cmnd. 7212, HMSO, London.

Warnock, M. (1988) *A Common Policy for Education*, Oxford University Press.

3.4

Taught helplessness? Or a say for disabled students in schools

John Swain

Introduction

In Ashdown School, a school for young disabled people from 3 to 19 years old, the idea that the students could have a greater say in the decision-making within the school has been a topic for discussion for some time, particularly as part of drawing up the school development plan and of the staff development programme. In spring 1991 a research project was used to further the debate in a broader context of views about the whole decision-making process within the school. It was undertaken at the request of the school by John Swain and Carole Thirlaway (from the local polytechnic) and involved the following steps:

- observation at five meetings of professionals and parents;
- open-ended discussions/interviews with seven groups of people in the school – that is, students, teachers, social workers, physiotherapists, medics (doctor and sister), parents and residential care workers (a total of 30 people);
- separate reports of the views of each of the groups to give them the opportunity for further comment;
- a full report for all participants, which included the reports for each of the separate groups;
- observation at subsequent meetings at which this full report was discussed.

The interviews were around a series of suggested topics: 'The say that you have in decisions which affect young disabled people's education and lives, and what limits the say that you have'; 'The say that others have'; 'The say that young people themselves have'; 'The implications of "disability" on the decision-making that determines young people's education and lives'; and 'What you see as the main priorities in terms of who has what say and in working with others in future decisions.' The present paper looks first at the general context of the discussions within Ashdown School and then outlines some of the issues that emerged from the research.

Student participation in decision-making

The notion of students having a say in decision-making – in planning, organising, managing and evaluating their education – pervades a vast array of positions and movements in education which come under a number of umbrella terms, such as 'alternative', 'radical', 'progressive' and 'libertarian' education. Educationalists have taken such stances throughout the history of compulsory schooling and they can trace the roots of their position at least as far back as the writings of William Godwin (1756–1836) and J. J. Rousseau (1712–78). Furthermore, the list of relevant topics is also seemingly endless, including: open classrooms; democratic schools; active and experiential learning; children's rights; student councils; and counter-hegemony, in which participation is directed at questioning the prevailing social order, social structure and power relations in society.

Nevertheless, despite the growth of the disability movement and the struggles of disabled people to control the decision-making processes which shape their lives, little attention has been given to the say that young disabled people have in controlling their education. Even in more recent statements relating to 'integration', still probably the dominant topic in the literature, no mention is made of young people themselves determining the process. They are the recipients (or not) of other people's decisions.

There are a number of arguments to promote student participation generally. In the light of the disability movement justifications which are particularly relevant to young disabled people reach beyond the school walls into broader social, economic and political realms. The central proposition of such arguments is that student participation in educational decision-making can contribute to, or be a force for, change in society, towards greater democracy and a more egalitarian society. Such arguments are not new. A seminal and key figure, at least in American education, has been Dewey, who was recommending in 1916 that schools should be organised as miniature democracies, and who saw education as a preparation for citizenship in a democratic society (Dewey, 1916). Closer to home, in their statement of educational principles, for example, a group of teachers from Wigan included the following: 'Education has the responsibility of operating within a democratic system; of respecting and nurturing democratic principles; of being open to change by democratic process; and, perhaps, most import-antly, of encouraging within the young those qualities and skills which enable them to participate in a democracy and ultimately to develop or change it' (Department of Education and Science, 1983, p. 27). This statement of intent from practising teachers concerns beliefs about the type of society in which people wish to live and how education can shape society. Hunter (1980) sees parallels with other pressures for change: 'arguments for participation in the classroom can be seen to be linked with the growing agitation for community participation in politics, industrial democracy and the feminist and anti-racialist movements' (pp. 231–2). Though generally overlooked, as in the above quote, links can also be made with the struggles and arguments pursued within the disability movement, including the establishment of a social definition of disability as a social status imposed by social barriers upon people with impairments and the rejection of stereotypes of 'dependency' and 'helplessness'. Democracy within education has the potential to promote the active involvement of young disabled people in their own interests and thus provide a basis for the development of confidence and identity as disabled adults who will join the struggle for broader social change.

Some dilemmas for professionals and parents

The concluding section of the final report for Ashdown began as follows:

> There do seem to be some concerns which recur throughout the interviews and seemed to be crucial to people's views about decision-making in the education and lives of young disabled people. These are not the points over which all or most people agree. These are the more controversial matters where sometimes people have conflicting views or there are dilemmas and contradictions for people.

Three themes were pinpointed and discussed in subsequent meetings. They seemed to go some way towards encapsulating the challenges that the notion of a shift of power to students holds for those immediately involved.

The first theme was, in different guises, consistently the main topic of debate for professionals. Concerning what may be termed the 'multi-professional approach', it was seen as a source of many difficulties for professionals and parents, some practical, some personal and some organis-ational. In part it involved differences in perceptions about the boundaries of people's work and what they contributed: in general, professionals and parents tended to see themselves as concerned with the young person and their life as a whole, but they saw others as being restricted in their work and concerned only with limited aspects of the young person.

There was a widely held concern to improve the effectiveness of professionals working together, and to involve parents more fully, so as to create a system in which there is openness, effective communication and negotiated decisions about priorities for young disabled people. The following two quotes, the first from a teacher and the second from a physiotherapist, are illustrative:

> I think the important thing is that we do establish with the other professionals within the school a real understanding about what we are trying to achieve, an agreement and, as far as possible, a sharing of values between us as to what we are trying to achieve with these youngsters.

> We've got to be able to set out the implications of the decisions, that may or may not be made, and priorities at a given time.

As indicated here, the perceived ways forward were varied, but it was agreed at the discussion meeting that 'improved communication' was at the heart of the matter.

Nevertheless, on the other hand it was widely felt that the system itself denied young people opportunities and circumstances in which they could have control over their own lives and education. The system was seen as creating dependency in that young people were passed from the hands of one professional to another, pressurised by the demands of each professional discipline, and had their 'needs' determined by others. Young people were caught up in a whirlwind of activity with, to quote a social worker, 'the teachers and the physios and the medics arguing out who has this square inch of this kid's time'. A physiotherapist compared it to 'a sausage machine'. The whole process of disempowerment was summarised by a social worker:

> I think they have very little say from the point of diagnosis to treatment or anything. They are made very dependent on a variety of specialists for information and advice . . . and in fact so are the parents. They're forced into a position of dependence and in fact how do you expect a disabled child to be independent when even their parents aren't?

Parents, too, voiced such feelings from their viewpoint:

> I honestly do not think my child is encouraged in any way, possibly because his life is short . . . to take charge of his life and I think this might be giving him an unspoken message that you don't count.

The second major theme concerned what the report called 'The "we-know-the-best-for-you" dilemmas'. It went on to explain:

> In fact they can be seen as the difficulties that are faced with young people generally: how far should they be allowed (encouraged?) to take risks and learn for themselves and how far should they be guided by those who 'know best'? With young disabled people the questions become more extreme because their lives are filled with so many more people who 'know best' (i.e. professionals) and who have power to control their lives. Furthermore their circumstances, such as pressures to be 'acceptable' and 'normal', do not allow young people to rebel against the control of others.

The doctor stated this succinctly: 'It's always a dilemma of how much you impose what you feel is best.'

It seemed to professionals and parents that there are certain ways in which young people can be helped: regimes they should follow; treatments that are essential to their well-being; skills and knowledge they require; and risks that they need to be sheltered from. Such forms of help were seen as enabling young people, in the long term, to have control over their own lives. A physiotherapist talked, for instance, of what she saw as the consequences of a young person complying or not with recommended regimes:

> If they followed the regime like some of the other young people, they would be a lot more mobile and more 'well' generally, because the implications of not doing some things affect not only the mobility but the actual kidney function, digestion and other things.'

Again, however, it was generally recognised that a life in which all decisions are imposed by others is disempowering. Relationships which impose such forms of help, it was felt, encourage apathy and passivity on the part of young disabled people. Young people observe that decisions are made by others and they learn to be controlled. So in later years, when opportunities might arise for young disabled people to have some choices and to have more say, they have no basis for such autonomy. Again, it was recognised that young people can either be helped or taught to be 'helpless'. (For a fuller discussion of the concept of 'learned helplessness', see Swain, 1989.) The same physiotherapist, for instance, simply stated that professionals 'make them more passive'. One teacher stated:

> I think that it is a problem that youngsters, in many respects, don't have much opportunity to actually influence their work. I think that probably they labour under a heavier burden in that, right from birth, in many cases, things have been done for them, to them and they have had very little control.

Another outlined what she saw as the consequences:

> Yes, I feel that it's very much a case that they have things done to them all the time and our pupils, a lot of them, are quite sort of apathetic in decision-making and are quite happy to accept, or appear to be happy to accept, whatever anybody decides should be done for them, to them.

The third and final theme centred on the definition or, more broadly, the meaning of 'disability'. Though discussed explicitly at times, this was more diffuse as a topic and was inherent in a wide range of concerns. Indeed, the dilemmas for professionals in their 'multi-professional approach' could be traced to paradoxes within their different understandings of the meaning of 'disability'.

In essence, 'disability' was consistently viewed, on the one hand, as a condition of the individual. Sometimes this was stated explicitly, as by a physiotherapist: 'I look on the disability as being the overall diagnosis . . . to me the children have got a disability, i.e. spina bifida, cerebral palsy, to me that's the disability. That's the underlying problem.' Others were more circumspect. The doctor, for instance, stated: 'I use the World Health Organisation classification of impairment, disability and handicap, and handicap is the social effect of the disadvantage suffered because of a person having disability which means a loss or an alteration of function due to impairment.' It is still clearly evident that the individual young person is the source of the 'problem'.

On the other hand, however, people tended to see themselves, in helping to overcome 'disability', as concerned with the young person as a whole, their lives as a whole, and, indeed, the barriers and opportunities faced by disabled people in our society. A physiotherapist stated, for instance: 'What we want to develop in them is the motivation to try and tackle society, take it head on so that they can actually say I want to go and do this, I want to go and do something else.' There were different nuances in terms of what people thought of as the barriers and how they thought they could be overcome. For one parent, for instance, it was public attitudes, in that 'people only see the disability': 'That's what's wrong with society as a whole: they don't see the person.' A social worker included professionals in creating 'disability': 'We cast the disabled person in a certain role. We fail to see them as people who have a voice, who have needs and feelings. I mean, they are very basic things but I think that we really don't acknowledge they are people who should be respected along with the rest of us.'

Professionals were in a position in which the interventions they engaged in denied young disabled people the very control over their own lives and education they were intended to promote. In the final report this was called a 'circle of disability':

> the more young people are thought to have 'special' needs → the more others help them by meeting those 'needs' → the more young people's lives are determined by others who 'know best' → the more passive or apathetic young people become → the more they become dependent on the help of others → the more they have 'special needs'.

This circle seemed to be locked by definitions of 'disability' which site 'the problem' within the individual young disabled person, who is thus dependent on interventions by others to achieve independence in every aspect of his education and life. In this paradox can be seen the dilemma experienced by professionals.

The voice of the students

The research also involved collecting and reporting the views of some students at Ashdown. Although the time-scale prevented an in-depth analysis of students' views, there were some indications that students seek greater control of their lives in school, as in the following quotes:

> You are treated very much as a child even when you're sixteen, seventeen, eighteen years old. They say you're an adult but because you are still in the school situation you still get treated as a child.

> I think we should have more say, now that we're older.

One instance of collective action was discussed by a small group of students:

> 'Except for the dinner queue, the dinner nannies always push to the front. The people in wheelchairs, it's fair enough that they can't get their own dinner, but they should at least go to the back of the queue like we have to, but they push straight to the front. There's not really much choice left by the time we get to the front of the queue.'
>
> 'And, like we've complained about it but nothing's been done.'
> 'To whom have you complained?'
> 'We drew a petition up to the headmaster but he hasn't done anything yet.'
> 'So what do you think you'll do next?'
> 'Talk to someone else. Try to work something out.'

Nevertheless, the involvement of the students in the whole school development programme was confined to these interviews. In policy-making meetings in which the School Development Plan is reviewed, in 'staff development' meetings at which 'student participation' is debated, and in the governors' meetings, the interests of students are represented by others. Furthermore, all the professionals at Ashdown are able-bodied (including the researchers) and no representative from a local group of disabled people has

been consulted or invited to contribute to the school development programme in any capacity. This, then, is a central paradox which underpins the
dilemmas facing professionals and parents at Ashdown: the argument for the
participation of disabled students in the decision-making processes which
shape their lives and education is largely pursued in the school by able-bodied
professionals.

A final note

The discussions within Ashdown School may lead to changes in organisation,
management and approaches which will involve a greater say for the
students. Certainly the intention is there on the part of the professionals. The
School Development Plan includes such phrases as: 'we aim to help pupils
learn and practise, from an early age, the skills of making choices and
decisions'; and 'which reflects the close involvement of both children and
their parents'.

Nevertheless, student participation challenges existing power relations and
structures, and there are possible dangers when such supposed shifts in power
are planned and controlled by others. There is the possibility that 'participation' will be a means of social control and manipulation, with students
ostensibly having a choice but all the options being determined by others.
Such 'choice' can be a means of motivating students to follow through the
decisions of others. Similarly students' attempts to control which have not
been predetermined by others may be deemed illegitimate – that is, as
'behavioural problems' or a lack of 'acceptance of disability'.

Ultimately it has to be asked whether able-bodied professionals, notwith-
standing their good intentions, prepare young disabled people for life as
disabled adults who are conscious of their identity as disabled people and of
the struggle for full participative citizenship within our society. Links with the
disability movement are not simply a part of the justification of student
participation, as argued earlier; they may also play an important role in
change within schools. The inclusion of representatives from local groups of
disabled people in the debates at Ashdown is not likely to provide simple
solutions to the dilemmas faced by professionals and parents, but it would
provide a different perspective which could help ensure that the interests of
the students as young disabled people were pursued. In this light, too, student
participation would become part of the struggle of disabled people in the
rejection of roles of 'helplessness' and 'dependency'.

Acknowledgement

Many thanks are due to the students, parents and staff at Ashdown School,
and to my co-researcher, Carole Thirlaway.

References

Department of Education and Science (1983) *Curriculum 11–16: Towards a Statement of Entitlement: Curricular Appraisal in Action*, HMSO, London.

Dewey, J. (1916) *Democracy and Education*, Macmillan, New York.

Hunter, C. (1980) 'The politics of participation – with specific reference to teacher–pupil relationships', in Woods, P. (ed.) *Teacher Strategies: Explorations in the Sociology of the School*, Croom Helm, London.

Swain, J. (1989) 'Learned helplessness theory and people with learning difficulties: the psychological price of powerlessness', in Brechin, A. and Walmsley, J. (eds) *Making Connections*, Hodder and Stoughton, London.

3.5

Conductive education: if it wasn't so sad it would be funny

Mike Oliver

The current fashion for conductive education has created a furore in the world of education. If it wasn't so sad, it would be funny. We have seen the creation of three new organisations aimed at furthering it, television programmes extolling its virtues, demonstrations at the House of Commons, picketing of the Spastics Society and the alleged poaching of conductors. To understand why all this is sad rather than funny, it is necessary to look at what conductive education claims to be and some of the wider issues that it raises.

So what is this conductive education that the furore is all about? Well, it isn't a medical treatment and it does not claim to cure the 'motor impaired' as its recipients are usually insensitively called. Rather it claims to be a method of enabling the motor impaired 'to function in society without requiring special apparatus such as wheelchairs, ramps or other artificial aids'. Well yes, but don't we all use artificial aids of one kind or another; try eating your dinner without a knife and fork or going to Australia without an aeroplane.

Its claims are built upon two underpinnings, one theoretical and one practical. Its theoretical underpinning is that under the right conditions 'the central nervous system will restructure itself'. Its practical underpinning is 'orthofunction': a teaching method which involves the whole person physically and mentally and which instils 'the ability to function as members of society, to participate in normal social settings appropriate to their age'. The word 'normal' crops up a lot in the writings of Dr Mari Hari, the leading proponent of conductive education, and her ever-growing band of disciples.

Unfortunately for them, the theory remains unproven for there is no evidence that the central nervous system of any human being has ever restructured itself in the manner suggested. But does that really matter if orthofunction as practical activity actually works? The evidence here is, perhaps, stronger; published studies indicate significant improvements in functioning in many motor impaired children, as do personal accounts

---

This paper was first published in *Disability, Handicap and Society*, 1989, Vol. 4, No. 2, pp. 197–200; Virginia Beardshaw's rejoinder was first published in *Disability, Handicap and Society*, 1989, Vol. 4, No. 3, pp. 297–99.

provided by the ever-increasing number of visitors to the Peto Institute in Hungary.

But, as any competent undergraduate social scientist will tell you, correlation does not prove causation. In other words, the relationship between the application of orthofunction and functional improvements may not be a causal one. It may well be that factors other than orthofunction are producing these improvements; factors such as better resourcing, a purposeful environment, the amount of time spent in active learning each day, or the one-to-one relationship with conductors, may be equally or more important than the specific application of the technique of orthofunction itself.

So, not only is conductive education theoretically unproven but also practically unsubstantiated. I would go further and suggest that it is also ideologically unsound. Its constant, uncritical use of the concept of 'normality' and its insistence on adapting individuals rather than environments flies in the face of much social scientific and educational wisdom, and, more importantly, the expressed wishes of many disabled people who want society to change, not themselves.

Unsound ideology can quickly turn into oppression and Dr Hari's views are certainly oppressive to a large number of disabled people. In one example, she endorses orthofunction as a way of teaching people with a spinal injury to walk, and adds that 'teaching must restore the will of the individual to do so'. As a person with a spinal injury, this view is oppressive to me, and other people with a spinal injury, in two ways. First, how dare she assume that our main goal is to walk, without consulting us in the first place. And second, how dare she imply that those hundreds of thousands of people with a spinal injury throughout the world are not walking because they lack the will to do so.

It is also interesting to note that Dr Andrew Sutton, director of the recently established Foundation for Conductive Education, can endorse these remarks as 'endearingly characteristic'. They are grossly offensive to me and many other disabled people, and it is symptomatic of the gap that usually exists between the consciousness of the able-bodied staff of many disability organisations and the disabled people they are supposed to serve.

Given that conductive education is theoretically unproven, practically unsubstantiated and ideologically unsound, why are we currently seeing many local education authorities and, indeed, the Spastics Society itself, besieged by angry parents demanding the provision of conductive education almost overnight?

To begin with, conductive education does offer a positive approach to a clear set of goals, whether you agree with them or not. That is something that special educators have, so far, lamentably failed to offer disabled children and their families. For far too long disabled children have been put away in special schools and been made to feel that there is something wrong with them, their disabilities are a burden and a thing of shame. While conductive education does offer an alternative vision, it is unfortunate that this vision implies the removal of burden and shame through the achievement of normality.

In addition, conductive education does offer higher expectations than those to which special education has aspired. Thus Andrew Sutton can comment that conductive education can produce results 'which seem quite beyond the expectations of children growing up with cerebral palsy and spina bifida elsewhere'. Given that the expectations of professionals about what disabled people can actually achieve has always been pathetically low, almost any intervention system which raises expectations is likely to produce similar results.

Throughout human history, disabled people have constantly confounded the low expectations of others, and how much better it would be for special educators to raise the expectations of disabled children and their families by giving them an understanding of this, by helping them to accept their disabled identities with pride, by helping them to understand their place in the world and their rights as well as giving them the practical skills to deal with these issues. Of course, in order to do this, special educators would need to understand these issues themselves.

Finally, it is sad but understandable that the parents of disabled children should clutch at the straw of conductive education as a means of resolving their own problems. To have a handicapped child in a society which has developed a fetishism for normality and which fails to even acknowledge the needs of these parents, let alone make any provision to meet them, is clearly a profoundly disturbing experience. But accepting the fetishism of normality can never even address these problems, let alone resolve them.

Those of us who were privileged to hear Paddy Ladd's moving account of the struggles and pride of the deaf community at last year's International Conference in Bristol, England, will long remember his response to a challenge from the floor that many parents regarded the birth of their deaf children as tragedies. He said that he understood this and was sorry, but could only add that the deaf community regarded the birth of each and every deaf child as a precious gift. We, as a society, could learn from that, and, if we regarded the birth of every disabled child as a precious gift and were prepared to provide the necessary resources to the children and their parents to allow these gifts to develop, then perhaps we would be spared the distressing sight of individual and groups of parents pursuing the latest fashionable cure for their child's blindness, deafness or other disability at whatever cost to themselves, their families and friends.

So, what kind of a world does conductive education envisage? One in which we are all exhorted to approximate to the walkie-talkie model of living, where physical and social environments remain unchanged and unchanging. I have an alternative vision, where difference is not just tolerated but valued, and even celebrated, and where physical and social environments are constantly changing to accommodate and welcome these differences. What is more, I think my vision is an achievable dream, that of conductive education an achievable nightmare.

My dream is achievable because all we have to do is stop doing some of the things we are already doing: stop using the productive forces we have developed to create disabilities through warfare, environmental pollution and industrial accidents; stop creating disabilities through poverty by using our vast wealth not in pursuit of capital accumulation and profit, but in ensuring that we all have the necessities to sustain material life; and stop judging and treating people on the basis of the contribution they can or cannot make to the development and operation of these productive forces.

The nightmare of conductive education is unachievable because nowhere in human history have the different been turned into the normal and neither medical science nor other rehabilitative techniques or educational interventions can assist in this process. The reason is simple; normality does not exist. Someone else, not very long ago, had a vision of normality associated with blond hair and blue eyes, and look where such a vision got him.

Conductive education: a rejoinder

Virginia Beardshaw

According to Mike Oliver, I am a 'straw-clutcher'. By deciding in late 1987 to take my daughter to Budapest's Peto Institute for a spell of conductive education I 'contributed to the distressing sight of individual and groups of parents pursuing the latest fashionable cure for their child's . . . disability' – in her case, cerebral palsy.

Of course, Dr Oliver is partly right. Learning to treasure my daughter's uniqueness in a world obsessed with 'normality' was – and still is sometimes – a very painful thing. Search for alleviation and cure is a very basic human reaction, as shrines from Lourdes to high-tech oncology clinics testify.

But by portraying those of us who have sought conductive education for our children as unthinking lemmings dashing off for a dose of Hungarian miracle water, Dr Oliver's polemic does us – and conductive education – less than justice. More importantly, by castigating conductive education he obscures some very important implications that the method has for the West.

The irony is that Dr Oliver has done more than most to document the real reasons why conductive education is attractive to parents from Britain and many other Western countries. He and other writers from the disabled people's movement have dissected the inadequacy of current approaches to disability. Together, they have criticised slipshod, ineffective and oppressive rehabilitation methods, and called for higher standards for the education of young people with disabilities. They have analysed the way that children with disabilities are encouraged to be passive recipients of care in our society, and have fought against this. Above all, they have emphasised the need for higher expectations from society as a whole about what disabled people can achieve, and have argued for the necessary resources to be devoted to helping them achieve them.

Conductive education is about high expectations. It is about motivating people with neurological damage to achieve things for themselves, and in so doing, get more control over their lives. For children with cerebral palsy it involves a focused yet holistic approach designed to stimulate them to move themselves out of the passivity that lack of control over their bodies has encouraged since birth. Doing so allows them to experience and interact with their environment and other people. That encourages experiential learning and socialisation in a way that few Western special education or therapeutic settings do.

Conductive education is also about setting ambitious goals, and then getting children to achieve them *because they want to for themselves*. Doing so requires great skill, and an integrated and wholly dedicated application of the techniques we know separately as physiotherapy, occupational therapy, educational psychology, speech therapy and teaching. For Dr Oliver to dismiss the knowledge and skill base of the method – which is breathtakingly more advanced than anything we have in the West – by claiming that conductive education is successful simply because it is an 'intervention system which raises expectations' is to ignore a number of important points.

But parents like me cannot afford to ignore them, even to permit Dr Oliver to find a totally ideologically sound approach to alleviating disability. Like him, and his many fellows in the disabled people's movement, we have had direct experience of the unfocused and frequently inept workings of rehabilitation professionals in this country. We know that, even given half-way decent funding, rehabilitation approaches and much of special education could never work well for our children because they start with low expectations, and are very unclear about what they are trying to achieve. What is worse still, they start from a wholly inadequate skill base which hinders more than it helps by carving up approaches which should be integrated into arbitrary professional divisions called 'occupational therapy', 'physiotherapy' and so on. In other words, we have already learnt the painful lesson that, despite all the kind words and good intentions, for most practical purposes society has already written our children off. It is unprepared to offer them the skilled attention that they need.

That is not good enough for some of us. And so – in my case very reluctantly, in a slow process of decision-making that took two years – we have taken the road to Budapest. There we have found not miracles but dedication, hard work, love and – the phrase repeatedly used by parents at the Peto – 'a lot of common sense'. I do not think that any one of us expects our children to walk out of the place 'normal', but we do know that it is the best place in the world for them to achieve their fullest potential. With its emphasis on self-motivation, active participation and problem-solving, the Peto method is their best chance of doing the best they can with what they have got.

To change tack slightly, I am not equipped to comment on Dr Oliver's critique of conductive education's theoretical base. All I will say is that in attempting to develop theories about the alleviation of neurological dysfunction as she has, Dr Hari has been one of very few medical scientists to address an important 'black hole' in the research agenda. Few others have been interested to devote resources and research talent to it, despite the fact that an estimated 1 in 500 children are born with cerebral palsy and that neurological disorders are one of the largest group of disabling conditions for adults. I think that this neglect is another part of the 'writing off' process that disabled people are still subject to.

I also think that before sitting in judgement on Dr Hari's 'uncritical use of the concept of "normality"', a social scientist of Dr Oliver's calibre might stop to think for a moment about the social context in which those remarks were made. Hungary is a much poorer country than Britain. Few of the flats in which most urban Hungarians live have lifts. Whole sections of Budapest, with its steep hills, have no pavements at all. Ramped access to public buildings is all but unknown. The public transport on which ordinary people depend is inaccessible to wheelchairs. During the 1980s, social security arrangements of all kinds have broken down. Hungary is a tough environment for all its citizens – able-bodied and disabled. Understanding this may make Dr Hari's remarks – delivered as they were in a foreign language – less 'oppressive'.

3.6

Participation and control in day centres for young disabled people aged 16 to 30 years

Colin Barnes

Introduction

This paper examines user involvement in structured activities, the decision-making process, and social control in a day-centre system for young disabled people aged 16–30 – the Contact group. Observations are derived from a 12-month empirical study conducted during 1986/7 of the interactions between users and staff in three day centres in a large northern town. The study highlights some of the problems associated with user participation in centres which purport to provide social and 'rehabilitative' facilities in an explicitly voluntarist framework.

The Contact group

The centres in which Contact operated had evolved along traditional lines. In common with the expansion of day services generally during the 1960s and 1970s (Carter, 1981) their development had been fairly *ad hoc* and unstructured. Segregative in both appearance and admission policies, they catered mostly for elderly disabled people. The facilities offered were commensurate with the phrase 'tea and bingo' (Kent *et al.*, 1984) and the 'warehouse' model of care (Dartington *et al.*, 1981).

Separate provision for young disabled adults did not emerge until the early 1980s, when a group, known as Contact, was formed to provide a more comprehensive facility than existing services. Offering a five-day service, the group was not based in one centre but used three. It had its own permanent staff; hence user–staff interaction was significantly greater than in other user groups.

Contact's staff were well qualified for this type of work. The two senior posts were held by women with experience in youth and social work. Six of the group's seven 'care assistants' were under 25 and on government-sponsored youth training schemes – having entered the caring industry to escape unemployment. Although their youth and lack of training were viewed with scepticism by other day-centre users and staff, this was not the case in Contact. Members, whose average age was 22.5 years, welcomed the opportunity to interact on a regular basis with non-disabled peers.

Such interaction was also viewed positively by Contact's senior personnel, as they were aware that most of the group's 22 male and 14 female members, one of whom was black, were unable to meet people of their own age outside the centres. Two members lived in local authority homes and 15 in households characterised by unemployment and chronically sick and/or lone parents. Of the remainder, only four were from homes where the head of the household was a non-manual worker. Overall, only three had managed to set up homes of their own.

Twenty-six users had attended segregated special schools. None had experienced higher education, but 19 had been on some form of post-16 provision. However, 16 of these placements were on segregated 'vocational' or 'independence'-type courses. Only 12 members had any academic qualifications, and the highest achievers were those from mainstream schools. Only seven people had experience of paid employment other than government work schemes, and four of these were employed before they acquired their impairment – they had not worked since.

All Contact's members were introduced to the idea of day-centre use by professionals working in either education or the health and social support services. Even though unemployment was a tacit factor, three main reasons accounted for their joining the group. Some wanted to maintain long-term friendships, having known each other from school or college. Others, although aware of the stigma attached to day centres, saw attendance as preferable to the extreme social isolation encountered when formal education ceased – a common problem for disabled young adults (Hirst, 1987; Kuh *et al.*, 1988; Martin *et al.*, 1988; Thomas *et al.*, 1989). The rest, mainly those with acquired impairments, believed that it would assist their rehabilitation.

The group's general ethos evolved from the interaction between staff and users. Its aim was to provide social and, in the non-medical sense, 'rehabilitative' activities within an explicitly voluntarist framework, consonant with the 'enlightened guardian' model of care. This approach has the advantage of accommodating in one framework the needs of dependent people as well as those of less dependent people. Alternatively, because these needs are contradictory it inhibits progress toward user participation and control (Dartington *et al.*, 1981). This was indeed the case in the context of the Contact group.

Structured activities

In principle Contact users had access to a wide range of structured 'rehabilitative' activities generally regarded as heightening independence and self-help. These included woodwork, sewing, cookery, music and drama, arts and crafts, literacy and numeracy classes, and an access course for further education, which was organised in conjunction with the local education authority. There were also occasional visits to local places of interest, such as art galleries, exhibitions and shopping centres, as well as spontaneous 'social' pastimes, such as games, listening to music, watching television and general socialising.

Access to many of these facilities was restricted, however, because of environmental and social factors. For example, woodwork, sewing and cookery were available at one centre only, which Contact visited three days a week. Places were limited, participation was determined individually on a first come, first served basis, and the centre's main client group, elderly disabled people, were given priority. Contact users were also reluctant to join these groups because, in common with young people generally (Brake, 1985; McRobbie, 1990), they preferred the company of their peers.

None the less, Contact staff were under pressure, albeit predominantly implicit, from three main sources – the local authority, users' parents and some users themselves – to 'encourage' user involvement in approved activities. To achieve this they employed strategies similar to those used by schoolteachers and referred to by Hargreaves (1975) as 'the liontamer', 'the entertainer' and the 'new romantic'.

The traditional 'liontamer' approach, where people are literally told what to do and how to do it, was most evident in the arts and crafts classes. These were held on Tuesdays at a centre where the manageress and her staff took the view that 'idle hands make idle minds'. No other activities were available at this unit. Users could either join in or sit and do nothing. These classes were very unpopular with Contact members. Tuesday was the day of the week with the poorest attendance levels – averaging about 17 users compared with an average of 26 for the rest of the week – and senior Contact staff had little control over the situation.

'The entertainer' approach is based on the assumption that motivation is latent and waiting to be tapped. Hence learning has to be fun or have some obvious use value. Apart from Tuesdays this was the strategy most in evidence in the centres and used to elicit participation in all activities. For example, a male tutor from the local college used this technique to cajole some of the male users into joining the bridging course. Because they were unenthusiastic about 'more education' he emphasised the social aspects of attending a mainstream college – notably the opportunity to meet girls.

Rooted in the belief that motivation is inherent and students will participate if they are interested, 'the new romantic' technique was used effectively by the literacy and numeracy teacher. She adopted an individually structured approach to teaching which allowed students to work at their own pace as and when they pleased. Between six and ten people (there were only ten on the class register) regularly attended these sessions.

Often there was scant evidence of academic activity, and this prompted criticism from some of those users who had been to mainstream schools.

Books were got out but little was done. Students would sit around chatting, leave if they felt like it, and not come back if they found something better to do. Commenting on a literacy, or 'English' class, Mathew, a male user who had had a 'normal' education, said: 'They were just sat about talkin'; some of 'em were drawin' when I went in. That's not English to me . . . they don't do owt in there.'

Inspection of users' books, however, showed that work had been done. Some had written letters to pop stars or relatives, others had written stories and all were doing elementary arithmetic. These were no mean achievements considering the nature of the subjects, the lack of literacy skills among users and their antipathy to formal controls and school in general. Indeed, it is doubtful whether the classes could have proceeded in any other fashion.

Moreover, most users saw the centres as somewhere to go to get out of the house rather than somewhere to learn. Although all expressed alarm about the lack of resources for facilities, only eight, the most autonomous in the group, felt that there was a need for activities specifically concerned with independence training and rehabilitation. Further, those who requested such facilities wanted them for others – those who had been 'mollycoddled' by their parents and by their teachers in special schools – rather than for themselves. They considered the activities available in the centres incompatible with their needs.

The decision-making process

Though the official rhetoric of organisations associated with day services often espouses a desire to maximise consultation between users and staff, meaningful participation is rare. One of the main reasons for this is undoubtedly economic. Sponsoring agencies, notably local authorities, have since the 1970s come under increasing pressure to control costs. This is reflected in the practices of senior day-centre staff whose primary loyalty is to their employer rather than to the users. The latter are rarely involved in the hiring and firing of staff and budgets are usually controlled by a central authority. Where user participation does occur it is normally limited to peripheral activities, such as trips and social events (Carter, 1981; Kent et al., 1984; Hampshire Centre for Independent Living, 1990).

Moreover, there are other difficulties associated with user involvement in day-centre management. Factionalism between user subgroups can cause friction which in turn neutralises the democratic process. This might be resolved with a written constitution and the formation of user committees; but committee members sometimes fail to comprehend that they represent the whole user body and only put forward their own ideas. Hence, committee membership can seriously aggravate existing user rivalry and conflict. This opens the way for staff to use their 'professional skills' to implement their own ideas rather than those of the users, which effectively renders the notion of user participation meaningless (Carr, 1987, personal communication; Jewell, 1975).

Similar difficulties were evident in the day centres studied. Excluding the Contact group, each of the three centres had user committees with written constitutions. Committee members were elected annually and meetings were held monthly. Staff did not attend committee meetings unless this was requested by members. The committees dealt with social issues such as trips and outings, and occasionally users' complaints about day-centre meals and day-centre staff – usually those on youth training schemes. They had no formal control over the staff or the centres' finances.

Users' attitudes regarding the value of these committees varied considerably. While some thought that they did a good job, a substantial minority felt that they were a waste of time. They pointed out that committee members were unrepresentative of the user body but got re-elected year after year. Some ascribed this to the fact that most people were not interested in committee membership because no one in the centres, including staff, had any real power. They believed that the real power base lay outside the centres in the social services central offices.

There were no representatives from Contact on any of these committees, although the group constituted almost one-third of the overall number of users at one of the centres and almost one-half at the other two. Any contribution to centre policy from Contact members had to be made either by senior Contact staff or individually. This was attributed by staff to the unique organisation of the group when compared with other user groups.

Until 1985 Contact had had its own user committee. It had performed similar functions to those described above, although there had been no formal constitution. Its principal members had been five of the most autonomous members of the Contact group. The committee's demise was generally attributed to factionalism and a lack of interest among other Contact users.

During the study period, however, two attempts were made to resurrect the user committee. Both were initiated by Billy, a 16-year-old with a recently acquired impairment who had only been with the group for a year. Sanctioned by staff, a group meeting was held at which Billy suggested setting up a new committee to 'get a few things sorted out'. His main concerns were the poor condition of the pool table and the need for more outings. After some persuasion on his part he managed to scrape together four reluctant nominees. But at the meeting's close there was no mention of a formal constitution, policy statement or even an agreed date for the first committee meeting.

Little was heard of the committee until six months later when Billy asked for another group meeting. His reason for calling it was unclear apart from vague statements about 'getting things moving'. Just over half the users present bothered to attend. Nothing came of the meeting and when it broke up there was much animosity between its organiser and the non-attenders.

Because of user non-participation, factionalism and the failure of user committees, periodic group meetings were organised by staff. There were seven during the study period. Their function was to discuss arrangements for forthcoming events, such as trips, holiday arrangements, structured activities, and so on. User involvement was usually limited to commenting on staff proposals. Finances were never discussed unless a user requested that the group buy a particular item. If funds were available the proposal was put to a vote. Senior staff's authority was rarely challenged during these discussions. As a result they were endowed with both the legitimacy of their official role and the popular support of the majority of users.

Social control

Although senior staff's authority went unchallenged, social control – the hegemonic and manipulative control of users during the course of daily interaction – was not a significant feature of day-centre life. It was only one of the staff's repertoire of tasks and when necessary was exercised through a combination of 'orchestration' and 'supervision', similar to techniques described by Bloor (1987) in his analysis of social control in a therapeutic community. Discipline was not considered a problem, but this was largely due to external factors rather than to the activities of senior staff.

The principle of individual user autonomy was sacrosanct in the day centres generally and the Contact group in particular. Apart from on Tuesdays, every effort was made by senior staff to ensure that an unfettered atmosphere prevailed. This was particularly evident in the delivery of personal services, an important area for disabled people because the body is the principal site of oppression, both in terms of cultural undervaluation and in respect of what is done to it (Abberley, 1987).

There were no 'bathing or toileting routines' for the convenience of staff. Users decided when and where these services should be provided. They were also responsible for their own medication – although it was common for users' families to ask staff to remind individuals to take it. Moreover, users had access to files or documents held by social services that concerned them as individuals.

But the principle of user autonomy was limited with regard to freedom to leave the building during opening hours. Officially users were not supposed to go outside the centres' grounds unaccompanied by staff without senior staff's permission. Although justified on the basis that the social services depart-ments, and by implication the staff, were responsible for users' safety during opening hours, this policy represented an explicit denial of users' freedom. It also undermined staff's attempts to encourage users' self-determination.

With this in mind senior Contact staff allowed Contact members to make their own decisions. Unfortunately most of the group were unable to exercise this right due to factors such as the hostile physical environment outside the centres, lack of resources – either money or essential mobility aids, such as electric wheelchairs – or parental overprotectiveness: some of the group were not allowed to go out alone or with disabled peers when at home. Moreover, because only a minority were able to leave the centres at will, this policy further aggravated the social divisions within the group. Some individuals resented the fact that 'some people can do what they like while others can't'.

Behavioural norms in the centres were subject to abstract principles of 'common sense'. Thus, what was viewed as acceptable was determined largely by the centres' main client group – elderly disabled people. Complaints about noisy behaviour were common, and this was a constant source of consternation for both Contact users and staff. It also meant that Contact was allotted a specific area in each centre and that generally group members stayed within it.

Not surprisingly, disruptive behaviour – shouting, swearing and general rowdiness – was sometimes evident. Generally perpetrated by the most physically independent male members of the group, antisocial activities were usually attributed by senior staff to extraneous socio-psychological factors and controlled through 'rehabilitative' activities. For example, one individual's aggressive behaviour was ascribed to his loss of able-bodied friends following impairment. Senior staff tried to resolve the problem through a combination of individual counselling sessions and by eliciting his help in a long-term project to repair the pool tables.

For 'serious' misdemeanours such as fighting, miscreants were asked to account for their actions in a formal setting: the manager's office. Besides emphasising the fact that certain behaviour was unacceptable, this ritual reaffirmed senior staff's superordinate position in the system. This was important because they had a predominantly 'social' rather than a 'professional' relationship with users, and it acted as a reminder that in the final analysis they had the power to impose sanctions when necessary.

However, this power was rarely used because both the main sanctions available to staff – contacting users' families and exclusion – have negative implications for both parties. For example, contacting users' families not only causes unpleasantness for the individual concerned but also damages the centres' carefully nurtured congenial atmosphere. With exclusion, users are denied access to a valuable social resource. For staff, because the process involves a protracted process of consultation with the local authority, sometimes other agencies, and the careful scrutiny of all relevant data by other personnel, internal policies might be seen as wanting and senior staff viewed as incompetent.

Conclusion

This paper has highlighted some of the main difficulties associated with user participation and control in a day-centre system providing social and rehabilitative facilities within an explicitly voluntarist framework. Clearly, Contact users had access to a range of facilities generally regarded as rehabilitative. Yet despite staff's efforts to orchestrate it, participation was low; users preferred social rather than didactic activities. Although 'swamping' by elderly disabled people was partly responsible for this situation, the lack of motivation is attributable to users' earlier life experiences: for the majority rehabilitation was inappropriate and for the rest the facilities offered were inadequate.

User participation in the decision-making process was evident in the centres generally, but it was largely tokenistic. Moreover, factionalism and misrepresentation by a vocal minority prevented its development in the Contact group and staff's authority went unchallenged. Yet, in contrast to official policy, Contact staff allowed users to come and go as they pleased in the centres. However, owing to, mainly, external considerations this policy aggravated social divisions within the group. Controls in the centres were kept to a minimum and despite environmental constraints on Contact's activities, social order was not considered a problem. However, when disruptive behaviour did occur staff controlled it through a combination of orchestration and supervisory control.

More involvement by Contact members might have been possible, with a radical reformulation of internal policies clarifying the group's primary function. But this would almost certainly have meant abandoning voluntarism in favour of some form of formal constitution demanding a greater commitment from users. Whether such changes would have been acceptable to Contact users is open to speculation since social interaction and individual autonomy were the group's main attractions. Given the environmental, economic and social constraints experienced by these young people in the community at large it is easy to understand why.

References

Abberley, P. (1987) 'The concept of oppression and the development of a social theory of disability', *Disability, Handicap and Society*, Vol. 2, No. 1, pp. 5–21

Bloor, M. (1987) 'Social control in a therapeutic community: re-examination of a critical case', *Sociology of Health and Illness*, March, pp. 305–24.

Brake, M. (1985) *Comparative Youth Cultures*, Routledge and Kegan Paul, London.

Carter, J. (1981) *Day Centres for Adults: Somewhere To Go*, George Allen and Unwin, London.

Dartington, T., Miller, E. J. and Gwynne, G. V. (1981) *A Life Together*, Tavistock, London.

Hargreaves, D. (1975) *Interpersonal Relations in Education*, Routledge and Kegan Paul, London.

Hampshire Centre for Independent Living (1990) *HCIL Papers 1990*, HCIL Hampshire.

Hirst, M. (1987) 'Careers of young people with disabilities between the ages of 15 and 21', *Disability, Handicap and Society*, Vol. 2, No. 1, pp. 61–74.

Jewell, P. (1975) 'Self-management in day centres', in Hatch, S. (ed.) *Towards Participation in Social Services*, Fabian Tract 419, Fabian Society, London.

Kent, A., Massie, B., Newman, B. and Tuckey, L. (1984) 'Day centres for young disabled people', Royal Association of Disability and Rehabilitation, London.

Kuh, D., Lawrence, C., Tripp, J. and Creber, G. (1988) 'Work and work alternatives for disabled young people', *Disability, Handicap and Society*, Vol. 3, No. 1, pp. 3–27.

McRobbie, A. (1990) *Feminism and Youth Culture*, Routledge and Kegan Paul, London.

Martin, J., White, A. and Meltzer, H. (1988) *Disabled Adults: Services, Transport and Employment*, Office of Population Censuses and Surveys, London.

Thomas, A. P., Bax, M. C. O. and Smith, D. P. L. (1989) *The Health and Social Needs of Young Adults with Physical Disabilities*, Blackwell, Oxford.

3.7

From Startrac to Leisure Choice: the first slow steps towards change

Marisa Lawton

Introduction

> We hope that the idea of Playtrac will spread. A mobile training resource based on the Playtrac model is being set up in the North East by Save the Children, in partnership with Mencap and The Spastics Society. This project will be called STARTRAC (Support Team for Advancing Recreation Training in The Community).

This quote from a chapter in the publication *Innovations in Leisure and Recreation for People with a Mental Handicap* (Denziloe, 1990, p. 317) sets the scene for the Startrac Project, established in April 1990, which was initially planned and controlled by the three voluntary service organisations mentioned. The project was to be funded for one year with money from the Telethon Trust, which paid for the author's post, that of development worker, as well as allowing a substantial budget; the overall aim was to establish a leisure service for disabled people within the Northern Health Region. Since the start of the project, however, this aim has been changed. The main aim of the project now is to make sure that the people who are on the receiving end of the services have more control and responsibility for the work which is being developed.

The project is not a shining example of a service that now fully involves disabled people and is controlled by them. We have been taking slow steps towards that goal and have faced a number of barriers along the way. These barriers must be recognised and taken account of by service-providers if they are serious about consulting and involving disabled people in the planning of services.

The changes that have been made may be small but they are significant. My own understanding of the role of services in the lives of disabled people has developed, and in the light of this I have reviewed my own working practices. Those people involved in the project have also gained an insight into the importance of establishing communication with disabled people and gaining advice from organisations of disabled people, *before* the setting up of services which are aimed at meeting their needs. It is hoped that the changes have also been important to the disabled people who are now involved in the work of the project; all of the quotes which appear in this chapter are theirs. A member of our group had this to say about the writing of this paper: 'It will be worth doing if it gets read by a lot of people. More groups like ours might get going to let disabled people have more say about what they want to do.'

The setting up of the project: erecting the barriers

The name 'Startrac' stood for 'Support Team for Advancing Recreation Training in the Community'. The words may sound very positive and impressive, but what do they actually mean? The name in itself gave no clues about the nature of the work being planned. The general aim of Startrac when it started out was to 'develop a resource within the Northern Health Region to promote leisure and recreation for children, young people and adults with special needs'. The stated objectives included:

● assessment of need
● integration into the widest possible range of leisure facilities
● support for carers – professional, family and volunteers
● looking for interagency co-operation and promoting community-based strategies.

'Can you put that into English?' was an understandable response. The language used to describe the project is difficult to understand. It is the language of professionals and others working within services, which can in itself be a barrier that stops people discussing those services which form a large part of their lives. The words we use to describe our services should be clear and without jargon. This is not always easy; we become skilled at using professional jargon and expect to hear it from others, but if we believe that people who use services should be involved in planning, then it is important that the language we use can be understood.

Startrac was well funded and well intentioned; the project set out to establish a service to meet the leisure needs of disabled people, but the way that it was set up was disabling in itself. The importance of disabled people being able to integrate into a wide range of leisure facilities in the community was recognised. The suggestion that disabled people should be consulted and included in discussions about the project had also been made but the implications of making this happen had not been considered. The professionals representing the three voluntary organisations involved were still very much responsible for control and decision-making within the project. There is much currently spoken about 'consultation with service-users' but this can all too easily become tokenistic without informed advice about how to realise this aim. The result is often the provision of a traditional service *for* disabled people to meet their 'special needs' with the only real changes being the words used to describe the service.

There was failure to take an important step when the project started its work. Disabled people had not been consulted about the way planning for the project should be arranged. This meant that the views of disabled people from the area were not taken into account and the informed opinion of the representative and organised voice of disabled people was not tapped.

A steering group had been brought together to advise and support the development of the project, but all the members were non-disabled professionals from a number of organisations including social services departments, the health authority and voluntary organisations. The decision that leisure should be the main focus of the project's work was also made by the service-providers; disabled people in the area were not involved in setting their own agendas to decide on the important issues as they saw them. Had disabled people been involved in the planning discussions for the project, perhaps even the main issues addressed would have been very different.

Since the start of the project I have spoken to a large number of disabled people who often begin by describing their daytime occupation or the type of work they would like to do. Barry Coombs had this to say: 'More jobs should be available for disabled people. If I was to get a job outside of the centre [occupational day centre] now and retired at 65 what would be the point of me getting a job?' Barry has already spent 21 years of his working life doing 'occupational therapy' in place of real work. He believes that there is little chance of him finding a job in the near future. I asked Barry why he felt it important to mention his long-term unemployment in this article about leisure. He answered: 'Jobs and leisure are all one thing aren't they – if you work you build yourself up for leisure.' What does leisure mean to people who have never had the chance to have real work opportunities? Unemployment may mean that people have more leisure time available but lack of money restricts the kind of activities they are able to participate in during their spare time.

Adult training centres are still often the only daytime occupation or 'work' available to disabled people, and the choice of activities within the centres can be limited: 'There's no jobs for the young ones leaving school in the adult training centres, they've got nothing to do, they're getting no jobs in – they just do jigsaws. When they do get jobs in they're finished straightaway and then there's nothing to do and you get bored to tears.' This is the very reason a member of the steering group gave for becoming involved in the project: 'It gives me something else to do, gets me out of the factory (adult training centre] and is less boring.'

There are many people wasting their lives wrapped up in services that have been set up to meet their so-called 'special needs'. It is these very services which can disable people, limiting the amount of real choice they have in their lives. Had disabled people been consulted and involved in the planning of the project from the start, the main emphasis of the work may well have been very different.

Three steps forward: shaking the barriers

The main focus of the project is still leisure, but there have been a number of important changes. As a starting-point the project's name has been changed to

'Leisure Choice' in the hope that it says a little more about the subject we are looking at. The membership of the steering group has also been changed. Eight people who are themselves disabled were invited to join the group, to match the number of professionals already involved, and to have a direct influence on the work which was being developed. People agreed to become involved for a variety of reasons. David Atkin, for example, was particularly interested in the issue of leisure opportunities: 'I want to find out how leisure activities can be improved because from what I've seen most disabled people in Hexham are fairly limited in being able to get out.' Sharon Harrington is a very active member of the group who has also been influential in the setting up of the Blyth Valley Self-Advocacy Group, which she now chairs. She makes the point that the new members have the most active roles within the group and are the most regular attenders of the steering group meetings. 'We livened the group up. I don't think you would have got anywhere if just professional people were involved.' Another member of the group, Tim Raine, refers to being part of a team that includes service planners and providers. He sees his involvement as an opportunity to have his views heard by people who have some control of the services: 'I liked the idea of working with people in authority. If you are not working with people in authority you are hardly likely to get things done.' The hope is that the professionals who are part of the group are not only listening to but also acting on the ideas that are put forward by members of the group.

The plan to invite new members to the group raised an important question. How do you bring a group of people together to work on an equal basis when half the members of the group are experienced non-disabled professionals who are used to taking control? A way to start to address this difficulty was suggested by the Strathclyde Equality Awareness Trainers, an organisation of disabled people. They organised a course for the steering group when the new members joined. The aim of the course was to get group members to think about disability issues in order to take a first step forward in working together.

The course was held over three days. During the first day the new members of the group followed the programme, which focused on the barriers that disabled people face in society. During the second day the professionals were taken through the same programme. On the third day of the course the group came together to share their experiences. A participant commented: 'I liked the last day when we teamed up with the professionals. I think they listened to us. It was actually disabled people doing the course and expressing their opinions and not the professionals.' The course was run by trainers who were themselves disabled, providing us with a real example of disabled people in a position of control.

Throughout the training programme we discussed the ways in which people are disabled – not by limited ability but by a number of barriers that keep them apart from the activities that the rest of their communities are involved in. This had a great influence on the issues that the steering group decided were most important for the project to work on. As one of the group

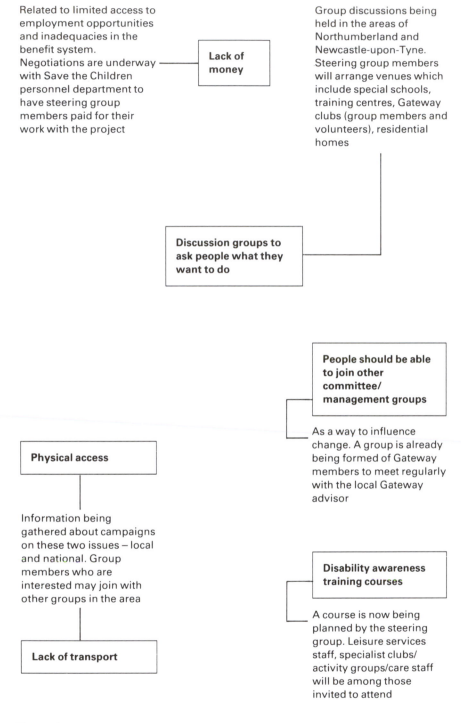

Related to limited access to employment opportunities and inadequacies in the benefit system. Negotiations are underway with Save the Children personnel department to have steering group members paid for their work with the project

Lack of money

Group discussions being held in the areas of Northumberland and Newcastle-upon-Tyne. Steering group members will arrange venues which include special schools, training centres, Gateway clubs (group members and volunteers), residential homes

Discussion groups to ask people what they want to do

People should be able to join other committee/ management groups

As a way to influence change. A group is already being formed of Gateway members to meet regularly with the local Gateway advisor

Physical access

Information being gathered about campaigns on these two issues – local and national. Group members who are interested may join with other groups in the area

Disability awareness training courses

A course is now being planned by the steering group. Leisure services staff, specialist clubs/ activity groups/care staff will be among those invited to attend

Lack of transport

Figure 1

put it: 'It made people think about what they wanted to do for the whole year.' The list of issues which the group came up with was so detailed that it was discussed over the following weeks. Given the time and resources available to the project it was agreed that we should concentrate on the topics shown in Figure 1.

Two steps back: the barriers remain in place

We have been working towards establishing a group where all the members have an equal say. We have equality in the number of disabled people involved and we believe that all should be equal members, but there is no room for complacency; the barriers are still in place. The amount of real control and involvement that disabled people have had in the work of the project has been affected by a number of familiar issues.

Access

The issue of access is just one of the barriers that we have not tackled as positively as we would have wished. Physical access to the building where Leisure Choice is based is difficult; other buildings have had to be used for our meetings. This issue is not only related to access into buildings. Inaccessible public transport systems have meant that a good deal of time and resources have gone towards enabling people to travel to and from meetings. People will remain disabled and dependent until they have access to the public transport systems which exclude them.

The lack of access that disabled people have to equipment is also significant. 'At the ATC [adult training centre] there's a new computer that none of the trainees have been shown how to use. There are some computers we can use but there's one special one we can't use – it's just for the staff.' Before working with the Leisure Choice group I did not appreciate the range of powerful tools that service workers can employ. Telephones, photo-copiers, word processors and computers are all there at our fingertips, allowing us to gain and share information. We have to allow disabled people access to this equipment, if we are serious about them taking part in the planning and evaluation of services. 'We've got the equipment down here at the training centre but the only people who have the knowledge of how to use it are the staff. We have had the chance of training courses but we get the information too late.' Not only does the specialist equipment have to be made available to disabled people; training and advice on how to use the equipment should also be provided. Perhaps if people were given access to this equipment they would find that they were able to spend their time in the centres a little more positively. As one group member said: 'What I'd like to see happening is this room set up with the computer and using it regularly to type up the notes from our meetings.'

My role: the professional person

I am not able to say that the steering group has achieved fair and equal representation of all its members. That is what we are working towards. As a non-disabled worker, or 'professional', I have been learning about releasing control of the work.

Throughout the development of the project I have had to step back and take an honest look at my way of working. As workers in the 'caring services' we need to ask ourselves certain questions: are we enabling and supporting people to take control of their own lives or are we disabling, taking the control for ourselves? We may not personally be responsible for many of the barriers in society that disabled people we work with have to face. We are, however, part of that society and it is essential for individual workers to examine their own working practices. I have certainly been challenged on a number of occasions. An example of this came during the disability awareness course. The trainers introduced an exercise that I believed was too complicated for a number of people in the group to understand. I spoke to one of the trainers about my concerns and was told not to worry. I sat back expecting to be proved right and watched as people joined in the discussion and debate. How often have I excluded people from discussion and decision-making because I believed the information was beyond their understanding? Of the many exercises we took part in during the course, this was in fact one which members of the group remembered most clearly. I remain the person with the control, the information, the equipment, the money. On a course recently someone suggested I had been talking too much and should be told to keep quiet. The reply was: 'No fear, she's the boss.' Just when I thought I was being so enabling.

Our aim should be to foster more equal relationships with disabled people. A way forward is to listen and value the opinions of disabled people we work with and to seek the informed opinion of groups of disabled people. We don't always have to agree; we should be open to both receive and give positive comment and challenges.

Time

The time available for the work of Leisure Choice was not enough to guarantee that no short-cuts were taken in terms of involving the steering group members in all parts of the project's work. Allowing a realistic amount of time is crucial if we are serious about asking people who are disabled to make informed decisions and choices.

People need time to learn about how organisations work and the way in which services are set up. Workers know the important information which enables them to take part in discussions, meetings and decision-making; disabled people need time to gain access to that information. The role of the non-disabled workers should be to allow the information to be passed on and to give support to people who want to develop skills and confidence to challenge the barriers they face.

More time is needed for meetings to make sure that everyone has the opportunity to participate fully. 'I do try to understand everyone in the group but I feel like I'm holding people up,' said one group member.

It should be made clear that if anyone does not understand what someone has said they should always ask, and that this is meeting time well spent. 'Like Graham, when you have spent a day with him you understand every word that he says.'

Summary

'It's a pity it's just been a year. If I could set something up in Northumberland it would be a good thing. But we weren't thinking about having professional people in our group – we might have a few to help us out but we'll pick our own.' When Sharon said this I immediately asked her if she would pick me. I asked because I wanted to know if I would be in a job if Sharon was in a position to employ me. How would the caring services react if we knew that our performance was being evaluated by the people we were serving, and if disabled people were always involved in deciding: which issues they felt were most important; how the money should be spent; and who they wanted to employ to support them to get the job done. These things should be happening if service organisations were really concerned with consultation, offering choices and quality services.

Acknowledgement

With thanks to steering group members: David Atkin, Jackie Beard, Barry Coombs, Sharon Harrington, David Knight, Kevin Pringle, Timothy Raine and Eileen Shell.

Reference

Denziloe, J. (1990) 'The Playtrac model of staff training', in McConkey, R. and McGiuley, P. (eds) *Innovations in Leisure and Recreation for People with a Mental Handicap*, Brothers of Charity Services, Chorley, Lancashire.

3.8

The dual experience of ageing with a disability

Gerry Zarb

Introduction

The population as a whole in Britain is an ageing one (Thompson, 1987). There is also a close association between old age and disability (Townsend, 1979; Martin *et al.*, 1988). However, the 'ageing population' is a far from homogeneous group; there are important differences between particular subgroups which need to be acknowledged and understood. One particular group of people which has been more or less completely overlooked are those who became disabled in childhood or adulthood, and who are now ageing with a disability.

Only within the last 20 to 25 years has there even been an identifiable cohort of ageing disabled adults; first, life expectancy for many types of impairments prior to this was low; second, people who became disabled as a result of injuries received during the Second World War are now entering older age; third, many children and young adults disabled as a result of the polio epidemics of the late 1940s and early 1950s are now in their 50s or older. Added to this, there are an unknown number of people with various impairments who may have been disabled since the 1920s and have simply been overlooked by researchers, policy-makers and service-providers alike.

Changing patterns of life expectancy and advances in medical technology, treatment and rehabilitation also mean that the size of this subgroup of older disabled people is increasing. While there are no completely accurate figures, the two national disability surveys carried out by the Office of Population Censuses and Surveys (OPCS) in the late 1960s and 1980s indicate that there are alive today just under 100,000 people aged 50 or older who have been disabled for 20 or more years, and that around another 200,000 will reach this age within the next 10 to 20 years (Harris, 1971; Martin *et al.*, 1988).

This increase in the numbers of people who are ageing with a disability is also differentially distributed according to both gender and race. Although the prevalence of a few types of physical impairments is higher among males, many of the largest subgroups of older disabled people contain more women than men. The most recent national survey estimates that there are a total of 3.6 million disabled women in Britain, compared with 2.5 million disabled men. Among those aged 75 or more, women outnumber men by a ratio of nearly 2½ to 1 (Martin *et al.*, 1988).

The present population of Britain also includes approximately 2.4 million people of minority ethnic origin. Again, there are no national figures but a number of local studies indicate a high incidence of certain physical and sensory impairments amongst black and Asian communities; the high incidence of sickle cell anaemia and thalassaemia among people of Caribbean and Mediterranean origin is also well known. (Wandsworth Council for Community Relations, 1978; Department of Health and Social Security Asian Working Group, 1983; Keeble, 1984; Shankland Cox, 1984). In addition, there are an unknown number of refugees from various countries, several of whom may have impairments associated with war, torture and so on. Largely because of migration patterns, the non-white population is also younger than the white population; for example, around 4 per cent (approximately 97,000) of the black and Asian populations had reached retirement age by 1986, compared with around 10 per cent of the white population (Patel, 1990). So, although it is not possible to state any overall figures, the prevalence of ageing with a disability among minority ethnic communities is also likely to increase significantly over the next decade and beyond.

Locating the dual experience of ageing with a disability within existing conceptual frameworks

Next to nothing is known about the experience of ageing with a long-term disability. While there may be some overlap between the experiences of people who are ageing with a disability and other ageing groups, there are also likely to be important differences. Among those ageing with a disability there are also likely to be differing experiences and concerns structured around race and gender.

In order to further an understanding of the various dimensions to ageing with a disability, we need a conceptual framework which takes account of the dual experience of both ageing and disability. While there are numerous conceptual models relating both to ageing and to disability, the problem lies in attempting to link the two together.

Early approaches to the study of ageing attempted to explain how people react to the ageing process in psychological or behavioural terms (Cumming and Henry, 1961; Neugarten, 1968). Such approaches have been criticised for failing to take account of external or structural factors which influence people's experience of ageing. More recent approaches have focused on issues such as the distribution of income, housing, access to services, and the needs and experiences of different groups of older people according to class, gender and race (Townsend, 1981; Norman, 1985; Phillipson and Walker, 1986; Arber and Ginn, 1991).

Neither of these two basic approaches provides a completely satisfactory framework for understanding the experience of ageing. Both share one major drawback: generality. Consequently, more recent approaches have placed greater emphasis on the qualitative study of individual experiences and needs. The concept of the 'biographical career' is central to this approach as it allows consideration of the uniqueness of individual biographies, the meanings which individuals attach to the concepts of age and ageing, and how these change over time (Johnson, 1978; Fairhurst and Lightup, 1982).

Clearly, this emphasis on subjective experience and meaning can help to further an understanding of ageing with a disability. However, the biographies of people who are both ageing and disabled will incorporate both the 'ageing career' and the 'disability career'. Prior experience of disability will be an important factor shaping people's perceptions of ageing, while their experience of ageing will also influence changing perceptions of disability.

We have used the concepts of 'biographical careers' and 'significant life events' in our research on the experience of long-term disability, and ageing with a disability (Oliver et al., 1988; Zarb et al., 1990; Zarb and Oliver, 1991, 1992). First, we suggested that the occurrence of disability as a significant event in an individual's life is only a starting-point for understanding the practical and personal consequences of living with a disability. Other factors, such as the social environment, material resources and – most importantly – the meanings which individuals attach to situations and events, are also essential to the development of an adequate conceptual framework.

Second, just as the onset of disability cannot be seen as a one-off life event, neither can the intervening impact of ageing be considered as a self-contained life event, or even a series of discrete life events. Thus, the concept of career is essential to an understanding of the impact of ageing on the experience of long-term disability as it allows consideration of how people's subjective experiences are shaped over time.

Building on these basic premises, we constructed a conceptual framework which integrates the dual experience of disability and ageing in what we have termed the 'disability/ageing career' (see Figure 1). Basically, the 'disability/ ageing career' is viewed as a series of physical, emotional and social processes punctuated by various 'triggering events' likely to occur in older age. For example, periods of ill-health, retirement, changes in family circumstances or bereavement, all of which can trigger a range of personal, physical and social consequences – such as an increased need for support. The consequences of such triggering events will usually be mediated by certain 'predisposing factors' (for example family circumstances), which may themselves have personal or social consequences.

The personal, social and physical consequences of ageing will, in turn, lead to both 'objective outcomes' and 'subjective outcomes' which relate to the meaning of such experiences to the individual. These outcomes can be either positive or negative, although, obviously, an individual's total life experience will usually be characterised by a mixture of both.

These outcomes will also be very much dependent on the personal, social and material resources available to the individual. In particular the level of social support, as well as financial and housing resources. However, these

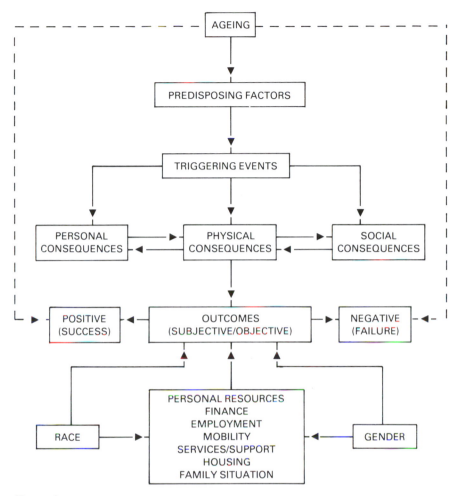

Figure 1

resources cannot be viewed separately from the meanings and values attached to them by the individual.

It is also important to keep in mind that both the objective and subjective dimensions of the disability/ageing career will be shaped by race and gender. First, social and material resources are differentially distributed among the ageing population (differential access to pensions, for example). Second, the ways in which disability is experienced subjectively throughout the disability career will be mediated by both race and gender. It follows, therefore, that such prior experience will also have a crucial influence on the subjective experience of ageing, and the values, expectations and meanings that people attach to any changes in their lives.

Drawing on the findings from three original research projects, the rest of this paper will illustrate some of the main features of the disability/ageing career, focusing in particular on people's subjective experiences of the ageing process and the perceived impact on their quality of life.

The first two studies examined the experiences of one particular subgroup: people with spinal cord injuries; the first (Oliver *et al.*, 1988) included 77 men who had been disabled for up to 15 years and the second included 42 men and 10 women disabled between 20 and 50 years (Zarb *et al.*, 1990; Zarb, 1991a). The third study (in progress) is examining the experiences of people with a wide variety of physical impairments or disabling illnesses, including diabetes, polio, multiple sclerosis, scoliosis, Parkinson's disease, muscular dystrophy and various forms of arthritis. The findings from this study are based on responses from 300 people (177 women and 123 men), 100 of whom have also been interviewed; this group has been disabled for between 20 and 80 years (Zarb, 1991b; Zarb and Oliver, 1991, 1992).

Physical changes/problems associated with ageing

Although the specifics vary between and within disability groups, there is a surprising degree of similarity in the kinds of physical changes experienced with ageing.

First, many people's experiences are consistent with the notion of 'premature' physical ageing; for them, ageing is characterised by a process of 'general deterioration' which appears to be more closely associated with the length of time since the onset of the impairment than with age itself. Typically, there is a noticeable 'downturn' in physical well-being and health status around 20 to 30 years from onset, regardless of chronological age.

Second, many of the physical changes that people experience are perceived as being long-term effects of their original impairments. For some groups, there are also common secondary impairments caused either by the original impairment, or the long-term effects of medical treatment or rehabilitation. The most common of these is the high incidence of arthritic and rheumatic problems; other specific examples include blindness and neuro-logical problems associated with long-term diabetes; chronic pain resulting from building up immunity to certain drugs, such as morphine (various groups); chronic respiratory problems caused by spinal deformity (scoliosis); and a variety of physiological problems coming under the heading of 'post-polio syndrome'.

Regarding the pattern of these physical changes over time, different kinds of impairments appear to have different 'trajectories', although there is also a certain degree of overlap in this. Some groups (for example people with long-term rheumatoid arthritis) typically experience a progressive deterio-ration which usually starts fairly early on in the disability career. Others (for example people with spinal injuries or polio) often experience a similar process of gradual deterioration, but only after many years of relative stability. For some, such deterioration may be increasingly progressive rather than gradual, while others (for example people with multiple sclerosis or Parkinson's disease) may also experience fluctuations between periods of deterioration and stability.

Perceptions of, and satisfaction with, the quality of life

The characteristic downturn in physical well-being and health status around 20 to 30 years from onset of impairment is often accompanied by a parallel downturn in satisfaction with the quality of life. For people who become disabled when they are young adults or when middle-aged, the first 10 to 15 years are usually marked by a steady increase in satisfaction levels, followed by declining satisfaction after 20 to 30 years (Zarb *et al.*, 1990; Zarb, 1991b).

This is also the same stage in the disability career when most of the physical consequences of the ageing process typically start to take effect. Thus, it seems that this 'downturn' in satisfaction is closely related to the perceived onset of the ageing process. For some people, satisfaction tends to rise again after around 30 years, but this is certainly not universal.

The situation for people disabled from childhood or from birth appears to be slightly different; there is the same pattern of increasing satisfaction preceding a downturn in later years, but the start of this upward trend often seems to be delayed until early adulthood. Often, negative experiences in institutions during childhood and youth play a major part in this. Further, women often describe these early experiences in noticeably more negative terms than men. Although the numbers are small, this appears to be related to women having been more likely to have lived in institutions during their childhood.

Many people describe the impact of ageing as representing the onset of a 'second disability'. Often, this realisation is quite sudden, being triggered by a particular problem or crisis. Sometimes these triggering events are related to physical ageing, but are just as likely to be related to personal changes, such as a death in the family. However, this kind of relatively sudden decline in levels of satisfaction is not necessarily permanent. Rather, while ageing is often experienced as a disruptive life event, some people find that they are able to accommodate themselves to the changes – both practical and emotional – in their lives.

Physical and emotional well-being are inextricably linked, not just in older age, but throughout the disability career. For many people, ageing is associated with a decline in emotional well-being. This can also become a vicious circle; the drain on their emotional reserves means that some people feel less able to cope physically, which, in turn, contributes to a further drain on both emotional and physical resources. On the other hand, some people with similar experiences may not view these in exclusively negative terms.

Many older disabled people may also perceive themselves as ageing more rapidly than their non-disabled contemporaries. This is closely related to perceptions of life expectancy; some people not only anticipate that they may age more quickly, but also that they may die at a younger age. Interestingly, most people's attitudes towards this appear quite accepting; often, the anticipation of dying seems to be less traumatic than dealing with the problems associated with ageing itself.

The meanings which people attach to issues such as their own mortality need to be seen in the context of perceptions of life expectancy throughout the disability career. At the time that many of the people participating in our research became disabled, life expectancy for people with various impairments was often very low. Several had been told, or simply assumed, that they would not survive adolescence, or would only live for maybe 20 or 30 years. This means that they had had a heightened awareness of their own mortality more or less throughout the disability career. At the same time, some people also said that although they were aware that they may face an early death, they also felt fortunate to have lived as long as they had. This reflects how expectations formed very early in the disability career can subsequently influence perceptions of the possible implications of ageing 20, 30 or more years later.

Ageing and independence

Perhaps the most important factor influencing changing perceptions of the quality of life among older disabled people relates to independence. Many older disabled people feel that their independence is threatened by physical and/or personal changes associated with ageing. In some cases this only extends to personal or physical independence, but for many people ageing represents a threat to their independence in the much wider sense of losing control over how they wish to live their lives. For example, several expressed concern about the possibility of having to make major changes in lifestyle, such as having more personal assistance or changing their living arrangements. Anxiety about the possibility of having to move into institutional care has a particularly strong influence on these perceptions – particularly for women.

Some people may even prefer the option of suicide or euthanasia, as such changes simply represent an unacceptable degree of compromise over how they wish to live. Others take a more philosophical view, regarding the provision of extra help as the best way of maintaining their independence, or at least avoiding any further loss of independence. On the other hand, some may never have placed such emphasis on independence in their lives, or never felt that they had very much independence in the first place. Consequently, the perceived disruptive effect of ageing may be minimal, or even non-existent.

The important common denominator is whether or not changes associated with ageing are compatible with how an individual wishes to live his or her life. It is very difficult to understand the significance and meaning of ageing without an appreciation of this crucial factor. It is also essential to place these contrasting perceptions in the context of attitudes towards independence, autonomy and responsibility that have developed throughout the disability career.

Many older disabled people perceive the achievement of independence (however they may define it) to be one of the most significant features of their lives throughout the disability career. Achieving this independence will often have taken many years and will certainly have involved a great deal of effort. Further, it is important to emphasise that 'independence' is not a fixed state, and maintaining control over their lives will often become increasingly hard as people grow older. Consequently, it is easy to see why the possibility of losing some of this control should be a source of great anxiety for many people. The fact that some see it as totally unacceptable, and view death as a preferable option, shows just how important it can be.

As stated earlier, subjective responses to ageing are also shaped by social and material resources. The availability of appropriate and acceptable support is particularly important in this context. The present structure of support provision fails to meet the needs of the majority of disabled people, let alone those who may have additional needs associated with ageing (Beardshaw, 1988; Fiedler, 1988). Consequently, many people who are ageing with a disability simply fall through the net.

When potential problems, such as lack of appropriate living options, inadequate pensions and enforced dependency on ageing carers, are added to this objective reality, it is not difficult to see why many older disabled people feel that ageing represents a threat to their independence.

Gender and race dimensions to ageing with a disability

Although practically all the issues discussed in this paper are of universal concern, it would clearly be mistaken to imply that the subjective experience of ageing is the same for men and women, or for people of different races and cultures.

Both old age and disability are dimensions of experience which are fundamentally linked to gender (Morris, 1991). Gender is also a particularly important factor in determining whether or not individuals are supported or prevented in their attempts to live independently. Because women are generally expected to take a more dependent role in society than men, disabled women face a particularly acute struggle to overcome the obstacles against them controlling their own lives, or even defining their own identities (Morris, 1989; Lonsdale, 1990).

It is not surprising, then, that many women place an even stronger emphasis on maintaining their independence in older age than men. Further, it is important to realise that many older women (disabled or not) are also supporting others. This is not to say that older men do not take on the role of 'carer', nor that the perceived threat to independence is only an issue for women. However, both of these issues are likely to be particularly important for women throughout the disability career and, consequently, are also likely to be crucial factors shaping their experience of ageing.

Practically nothing is known about the race dimension to ageing with a disability. However, what evidence there is highlights a number of ways in which – relative to older whites – black and Asian elders are disadvantaged (in income, housing, health and access to services), and are part of a minority group which clearly suffers racial discrimination. There is also considerable evidence of unmet support needs among disabled black and Asian people of all ages (Greater London Association of Disabled People, 1987; Ahmad, 1988).

This has led to the conceptualisation of older people from minority ethnic communities as being in 'double jeopardy' (Dowd and Bengtson, 1978). Class and gender are also seen as important dimensions of inequality in addition to race and age; the cumulative effect of these factors has, in turn, led to consideration of triple or 'multiple' jeopardies in describing the experience of different subgroups, particularly within the black population (Norman, 1985).

Concluding comments

If pushed too far, there is a danger that characterising people's experiences in terms of multiple jeopardies may only serve to marginalise their experiences even further and divert attention from common concerns and issues. Many older disabled people feel that their needs – and even their existence – has been overlooked. While the particular experiences shaping these perceptions may vary, there is also a considerable degree of similarity to the objective situation in which many disabled people find themselves as they age.

Clearly, there will also be some overlap between the experiences and concerns of different groups within the ageing population, and between disabled people of all ages. However, this paper has attempted to demonstrate that there is a whole range of dimensions to the experience of ageing with a disability, and also that both the subjective and objective reality of ageing can be understood only in the context of prior experience. A conceptual framework based on biography, identity and meaning is, therefore, essential to the development of an understanding of the dual experience of ageing with a disability.

References

Ahmad, A. (1988) *Social Services for Black People*, National Institute for Social Work: London.

Arber, S. and Ginn, J. (1991) *Gender and Later Life: a Sociological Analysis of Resources and Constraints*, Sage, London.

Beardshaw, V. (1988) *Last on the List: Community Services for People with Physical Disabilities*, King's Fund, London.

Cumming, E. and Henry, W. (1961) *Growing Old: the Process of Disengagement*, Basic Books, New York.

Department of Health and Social Security Asian Working Group (1983) *Report of the Stop Rickets Campaign*, Save the Children Fund, London.

Dowd, J. and Bengtson, V. (1978) 'Ageing in minority populations: an examination of the double jeopardy hypothesis', *Journal of Gerontology*, Vol. 33.

Fairhurst, E. and Lightup, R. (1982) 'Growing older: issues in the use of qualitative research', in Taylor, R. and Gilmore, A. (eds) *Current Trends in British Gerontology*, Gower, Aldershot.

Fiedler, B. (1988) *Living Options Lottery: Housing and Support Services for People with Severe Physical Disabilities*, Prince of Wales Advisory Group on Disability, London.

Greater London Association of Disabled People (1987) *Disability and Ethnic Minority Communities: a Study in Three London Boroughs*, GLAD, London.

Harris, A. (1971) *Handicapped and Impaired in Great Britain*, HMSO, London.

Johnson, M. (1978) 'That was your life: a biographical approach to later life', in Carver, V. and Liddiard, P. (eds) *An Ageing Population: a Reader and Sourcebook*, Hodder and Stoughton, Sevenoaks/The Open University, Milton Keynes.

Keeble, P. (1984) *Disability and Minority Ethnic Groups: a Factsheet of Issues and Initiatives*, Royal Association of Disability and Rehabilitation, London.

Lonsdale, S. (1990) *Women and Disability*, Macmillan, London.

Martin, J., Meltzer, H. and Elliot, D. (1988) *OPCS Surveys of Disability in Great Britain, Report 1: The Prevalence of Disability Among Adults*, HMSO, London.

Morris, J. (ed.) (1989) *Able Lives: Women's Experience of Paralysis*, The Women's Press, London.

Morris, J. (1991) *Pride Against Prejudice: Transforming Attitudes to Disability*, The Women's Press, London.

Neugarten, B. (ed.) (1968) *Middle Age and Ageing: a Reader in Social Psychology*, University of Chicago Press.

Norman, A. (1985) *Triple Jeopardy: Growing Old in a Second Homeland*, Centre for Policy on Ageing, London.

Oliver, M., Zarb, G., Moore, M., Silver, J. and Salisbury, V. (1988) *Walking into Darkness: the Experience of Spinal Cord Injury*, Macmillan, London.

Patel, N. (1990) *A Race Apart*, King's Fund, London.

Phillipson, C. and Walker, A. (eds) (1986) *Ageing and Social Policy: a Critical Assessment*, Gower, Aldershot.

Shankland Cox (1984) *Initial Demographic Study*, Royal National Institute for the Blind, London.

Thompson, J. (1987) 'Ageing of the population: contemporary trends and issues', *Population Trends*, No. 50, Winter.

Townsend, P. (1979) *Poverty in the United Kingdom*, Penguin, London.

Townsend, P. (1981) 'The structured dependency of the elderly: the creation of social policy in the twentieth century', *Ageing and Society*, Vol.1, No. 1, pp. 5–28.

Wandsworth Council for Community Relations (1978) *Asians and the Health Service*, Campaign for Racial Equality, London.

Zarb, G. (1991a) 'Creating a supportive environment: meeting the needs of people who are ageing with a disability', in Oliver, M. (ed.) *Social Work: Disabled People and Disabling Environments*, Jessica Kingsley, London.

Zarb, G. (1991b) 'Forgotten but not gone: the experience of ageing with disability', paper presented to British Society of Gerontology Annual Conference, UMIST, Manchester.

Zarb, G. and Oliver, M. (1991) *Ageing with a Disability: the Dimensions of Need – Preliminary Findings*, Thames Polytechnic, London.

Zarb, G. and Oliver, M. (1992) *Ageing with a Disability: the Dimensions of Need*, Thames Polytechnic, London.

Zarb, G., Oliver, M. and Silver, J. (1990) *Ageing with Spinal Cord Injury: the Right to a Supportive Environment?* Thames Polytechnic/Spinal Injuries Association, London.

SECTION 4: IN CHARGE OF SUPPORT AND HELP

4.1

The crafting of good clients

Ken Davis

Becoming disabled brings us into some odd relationships with people. One that most of us are familiar with is the doctor–patient relationship. When we're in it, we play a role, the sick role. We're expected to play it whether we're sick or not. Most of us know that it is in our best interests to play it – we've never been taught the lines, but we soon catch on to what we're supposed to say.

Soon enough, we're bumping into the disability 'professionals'. There are lots of them, they have different titles and work for different agencies, and often we get a bit confused as to who they are. They learn about disability by doing courses and reading books. Some of them are given diplomas for doing this, so they can then prove how expert they are in disability matters. These paper qualifications help them get jobs and make careers out of our needs.

Sometimes these 'professionals', such as occupational therapists and social workers, call us their 'clients'. Even people who help us to keep our homes clean such as home helps, or people who work in day centres, also call us their 'clients'. This confuses us even more.

Most of us probably thought that becoming a client was a matter of personal choice. Like going to a solicitor if we can afford it – or if we can't afford not to. Solicitors, accountants, consultants of all kinds, they too are regarded as professional people – but should we use their services, we have the choice, we decide. If they don't come up to scratch, we can complain to their professional body and seek redress. Or we take our custom elsewhere.

But the situation with disability 'professionals' is different. Well, yes, we can complain about their performance and we may or may not get redress via their employers. But if we decide to take our custom elsewhere – well, unless we're very well-heeled, it's best to forget it. To all intents and purposes, these denizens of the disability industry are the gatekeepers to the services we need. We either go through them, or do without. Take it or leave it.

This paper was first published in *Coalition*, September 1990, pp. 5–9.

No wonder many of us get confused. We grow up to expect that, if we become a client of some professional service or other, that it is a voluntary thing, something we do as a matter of choice. But, in terms of disability services, the choice available to us amounts to little more than Hobson's choice. The law gives local authorities the power to decide and they, in turn, define the kind of workers they want. Various schools, universities and other training establishments churn out the 'professionals'. Together they decide what we get.

Whether we're happy or unhappy about this situation is merely academic. Going over the top of our heads is well-rooted and par for the course. Despite the growth of the disabled people's movement these paper professionals still think it quite normal to sit down round the table and decide what's best for us. So it is quite natural that, along with all their other decisions, they should define the nature of their relationship to us.

Given that this is the case, it is interesting and instructive to reflect on why it is that these people have decided to call us their 'clients'. I mean, they know just as well as disabled people what is usually understood in terms of the professional–client relationship. So why have these workers been so keen to graft their ambitions on to terminology, the Latin root of which lies in patrician–plebian; master–slave; patron–dependant subservience?

One possibility is that they do actually see themselves as superior – as opposed to seeing us as inferior or helpless. Maybe they do think of themselves as being professional in the same, or similar, sense to that which is commonly understood. Or maybe they have forgotten that they are involved in a relationship, and that the consequence of setting themselves up as 'professionals' automatically cast us in the role of 'client'.

Hearing some of these people explaining the terminology can be equally interesting. For example, they may say that 'client' is a nice easy word, which avoids the anonymity of 'person' or 'disabled person'. Or that you can't use 'person with a physical impairment' all the time because the phrase is too long! Or that 'client' gives a disabled person some dignity, some status. That one is particularly pleasing, as it conveys the idea of equality wrapped up in more recent connotations which assign customer status to both patron and client. A very neat bit of professional sleight of speech, suggesting equivalence in choice and control, even though they and we know that the reality is very different.

When you look more closely at this apparently innocent use of words, it is easy to see that it is all part of a very carefully engineered process. Just how consistent it is with the prevailing relationship of disabled people to our able-bodied society comes clear when you look at some of the many questions which can be raised. For example, how did these so-called professionals come to get involved with us – and what is at stake for them in the way they define their relationship to us?

The first question begs many others – but those of us who are familiar with some of the history of the disabled people's movement will recognise that today's 'disability professionals' are on a career path which has been carefully and painstakingly carved out by generations of their predecessors.

Aware that society has been constructed by able-bodied people in ways which serve and perpetuate their own interests, these people have used our consequential marginalisation and dependence not as a starting-point for developing with us a struggle for social change and equal opportunities, but as a handy and convenient fact to justify the development of all the inappropriate disability services with which we are now so familiar.

This disingenuous acceptance of the status quo, pregnant with career opportunities, is basic to those who feed on the effects of social problems rather than engage in the struggle to deal with causes. It is a well-established form of parasitism, resting on bits of biblical dogma such as 'the poor always ye have with you' (John, xii.8). The updated version of the old Poor Law, which sustains most of today's welfare professionals, depends for its continuity on such counsels of despair. It has become, let's face it, a nice little earner.

Nowadays, these people have got it made. As a body, they have influenced government and secured their future so effectively that they and their agencies are written by name into the Statute Book. For our part, the barrier-ridden, able-bodied world of inaccessible streets, buildings, transport and information – coupled with limited services of personal assistance – has severely inhibited the extent of disabled people's own influence. Nevertheless, our movement is growing rapidly, as a reaction against these oppressive social conditions. But we have yet to eclipse the influence of these professional disability parasites. Although the day will inevitably come, we have yet to secure legislation appropriate to our real needs.

At this juncture, our lives are still substantially in their hands. They still determine most decisions and their practical outcomes. Their control over the decision-making process has been carefully reinforced by ensuring that the climate of ideas which surround the making of disability policy is also under their influence. Which brings us back once more to the web of words they have spun to entrap us.

Effective control of the climate of ideas requires a thoughtful approach to the choice of words. This is why the selection of 'professional' and 'client' can never be dismissed by disabled people as irrelevant or innocuous. There is, to address the second question, much at stake for the disability industry, in terms of jobs and status, pay and conditions, and career opportunities, if they begin to lose their grip.

To obviate this, they need to contain the idea of their dominance and our dependence within a coherent philosophical framework designed to encapsulate, reinforce and sustain the interests of the industry. Such a framework needs to be flexible enough to move with the times, keep abreast of public sympathy, but ensure that their control over our lives remains essentially untouched. Thus, it has come to be that the disability 'professionals' and us, their 'clients', live within the carefully crafted, mechanical embrace of 'care'.

Today's generation of 'professionals' are packing this artificial ethos with endearing little catchprases such as 'community care' 'caring professionals' and the soon-to-be-foisted-on-us 'care managers'. The idea of 'care' has been carefully nurtured until it has become the hallmark of solid acceptability, the key to political creditworthiness, and the disability industry's SDI designed to shield their programmes of social control from criticism.

It is an increasing obligation on our movement to challenge both the mythology of care and the reality of their manipulation of disability policy and decision-making. Part of the process of gaining control over our lives involves us in resisting their attempts to box us in the pigeonhole of 'client' – and to expose their self-styled, self-seeking efforts to elevate their second-hand knowledge about disability into a 'profession'.

The disabled people's movement has already done much solid work in redefining disability and in creating the basis of a new hegemony of ideas which rests on direct experience of the problems we face in our daily lives. We have carried some workers in the disability industry along with us. In supporting our own active participation in, and control over our own affairs, such people are giving us the right kind of help. However, for the majority of the 'professionals', despite their need to cling to power, their careful crafting of our dependence is disintegrating before their very eyes.

4.2

Experiences of disabled health and caring professionals

Sally French

It is frequently argued that having personal experience of an event gives a dimension of knowledge that others cannot fully share. Childbirth is an example of this, where mothers may assume that neither men nor childless women can fully appreciate the experience. Various self-help groups have been formed because of dissatisfaction with the help that professionals provide or a realisation that such help is limited. Many believe that minority group members have better insight, more commitment and greater rapport with similarly affected people than does the general population (Shearer, 1981) and that people with extensive professional training do not necessarily help those who are disabled (McKnight, 1981).

Disabled people are widely discriminated against in most types of employment including the health and caring professions. Chinnery (1991) points out that there are far fewer people employed in the caring services in the United Kingdom than the recommended 3 per cent, and that most of them manage to 'pass' as able-bodied. In a content analysis of the career literature of 26 health and caring professions and occupations (French, 1986a) it was found that disabled people were never specifically invited to apply, yet 10 of these occupations explicitly sought candidates with the ability to empathise and understand ill and disabled people. The radiography profession, for example, was seeking people who displayed tact and empathy (College of Radiographers, 1985) and the audiology technician was required to have 'a sympathetic and understanding personality' (British Society of Audiology, n.d.). These are qualities which disabled people, by virtue of their experiences, are likely to possess. Burnfield (1985), a psychiatrist with multiple sclerosis, states: 'I believe that having MS has helped me to become more sensitive to the needs of others and that it has enhanced my skills as a healer. I often think of myself as being doubly qualified, firstly as a patient and secondly as a doctor – the order is important.' Similarly, a blind physiotherapist said: 'The frustrations of disability are much the same inasmuch as it is a physical limitation on your life and you think "if only" . . . Having to put up with that for

---

This paper is an edited version of S. French (1988) 'Experiences of disabled health and caring professionals', *Sociology of Health and Illness*, Vol. 10, No. 2, pp. 170–88.

Table 1

	Number
Professions	
Medicine	4
Physiotherapy	7
Occupational therapy	3
Social work	4
Nurse/nurse tutor	1
Prosthetics	3
Counselling	2
Occupational therapy/physiotherapy	1
	—
	25
Impairments	
Visual impairment	4
Cerebral palsy	1
Cerebral palsy/visual impairment	1
Cerebral palsy/hearing impairment	1
Lower limb amputation	4
Tetraplegia	1
Multiple sclerosis	1
Epilepsy	1
Ileostomy	1
Achondroplasia	1
Hearing disability	3
Shoulder/cervical abnormalities	1
Recurrent dislocation of patella	1
Rheumatoid arthritis	1
Ankylosing spondylitis	1
Spina bifida	1
Liver disease	1
	—
	25

so long I know ever so well what patients mean when they mention those kinds of difficulties' (French, 1990).

Most of the overt justification for the exclusion of disabled people from the health and caring professions is in terms of the disabled people themselves. Their presumed inability to cope, the adverse effect they are presumed to have on patients and the assumption of proneness to accidents (Browning, 1980; Chickadonz, 1983; Libman, 1983). Others believe, however, that disabled people have unique assets to offer these professions (Hutchins, 1978; Biehn, 1979; Gavin, 1980; Bueche, 1983; Turner, 1984; Wainapel, 1987; O'Hare and Thomson, 1991). Negative attitudes are sometimes rationalised and disguised as concern, emphasising that disabled people may damage themselves by undertaking such demanding work (Safilios-Rothschild, 1976; French, 1986a).

To my knowledge there has been no research specifically addressing the experiences and perceptions of people who have become health and caring professionals despite being substantially disabled. It is hoped that the following study goes a small way towards describing their experiences and situation, as well as highlighting what the inclusion of disabled professionals reveals about the orthodox professional/client relationship.

Method

In this study 24 disabled people currently employed or training in the health and caring professions were interviewed, and one person, who was working abroad, sent a written account of her experiences using the interview schedule as a guide. The sample consisted of nine men and 16 women and represented eight professions and 17 types of impairment; two people had dual qualifications. All but two people were accepted for training as disabled people, the others acquiring their impairments during training; 10 people had trained within the last five years and 14 within the last 10 years. The professions and impairments represented were as shown in Table 1.

Findings

Perceived advantages and disadvantages of being disabled

All the disabled professionals could see advantages relating to being disabled in the work context. The most common response was that they felt better able to empathise with their patients and clients and understand the social and psychological implications of disability.

Some of the professionals believed that they had greater patience than their able-bodied colleagues, and often pointed out that their patients and clients had greater confidence in them and were more likely to take their advice. One person said: 'Many clients thought they'd get a slightly better deal through having a blind social worker because they thought I was having to pull out all the stops to prove that I was good and therefore they would get a spin-off.' Most people felt that they could empathise with and understand those with a similar impairment best. A partially deaf therapist stated: 'I've got a lot more patience with deaf people and I get more out of them. The doctors say "Forget it, ask a relative" but I speak to them.'

All the deaf people found the ability to lip-read helpful. One mentioned her skill at communicating with patients who had had a tracheostomy and another found that she could lip-read patients when nobody else could understand them. One spoke sign language fluently and was sometimes used as an interpreter. Most of the disabled professionals believed that they had more knowledge of disability than their colleagues. A prosthetist who had a lower limb amputation himself stated: 'They [patients] want to pick your brain for every bit of knowledge they can get. They're very interested to find out how you coped.' He found that he was able to identify the causes of patients' problems, especially the small, less obvious ones which other prosthetists might miss or regard as trivial.

Many reported that their patients and clients frequently commented on the advantage of the disability from their own point of view. A prosthetist with an amputation himself remarked, 'Patients say, "You've got one, you know what I mean."' Similarly a doctor said: 'Very many people have told me they can talk to me because I know what it feels like to have an illness. Once you get over that hump of being accepted [for training] then you can use your disability.'

Many people found that being disabled helped to break down professional barriers. A deaf therapist said: 'They don't see me as a health professional who knows it all, but who doesn't really understand; they see me as a disabled person.' A doctor found his patients' interest in his electric wheelchair useful in this respect, and a social worker found that his guide dog helped: 'Even when there's an awful atmosphere he's wagging his tail. He's definitely an ice-breaker.'

Several people spoke of the advantage of needing help from their patients or clients. A counsellor explained, 'By me needing help it's actually saying "This is a partnership".' Similarly a blind social worker commented: 'I'm able to say to my clients, "I'll help you, but there are certain ways in which you are going to have to help me", and the client doesn't feel totally taken over or totally worthless.'

Some people mentioned that they acted as models to their patients. A counsellor said that many of her clients would say, 'If you can do it, so can I', and a physiotherapist found that the misconception that all physiotherapists are very fit helped because her patients assumed that this applied to her even though she was disabled. Several people mentioned that fellow students had learned a great deal about many aspects of disability through having them in the peer group.

Many people felt that the advantages of being disabled not only cancelled out any disadvantages there might be but actually outweighed them. A doctor commented: 'MS has been something I've used. Having MS has been an added dimension in my training, in my understanding of people, and in the development of my expertise and skills.' And a prosthetist said: 'You have a great understanding of their problems because no matter how good a prosthetist is, if he's got two legs he falls short of really knowing what it's like.' However, two of the disabled professionals firmly believed that being disabled gave them no additional insight into other people's disabilities, and one congenitally disabled person said she had no special understanding of acquired disability.

Some people pointed out the advantages of their work from a personal point of view. Several physiotherapists mentioned that the active nature of the job benefited them physically and a number of people with sensory impairments believed that the nature of the work prevented them from becoming isolated. A profoundly deaf therapist said: 'I do feel that if I didn't have this type of job where I'm meeting different people every day I would withdraw very quickly into myself.'

Many people had been asked to counsel patients or clients who were similarly disabled or to demonstrate their ability to cope. Many others helped their patients and clients informally, especially if they appeared anxious. Several people said that they had been asked to lecture to a wide range of students and colleagues on the subject of their particular disability, or disability in general. A number of the disabled professionals were actively involved in disability issues. Several had written books and articles and others were involved in voluntary work. Some had given radio talks and one had founded a society for people with his own impairment.

In contrast, a few people pointed out the disadvantages that could arise as a result of being disabled when interacting with patients or clients. One blind person found lack of non-verbal communication a problem, though others felt able to compensate and even viewed blindness as helpful in some situations. For example, a social worker felt that clients could speak more openly to him because they knew he could not recognise them in other contexts, and a counsellor reported that her clients would sometimes say that they could speak more openly knowing that she could not see them. A few people found that being disabled had the effect of trivialising patients' problems. This could be a disadvantage but sometimes served as a motivator. A disabled doctor reported that patients would say, 'I'm off work with a sore knee and there you are working on your crutches.'

Another doctor found that his severe disability inhibited psychiatric patients from discussing their problems, and an occupational therapist found that elderly confused patients occasionally lacked confidence in her but she managed the situation by reassuring them and immediately focusing attention back on them. The prosthetists with amputations noted that patients could be discouraged by seeing them cope so well. They would sometimes say, 'If only I could walk like you.' The prosthetists were, however, acutely aware of this problem and were very careful never to compare themselves with their patients.

Access to training

Of the 23 disabled professionals who had been accepted for training as disabled people, eight reported that their entry qualifications were better than average, and five thought that this had been a major factor in their acceptance for training. A further eight people said that they had been helped to gain access to training by an influential person. Such people were either doctors of high status who knew the individual personally, or someone on the selection panel with particular knowledge of or interest in disability; for example, a person interviewing a blind candidate had had a visually impaired son. Twelve people felt that their acceptance for training had been strongly influenced by one of these two factors. In addition a doctor mentioned the advantage of his privileged background and several people indicated that they came from medical families.

All but one person had revealed that they were disabled before interview. Several, especially those with relatively hidden disabilities, were uncertain of the wisdom of this and spoke of being in a dilemma over the issue. A profoundly deaf person felt that it was best to reveal her disability after contact had been made because of the 'funny ideas' people have about deafness.

Of the 23 health and caring professionals who had been accepted for training as disabled people, eight had experienced difficulty. An occupational therapist stated: 'It didn't matter what I said, they said I couldn't cope', and a physiotherapist recalled that: 'His parting words were "Nobody will accept you as a physio, no school's going to accept you."' Interestingly she was later accepted by the very person who said this. Several people mentioned that getting as far as the interview was the main problem. A counsellor concluded that professionals 'Have conditioned themselves to believing that the disabled person is the person who should be helped rather than the helper.' It must be emphasised, however, that the majority of the disabled professionals, 15 of the 23, had experienced no problems regarding their acceptance for training.

Attitudes of tutors

Some people had experienced negative attitudes from their tutors. The most common complaint was a general lack of adaptation of teaching strategy to meet their needs. A physiotherapist recalled: 'They weren't obstructive, but they didn't go out of their way to be helpful either.' And a deaf therapist said: 'I couldn't follow the lectures at all, yet I didn't feel I could keep saying, "I'm deaf, will you look at me?"'

Some felt that they were viewed in terms of being disabled while others mentioned that their tutors lacked confidence in them. Several blind people complained of the excessive concern over their inability to make eye contact with clients and the difficulty they had convincing teaching staff that they could cope.

A doctor who acquired his impairment during training felt unable to confide in the staff. He stated: 'I was very frightened that if I had a disease like that they might suggest that I wasn't able to continue the training and that I wouldn't qualify. I felt if I mentioned them [the symptoms] they'd think I was skiving or malingering or being a hypochondriac or neurotic, and I wasn't going to be labelled as those things.' Similarly, a physiotherapist said: 'I had to try and keep a brave face on it and not let on. I thought it might affect my career, they might just chuck me out.'

Only two of the 25 disabled professionals were given substantial concessions during their training. Some people were openly informed that there would be no special help. A deaf therapist said: 'They felt that if I wanted to be on the course, I'd got to manage the same as everyone else. The foreign students got more help.' Their feelings about concessions were, however, mixed. A blind person remarked: 'If someone said to me "You'd better not do this placement" then I'd rather walk to Australia on my hands than admit that I couldn't.' Despite all these problems, only six people failed to complete their courses in the minimum possible time.

Twelve of the disabled professionals could recall negative attitudes from their tutors, although they all related instances of positive attitudes too. The remaining 13 regarded the attitudes of their tutors as either neutral or good. A physiotherapist said that she could not recall any aggravation at any level, and an occupational therapist said: 'It didn't matter what problems I had, I just had to go to them and they'd say "OK, there's a way round it."'

Employment

The attitudes of colleagues were reported as being overwhelmingly good, although a few people mentioned a certain lack of understanding, saying that their colleagues tended to forget or deny that they were disabled, which could create difficulties.

Both during training and after qualifying some people said that they had been encouraged by senior colleagues to work with disabled people or in areas of medicine of low prestige. A blind person was accepted for a post on the condition that initially he would work with blind clients. A counsellor commented: 'They always assumed I'd do disability counselling; they were hanging a label round my neck.' A physiotherapist was asked, 'Don't you think you should be working with the young chronic sick?' and an occupational therapist was advised to work in psychiatry. After successfully qualifying, two people were advised by members of their own profession to do full-time voluntary work.

Some people decided to work with those having the same type of impairment as themselves. This could lead to suspicion: two people complained that colleagues thought they might 'over-identify' and therefore lack objectivity. Most people, however, had met with very positive attitudes at work. A deaf therapist commented: 'I depend a little on the staff but they never seem to mind, they never force me into anything.' Only three people reported any instances of negative attitudes from patients or clients.

Just four of the disabled professionals had had difficulty in finding work. However, a few had met with negative attitudes in the process. At her first interview in a large London teaching hospital, an occupational therapist was told: 'I must be perfectly honest, I don't see any point in showing you round.' One problem encountered was the expectation in some of these professions that newly qualified staff should 'rotate' to different medical specialties thereby gaining varied experience, a practice not possible for all the disabled professionals. Some people observed that working in senior posts was easier. A deaf person spoke extensively of the advantages of being in charge. She explained: 'I'm the boss and I delegate what I can't do. I'm in control and I know what's going on; all communication comes through me.'

Many people felt that in order to cope, both during training and at work, it was necessary to work harder and be more determined; they spoke of a need to 'prove' themselves. Others had come to the conclusion, however, that these feelings originated from within themselves: a blind person had started to ask himself, 'To whom am I proving what?'

Where possible, people had tended to specialise early. They tried to find work where they could function well; for example, a deaf person said she would avoid a position which involved treating patients in groups and would never work in a very large hospital. However, people with the same type of impairment had differing views concerning the suitability or unsuitability of various areas of work. This variation seemed to be due both to the severity of the impairment and to personality factors; it would therefore be simplistic and unwise to make generalisations based entirely on impairment.

Fifteen of the disabled professional were restricted in the type of work they could do. For example, the doctor who used crutches said that he would find surgery difficult and could not visit patients at home because of access problems. However, by choosing their specialties and places of work carefully, most people reported that they could fulfil all of their work obligations.

Conclusion

This research indicates that the majority of the disabled professionals had, in the main, received positive treatment from colleagues, clients and patients during training and at work. A sizable minority, however, had experienced some degree of negative discrimination as a result either of work structures or of their colleagues' attitudes and lack of understanding. Most of these problems had occurred when people were attempting to gain access to training and during training.

There is much evidence to suggest that disability may be just one attribute which is considered undesirable in members of the health and caring professions; race and class discrimination are well documented (Young, 1981; Watkins, 1987; Baxter, 1988) and gender discrimination is also marked (Young, 1981). In addition French (1986b) found that various characteristics which go against the stereotyped image of the physiotherapist are stigmatised by that profession; for example, to be very overweight was considered more of a barrier than blindness or needing to use a wheelchair. The social acceptability of a disability may, therefore, be more important than the limitations it may give rise to. But not all professionals subscribe to the view that disabled people are unsuitable as health professionals. Turner (1984) notes the hypocrisy of excluding disabled people from these professions, stating: 'How can we tell patients they can lead normal lives when we don't allow their peers to become our colleagues? Though not yet illegal to discriminate on health grounds, there can be no doubt that it is immoral and unethical to do so.'

The degree of discrimination against disabled people working in the health and caring professions cannot be fully answered by this research. Dissimilar professional ideologies might suggest that there would be different levels of discrimination among the professions. This was not found to be the case, although the number of people in each profession was far too small for this finding to carry much weight. It also remains unclear to what extent disabled people working in the health and caring professions have a better understanding of illness and disability than their able-bodied colleagues, although it can be argued that this should not be a central issue as disabled people should not be expected to perform better than other people in order to be acceptable.

It is evident that further research is needed in this little-researched area. This small study does, however, suggest that disabled professionals are no less capable than their able-bodied colleagues and may have unique assets to bring to these professions. However, their presence may well undermine traditional professional values and beliefs, and there is little evidence that the senior members of these professions are actively seeking to recruit disabled people.

References

Baxter, C. (1988) *The Black Nurse: an Endangered Species*, National Extension College for Training in Health and Race, London.

Biehn, J. (1979) 'Psychiatric illness in physicians', *Journal of the Canadian Medical Association, Sociology of Health and Illness*, Vol. 2, p. 1342.

British Society of Audiology (n.d.) *Employment and Training of Audiology Technicians*, British Society of Audiology, London.

Browning, H. K. E. (1980) 'Careers for diabetic girls in nursing', *British Medical Journal*, Vol. 255, p. 307.

Bueche, M. S. (1983) 'Student with a hearing loss: coping strategies', *Nurse Education*, Vol. 3, No. 4, p. 7–11.

Burnfield, A. (1985) *Multiple Sclerosis: a Personal Exploration*, Souvenir Press, London.

Chickadonz, G. H. (1983) 'Educating a deaf nursing student', *Nursing and Health Care*, Vol. 4, No. 6, p. 327–33.

Chinnery, B. (1991) 'Equal opportunities for disabled people in the caring professions: window dressing or commitment?' *Disability, Handicap and Society*, Vol. 6, No. 3, pp. 253–8.

College of Radiographers (1985) *Radiography – Your Career?* College of Radiographers, London.

French, S. (1986a) 'Handicapped people in the health and caring professions – attitudes, practices and experiences', M.Sc. Dissertation, South Bank Polytechnic, London.

French, S. (1986b) 'Obesity – a greater stigma than disability', *Therapy Weekly*, Vol. 13, No. 17, pp. 5–6.

French, S. (1990) 'The advantages of visual impairment: some physiotherapists' views', *New Beacon*, Vol. 75, No. 872, pp. 1–6.

Gavin, A. (1980) 'Meeting the challenge of professional social work: education of the hearing impaired', *American Annals of the Deaf*, Vol. 125, December, pp. 1086–90.

Hutchins, T. V. (1978) 'Affirmative action for the physically disabled in social work education', *Journal of Education for Social Work*, Vol. 14, No. 3, pp. 64–70.

Libman, G. (1983) 'Doctor who overcomes deafness', *Synapse*, Vol. 4, No. 5, pp. 2–3.

McKnight, J. (1981) 'Professionalised service and disabling help', in Brechin, A., Liddiard, P. and Swain, J. (eds) *Handicap in a Social World*, Hodder and Stoughton, Sevenoaks/The Open University, Milton Keynes.

O'Hare, C. and Thomson, D. (1991) 'Experiences of physiotherapists with physical disabilities', *Physiotherapy*, Vol. 77, No. 6, pp. 374–8.

Safilios-Rothschild, C. (1976) 'Disabled person's self-definitions and their implications for rehabilitation', in Finkelstein, V. (ed.) *Rehabilitation: Supplementary Readings*, The Open University Press, Milton Keynes.

Shearer, A. (1981) *Disability: Whose Handicap?* Basil Blackwell, Oxford.

Turner, C. (1984) 'Who cares?' *Occupational Health*, Vol. 36, No. 10, pp. 449–52.

Watkins, S. (1987) *Medicine and Labour*, Lawrence and Wishart, London.

Wainapel, S. F. (1987) 'The physically disabled physician', *Journal of the American Medical Association*, Vol. 257, No. 21, pp. 2936–8.

Young, G. (1981) 'A woman in medicine: reflections from the inside', in Roberts, H. (ed.) *Women, Health and Reproduction*, Routledge and Kegan Paul, London.

4.3

Medical responsibilities to disabled people

John Harrison

As a profession, we in medicine do not spend much time thinking about our philosophy. We are constantly approached by people who want our help, and we respond in the best way we can. If our patients have problems we cannot cope with, we usually say so; we may then simply advise going elsewhere, or we may act as advocates to ensure that the issues are properly taken on by others. It is a matter of professional honour to keep our standards as high as possible. We are usually open to proposals for improvement or change.

Anyone with an illness or injury of any severity is disabled for as long as the condition lasts. In that sense medicine and disability are inextricably linked, yet the approaches of physicians and surgeons to disabled people are criticised as well as praised. Why the criticism, and why do we often get things wrong?

The medical culture

Medical students learn to distinguish 'acute', which means something of recent onset, from 'chronic', which means a condition which has lasted and will probably continue for a substantial time. Doctors are essentially interventionists, trained to diagnose, treat and either cure or admit defeat. This ethos fits the 'acute' model far better than the 'chronic' one.

Until the 1960s disability had a limited meaning: it referred to the effects of injuries but not often the effects of illness. People who were 'chronically sick', on the other hand, were familiar: they had failed to benefit from medical treatment and were therefore a problem, usually best left to themselves or to others to cope with. Medical education is rooted in the natural sciences. The rule has been that young people intending to study medicine must forsake the humanities and social sciences for physics, chemistry and biology. In their undergraduate years they are drilled in factual knowledge and scientific method, and rarely see patients outside hospital buildings. Interpersonal skills are usually expected to develop without formal training, or are just taken for granted.

In acute illness, doctors take full responsibility for treatment and develop the habit of making decisions which their patients do not wish to challenge. In hospital wards, short admission–discharge sequences reinforce the acute model, even if the condition being treated is not acute at all. It is a poor environment for learning correct approaches to disability.

Hospital outpatient clinics are better: many people attend regularly, precisely because they do have chronic illness and are therefore likely to be disabled. Many clinics are beyond reproach but others, while giving doctors the opportunity to monitor their patients' progress, can appear unhelpful to the patients themselves.

For more than ten years, general practice has required that doctors must now undergo further training. Together with inevitable involvement with patients and their families over long periods, this encourages a change of emphasis from diagnosis/treatment/cure to assessment/assistance/care. But specific education about disability and rehabilitation remains uncommon.

Why do disabled people need medicine?

A person with an established, stabilised impairment who develops a complication of that impairment, or suffers an independent illness or injury, will seek medical advice and treatment in the same way as anyone else. A person may also elect to undergo medical or surgical treatment to help correct the impairment, without being at all ill: hip replacements, and lens implants to replace cataracts, are obvious examples.

People whose disabilities begin with severe illness or injury find themselves in medical hands whether they like it or not. Once their condition has stabilised they may have to face a whole range of issues: new restrictions; new sensations; new embarrassments; new lifestyles. They do not expect the medical profession to be disinterested, and are disappointed if it does not provide advice and support.

People with progressively severe impairments, due to illness such as multiple sclerosis or rheumatoid arthritis, must constantly cope with new problems. Medical treatment may be relatively ineffective but also may not be useless: advice on therapies, equipment and future outlook in health terms may be invaluable. New problems may take the form of crises, such as sudden and/or final loss of ability to walk, or the development of pressure sores.

Crises may, of course, be primarily social: leaving school; loss of employment; illness of a close partner; separation or bereavement are examples. Medical help is not then the main requirement, but it may be relevant: advice, advocacy and co-operating to make new resources available may all be deeply appreciated.

Disabled patients who speak well of their doctors often say that they spend time with them, they listen, are helpful, visit regularly and are reliable. This doctor/patient relationship, so essential to good medical practice, belongs to what has traditionally been called the 'art' of medicine as distinct from its science.

The gatekeeper role and limitations of choice

More controversial is the command of access to resources. The growth of options for disabled people has been relatively recent. Forty years ago the National Health Service was almost the only establishment they could turn to. Even now, disabled people find themselves in hospital because it is the only place that will look after them and for that reason alone. A common institutional response is to be intolerant, not of the circumstances but of the patients and their families. Doctors such as geriatricians and psychiatrists have been cast in the role of fixers and gatekeepers to protect the institutions.

That unpleasant responsibility is less necessary than it was but the habit of mind, in society as much as with the professions, lingers on. Hospital doctors, for example, are still expected to have the last word about their patients' discharge dates, or about their transfer to other institutions, or to decide whether they should be offered facilities such as regular readmission to relieve carers. These are not necessarily medical decisions, but the constant demands on the hospital service require someone to take responsibility.

Other assessment and gatekeeper roles exist because, at least in the past, there have been few alternatives to doctors as sufficiently skilled and entrusted guardians of limited public resources. Assessments for benefits and equipment, still widely delegated to doctors, are now matched by other professionals' assessment procedures, for example when housing adaptations are required. The real problems are the need for assessment at all, and that doctors who undertake the responsibility may not be adequately trained (or experienced) for the task.

Teamwork

The practice of medicine has always depended on nursing, and the therapy professions have grown up to supply new kinds of skills. Most of the 'paramedicals' are relatively specialised, but a disabled person may have many requirements and many people may therefore be needed to meet them. Success depends on working together, with the added advantage that teamwork brings a variety of personal perspectives.

Some brief case histories may illustrate why disabled people make use of hospital help, and the scope for teamwork response.

Arthur B had just passed retirement age when he suffered a very severe stroke. Depressed and bewildered because it had inexplicably impaired his ability to think and concentrate, he soon guessed that his paralysis and clumsiness would make him always dependent on a wheelchair. His wife and family were as supportive as they could be, but found the staff in his first hospital ward uncommunicative and discouraging. The staff of the rehabilitation unit, on the other hand, where he spent several months before returning home, became their close partners and friends. Back home, Mr B experienced frequent complications including pain, embarrassing incontinence, uncontrollable temper, and frustration because of being housebound, but he also regained most of his old mental ability. The team remained supportive yet in many ways felt powerless because of social factors beyond their control. Medical involvement was continuous, mainly because his physical and mental health (and the couple's emotions) remained unstable.

Judith C had been disabled since birth, getting about with sticks and, for much of her life, leg calipers. The medical diagnosis was cerebral palsy. As a child her health had been well supervised: she attended an ordinary school and at the age of 19 obtained an office job. The network of health and social work support she had enjoyed fell away, but she led a full life and drove her own car, though she still lived with her parents. Then her legs developed new spasms and new deformities: she gave up her job and stopped driving. She agreed to undergo corrective surgery but the result disabled her further. She became depressed and lethargic, asking (with her parents) for more medical advice. She needed careful, patient help from an interdisciplinary team, together with 'time out' in a residential institution, before she was ready to embark on an independent wheelchair life in a home of her own. Medical involvement was mainly in the background, but it included expert knowledge of abnormal neuromuscular function and its alleviation.

Mary D had multiple sclerosis. When she first developed her symptoms the doctors had told her it was 'neuritis', and she discovered the diagnosis herself by picking up a magazine article in a cafe. Years later her increasing helplessness was causing unhappiness at home, yet there was still no one to whom she could turn: her parents had died; her children had left her; her sister was in Canada; the family doctors and hospital doctors were uninterested; and, apart from arranging adaptations to her house, social services were too overworked to be accessible. Sudden and final loss of ability to walk turned a chronic problem into a crisis: emotionally she could not face this added challenge, and her marital relationship collapsed. Almost too late to be of real use, a rehabilitation unit took her in and began the slow, hard work of helping her and her family reconstruct and make sense of their situation. Again this could only be achieved by teamwork, the medical component as important as all the others.

Agnes E lived alone, had reached her ninetieth year and had retained her independence of mind. For some years her vision had only enabled her to find her way about her house: she could not read and could scarcely see her television. One day she fell and broke her hip: it was repaired in hospital but she remained in some pain and was even more precarious on her feet. Her family believed she should be 'in a home' but she did not: though just a little forgetful, with the help of an interdisciplinary team she showed that she had kept enough living skills to get home again. There she stayed, with the help of the home care service and a watchful nurse specialist; one short illness a year later was managed by the hospital team which already knew her. She carried on for another year and then died suddenly from a heart attack. One of the medical responsibilities had been to assess the 'risk', advise the family and allay fears, and reinforce confidence that the hospital team would never let them down.

Interdisciplinary teamwork is now widely practised within hospitals and rehabilitation centres but is still rather unusual elsewhere. The same principles need to extend throughout community care, so that the medical approach to disability becomes just one part of a response involving a whole range of agencies, professions and interests. And the team must always include the disabled person in question, besides key members of the family and friends.

Concepts of disability

Population surveys of disabled people help governments and service-providers to be aware of numbers and needs. The extension of the idea that disability confers the right to certain benefits, to the identification of a group with civil rights of a more comprehensive kind, moves the concept of a disability a very long way from chronic sickness. Yet people with more or less stable impairments, struggling to make their way as oppressed citizens, do not usually appear in professional eyes to have much in common with the majority of bewildered, vulnerable people who seek medical help.

Public health, and monitoring the health status of populations, are part of the medical culture. Most surveys of disability have made use of medical advice in identifying the responsible injuries and diseases, which usually helps to confirm the pluralistic nature of the disabled population. For example, arthritis and deafness are the commonest impairments. Most disabled people are old (and the distinction between old age and disability is regularly confused). Young adults (aged 16–29) amount to only 5 per cent of the disabled population if everyone is included, a little more than that among the most severely impaired. Mental illness and loss of mental function are impairments too.

Although disabled people as a group experience many difficulties in common, specific problems are linked to specific conditions. Asthma, multiple sclerosis, osteoarthritis or Parkinson's disease, for example, each carry their own set of implications for disabled living, and yet, of course, this is only part of the picture. The enormous complexity helps explain why different groups have evolved different concepts of what disability really is.

With the aim of clarification, medical epidemiologists have introduced the impairment/disability/handicap triad: loss of function or loss of part of the body (impairment) leads to difficulty with the tasks of daily living (disability), resulting in economic and social disadvantage (handicap). Challenged by disabled people as disregarding the physical and social environment, and still not widely known within the medical profession, the triad does emphasise important issues and is useful in the education of professionals and as an adjunct to practice.

The fact remains that most health professionals would still speak of and regard someone like Arthur B as an old man with a stroke, not a disabled person with rights and entitlements. A great deal of work is needed to close that conceptual gap.

Rehabilitation medicine

In spite of the relatively poor understanding of disability in medical and hospital practice, health professionals cannot remain aloof. Many examples of good rehabilitation practice have developed simply because medical teams have seen obvious need: cardiac rehabilitation, or the support given to people on long-term dialysis or those who have undergone organ transplants, are a few examples.

But although doctors know that they must do all they can for their patients, the limits of their responsibilities have never been, and perhaps never can be, defined. Physicians and family doctors vary in the extent to which they feel comfortable outside the strict limits of medical treatment; for psychiatrists, on the other hand, this is the essential nature of their work.

The medical commitment to disabled people still lacks a generally agreed term with which best to describe it. 'Disability medicine' has not found wide support, if only because it has been (wrongly) interpreted to imply the medicalisation of disability. 'Rehabilitation medicine' at least sounds more positive, provided that it is recognised to mean far more than physical therapy and more than helping someone to recover from a single injury or illness. It hardly suits disabled children who have to learn about life as they experience it and cannot recover something that they never possessed.

But for everyone, rehabilitation is at least partly a learning process. Many people achieve it on their own, within their families, or with the help of friends or untrained helpers. Equally, the value of professionals who are trained and experienced in rehabilitation can hardly be in doubt, and all doctors should at least understand the basic concepts.

If they did, and if they understood them thoroughly, rehabilitation medicine as a speciality might not be needed. But in hospitals the extent of technical specialisation makes delegated expertise in medical aspects of rehabilitation virtually essential. One difficulty is that, like geriatric medicine, rehabilitation medicine in the past has been regarded within the profession as a 'soft option' bringing limited benefits, being unexciting and scarcely medicine. Such negative attitudes hardly encourage success.

Yet the climate of opinion is slowly changing, reflecting the gradually widening appreciation of disability in society as a whole. The medical Royal Colleges, as guardians of high standards of practice, are adding their influence. Public opinion does not go unheeded, and disabled people are not the only group which is asking for its own wishes and opinions to be recognised. There are grounds for cautious optimism.

Conclusions

We in medicine are privileged to be members of an influential profession, and society will probably ensure that we always will be. It is unthinkable that we should be unconcerned about the difficulties that our disabled patients face: it is essential that we are better informed and respond to them more appropriately. And that includes constant readiness to do so on their terms.

4.4

A social model in a medical world: the development of the integrated living team as part of the strategy for younger physically disabled people in North Derbyshire

Louise Silburn

A young disabled unit: to be or not to be?

In 1985 North Derbyshire Health Authority started planning how to spend the £430,000 they had been given for services to younger disabled people. They assumed that they would do as most of their neighbouring authorities had done and build a younger disabled unit (YDU), the only uncertainty being about its size. A newly formed joint planning group, including representatives of the Derbyshire Coalition of Disabled People and the Derbyshire Centre for Integrated Living (DCIL), was asked to discuss the issue.

Senior nurses and the district medical officer felt very strongly that a small YDU was needed in North Derbyshire in order to cater for people they felt were inappropriately cared for on wards for elderly people and for rehabilitation purposes. The Coalition and DCIL put forward equally strongly the view that putting money into such a unit kept vital resources away from the community services that disabled people needed in order to stay out of such units. The ideas, language and experience of the two groups were miles apart, and the early stages of planning were fraught with conflict.

Disabled people's needs and priorities: a survey

The short-term planning solution was to commission a survey of need which would establish what the expressed needs of disabled people in North Derbyshire were. The research was carried out by the University of Nottingham (Silburn, 1988) and was based on seven needs as defined by disabled people in Derbyshire (see Appendix 1) as well as planning issues facing health and social services. The seven needs were: information;

housing; technical aids; counselling; transport; personal assistance; and access. Particular services, such as physiotherapy; chiropody; drugs; day services; and domiciliary services, were also scrutinised. The interviews were carried out by independent researchers on a one-to-one basis where possible, and the survey provided both statistical analyses and case study reports in people's own words.

What the survey showed was that disabled people wanted community services; they thirsted for information, and wanted more generally based services in areas such as peer counselling, rather than specific professional services. The survey results strongly indicated the interlinking nature of the seven needs and the necessity to plan services in an integrated way.

Residential solutions did not play a part in the way disabled people viewed ideal services.

The development of a community strategy

The planning group began to plan community services to reflect the needs as perceived by its population of disabled people. This emphasis was very unusual and highly challenging to many health professionals who were used to being in control of decisions of this nature. Direct experience of living in a YDU as set against observation of people living in YDUs became the key debate once the choice of community strategy or YDU became clear. Eventually a community strategy was agreed, with a proportion of the available finance being set aside for an integrated living co-ordinator and a flexible budget which would plug the gap perceived by the health professionals and ensure that disabled people did not block beds in acute services.

The integrated living team: planning and philosophies

Once the decision had been taken to employ an integrated living co-ordinator to manage a flexible budget which would help people to move out of hospital quickly and also stop them being admitted inappropriately, the planning group decided to use some of the money in the budget to pay for therapists and include one occupational therapist, one speech therapist and one physiotherapist working in a team. The co-ordinator could be from any relevant background.

Initially there were strong feelings that each therapist should be managed by her own departmental head; a compromise was eventually reached whereby although each therapist would be supervised by her own district head, the day-to-day management of work would be carried out by the co-ordinator. Once appointed, however, the co-ordinator took over full management responsibility for all team members. On the whole, this arrangement has been accepted by most people. One consultant, however, still complains that the team 'freewheels' through acute and community services without any clinical accountability.

I was appointed to the post of co-ordinator with a background of work as joint director of the Derbyshire Centre for Integrated Living. My colleague Richard Wood went on to become director of the British Council of Organisations of Disabled People, and my knowledge and experience of planning and providing services for disabled people came from the disability movement. As a result of this appointment therefore, the health service was endorsing the creation of a team whose philosophy and practices were firmly rooted in the social model of disability.

The role of the integrated living team member

It is accepted by all team members that the people with whom we work have requirements which need to be fulfilled as quickly as possible and in a way which gives them control over the process of achieving integrated living. It is therefore necessary to adopt a key-worker approach whereby one team member is responsible for working with a disabled person on all aspects of their move out of hospital or on helping them remain in the community if they are at risk of inappropriate hospital admission. They use each other's professional expertise in discussion and advice and from time to time conduct joint visits if specialist assessments are needed. As the team members grew in confidence and commitment to this new way of working, they tried to drop any reference to their original professional title. This practice has caused much discomfiture among health service staff in other areas, whose habitual first question to the team members and myself is 'What are you?'

The bulk of the work of the team revolves around the seven needs which are used as the basis of service planning. The disabled people with whom the team works may have health needs which are being met by hospitals or primary health care services, but the reason they need help from the team is because they do not have access to the appropriate non-medical services they require to live comfortable and secure lives in the community.

When a team member visits someone for the first time, he or she assesses the services required by reference to the seven needs; only the most basic and immediately relevant details about medical and personal factors are used in the initial assessment. The service the team provides does not have to conform to the procedures laid down by a department or by the boundaries imposed by a professional qualification; it has been developed to be specifically useful to disabled people in particular circumstances.

Criteria for referral to the team

The team will work with 'anyone aged between 16 and 64 who is severely physically impaired, in hospital and needing to move out or in the community and at risk of inappropriate hospital admission'. 'Inappropriate' means, in this context, that the person is not ill and in need of medical attention in hospital. Another way of looking at this is to define our criteria as being that the person would have been admitted to a YDU had there been one in the district. The criteria are clearly defined and adhered to in order to allow the team members the time and money to work with those people whose 'health' needs are greatest. The 'health' needs in this instance are that they would normally have to call on a health authority budget, although, as will be demonstrated later in the paper, these needs are, in fact, social.

Flexible budget

The budget is the key to creative working by the team members. It frees them to discuss different options with the disabled people with whom they work, and allows them to have access to the funds necessary to finance their choice of solution. In 1990/1 the budget was £78,000 per annum. It is mainly used for non-recurrent expenditure, such as technical aids which are unavailable from other aids services, adaptations, personal assistance in the home, transport and holidays. However, it can be used for anything the team considers appropriate to help someone remain in the community or to enable someone to move out of hospital.

It is often used in conjunction with other sources of funding to make the best use of the available money each year. It can therefore be used to top up disabled facilities grants, to make major adaptations a reality for people for whom means-testing would otherwise make changes to their home imposs- ible. It can be used to pay for personal assistance in someone's home for an interim period until social services have recruited full-time staff to continue with the long-term commitment. It has also been used as a successful stop-gap while people have awaited Independent Living Fund money.

The existence of this budget as a spur to the spending of money on a long-term basis has sometimes caused problems with social services depart- ments, who have much longer lead times than ourselves for decisions over the spending of money and recruitment. On one occasion, when the team's money was due to come to an end, we insisted (with the permission of the person concerned) that the staff would be withdrawn whether or not the social services department had put their own staff in place. Miraculously they managed to find some staff in time, but afterwards there was a long period during which we received no referrals from that area.

A regular use of the money is to pay for holidays for disabled people who were previously taking 'respite' breaks in hospital, or for people for whom the provision of a holiday each year was dependent on the state of the County Council's finances. The use of the budget to book set holidays a number of times a year relieves the uncertainty and thus ensures that both carers and disabled people can look forward to their break rather than worry about whether or not they will get one.

Examples of work

The team's work with disabled people can be broken down into five groups.

(1) Some people are admitted to hospital following some kind of trauma that results in physical impairment. This could be a stroke or illness or accident resulting in amputation, spinal injury or head injury. They will require varying degrees of medical treatment before they go home and may be transferred to a specialist inpatient rehabilitation facility such as a spinal or head injury unit.

People in this group often require substantial adaptations to their home before they can return to it, or their family circumstances may change as a result of reactions to the trauma, and returning to their original home may no longer be an option for them. They can remain, therefore, inappropriately in hospital wards although they are no longer in need of the medical care provided, blocking beds which could be used for other people.

For the integrated living team this group of people, though only one-quarter of those we see, represents a political challenge; moving them out of expensive resources is seen as the reason for the team's existence. If we can do that, we are worth the money.

Most of the people we have helped to move out of hospital have gone home fairly quickly and services have gradually been developed around them. For some this is not possible: this may be because they are homeless, or because their home is unsuitable even for temporary occupation. For these people, we have embarked upon complex joint projects with council housing departments and environmental health departments, drawing up plans with the disabled person, their family and the health authority works department. The process for some people is frustrating and slow, despite our budget and time. Yet involvement in the process has been helpful to people adjusting to a changed body, a new sort of life and new challenges.

One man who had to go through this process began it with a grudging acceptance that if he couldn't stay in hospital all his life, which was what he wanted at that moment, then he had better plan his kitchen. When he moved into the flat, planned to his specification and decorated to his taste, down to the black sitting room with red ceiling, he said he never wanted to see another magnolia-painted hospital wall in his life.

(2) Another group of people with whom the team works are those who are in hospital because they have been inappropriately admitted; for example, they may have been admitted to be 'sorted out'. 'Sorting out' means that their drugs are reviewed, the hospital occupational therapist and physiotherapist works with them, and they have a rest in hospital while their carer has a rest at home.

As a result of this stay in hospital it often becomes evident that the root of the problem is a lack of accessible housing, poor technical aids and not enough support for either the disabled person or the family carer in the form of practical help or emotional/social release. The hospital social worker will be asked to arrange things at home so that the person can be discharged back to a more suitable environment. The social worker contacts the integrated living team, who then start to 'sort out' the social environment which is disabling that person.

The results of such admissions are that stress on both the disabled person and their carer is increased by the normal anxiety experienced by any family on admission to hospital. Sometimes extra pressure is put on the team to provide a certain level of service in the home before the disabled person can be discharged, which means that less than ideal solutions have to be 'cobbled together' in haste while more money is spent on longer-term solutions.

(3) For some people with degenerative, terminal diseases, such as motor neurone disease (MND), a joint approach to services has been developed. The hospice in Chesterfield will take people with MND into their day hospital and then later for respite care and the final stages of illness. The integrated living team can work with people from diagnosis of MND onwards, to ensure that they stay at home for as long as possible, anticipating communication needs, personal assistance requirements and planning any adaptations that may be necessary.

The team set up groups of helpers drawn from the local community to support a husband caring for his wife who had MND. The helpers were neighbours, paid to come in for a few minutes at a time to help her get a drink or go to the toilet, but not to overwhelm her with a caring presence which she did not want. This freed her husband for parts of the day, but allowed him to look after her himself, which is what he wanted to do. The hospice then provided a bed for a week on and a week off, so that her admission to it was not seen as the failure of either of them to cope with living at home.

(4) Working with people who are at risk of inappropriate hospital admission accounts for over half of the team's work. A disabled person can be inappropriately admitted because of the illness of a carer or the possibility of a carer leaving altogether. Another reason could be a deterioration in the person's physical state which is not matched by an increase in support at home, perhaps in the form of personal assistance or aids and adaptations. Sometimes the cause is emotional or relationship problems that have come to a head.

When first visiting someone at home the team member will have some idea about what is threatening to make their admission to hospital likely, but working through the seven needs with people will reveal a much broader picture of their lives and point up the delicate framework of dependencies on an often haphazard group of services. If the primary requirement is the relief of stress, the team will often organise a holiday, to be taken fairly quickly, and then spend longer looking at personal assistance, counselling, technical aids and housing issues which might have created the stress in the first place.

For some people, just the provision of a decent hoist, the organisation of three holidays a year or a home care aide booked to come to their home every week is enough. For others, the identification of one need will lead on to another, and the team can work with someone for a long time. Many people we will always stay in touch with, particularly those whose physical condition is not static.

(5) The final group of people consists of those for whom ill-health is the result of the social problems discussed earlier. For most people, such ill-health would not warrant admission to hospital. For disabled people it often does because it is the emergency response forced on to GPs who are given neither the role nor the resources to tackle the root cause. Also, for disabled people, ill-health can lead to complaints that are more serious and difficult to treat. Poor pressure relief, resulting from inadequate wheelchair cushions, unsuitable mattresses, lack of assistance in turning, or a poor diet, owing to lack of money, mean that disabled people may be admitted to hospital for treatment for pressure sores which need never have existed.

The team has successfully worked with people who were frequently being admitted to hospital so that they can stay in the community in better health as a result of better organised and higher-quality services.

The way forward: rehabilitation or integrated living?

The integrated living team is operating at the interface of social and medical models of care. The medical model is the rehabilitation service, which still dominates the health service's view of what disabled people need from it. It strives to produce normally functioning individuals, with the definition of 'normal' being 'as they were before they became disabled'. A normally functioning person does not have to grapple with the social (or administrative) model of disability which is made up of a complex interrelationship of poor access, inadequate housing, insufficient income, cash-starved social services and professional control over their life.

Rehabilitation is a vast area in the health service, underpinned by departments in universities, consultants in hospitals and special units, physiotherapy departments, occupational therapy departments, multi-disciplinary teams and international institutes. If you want to read about disabled people in terms of health services, you have to look them up under 'rehabilitation'. The idea that someone may not be rehabilitated, or may fail in the process is rarely addressed in service planning. The concept of the disabling society is not one which is seriously considered when delivering health services to disabled people.

Yet it is questionable to what extent disabled people would want to be rehabilitated if they lived in a world where the struggle to learn to walk a few yards on crutches was made pointless by decent wheelchairs and a barrier-free environment. The work of the integrated living team is based firmly in the realm of creating for disabled people as barrier-free an environment, in the widest sense, as possible, to enable them to live secure and integrated lives. Therefore rehabilitation is not practised by the team and this is what makes it so threatening for health professionals rooted in the rehabilitation tradition.

The team's insistence on working within a social model of disability – empowering, offering choices and focusing on society as the problem, rather than the individual has led to some problems in work with individuals where other services have had a different approach. In terms of the creation of the service in a planned strategy, and the development of that strategy for the future, the team's model of working has been seen by some doctors as wrongly situated in the health service. Indeed, the team has been accused of creating 'anarchy' in the health service. The most painful example of this was the occasion on which the team had to submit to an 'audit' of its handling of a situation where the team member refused to plan a young disabled man's admission to a residential home without his being present at the consultant-led case conference.

Yet despite this, opposition is actively voiced by only a very few people. The team rarely needs to confront the issues set out here and can work co-operatively with the professional rehabilitation staff in the district. That way the team obtains services for people, and survives in a medical world.

The medical/rehabilitation world can be a comfortable place, and some of its most powerful exponents can treat those of us living outside it with barely disguised contempt. It is sometimes hard for all of us in the team to resist the temptation to be part of that world by seeing disabled people's bodies as the problem and denying the disabling society. Yet in Derbyshire we work closely with disabled people for whom the disabling society is a reality, and through them derive support for our belief that working with a social model of disability is the most helpful service we can offer.

References

Silburn, R. (1988) *Disabled People: Their Needs and Priorities*, Benefits Research Unit, Department of Social Policy and Administration, University of Nottingham.

Appendix 1   The seven needs

Information

Disabled people need information about all aspects of life, including benefits, employment opportunities and other services available to them. Information sources need to be accessible to all disabled people.

Access

Lack of access to everyday facilities open to non-disabled people cause disabling barriers.

Housing

Disabled people need a range of accommodation which is barrier-free, designed to suit individual needs and promote independence.

Technical aids

Technical aids, such as hoists, eating aids and wheelchairs, when selected on the basis of good information can promote independence and be valued tools in people's everyday life.

Personal assistance

Just as housing and technical aids can promote independence, so can personal assistance which is available when required by disabled people and, where possible, controlled by disabled people.

Counselling

Disabled people need access to counselling services for the same types of problems as non-disabled people. However, many counselling services are inaccessible to disabled people, either because of physical or attitudinal barriers.

Transport

'Public transport' is not often available to disabled people, adapted or barrier-free transport is expensive. Services, benefits and vehicles do exist, however, which mean that disabled people can have freedom to travel.

The integrated living team works to ensure that these seven needs are covered and solutions found to the problems that can be encountered in each area.

4.5

Setting a record straight

Sally French

Many physiotherapists, along with other health professionals, have adopted the problem-orientated medical record system (POMR) proposed by Weed (1969) to assess and monitor the progress of their patients. The system seeks to standardise medical records in order to improve the reliability of the information obtained and to make it suitable for computerisation. Medical records have tended to be so poorly written that they have lacked intelligibility and have been of little value for managerial, educational, legal and research purposes. It was hoped that the adoption of the POMR system would help to rectify this situation.

The POMR system

An outline of the POMR system is given below. It must be appreciated, however, that the details vary from place to place and according to speciality. The records are generally organised in four main sections:

1 The data base – where all the relevant information, obtained from the patient and through the clinical examination, is documented.
2 The problem list – where the problems the patient is experiencing are listed, having been extrapolated from the data base.
3 The initial plan – where a plan is made of the patient's treatment programme by reference to the problem list.
4 The progress notes – which are written under four subheadings – 'subjective', 'objective', 'assessment' and 'plan' – and are thus frequently referred to as SOAP notes. According to Heath (1978) and Coates and King (1982), what the patient says about his or her problems are documented under 'subjective', while the physiotherapist's observations and measurements are documented under 'objective'. Under 'assessment' the therapist states her goals and recommendations, and the 'plan' gives an account of the implementation and development of the treatment programme. For a detailed discussion of the POMR system readers are referred to Petrie and McIntyre (1979).

This paper is an edited version of S. French (1991) 'Setting a record straight', *Therapy Weekly*, Vol. 18, No. 1, p. 4.

Many extravagant claims have been made for the POMR system. It has been argued that information obtained in this way can be used to evaluate clinical practice, thereby enhancing the quality of patient care. The system is said to have educational benefits for physiotherapists and physiotherapy students by helping them to develop their analytic skills and their ability to think strategically rather than intuitively about their patients' problems (Scholey, 1985). It seems, however, that far less impressive claims than these can be confidently made. For example, Fletcher (1974) compared problem-orientated medical records with conventional records and found no significant difference either in the time it took doctors to read them or in their comprehension of them. Neither did the number of errors they recognised differ. This finding applied to those doctors who favoured and regularly used POMR as well as those who did not.

The language of POMR

Carson (1973) states that terms such as 'data base' have a 'pseudo-scientific ring', giving the impression that the information gathered is more objective and factual than is really the case. Goldfinger (1973), expressing a similar view, spoke of the 'fallacy of misplaced concreteness' whereby our abstractions are mistaken for reality, and Grieve (1988) is of the opinion that the division between 'objective' and 'subjective' information in the SOAP notes is very misleading. He states: 'While we may not welcome the prospect, the lack of scientific certainty does suggest that most clinical examination procedures are more subjective than objective.'

Are we are not deluding ourselves by thinking that our measurements and observations are objective while the patient's are not? Students, and perhaps most of us, tend to be motivated to perceive our work in terms of 'facts' and clear-cut theories, thereby reducing the chaos of the clinical world. The language of POMR encourages a tendency which should surely be discouraged, for as Laing (1983) reminds us, 'there is nothing as subjective as objectivity blind to its own subjectivity'.

The term 'problem-solving' is at the heart of the POMR system and is something of an 'in' term in medicine at the present time. McKnight (1981) points out that this term implies that patients' problems can be solved by medical professionals, whereas in reality they are more often the result of political and economic factors beyond medical interest or influence (see Smith and Jacobson, 1988; Turshen, 1989). Theoretically we have broadened our notions of illness and disability beyond the medical model to include social, psychological and political models. This leaves us in no doubt that professional intervention is just one source of influence in a much wider process, but, despite this, the narrow view that health professionals can 'solve' what are perceived as patients' problems prevails and is encouraged by POMR language.

Critical analysis and clinical decision-making

Finkelstein (1980) believes that the analysis of complex problems is something that all human beings are engaged in throughout their lives. Similarly Brechin and Liddiard (1981) claim that citing a problem and proposing solutions to it, 'is the kind of process that most of us think of as using our common sense'. It is surely naive to assume that our powers of critical analysis, which as human beings we exercise constantly, will be significantly altered by merely complying with the format of a medical record, much less that these powers will be enhanced to the extent that patient care will be influenced, as proposed by Coates and King (1982). Cantrill (1979) believes that the POMR system helps us to apply logic to our choice of treatment and its progression, but how far is this 'logic' artificially created by the system? The notion that meticulous attention to the POMR system will necessarily help in clinical decision-making is misleading. As Goldfinger (1973) states: 'Anxieties about the huge body of knowledge required to practise excellent medicine should not be allayed by the assurance that a well kept record will somehow miraculously guide one to the right answers.' Feinstein (1973) believes that the arrangement of the data determines not whether the concepts themselves are correct, but whether the individual has complied with the system, and Carson (1973) believes that it is the ability to comply with the system that is 'audited' rather than the quality of patient care. Concern has also been expressed that compliance with the POMR system will become an end in itself (Brechin and Liddiard, 1981).

Downie and Calman (1987) believe that technical models of decision-making, used by health professionals, are simplistic because they tend to ignore the all-important moral dimension of the process, sometimes to the extent that the patient's own wishes and opinions are not fully taken into account. They believe that an adequate understanding of another person requires, 'a kind of sympathetic and imaginative awareness of what it is like to be a patient or client in a given situation' and that this involves 'the sort of understanding which a friend shows to a friend'.

Research

Scholey (1985) believes that the POMR system will provide a valuable source of research data for the evaluation of clinical practice. In rehabilitation few of our measurements are entirely objective or reliable, and this, as well as the enormous complexity of the clinical situation, makes controlled experimental research extraordinarily difficult. Surely the use of information which has been gathered in an uncontrolled fashion in ordinary working conditions will only serve to compound these problems. I am not suggesting that such information is of no research value, but I believe we are in danger of ignoring the fact that it remains as subjective as it ever was. Feinstein (1973), when considering the POMR system, states: 'Students and house staff may begin to believe that a problem in patient care has received a scientific solution when the data are precisely catalogued, the problem is clearly stipulated and a selected expert has delivered his anecdotal opinion on what to do next.'

There is also no guarantee that the people collecting the information are necessarily committed to accuracy or interested in research. Official and semi-official records are notoriously unreliable and low in validity and my past experience of collecting 'numbers' in physiotherapy departments leads me to believe that they would be similarly unreliable. Slattery (1986) states: 'Official statistics on such topics as crime, suicide and unemployment are often more a reflection of the attitudes, values and behaviour of officials than of the people they claim to be representing.' Goldfinger (1973) found that workshop activities in which competent physicians were asked to produce a 'problem list' from an identical 'data base' yielded as many different problems lists as there were participants. Inter-participant reliability was clearly very low, but, more profoundly, there was marked disagreement about the very definition of the problems themselves. Achieving reliability, though very difficult, is largely a technical matter, but when considering validity the very nature of reality is questioned. In the POMR system the treatment is based on the problem list, but can we be sure that these problems are valid? There is considerable evidence to show that definitions and perceptions of illness and disability differ between lay and professional people as well as indications of a growing dissatisfaction with the power of professionals to promote their particular version of reality (Oliver 1991; Morris, 1989). Brechin and Liddiard (1981) describe the use of Kelly's Repertory Grid to compare the perceptions of health professionals and disabled people regarding the latter's 'problems'. Generally speaking, health professionals tend to view the problems in terms of the individual, whereas disabled people tend to view them in social terms. Overall there appeared to be little agreement between them. Brechin and Liddiard (1981) claim that professionals tend to have a narrow, specialist focus and that their assessment procedures have 'evolved around the assumption that within the individual lies the problem and the solution'. (For details of Kelly's Repertory Grid technique see Fransella and Bannister, 1977).

Co-ordination of the team

According to Heath (1978) the POMR system helps to co-ordinate the health care team. A glance at any account of group dynamics will, however, suggest this to be unlikely (see Brown, 1988). Feinstein (1973) points out that the problems of communication among health workers are far too complex a matter to be resolved by merely revising the format of a medical record. Cantrill (1979) claims that the system seeks to avoid contradictory plans amongst team members and that the data can be used to influence and improve patient care 'by altering the behaviour of deficient health care providers'. The notion that it is desirable for the team to 'speak with one voice' is however, debatable (Brechin and Liddiard, 1981). It may have the advantage of avoiding confusion but it can also stifle ideas and innovations, as well as being oppressive to team members, including patients, who disagree with the team's definition of the situation. Brechin and Liddiard (1981) make the point that the patient is typically not in a position to influence the team significantly.

Conclusion

It seems unlikely that the reformulation of any medical record, however sophisticated it may seem, can meet any of the grand claims that have been made for the POMR system. Furthermore, the very idea that it can meet them has the potential to inhibit creative thought which reflects the true complexity of the problems faced by people who consult health professionals, as well as their possible solutions.

References

Brechin, A. and Liddiard, P. (1981) *Look At It This Way: New Perspectives in Rehabilitation*, Hodder and Stoughton, Sevenoaks.

Brown, R. (1988) *Group Processes*, Basil Blackwell, Oxford.

Cantrill, S. V. (1979) 'Computerisation of the problem orientated medical record', in Petrie, J. C and McIntyre, N. (eds) *The Problem Orientated Medical Record*, Churchill Livingstone, Edinburgh.

Carson, P. (1973) 'Problem orientated medical records', *British Medical Journal*, Vol. 2, pp. 713–14.

Coates, H. and King, A. (1982) *The Patient Assessment*, Churchill Livingstone, Edinburgh.

Downie, R. S. and Calman, K. (1987) *Healthy Respect: Ethics in Health Care*, Faber and Faber, London.

Feinstein, A. R. (1973) 'The problem of the problem orientated medical record'. *Annals of Internal Medicine*, Vol. 78, pp. 751–62.

Finkelstein, V. (1980) *Know Your Own Approach: The Handicapped Person in the Community* (course workbook), The Open University Press, Milton Keynes.

Fletcher, R. H. (1974) 'Auditing problem orientated and traditional records: a controlled experiment of speed, accuracy and identification of errors in medical care', *New England Journal of Medicine*, Vol. 78, pp. 751–62.

Fransella, F. and Bannister, D. (1977) *A Manual for Repertory Grid Technique*, Academic Press, London.

Goldfinger, S. E. (1973) 'The problem-orientated record: a critique from a believer', *New England Journal of Medicine*, Vol. 288, pp. 606–8.

Grieve, G. P. (1988) 'Clinical examination and the SOAP mnemonic', *Physiotherapy*, Vol. 74, No. 2, p. 97.

Heath, J. R. (1978) 'Problem orientated medical systems', *Physiotherapy*, Vol. 64, No. 9, p. 269–70.

Laing, R. D. (1983) *The Voice of Experience*, Penguin, Harmondsworth.

McKnight, J. (1981) 'Professionalised service and disabling help', in Brechin, A., Liddiard, P. and Swain, J. (eds) *Handicap in a Social World*, Hodder and Stoughton, Sevenoaks/The Open University, Milton Keynes.

Morris, J. (1989) *Able Lives*, The Women's Press, London.

Oliver, M. (1991) (ed.) *Social Work: Disabled People and Disabling Environments*, Jessica Kingsley, London.

Petrie, J. C. and McIntyre, N. (1979) (eds) *The Problem Orientated Medical Record*, Churchill Livingstone, Edinburgh.

Scholey, M. E. (1985) 'Documentation: a means to professional development', *Physiotherapy*, Vol. 71, No. 5, pp. 276–8.

Slattery, M. (1986) *Official Statistics*, Tavistock, London.

Smith, A. and Jacobson, B. (1988) *The Nation's Health*, King Edward's Hospital Fund for London.

Turshen, M. (1989) *The Politics of Public Health*, Zed Books, London.

Weed, L. L. (1969) *Medical Records, Medical Examination and Patient Care: Year Book*, Medical Publishers, Chicago.

4.6

Do disabled people need counselling?

Joy Lenny

There can be no simple answer to what is essentially the simple question of the title: do disabled people need counselling? There are many reasons for this but most important is that counselling involves a one-to-one relationship between a counsellor and a client. Underpinning this relationship is the assumption that the client has an emotional, psychological or personal problem that needs to be worked through and that counselling should facilitate this process.

On the other hand, in recent years disabled people have increasingly come to confront and reject both general views and professional assumptions that disability is a problem for impaired individuals. Instead they have argued that disability is a problem of the disabling society; that impaired individuals are disabled by a society which is not organised for, and takes little account of, their needs.

If this is the case, and I shall argue that it is, then the answer is that while disabled people may need political action, self-help groups, community work, social programmes and the like, *they unequivocally do not need counselling*. Yet as disabled people have begun the process of collective empowerment, they have articulated a need for counselling; not for more social work, physiotherapy or occupational therapy or other individually based professional interventions, but for counselling.

It is to the paradox contained in this situation that the rest of this paper will be addressed.

The problem of adjustment

Whatever the psychological theory utilised in an attempt to understand personal responses to disability, they all make a common assumption; they assume that the onset of disability not only brings about physical changes but emotional ones as well. They assume that the mind has to adjust to these bodily changes in order for the individual to come to terms with a changed body-image. It is only through the process of coming to terms that the disabled individual can become psychologically whole again, and that professional help is often a key element in this.

Ironically, it is often further assumed that people who appear not to need this help are, in reality, those who need it the most. A classic statement of this view is given below:

> Occasionally a newly disabled person does not seem to be particularly depressed, and this should be a matter of concern. In almost all instances something inappropriate is taking place. A person should be depressed because something significant has happened, and not to respond as such is denial.
>
> (Siller, 1969, p. 292)

This classic psychological response of denial places disabled people in a Catch-22 situation; to deny that adjustment to their disability is a problem for them shows just how great their adjustment problem really is.

Following from the normative assumptions built around the concept of adjustment, the idea of loss comes to occupy a central place in the theoretical model that is being built. It can explain so many things: disabled people have lost some or all of their functional capacities, including the ability to express their sexuality; they have lost their familial, their economic and social roles; and so on. No wonder they have problems of adjustment, even if they deny that they do.

Equally important from a psychological perspective, they have lost their perfect bodies of body-image theory. And this body-image problem remains a psychological one rather than a cultural one based upon imposed norms surrounding the body beautiful. It remains a problem despite the increasing denials by disabled people themselves, as by one of the leading disability activists who not only claims that 'I'm in love with my body' but also attacks the medical intrusions that are part of all disabled people's lives.

> My body's got self-dignity
> My body's got self-respect
> No-one can take that away from me
> In this world or the next.
>
> (Creschendo, 1989, p. 16)

The theoretical edifice which has grown up around the problem of adjustment has borrowed from other psychological theories – namely grief and stage theories – and these have combined to produce a series of fixed stages through which disabled people must pass before they can become psychologically whole.

Stage theories have an impressive pedigree going back to Freud, Piaget and Erikson, and they continue to have a significant impact on professional interventions despite the fact that research has failed empirically to demonstrate their existence (Silver and Wortman, 1980). Not only do they not accord with the experience of disabled people but, rigidly applied, they become oppressive, and disabled people come to see themselves as victims of the professional interventions on which they are based (Trieschman, 1980).

The ideology of stage theories is deeply oppressive to disabled people, as a disabled social worker explains in terms of her own exposure to such theories when she was training.

> we continued to use the Erik Erikson model of human development that emphasised bladder and bowel continency as a precursor to the development of a sense of competency. There was no contradiction because we had no knowledge of those disabled adults who would never have control over these functions, but who were obtaining an impressive level of personal competency and positive self-image. Their new self-confidence was propelling them towards a confrontation with society's negative evaluation of their abilities and rights.
>
> (Owen, 1985, pp. 397–8)

When grief theories are added to fixed stages, the problem of adjustment becomes even greater. In order to overcome their loss, disabled people must grieve, go through the process of mourning and express feelings of anger and even denial before they can become psychologically whole.

A classic statement of this position, linking loss to emotional trauma and stages of adjustment, is to be found in an article in a leading social work journal which claims to be 'a comprehensive review of the diverse literature on human response to traumatic loss and disability' (Berger, 1988). There are a number of dimensions to this position which can be summarised as follows: loss is a universal experience of all disabled people across all disabilities; denial is a common response to such loss; disabled people and their families pass through stages before they are 'able to gradually integrate the reality of the situation'; and subsequent actions and behaviours can be explained in terms of 'delayed traumatic stress syndrome'.

Berger sees three counselling approaches as being appropriate to those who have suffered traumatic loss; religious counselling for those who think that 'God did this to me because I'm a bad person'; assertiveness training for those who experience their disabilities as a threat to their self-image; and the sharing of experience because 'survivors of loss struggle to give meaning to their pain by sharing it with others, in the hope that their experience will not have been in vain'.

On empirical grounds there have been many studies which clearly demonstrate that not all disabled people experience their disabilities as loss (Campling, 1981; Sutherland, 1981; Oliver *et al.*, 1988; Morris, 1989). In addition the denial mechanism is tautological and explains nothing and everything at the same time. Further, there is little empirical support for stage theories so far as disabled individuals (Trieschman, 1980) or families (Vargo and Stewin, 1984) are concerned. Finally, loss models lock disabled people into stereotypes as pathetic victims overwhelmed by, or superheroes battling to overcome, this loss.

From what has been said, it would appear that psychologically based understandings of adjustment do not offer a promising basis for developing counselling services for and with disabled people. Does this mean that we have to abandon the very idea that counselling is useful to disabled people (despite their expressed wishes) or that we have to search for more appropriate models of the counselling process?

Counselling disabled people?

Most counselling approaches are dependent upon a pre-existing psychologi-cal theory or paradigm, and while there are many ways to divide up the world of psychology, for the purposes of this paper I shall divide the world into three: psychoanalytical; behavioural; and humanistic.

The psycho-dynamic process is one of exploring and developing links between the conscious and the unconscious and ensuring that the id, the ego and the super-ego are in balance. The aim of psychoanalytically based counselling, therefore, is 'to strengthen the client's ego by lifting childhood repressions, filling in gaps in memory and allowing acts of judgement to be made through the ego's present strength rather than its previous weakness' (Nelson-Jones, 1982, p. 84). Because thinking on the problem of disability has been underpinned by personal tragedy theory, it seems not unreasonable to see the onset of disability as a powerful assault on the ego and hence to think that psychoanalytically based counselling can repair the damage to the egos of disabled people. The problem is that few, if any, studies of the experiences and effects of disability have found evidence of this damage.

It is important to emphasise here that I am not arguing that psychoanalysis is never appropriate for disabled people; a few may experience their disability as an assault on their ego and other disabled people may have damaged egos for a variety of reasons unconnected with their disabilities. The point I am making is that psychoanalytic theory can never provide a basis for under-standing the experiences of disability in general, and that attempts to use its skills and techniques uncritically may end up doing more harm than good.

Behaviourism is more concerned with the ways in which the outside world rather than the effects of past experiences may structure the consciousness of individuals. Behaviourist counselling is therefore concerned with developing techniques and skills to enable people to deal with the external constraints on their behaviour. Thus for behaviourists the well-adjusted person is one who is able to control these external forces and the outside world and to make appropriate choices and decisions.

As far as disability is concerned, behaviourist assumptions centre on the idea that because disability imposes functional limitations on individual disabled people, then their capacities to control these external forces are impaired. As a consequence disabled people experience a phenomenon called 'learned helplessness' (Seligman, 1975) and become passive, depen-dent and unable to make decisions for themselves.

It is certainly true that many disabled people do exhibit traits which could be indicative of learned helplessness. Where I would take issue with behaviourist theories is in the explanation of this as stemming from the functional limitations of individuals. Where I would take issue with behaviourist counsellors is in their attempts to equip disabled people with the abilities to overcome their functional limitations.

It is not because of their functional limitations that disabled people are unable to take control of their own lives; it is because every aspect of the world in which they live denies them any form of control over their lives. Whether it be inaccessible built environments, patronising welfare legislation, negative and distorted images of disability peddled by charities or the theories and practices of a whole range of professionals, the message is always the same and becomes a self-fulfilling prophecy: disabled people are helpless.

Clearly counselling which seeks to help disabled people to take control over their lives is urgently needed; my criticism of behaviourist counselling is that it continues to focus on the functional limitations of disabled individuals rather than the collective experience of disability in a hostile world.

Humanistic psychology and person-centred counselling, on which it is based, tends to be less dogmatic in its theoretical imposition and is much more concerned with enabling people to explore their own situations and circumstances and the meanings these have for them. Counselling within this paradigm is about enabling people to fulfil their 'self-actualising tendencies' as part of 'an active process representing the inherent tendency of the organism to develop its capacities in the direction of maintaining, enhancing and reproducing itself' (Nelson-Jones, 1982, p. 19). Given the criticisms of psychoanalysis and behaviourism in terms of developing an appropriate understanding of disability, humanistic psychology, which starts from the perspective and experience of the disabled individual, would seem to offer a way forward. Not only does it not impose meaning, as psychoanalysis does, it also accepts the existence of learned helplessness because 'The person-centred philosophy in many aspects is one of self-control, self-help and personal power' (Nelson-Jones, 1982, p. 32). In many ways these issues of control, self-help and power are ones with which disabled people themselves are currently struggling. The issue for us, however, is whether person-centred counselling, because of its focus on the individual, can address these issues in the ways that disabled people would wish them to be addressed.

The crucial issue this raises is why does the concept of adjustment exert such a powerful influence over what professionals actually say and do about disability? It is clear that this influence cannot be accounted for in terms of theoretical coherence or empirical grounding, for, as one disabled sociologist has pointed out, reflecting upon his own experience of disability,

> I realised how meagre are our attempts to write and do research about adjustment and adaptation. It would be nice if, at some point, growing up ends and maturity beings, or if one could say that successful adjustment and adaptation to a particular difficulty has been achieved. For most problems, or perhaps most basic life issues, there is no single time for such a resolution to occur. The problems must be faced, evaluated, re-defined, and readapted to, again and again and again. And I knew now that this applied to myself. No matter how much I was admired by others or by myself, there was still much more I had to face. 'My Polio' and 'My Accident' were not just my past; they were part of my present and my future.
>
> (Zola, 1982, p. 84)

In recent years a link has emerged between these professional constructions of disability as adjustment and cultural images of disabled people.

> The most prevalent image in films and especially in television during the past several decades has been the maladjusted disabled person. These stories involve characters

with physical or sensory, rather than mental, handicaps. The plots follow a consistent pattern: The disabled central characters are bitter and self-pitying because, however long they have been disabled, they have never adjusted to their handicaps, and never accepted themselves as they are.

(Longmore, 1987, p. 70)

Thus, it is disabled people who have the problem. They treat their families and friends badly until, long-suffering enough, they confront these disabled people, giving them 'an emotional slap in the face'. The disabled person then realises that it is him or her that has the problem, accepts the rebuke and becomes a well-adjusted adult.

Hence, professionals are clearly influenced by cultural images and ideological constructions of disability as an individual, medical and tragic problem. The issue of adjustment, therefore, became the focus for professional intervention and reinforced these very images and constructions by rooting them in practice.

The problem with these cultural images, as with professional constructions, is that they ignore issues of social prejudice and institutional discrimination. The non-disabled have little trouble in accepting disabled people and indeed understand the problems of disability better than the disabled people themselves. This, of course, as disabled people know, is exactly the opposite of reality.

Social adjustment: a sociological approach

Thus psychological approaches fail to provide an adequate account of the experience of disability, and there have been attempts to develop alternative frameworks using the concepts of social adjustment and social oppression. These attempt to locate the experience of disability within a wider social context and to consider the wider social forces which structure the experience of disability.

In a study of men with a spinal-cord injury (SCI), the concept of social adjustment was developed to facilitate an understanding of the wide variety of personal responses to spinal injury:

> understanding the consequences of SCI involves a complex relationship between the impaired individual, the social context within which the impairment occurs and the meanings available to individuals to enable them to make sense of what is happening. This is what we mean by social adjustment; it is more than simply the functional limitations that an individual has or the social restrictions encountered; it is a complex relationship between impairment, social restrictions and meaning.
>
> (Oliver *et al.*, 1988, pp. 11–12)

The experience of spinal-cord injury, therefore, cannot be understood in terms of purely internal psychological or interpersonal processes, but requires a whole range of other material factors, such as housing, finance, employment, the built environment and family circumstances, to be taken into account. Further, all of these material factors can and will change over time, sometimes for the better and sometimes for the worse, giving the experience of disability a temporal as well as a material dimension.

Hence the personal responses of individuals to their disabilities cannot be understood merely as a reaction to trauma or tragedy but have to be located in a framework which takes account of both history and ideology. Thus 'a materialist understanding of the individual must centre upon two aspects of the ensemble of social relations of which the person is constituted: the performance of labour and the incorporation of ideology' (Leonard, 1984, p. 180). If this is the case, and I would argue that it is, then whether counselling is of any use to disabled people becomes a crucial question.

Resolving the paradox

The paradox in general terms concerns the relationship of the individual to society; the paradox in specific terms of disability concerns the relationship between individually experienced impairment and socially imposed disability. These relationships, general and specific, can be mediated through politics, through empowerment, through therapy or any number of other approaches. Hence, as the relationship between impaired individuals and disabling society has come more sharply into focus, it is inevitable that appropriate mechanisms for making sense of this should come into being.

In recent years counselling has become an important mechanism for addressing, if not resolving, the paradox between the individual and society. Therefore it is not surprising that disabled people should see counselling as a way of dealing with the relationship between their individual impairments and their disabling society. The crucial question posed at the beginning of this paper, however, was: can counselling do it? Do disabled people need counselling?

As I have demonstrated, not *all* counselling can, but I believe that person-centred counselling has a substantial contribution to make because, by its very nature, it does not make judgements about how people adjust to their disabilities. It does not impose its own meaning on situations, does not make judgements in advance or put labels on people. It is not about someone's impairment or their disability but about helping them to make sense of the relationship between the two. Carl Rogers (1980, p. 42), the guiding influence of such an approach, provides a quote from Chinese philosophy which captures the essence of what this form of counselling can provide and is not a million miles away from what disabled people need in order to make sense of their worlds.

> If I keep from meddling with people, they take care of themselves,
> If I keep from commanding people, they behave themselves,
> If I keep from preaching at people, they improve themselves,
> If I keep from imposing on people, they become themselves.
>
> (Lao-Tsze)

References

Berger, R. (1988) 'Helping clients survive a loss', *Social Work Today*, Vol. 19, No. 34.

Campling, J. (ed.) (1981) *Images of Ourselves*, Routledge and Kegan Paul, London.

Creschendo, J. (1989) 'I'm in love with my body', in 'Johnny Creshcendo Revealed', unpublished.

Leonard, P. (1984) *Personality and Ideology*, Macmillan, London.

Longmore, P. (1987) 'Screaming stereotypes: images of disabled people in television and motion pictures', in Gartner, A. and Joe, T. (eds) *Images of the Disabled: Disabling Images*, Praeger, New York.

Morris, J. (ed.) (1989) *Able Lives: Women's Experiences of Paralysis*, The Women's Press, London.

Nelson-Jones, R. (1982) *The Theory and Practice of Counselling Psychology*, Cassell, London.

Oliver, M., Zarb, G., Moore, M., Silver, J. and Salisbury, V. (1988) *Walking into Darkness: the Experience of Spinal Injury*, Macmillan, London.

Owen, P. (1985) 'A view of disability in current social work literature', *American Behavioural Scientist*, Vol. 28, No. 3.

Rogers, C. (1980) *A Way of Being*, Houghton Mifflin, Boston.

Seligman, M. (1975) *Helplessness: On Depression, Development and Death*, W. H. Freeman, San Francisco.

Siller, J. (1969) 'Psychological situation of the disabled with spinal cord injuries', *Rehabilitation Literature*, Vol. 30, pp. 290–6.

Silver, R. and Wortman, C. (1980) 'Coping with undesirable life events', in Gerber, J. and Seligman, M. (eds) *Human Helplessness: Theory and Applications*, Academic Press, London.

Sutherland, A. (1981) *Disabled We Stand*, Souvenir Press, London.

Trieschman, R. (1980) *Spinal Cord Injuries*, Pergamon Press, Oxford.

Vargo, F. and Stewin, L. (1984) 'Spousal adaptation to disability: ramifications and implications for counselling', *International Journal for the Advancement of Counselling*, Vol. 7, pp. 253–60.

Zola, I. (1982) 'Social and cultural disincentives to independent living', *Archives of Physical Medicine and Rehabilitation*, Vol. 63.

4.7

Access to new technology in the employment of disabled people

Alan Roulstone

Introduction

This article is based upon the author's research in new technology and the employment experiences of disabled people, in which a 'barriers' approach is used to access the range of employment experiences of a nationwide sample of disabled workers.

The significance of new technology for the disabled worker

The potential of new information and communication technologies for disabled people is gaining increasing recognition in both the rehabilitation and disability studies fields. To date, the rehabilitation approach has emphasised the way in which technology corrects or normalises the impaired person. Such terms as 'augmentative technology', and 'compensation' are commonplace in the literature. 'Technology is . . . Providing the ability to manufacture devices which offset many handicaps' (Steventon, 1983, p. 45). The American writer Frank Bowe notes how desktop technologies can now help the blind to 'see', the speech-impaired to 'speak' and the hearing-impaired to 'listen' (Bowe, 1990; see also Cornes, in Oliver, 1991a, pp. 99–114). The primary emphasis here is on what Giannini calls a 'promising alliance' (in Hazan, 1981) between the corrective functions of technology and the deficits of the disabled person.

The 1980s have also witnessed a growth in the output of optimistic work from disability studies writers whose emphasis is upon the enabling potential of new technology (although there are dissenting options; see Oliver, 1990, p. 125). The positive scope of new technology is said to offer:

1 a wider range of employment options as more jobs are computerised
2 a wider range of tasks in any given employment
3 flexible working arrangements, with, for example, the potential for home-based employment

4 enhanced quality of working life, with less physical demands allowing for a
   concentration of energies into other tasks
5 the abilities of disabled workers to be emphasised, and (in theory) shifting
   perceptions as to what disability is.

At its most optimistic such a viewpoint suggests that: 'microprocessor devices
and computer designs extend the disabled person's sense of autonomy and
self-reliance and enable him or her to be more active in society' (Weinberg,
1990, p. 128). Whilst others have provided a picture of new technology
applications (Schofield, 1981; Rajan, 1985; Sandhu and Richardson, 1989;
Cornes, in Oliver, 1991a, pp. 99–114) it is important to outline these benefits.

At a general level, obvious potential exists for the further use of desktop
computing applications which can reduce the amount of physical activity
required in filing, walking around large buildings, climbing stairs and
retrieving documents. Networked computing allows ease of access to
databanks, and can also allow easier communication via electronic mail. The
ability to perform a number of varied functions from one workstation can have
major implications for reducing the barriers inherent in large and difficult
buildings. Electronic facsimiles, or faxes, can save valuable energy, especially
where one is sending information of a technical kind which would be difficult
to transmit over the phone.

The massive potential of desktop technology, even for the less severely
impaired worker, is summed up in the following quote from the author's own
research: 'Using the personal computer means that I can let my fingers do the
walking.' Electronic print scanners, braille keyboards and speech synthesisers
enable visually impaired workers to read, produce and transmit documents.
This can open up the working world, based on text, and offer greater potential
for more equal employment opportunities. The speech synthesiser (along
with the pocket-sized personal communicator) also allows people with
speech impairments to communicate.

There are now a number of applications, of both hardware and software,
which allow formerly excluded workers with limited motor control to operate
computers with head, tongue, chin, pneumatic and light-beam operation.
However, there is little evidence of widespread employment allowance for
such forms of operation. Many remain within the school, college or
training-centre area.

One of the most significant aspects of microchip technology is the ease of
applying sophisticated communications devices which allow 'remote' working, especially for homeworking. This makes it possible to change the way
employment is organised so that work comes to the employee and not the
other way around.

However, whilst evidence of wider employment opportunities and enhanced employment is available (Ashok *et al.*, 1985; Rajan, 1985; Cornes,
1987), little evidence exists to show that new technology is redefining the
notion of disability. It is worth looking at this idea in more detail.

Placing information and communication at the disabled worker's fingertips not only provides ease of access to the workplace and information, but allows for a more focused operation of tasks that is based *less on physical prowess*. This questions fundamentally the root or source of disability, and suggests that disablement is to be located squarely in environmental and attitudinal barriers.

A question of access: factors enhancing and limiting access to technology and technology-based employment

Factors enhancing access

The realisation among educators, rehabilitation practitioners, disablement resettlement officers and disability activists of the particular benefits of new technology in the training and employment of disabled people has begun to filter through into training and resettlement programmes. A growing number of colleges for disabled children and young adults are making conscious efforts to include technology education and training, so that training in word processing, spreadsheets, computer-based learning and in some cases basic programming, forms an integral part of the syllabus. Any comparison with what was provided 10 years ago would indicate the changes that have occurred (see, for example, National Foundation for Educational Research, 1982, pp. 2–6).

The diffusion of technology into white-collar work has occurred at an astonishing rate; although a debate rages about the impact on employment/ unemployment of new technology, the total number of potentially accessible jobs is set to rise as more jobs are computerised.

The reduced cost of personal computers not only makes the adoption of equipment more attractive for employers, it also allows more unemployed disabled people to become familiar with such technology. Research undertaken by the author suggests that many disabled workers have at home technology which was beneficial to their early experiences with technology at work.

As more disabled people are employed, the potential for a knock-on effect exists. This has yet to be seen, but the possibilities for employing disabled people who use technology should expand as their abilities are realised. Whilst attitudinal change should not be overstated, the practicalities of employing formerly excluded workers should become ever more obvious.

Factors inhibiting access

Although computers are getting cheaper, business-standard equipment, especially for small businesses, may still represent a major overhead. Even if a worker were to become impaired whilst employed for a given company, the costs of locating to a new technology-based job may still be inhibitory. In addition, where technology is bought relatively cheaply for home use, it may not be compatible with business equipment.

The increasingly technology-inclusive education and training may fail to benefit those made redundant in the traditional employment sectors. In addition, as the recent Office of Population Censuses and Surveys (1989) study on employment and disability notes, the majority of disabled people now employed, are employed in lower-grade manual work. The implications are that disabled workers would be ill-prepared to shift to technology-based white-collar work. There is also ample scope here for 'technofear', where exposure to technology occurs for the first time.

The rapid changes in computing, the often impenetrable instruction manuals and the patchy provision of adult computer training for disabled workers/ex-workers all militate against ease of access where a career change is necessary.

The restrictions that surround the state benefits system, particularly invalidity benefit, Severe Disablement Allowance and the therapeutic earnings rule, have all been criticised for limiting the scope for combining benefits with part-time work. This is especially true where a gradual re-entry into employment is sought. Although computer-based work offers greater flexibility, the 'fit for work' rulings mean that the opportunities for entry into new areas of work are extremely difficult. The new Disability Working Allowance aims to break down the rigidities of the benefits system.

A fundamental factor that hinders access to new technology work is the mis-match between the requirements of the more intellectually demanding forms of computer work – programming and systems analysis – and the life experiences of many disabled people. The dependency relationship foisted upon many disabled people (Barton, 1989, pp. 1–5) and the helper–helped relationship (Finkelstein, in Brechin *et al.*, 1981, pp. 58–63) may not be well suited to work which demands self-confidence and assuredness; as Croxen notes, 'The demands for the particular skills of the microtechnological environment puts the disabled at a particular disadvantage. A career in disability does not generally make for independent autonomous thinking' (Croxen, 1982, p. 15). A less tangible factor inhibiting access to technology in employment is the issue of attitudes. There is nothing inherently egalitarian about technology, and evidence suggests that the way computers are introduced and used varies widely across organisations (Child, 1987, pp. 76–97). Even when disabled workers work with technology there is no guarantee that the technology will be used in an enabling way. This is particularly evident during the early stages of employing disabled people with new technology; here the newness of the employment (or redeployment) can lead to an inappropriate, disabling use of technology. An example of this is where disabled employees are given such work because it is thought that it equates with the 'backroom' perceptions of the kind of work disabled people do. Perhaps the most disturbing element of the employment of disabled technology-users is that although workers themselves realise the particular benefits that technology has for them, the employer may be oblivious to these benefits. The main message coming from a discussion of inhibitory factors is that access to technology is generally not a conscious process.

The Special Aids to Employment scheme: a special case

The Department of Employment's Special Aids to Employment scheme (the SAE scheme) warrants particular attention because it acts as the main gatekeeper of technological resources. The provision is especially significant as it forms a part of the employment welfare measures of the post-war era; this places the scheme outside the direct forces of supply and demand characteristic of the capitalist labour market. Most disabled workers who use technology in their work have had little or no contact with the scheme. However, the main users of the scheme are severely impaired workers who face substantial barriers in the working environment.

The scheme is a product of the 1944 Employment (Disabled Persons) Act, whilst the present service is the outcome of piece-meal alterations to the 1944 provisions. This Act attempted to assist the return of disabled persons to the employment arena (for a full assessment of the Act, see Topliss, 1982).

The aim of the scheme was to provide equipment according to the Department of Employment's (the then Ministry of Labour) own assessment process as to who might benefit from such support. The scheme falls within what Finkelstein calls the 'administrative' tradition of social policy (Finkelstein, in Oliver, 1991a, pp. 19–39), in that improvements to the scheme are limited to questions of numbers benefiting, and the matching of technologies to 'disabilities'. No attempt is made to question the basic principle or premises of the scheme, nor does the scheme allow representations from disabled people about its form or efficacy.

The main assumption behind the scheme is that equipment serves to 'correct' the deficits of the disabled person. This assumption lies firmly within the individualising notions at the heart of rehabilitative and medical models of disability.

Recent developments have meant that the scheme is now run by the Employment Department (formerly the Manpower Services Commission). The staffing of the scheme, and the development of the Disablement Advisory Service (DAS) as a discrete organisation, provides recognition of the potential that technological and technical aids can have for disabled workers.

The inbuilt limitations of the SAE scheme

By taking a corrective view of technical aid, the onus is placed upon disabled people to acquire technology, as they are seen as the root of the problem. A 'barriers' approach, in contrast, would logically lead to the notion of technology as a *right*, given its ability to equalise opportunity by making the working world accessible. At present the 1944 Act and its provisions provide the Secretary of State with the 'power' to provide aids and equipment. The eligibility for 'assistance' has meant that those for whom it is thought no 'correction' is possible will not be eligible. This contrasts heavily with a scheme based on rights, where eligibility relies upon the potential for technology to surmount workplace barriers.

One of the most glaring problems with the SAE scheme is that applicants are only eligible for technological assistance if they have, or are very likely to obtain, work. This can operate as a 'Catch 22', where no employment is available without the offer of techno-support, whilst no offer of help is likely unless one has, or is very likely to gain, employment. Another, related, issue is that disabled people who seek work (or useful forms of non-paid employment) but who are unemployed could still benefit from having equipment on a loan basis. Findings from the author's own research suggest that this would allow familiarisation with and competence in desktop technology, especially where a basic training course has already been followed. This could make all the difference between simple computer-competence and computer-confidence.

Another important barrier is the bar on technological provision where it is felt that the equipment requested is used as an everyday item in the applicant's workplace. The assumption is that the employer should provide the equipment, where such equipment is otherwise available. Whilst this approach may have been designed to avoid wholesale abuse of the scheme, it can mean that the disabled employee or job-seeker is stuck between intransigent employers and DAS officials.

Perhaps the most extraordinary aspect of the scheme, one which reflects the scheme's disabling premises, is that the equipment provided should have 'unique' benefits for the disabled worker, which are not evident for able-bodied workers. The consequence of this is that technology may not be provided for the large number of disabled workers/job-seekers who are less severely impaired. The confusion here is between 'particular' and 'unique' benefits. Arguably technology has benefits for able-bodied workers also; however, such benefits are not central to the worker's ability to overcome physical barriers in the workplace. Therefore the scheme operates to exclude large numbers of would-be beneficiaries who could claim particular benefits of technology in their work. By loading emphasis on the need for 'unique' benefits, not only is the scheme emphasising unnecessary differences, but it is also guaranteeing its own limits to expansion.

Whilst new technology has the potential to increase employment options and flexibility, the uncertainty that surrounds the transferability of equipment means that recipients may find themselves trapped in a particular job, and afraid to move for fear of losing the technology provided. Although opposition to transfer has not yet been observed, a number of beneficiaries have noted their uncertainty about the effects of moving jobs, as the technology remains the property of the Department of Employment.

Conclusions

There are several important issues concerning access to technology in the employment of disabled people. First, much of the discussion on the potential of new technology is couched in terms of *technical* possibilities, where the latest device is heralded as the new saviour for disabled people. Whilst such thinking may be laudable, it can serve to obscure the equally significant issue of *access* to technology. The ability to access technology is of crucial importance if new technologies are to realise their potential for disabled workers.

Second, the employment of disabled people in technology-based work is not seen as a guarantee that the particular benefits of technology for disabled workers will be noticed. In our research many workers, whilst appreciating the benefits themselves, note that these go unnoticed by most employers. This is perhaps a comment on the employment relationship generally, especially where the employee is not a 'core' worker (for example if they work part-time; see Oliver, 1991b, pp. 132–47). The fact that technology is not designed, constructed and used in a social vacuum suggests that employers have a central role in realising the 'promising alliance' between disabled workers and new technology.

The final and fundamental point is that technology has generally been seen to 'correct' the deficits of the impaired individual, rather than the prime focus being on the impact of technology on employment barriers (physical and attitudinal). It seems clear that this permeates most mainstream areas of provision, from rehabilitation to the government-backed SAE scheme. Arguably, not only does the focus need to shift to an emphasis upon the impact on barriers, but, in terms of the SAE scheme, this can only be achieved by seeing new technology as a *right*, where it is used to open up the employment domain and create an environment in which the chance for expression of abilities is optimised.

References

Ashok, H., Hall, J. and Huws, U. (1985) *Home Sweet Workstation: Homeworking and the Employment Needs of People with Severe Disabilities*, Greater London Council, London.

Barton, L. (ed.) (1989)] *Disability and Dependency*, Falmer Press, London.

Bowe, F. (1990) 'Disabled and elderly in the first, second and third world', *International Journal of Rehabilitation Research*, Vol. 13, pp. 1–14.

Brechin, A., Liddiard, P. and Swain, J. (eds) (1981) *Handicap in a Social World*, Hodder and Stoughton, Sevenoaks/The Open University Press, Milton Keynes.

Child, J. (1987) 'Managerial strategies, new technology and the labour process', in Finnigan, R., Salaman, G. and Thomspon, K. (eds) *Information Technology: Social Issues. A Reader*, Hodder and Stoughton, Sevenoaks/The Open University Press, Milton Keynes.

Comes, P. (1987) *The Impact of New Technology on the Employment of Persons with Disabilities in Great Britain*, Rehabilitation International and the Commission of European Communities.

Croxen, M. (1982) *Disability and Employment: Report to the Commission of European Communities*, Commission of European Communities, Brussels.

Hazan, P. (1981) *Computing*, January, pp. 12–13.

National Foundation for Education Research (1982) *Young Disabled People: Their Further Education, Training, and Employment*, Nelson, Windsor.

Oliver, M. (1990) *The Politics of Disablement*, Macmillan, London.

Oliver, M. (ed.) (1991a) *Social Work, Disabled People and Disabling Environments*, Routledge and Kegan Paul, London.

Oliver, M. (1991b) 'Poor Work', in Brown, P. and Scase, R. (eds) *Disadvantage and the Division of Labour*, The Open University Press, Buckingham.

Office of Population Censuses and Surveys (1989) *Disabled Adults: Services, Transport and Employment*, Report No. 4, Social Survey Division.

Rajan, A. (1985) *Information Technology and Disabled Young Workers*, OECD/Institute of Manpower Studies, University of Sussex.

Sandhu, J. and Richardson, S. (1989) *Concerned Technology: Electronic Aids for People with Special Needs*, CT 89.

Schofield, J. M. (1981) *Microcomputer Based Aids for the Disabled*, Heyden/British Computer Society, London.

Steventon, J. (1983) *International Journal of Rehabilitation Research*, Vol. 6, No. 4.

Topliss, E. (1982) *Social Responses to Handicap*, Longman, Harlow.

Weinberg, N. (1990) *Computers in the Information Society*, Westview Press, London.

4.8

A four-way stretch? The politics of disability and caring

Gillian Parker

The past few years have seen a blossoming of research and comment about the provision of 'care in the community' to enable disabled and frail older people to remain in their own homes. Implicit in many of the government policy documents in this area is the assumption that 'care in the community' cannot be achieved without the (substantial) involvement of 'informal carers': the family, friends and neighbours of disabled and older people.

While the majority of frail older and disabled people are indeed supported primarily by members of their informal networks, is this situation inevitable and, indeed, is it 'right'? Argument and debate in this area is characterised by a number of apparently irreconcilable positions. First, there is a developing social policy of community care which sees the informal provision of the majority of help and support to disabled and older people as 'right' and to be encouraged. Second, there are the organisations of disabled people who argue that disabled people do not want 'care', and, by extension, do not want informal carers (Wood, 1991). Rather, they want redirected and/or increased resources and self-directed services that will give them the freedom to arrange their own lives. Third, organisations of and for informal carers argue that they want recognition for carers and services and support which will help them in the role but without fundamentally altering the relationship between the carer and the disabled person. Finally, there are feminist writers who challenge family-based models of care which, they argue, inevitably mean that women become the major providers of (unpaid) help and support to disabled people. The solutions they suggest are residential or communal forms of care for older and disabled people.

In this paper I hope to unravel some of these positions and ask whether they are really as far apart as they seem. To do this, we have to start with some understanding of current policy on community care for disabled and older people and the way in which this prompted a feminist critique of reliance on informal care as a means of delivering the policy.

Community care policy

The notion of 'community care' has existed in British health and welfare policy since at least the turn of the century. Although it was originally concerned primarily with people with learning disabilities or mental health problems, the concept broadened during the century to include other people seen to be in need of some degree of physical or social support (see Parker, 1990).

Until recently, the impetus to promote community care has been based on assumptions that living outside large-scale, segregated institutions, and preferably with family members, is in the best interests of disabled people and accords with their wishes and those of their families and friends. The aims of policy have been both to promote independence among people in long-stay residential establishments to enable them, wherever possible, to move into the 'community', and to promote independence among those currently living in the community who might be at risk of entering residential care. These aims, however, have been clouded by other, both covert and overt, policy issues. One of these has been that of cost. Since the mid-1970s, official policy statements have increasingly argued not only that the state cannot bear the costs of 'expensive' residential care but also that it cannot afford to provide a comprehensive network of health and welfare services to support the many older or disabled people who live outside formal institutions:

> Providing adequate support and care for elderly people in all their varying circumstances is a matter which concerns – *and should involve* – the whole community . . . Public authorities simply will not command the resources to deal with it alone.
> (Department of Health and Social Security, 1981, paragraph 1.11; my emphasis)

A second issue (although one which is closely related to that of cost) has been an assertion of family and community 'responsibility' for providing help and support to older people living in the community. This was given quite explicit emphasis in the 1981 White Paper on services for older people, *Growing Older*, which asserted that:

> the primary sources of support and care for elderly people are informal and voluntary. These spring from the personal ties of kinship, friendship and neighbour-hood . . . It is the role of public authorities to sustain and, where necessary, to develop – but never to displace – such support and care. Care *in* the community must increasingly mean care *by* the community.
> (Department of Health and Social Security, 1981, paragraph 1.9; original emphasis)

More recently, Sir Roy Griffiths' *Agenda for Action* on community care stated that families, friends, neighbours and other local people would 'continue to be the primary means by which people are enabled to live normal lives in community settings' (Griffiths, 1988, paragraph 3.2). Again, the primacy of the informal provision of help and support was emphasised, but this time a stance which was previously articulated only in relation to older people was carried over into policy prescription for *all* disabled people (see also Department of Health, 1989).

These developments have led to an inevitable shift in emphasis from statutory provision (which is seen as expensive) to informal and voluntary provision (which is seen as cheap or even 'free') as a means of implementing policy. As a result, the 'first task of publicly provided services' has become 'to support and where possible strengthen' informal networks (Griffiths, 1988, paragraph 3.2).

The new role for the state, then, is not to encourage self-directed independence for disabled and older people, but rather to maintain dependence on family and other informal networks, or, in some cases, to effect a transfer of dependence from the state to the family or neighbourhood.

Informal care and disability

Since the early 1970s there has been a substantial stream of empirical research about informal carers. This started with studies of the families of disabled offspring, both children and adults (for example Bayley, 1973; Wilkin, 1979; Bradshaw, 1980; Glendinning, 1983, 1985; Baldwin, 1985) but swiftly moved on to those caring for frail older people (for example Hunt, 1978; Nissel and Bonnerjea, 1982; Levin *et al.*, 1983; Wright, 1983; Wenger, 1984; Ungerson, 1987; Lewis and Meredith, 1988; Qureshi and Walker, 1989).

This research has led in two completely different directions. First, there has been the development of a feminist critique of reliance on informal care. This points to the extent to which women are the principal providers of help and support in the community and demonstrates the negative impact that this has on their employment, finances and social and emotional lives. This critique has largely seen women's responsibilities for informal care as rooted in and growing out of their conventional responsibilities for domestic service and child care. The 'solution' to reliance on informal support which follows from this analysis is to challenge and look for alternatives to family-based models, involving either communal or residential provision for older or disabled people (Dalley, 1983, 1988; Finch, 1984).

The second effect which this research on informal carers has had is to bring this group increasingly into the limelight; a process capped by their specific inclusion, for the first time ever, in British health and social services legislation – the Disabled Persons (Services, Representation and Consultation) Act 1986 and the National Health Service and Community Care Act 1990. This process has been accompanied by a growth in organisations representing carers' interests. Those who campaign for carers are looking for very different solutions from those which would be seen as appropriate by feminist writers. Instead of a challenge to family forms, carers' campaigners are looking for improvements at the margin which would improve both carers' and disabled people's lives but which would, by and large, leave the fundamental relationship between them unchanged (Pitkeathley, 1991).

This incorporation of informal carers into the policy arena has not been accompanied by questions about why so many disabled and older people have to rely on informal carers or suggested alternatives to this reliance. Rather, informal carers are increasingly seen as part of the 'natural' background; a given source of support for disabled people (Twigg, 1989).

This further alarms feminist commentators who see the possibility of *informal* carers becoming a *formal* part of the 'care packages' which are at the heart of the new community care arrangements (Land, 1991; Parker, 1991).

At the same time as feminists have been developing their analysis of caring, disabled writers have been developing their analysis of disability. This has been described in depth elsewhere (Oliver, 1990; Keith, 1991; and throughout this book). Debate about the nature of dependence, independence and interdependence, and, related to these, issues of power, choice and control have been central to disabled people's arguments. These are the very areas, however, which bring the disabled people's movement and the feminist analysis of informal caring most obviously into opposition.

An analysis which points to the ways in which disability is both socially constructed and socially created challenges conventional notions of dependence and independence. Independence is about control, not about abilities (Oliver, 1990).

> We do not use the term 'independent' to mean someone who can do everything for themself [*sic*], but to indicate someone who has taken control of their life and is choosing how that life is led . . . The most important factor is not the amount of physical tasks a person can perform, but the amount of control they have over their everyday routine. The degree of disability does not determine the amount of independence achieved.
>
> (Brisenden, 1986, p. 178)

The way in which dependence is constructed in the feminist debate generally fails to acknowledge this issue and rarely sees that the 'dependent person' may be giving as well as receiving help and support. For disabled women, who may be the major providers of 'care' in their homes, this second failure is one that is particularly galling (Keith, 1991; Morris, 1991).

Solutions put forward by some feminist writers to release women from the obligation to provide care, particularly the provision of enhanced forms of residential care or communal forms of living, are those which few disabled people would support:

> Disabled and older people experience daily the inadequacies of 'community care' and would agree with everything that feminists . . . say about the isolation, poverty and sheer hard work which too often characterises both their lives and that of their carers. However, disabled and older people as individuals and through their organisations have almost without exception put their energies into achieving a better quality of life *within* the community (taking this to mean outside residential care) and have maintained a (critical) support of community care policies.
>
> (Morris, 1991, p. 153)

A four-way stretch or a common agenda?

Is there any scope at all for the development of a common agenda between these apparently irreconcilable positions? Before attempting to identify any common ground, it is important to outline the weak points in each of the positions. This involves some major over-simplification, but might be helpful.

There are a number of implicit assumptions about the existing nature of 'care in the community' and its potential for expansion as a source of support for disabled and older people in recent policy documents. One of these is that 'the community' (which is rarely defined) does not do as much as it should to help disabled and older people. Related to this is the notion that there exists a large, untapped and dormant reserve of help within kinship, neighbourhood and friendship networks which, if only given the right sort of encouragement, would spring into life, thus doing away with the need for statutory services. A further assumption, and one which is particularly important here, is that reliance on informal, rather than formal, sources of help is what all disabled or older people themselves want. None of these assumptions is actually upheld by the available evidence (Parker, 1991, 1992).

The position maintained by organisations of disabled people is that, as disability is socially created, social and economic change can prevent individuals with impairments becoming disabled. Such change, and particularly the provision of 'personal support services which are directly under [the disabled persons'] control, or that of a chosen advocate' (Wood, 1991, p. 202), would thus remove the need for informal carers. There are three main problems with this position. First, the provision of personal support services from outside is likely to threaten certain sorts of relationships, particularly established marriages, and run counter to what some disabled people in those relationships want (Parker, 1992). Second, this position ignores the existing power dynamics within relationships which will influence 'choice' about preferred sources of support. Some women, in particular, may remain the main providers of personal support services because that is the wish of those they are close to. Third, this position is one which is more likely to meet the needs of younger, independent disabled people than those of, say, frail older people who have mental impairments, or those who are very ill as well as disabled.

The arguments of carers' organisations are weak because, while they acknowledge the needs of disabled people, they do not challenge the social creation of disability and, therefore, of carers. Such arguments do, however, acknowledge that disability and caring take place within existing relationships, that the dynamics of these relationships can be important, and that the needs of the disabled person and the carer may conflict.

The feminist challenge to the question of informal care, as we have seen, involves the development of residential and communal alternatives to family models of care. This fails to take into account the expressed wishes of most disabled and older people and, as Morris (1991) has argued, puts disabled people at the forefront of a challenge to forms of family life to which they have rarely had equal access. As the social creation of disability is not presented as central to this analysis, solutions which might reduce disability, *per se*, are not seen as central to the feminist agenda.

As Croft (1986) has pointed out, there is a real danger that current community care policies will increase 'divisions and conflicts of interest between [carers and disabled people] instead of encouraging alliances and solidarity' (p. 34). Energy which could be put into challenging the effects of community care policies might, instead, be diverted into a conflict between disabled people and informal carers as each group argues its pre-eminence.

Feminists searching for an alternative to reliance on female informal carers have looked in the wrong direction for their solutions mainly, some would argue, because they have cast the disabled or older person in the postion of 'other' (Keith, 1990). Thus while:

> Feminist research on carers is a valuable application of the principle 'the personal is the political' . . . the failure to include the subjective experience of 'the cared-for' has meant that the feminist analysis and strategies stemming from the research have a number of limitations. Most importantly it has resulted in a dilemma being posed between 'care in the community' *or* residential care, which is in many ways a false dichotomy.
>
> (Morris, 1991, p. 156; original emphasis)

Similarly, Graham (1991) points out that both community care policy-makers and the feminists who criticise them have failed to distinguish conceptually between 'the location' and 'the social relations of care'. Thus the home-based provision of support for disabled people and the involvement of informal carers have been analysed in ways that *assume* that they are inextricably and unavoidably linked. What ways forward are available which *unlink* the two and make the creation of a common agenda possible?

The first step is to acknowledge that disability is socially created and that action committed to reducing the effects of a disabling social, economic and physical environment will also reduce the need for anyone, man or woman, to provide informal care. Within this commitment, however, there has to be a recognition that the existing dynamics of relationships, and women's position in them, would be unchanged. Different people – women, black people, older people, those who are ill as well as disabled – may have their disability created in different ways. The agenda will not be the same for all, and neither will the way in which they wish to have their needs for personal support met.

That some people *will* wish to have their personal support needs met through informal relationships means that there will still be informal carers. A continuing feminist analysis is needed to point out why, in many cases, it will still be women who become carers, but it must also start to incorporate growing evidence about the involvement of men (Parker and Lawton, 1992) and how this can be encouraged (Baldwin and Twigg, 1991). Further, this analysis will have to acknowledge 'the reciprocity involved in caring relationships and the threats to that reciprocity . . . because it is the loss of reciprocity which brings about inequality within a relationship – and disabled and older people are very vulnerable within the unequal relationships which they commonly experience with the non-disabled world' (Morris, 1991, p.163). As Morris also points out, dependence on a partner or family member is exploitative to *both* sides if it is necessary because of a lack of any alternative.

Finally, because some people will continue to provide unpaid help and support – the parents of young disabled children, some spouses, some offspring of frail older people, for example – there will be a continued need for recognition of their contribution and support for *them* as well as for the person they help.

Conclusion

The new community care arrangements and the policy documents which preceded them emphasise a system which is needs-led rather than service-led – where the identified needs of disabled and older people and carers determine the shape of service-led provision, rather than the other way around. If this really did become the guiding principle behind the changes then much of the tension between the positions outlined above could be resolved. However, given the context within which the new arrangements have been introduced, particularly the expected reliance on informal networks to deliver the majority of 'community care', it is difficult to see how this principle *can* be applied to all. There is a danger, therefore, that an even greater wedge will be driven between the disabled people's movement, carers' organisations and feminist commentators. As argued here, developments at both a theoretical and a practical level are needed if this is to be avoided.

References

Baldwin, S.M. (1985) *The Costs of Caring*, Routledge and Kegan Paul, London.

Baldwin, S. and Twigg, J. (1991) 'Women and community care – reflections on a debate', in Maclean, M. and Groves, D. (eds) *Women's Issues in Social Policy*, Routledge, London.

Bayley, M. (1973) *Mental Handicap and Community Care*, Routledge and Kegan Paul, London.

Bradshaw, J. (1980) *The Family Fund: an Initiative in Social Policy*, Routledge and Kegan Paul, London.

Brisenden, S. (1986) 'Independent living and the medical model of disability', *Disability, Handicap and Society*, Vol. 1, No. 2, pp. 173–8.

Croft, S. (1986) 'Women, caring and the recasting of need – a feminist reappraisal', *Critical Social Policy*, Vol. 6, No. 1, pp. 23–39.

Dalley, G. (1983) 'Ideologies of care in a feminist contribution to the debate', *Critical Social Policy*, Vol. 8, pp. 72–82.

Dalley, G. (1988) *Ideologies of Caring*, Macmillan, London.

Department of Health and Social Security (Scottish Office/Welsh Office/Northern Ireland Office) (1981) *Growing Older*, Cmnd. 8173, HMSO, London.

Department of Health (1989) *Caring for People: Community Care in the Next Decade and Beyond*, Cm 849, HMSO, London.

Finch, J. (1984) 'Community care: developing non-sexist alternatives', *Critical Social Policy*, Vol. 9, pp. 6–18.

Glendinning, C. (1983) *Unshared Care*, Routledge and Kegan Paul, London.

Glendinning, C. (1985) *A Single Door*, George Allen and Unwin, London.

Graham, H. (1991) 'The concept of caring in feminist research: the case of domestic service', *Sociology*, Vol. 25, No. 1, pp. 61–78.

Griffiths, R. (1988) *Community Care: an Agenda for Action*, HMSO, London.

Hunt, A. (1978) *The Elderly at Home*, OPCS Social Survey Division, HMSO, London.

Keith, L. (1990) 'Caring partnership', *Community Care*, 22 February.

Keith, L. (1991) 'Some thoughts on the current debate on disabled and elderly people and carers', paper given to Disability Research Seminar No. 4, June 1991, held at the Policy Studies Institute, London.

Land, H., (1991) 'Time to care', in Maclean, M. and Groves, D. (eds) *Women's Issues in Social Policy*, Routledge, London.

Levin, E., Sinclair, I. and Gorbach, P. (1983) 'The supporters of confused elderly people at home: extract from the main report', National Institute for Social Work Research Unit, London.

Lewis, J. and Meredith, B. (1988) *Daughters Who Care: Daughters Caring for Mothers at Home*, Routledge and Kegan Paul, London.

Morris, J. (1991) *Pride Against Prejudice: Transforming Attitudes to Disability*, The Women's Press, London.

Nissel, M. and Bonnerjea, L. (1982) *Family Care of the Handicapped Elderly: Who Pays?* Policy Studies Institute, London.

Oliver, M. (1990) *The Politics of Disablement*, Macmillan, London.

Parker, G. (1990) *With Due Care and Attention: a Review of the Literature on Informal Care*, 2nd edn, Family Policy Studies Centre, London.

Parker, G. (1991) 'Whose care? Whose costs? Whose benefit? A critical review of research on case management and informal care', *Ageing and Society*, Vol. 10, pp. 459–67.

Parker, G. (1992) *With This Body: Caring, Disability and Marriage*, The Open University Press, Buckingham.

Parker, G. and Lawton, D. (1992, forthcoming) *Different Types of Care, Different Types of Carers*, HMSO, London.

Pitkeathley, J. (1991) 'The carer's viewpoint', in Dalley, G. (ed.) *Disability and Social Policy*, Policy Studies Institute, London.

Qureshi, H. and Walker, A. (1989) *The Caring Relationship: Elderly People and Their Families*, Macmillan, London.

Twigg, J. (1989) 'Models of caring: how do social care agencies conceptualise their relationship with informal carers?', *Journal of Social Policy*, Vol. 18, No. 1, pp. 53–66.

Ungerson, G. (1987) *Policy is Personal: Sex, Gender and Informal Care*, Tavistock, London.

Wenger, C. (1984) *The Supportive Network: Coping with Old Age*, George Allen and Unwin, London.

Wilkin, D. (1979) *Caring for the Mentally Handicapped Child*, Croom Helm, London.

Wood, R. (1991) 'Care of disabled people', in Dalley, G. (ed.) *Disability and Social Policy*, Policy Studies Institute, London.

Wright, F. (1983) 'Single carers: employment, housework and caring', in Finch, J. and Groves, D. (eds) *A Labour of Love: Women, Work and Caring*, Routledge and Kegan Paul, London.

SECTION 5:
CREATING A SOCIETY
FIT FOR ALL

5.1

'Talking to top people': some issues relating to the citizenship of people with learning difficulties

Jan Walmsley

Introduction

Citizenship is now a fashionable topic. Ruth Lister (1990) and Ralf Dahrendorf (1990) have called the 1990s the 'decade of the citizen'. The rhetoric of citizenship has been seized upon by both the right wing – the Conservative government's 'moral crusade' for active citizenship – and the left wing – Charter 88 and demands for the European Convention on Human Rights to be incorporated in British law (Knight, 1990).

The limitations on the exercise of *de jure* citizenship rights by particular groups have begun to be addressed. Lister (1990) discusses women; Smith (1989) discusses 'race'; and Driedger (1989) has dubbed Disabled Peoples' International 'The last civil rights movement'. In this paper, however, I propose to focus on the citizenship of people with learning difficulties (mental handicap) and suggest ways in which their citizenship claims can be furthered.

There are specific reasons for focusing on the situation of people with learning difficulties.

First, people with learning difficulties present a particular challenge if we are to create a citizenship model to 'provide everyone with the wherewithal to enjoy and participate in the benefits of pluralism' (Harris, 1987, p. 184) yet they are rarely considered. In seven publications which discuss citizenship, significant reference to people with learning difficulties is made in only two (Rankin, 1989; Heginbotham, 1990), and significantly these two are concerned with citizenship in the context of volunteering rather than making

This paper is an edited version of J. Walmsley (1991) ' "Talking to top people": some issues relating to the citizenship of people with learning difficulties', *Disability, Handicap and Society*, Vol. 6, No. 3, pp. 219–31.

claims to a broader justification of citizenship (the others are Turner, 1986; Harris, 1987; Hindess, 1987; King, 1987; Barbalet, 1988).

This is not surprising. People with learning difficulties have often been marginalised, and treated as in effect subhuman, beneath coinsideration (Wolfensberger, 1975). The study of mental handicap has historically been segregated, like people with learning difficulties themselves. Citizenship, as it has traditionally been conceived, has seemed an impossible status for people with learning difficulties.

Second, recent developments in the learning difficulties field suggest that citizenship for people with learning difficulties is not an empty dream. Despite ideological and structural barriers, which will be examined later in this paper, some people with learning difficulties are learning skills which enable them to participate in a meaningful way in decisions about their own lives, and in activities which might be categorised as pertaining to citizenship. Self-advocacy (Crawley, 1988) is about increasing the confidence and skills of individuals both to effect change for themselves, and to effect change in the world outside (Williams and Walmsley, 1990). Examples of the latter are increasingly common: the Nottingham Advocacy in Action project, for example, chronicles the following achievements of learning disabled co-workers in its Annual Report for 1989–90 (Advocacy in Action, 1989):

● working alongside the Open University to run training events in the East Midlands
● teaching social work students at the University of Nottingham
● training volunteers in disability awareness
● representing the interests of people with learning difficulties on social services committes.

Since the Annual Report the project has won a Social Work Today Partnership Award in competition with all comers. The skills practised by members of the Nottingham Advocacy in Action include 'talking to top people', the phrase which gave this article its title. It is clear from examples such as this that active citizenship is not an empty dream for people with learning difficulties. If this is the case, the reader might ask why an article such as this is needed. I believe the answer lies in the following:

● There are considerable ideological and sociostructural barriers to the exercise of citizenship rights by people with learning difficulties. Examples such as that of Nottingham Advocacy in Action cited above, though heartening, are rare, and tend to be achieved outside the family and service settings which frame the lives of most people with learning difficulties.
● The feminist critique of citizenship (Lister, 1990) emphasises the limitations that acting as carers places on the citizenship of women. However, on the face of it, liberation for carers may actually conflict with the claims of 'dependent' groups for citizenship, for example by reintroducing institutional care.
● Where is the place for people with learning difficulties in the Conservative government's concept of the active citizen? This emphasises the obligation

imposed upon citizens to contribute not only through taxation but also through charitable giving, and active volunteering (Patten, 1988). As it is currently conceived it is likely that active citizenship will require passive non-citizens to receive the bounty of such volunteering. People with learning difficulties are ideally placed to become subjects, rather than actors in such a scheme. However, people with learning difficulties can and do act as 'active citizens'. They give to, as well as take from, the community. Citizenship theory must also take this on board.

Citizenship and people with learning difficulties: an overview

A historical perspective

Within the broad literature on citizenship the assumption is that everyone is *de jure* a citizen (Smith, 1989), and that this is the product of a long and unfolding historical process, at least in Western democracies (Turner, 1986). But the concept of citizenship, stemming as it does from the Ancient Greek *polis*, carries with it a sense of privilege, and consequently a sense of exclusion. Citizenship was very much the prerogative of the Athenian property-owning male. It was not a status enjoyed by slaves, by women, or by non-Athenians (Bowle, 1947, ch. 4). It was T.H. Marshall's role to alter this ancient formulation of privilege, to provide a theoretical justification for redrawing the citizenship boundary to encompass the working class. Perhaps we could see them as the modern equivalent of Aristotle's slaves.

Most modern discussions of citizenship begin with Marshall's highly influential work (see, for example, Turner, 1986; Barbalet, 1988). Marshall's (1950) *Citizenship and Social Class* defined citizenship primarily in terms of equality of status and of the rights and duties stemming from full participatory membership of community. Marshall (1981) described three elements of citizenship: civil/legal, political and social. He traced the development of modern citizenship and characterised its development as sequential, thus the eighteenth century saw the securing of civil rights, the nineteenth, political rights and the twentieth, social rights. This does not appear to reflect the experiences of people with learning difficulties. As industrialisation proceeded, the need to define and make provision for disability grew. While citizenship rights may have developed for the majority, for people with learning difficulties they apparently diminished. In the late nineteenth and early twentieth centuries people with learning difficulties, or the 'feeble-minded', were perceived as unable to work, and a social problem (Barker, 1983; Jones, 1986). Civil rights, such as the right to own property, and equality before the law, were not secured for 'idiots'. Indeed, the nineteenth century saw an erosion of any civil rights that people with learning difficulties may have had, culminating in the passage of the 1913 Mental Deficiency Act which gave local authorities the power to place mental defectives in institutions or under guardianship on the say so of two doctors (Jones, 1972).

Though by no means all people with learning difficulties were institutionalised under the Act, instances of people losing their liberty for many years, and sometimes for life, under the terms of this Act, are not uncommon (see Potts and Fido, 1990, for some individual accounts).

The nineteenth and early twentieth centuries saw the gradual increase of political (suffrage) rights to virtually the entire population. By 1929, all British citizens over the age of 21, male and female, were entitled to vote: with one qualification, namely that they were of sound mind. Residents of mental hospitals were not, and are not, entitled to exercise their right to vote. As described above, the 1913 Act had given local authorities sweeping powers to compulsorily detain those deemed to be mentally defective. At the same time, though not necessarily intentionally, they also deprived people of their political rights under the terms of the same Act. Effectively, in the early twentieth century, many people with learning difficulties were denied both political and civil rights, at the same time, according to Marshall, as those rights were being secured for the populace as a whole.

Citizenship today: civil and political rights

What of civil and political rights today? In many respects people with learning difficulties are less well off than others in claiming civil and political rights. Political rights may exist formally, but in practice are often meaningless, if only to the extent that many polling stations are physically inaccessible to people with limited mobility (Oliver and Zarb, 1989; Lonsdale, 1990).

Civil rights are even more problematic. There is no legislation to protect people with learning difficulties from discrimination as there is for women and ethnic minorities (Lonsdale, 1990). Disabled people can legitimately be excluded from places of public entertainment in a way that is illegal for women and ethnic minorities. While Leach (1989) argues that disabled people are low on the Equal Opportunities shopping list, people with learning difficulties do not figure at all. It is not unusual for women with learning difficulties to be subject to compulsory sterilisation (Heginbotham, 1987; Jenkins, 1989). Whilst the UN Declaration on the Rights of Mentally Retarded Persons (1971) expects a guardian to be appointed if someone with a mental handicap is incapable of decision-making, 'This call is not fulfilled in England', as Gunn (1986) laconically comments, though he argues that a well-constructed form of guardianship could solve some of the problems created when a person is incapable of decision-making.

Social rights: ideological and structural limitations on the citizenship of people with learning difficulties

Formal political and civil rights are at best uncertain for people with learning difficulties. What of social rights? Before moving on to discuss this it is important to define what social rights consist of. Dahrendorf (1990) describes social rights as those which enable people to make use of the other two sets of rights, political and civil, and quotes two examples, the 'right not to fall below a certain level of income and the right to an education'. At one level, this makes a nonsense of discussing social rights for people with learning difficulties, as the burden of the argument so far is that these civil and political rights have been barely existent for people with learning difficulties. However, social rights are at least notionally in existence for people with learning difficulties, though the way these are structured perpetuates their economic dependency.

Regarding social rights Barbalet (1988) comments that social rights refer to individuals as consumers, not actors (p. 20). Not only this, he argues, but they are vulnerable, in a way civil rights are not, to economic recession. They can be readily withdrawn.

Crucially for people with learning difficulties, the 'social rights' to which they are entitled within the welfare state create a powerful, and often controlling, bureaucratic and professional layer to administer them (Oliver, 1990). That this is so is evident from the experiences of people with learning difficulties within the social security system. To obtain Mobility Allowance, for example, disabled people are subject to a medical examination to judge whether they are sufficiently immobile to warrant the allowance. Any improvement in their capacity to walk jeopardises their entitlement. 'Rights' are dependent on incapacity, and this incapacity is the subject of a medical judgement.

In addition, the way social security benefits are organised in Britain ensures that people with learning difficulties are both stigmatised and often in poverty. Few people with learning difficulties are eligible for an income based on National Insurance contributions, for the simple reason that they are not often in paid employment. Instead, if they live outside the family, they are dependent on Social Security benefits set at levels which ensure poverty. Thus their dependency is enshrined in the ideology of the welfare state, equally as forcibly as is the dependency of married women.

Poverty is also a restriction on the lives of people with learning difficulties. Those who live independently often rely on state benefits which are low: Flynn (1989) found that the average weekly income of 88 people in her study was £39 in 1985. In addition many people with learning difficulties live with their families well into adult life, approximately 60,000 in 1971 (Flynn and Saleem, 1986). This is also likely to be a barrier to full citizenship. For example, the family may come to rely on the income from the person with learning difficulties, particularly as caring for that person often inhibits family members, usually women, from taking paid work (Abbott, 1990). Seven of the 12 adults in Flynn and Saleem's study even handed over their meagre (£4 a week) earnings from the adult training centre (ATC) over to parents. The move away from institutional care to 'care in the community' is likely to increase the dependence of people with learning difficulties within the family – like young people without work (Wallace, 1987) people with learning difficulties are between the family and the state, dependent on both, independent of neither.

Feminist perspectives on citizenship: common ground and contradictory claims

Common ground

In an important article Ruth Lister (1990) has opened up a debate on the citizenship claims of women. Though, as she says, 'on the face of it, the language of citizenship appears to be gender-neutral', in effect, she argues, women's ability to exercise citizenship rights is limited.

Theoretically, the modern boundaries of citizenship do encompass women. Turner (1986) cites the Matrimonial Causes Acts and changes in the divorce laws as 'having had the consequence of not only equalising the relationship between men and women in marriage but also constituting women as legal personalities' (p. 96). However, this seems a superficial judgement. Lister argues that many women are not full citizens in practice. This is partly a consequence of their role as carers within the private world of the family, a role which leaves them little time or opportunity to participate actively in the public political realm.

A second issue for women, says Lister, is poverty. In this they also share some of the restrictions experienced by people with learning difficulties. Married women do not enjoy an income as of right, but one mediated by their place in the family, through their male partners. The effect is that women are very much 'second-class citizens'.

We can see here some parallels with the situation of people with learning difficulties. They too are often confined to the private world of the family. They too are excluded from full participation in the community partly through lack of the means by which to exercise 'citizenship' rights. Time is less likely to be a problem, but opportunity is: through lack of transport, lack of information and indeed lack of confidence to attend meetings and exercise political rights. Poverty, too, characterises the lives of many people with learning difficulties, excluded from paid work, and dependent on state benefits. Dependency, in the case of people with learning difficulties, is structured not through marriage, but through the family or services which control their often meagre income, and indeed restrict their freedom of movement: care can also be control (see, for example, Jahoda *et al.*, 1988; Richardson, 1989; Williams and Walmsley, 1990).

Contradictory claims?

It is important to note here that the interests of women as citizens are currently likely to be in conflict with the interests of people with learning difficulties as citizens. It is, in Lister's view, women's role as unpaid carers that is a major limitation on their opportunity exercise full citizenship rights. People with learning difficulties are likely to make heavy and continuing demands for care from their families, particularly as under-resourced care in the community becomes the norm (Abbott, 1990). In the current climate the way care is structured means that people with learning difficulties and other dependent groups are seen as limiting the opportunities for citizenship for carers. If women are to have their claims to citizenship recognised other means of caring for dependents will be needed. Yet providing alternatives to family-based care has traditionally meant institutionalisation for people who require care: and, potentially at least, this erodes their autonomy and their citizenship. Indeed Finch (1984) has advocated the reintroduction of residential care as less oppressive to women.

It would be unfortunate indeed if the claims of women to full citizenship are seen as being based on the denial of citizenship rights to people with learning difficulties and other dependent groups. Indeed, it would be non-sensical, for as Williams (1990) has pointed out, 'women with learning difficulties are women too'.

Duties and obligations: the active citizen

'Duties, the "other side" of citizenship, have stimulated a considerable amount of political conflict in the post war West' (Roche, 1990). Arguably, the denial of rights to people with learning difficulties is notionally justified on the grounds that they fall within the 'needs' rather than the 'work' group in society (Stone, 1985). Conceived of as net takers, rather than contributors to the community, they are susceptible to political or legal decisions which can amount to a denial of citizenship rights. The most extreme conclusion of this can be abortion of foetuses deemed to be severely handicapped, which arguably undermines the right of disabled people to exist (Davis, 1987). However, less dramatic examples, such as the poll tax issue referred to above, suffice to make the point.

In view of the work of Mead (1986) and others, the apparent failure of people with learning difficulties to contribute to society through the medium of paid work is likely to undermine any claims they may have to full citizenship rights. Mead's view that members of the underclass, the workshy, the long-term unemployed, should be resocialised into 'the social obligations of citizenship' suggests that for people with learning difficulties the only salvation is through 'normalisation', struggling to compete in the world of the able-bodied and able-minded.

However, Oliver (1990) argues that a different set of ideologies could allow disabled people to be seen to be making a material contribution to society. Some examples he quotes include people with learning difficulties undertaking work in ATCs which is paid at slave labour rates even by the standards of the Third World. With regard to another group of 'dependents', older women, Walker (1983) found a good deal of reciprocity in caring relationships: the older people gave as well as took. It is not difficult to find instances of such reciprocity existing in relationships between people with learning difficulties and others. Evidence from Atkinson and Williams (1990),

Potts and Fido (1990), Barron (1989) and Etherington *et al.*, (1988) shows that:

- many women with learning difficulties have informal roles as carers, for elderly parents, for brothers, for peers in group homes (though rarely for children)
- people with learning difficulties work in hostels at domestic tasks which in other situations would be classed as paid work, and historically hospital residents have undertaken unpaid hard manual labour, in laundries, hospital kitchens, gardens and hospital workshops, or, indeed, caring for other residents/patients
- some people with learning difficulties undertake voluntary work in the community, at old people's lunch clubs, day centres for stroke victims, etc.
- people with learning difficulties do undertake low-paid jobs which are not easy to fill by non-labelled people, in day centres, horticulture and as home helps.

If we add to the list of ways in which people with learning difficulties give as well as receive, by reference to the contribution people with learning difficulties make to the livelihood of professionals (Oliver, 1990), by their very existence, and their role as consumers of goods and services, the picture of them as givers to, as well as takers from, society is less bleak than at first sight it appears. For people with learning difficulties, like women, a lot of the work they do is invisible, taken for granted, and somehow does not count as work.

Ways forward: reconceptualising citizenship

It is impossible to undertake here the task of fully refashioning the concept of citizenship to incorporate all groups in society. However, here are some suggestions for action arising from the discussion in this paper:

- There is a danger that the citizenship rights of carers will, if they are fully recognised, be achieved at the expense of people regarded as dependents, including people with learning difficulties. Some people with learning difficulties are also women. Their claims must be promoted alongside the claims of carers.
- A range of support for people with learning difficulties is required as alternatives to community (family) care so that the needs of women and other informal carers are not in opposition to the needs of people with learning difficulties and other dependent groups.
- The benefits system needs to take into account the needs of people who can obtain part-time or low-paid jobs to receive top-up support from state benefits along the lines of the Danish Arhus (Lonsdale, 1990).
- Wherever possible self-advocacy, rather than advocacy, should be seen as the goal. When people with learning difficulties learn to 'speak for themselves' the possibilities of their being recognised as 'active citizens' become obvious.
- Where people are genuinely unable to make informed decisions a system

of legal guardianship such as that stipulated in the UN Charter should be set up.

- Anti-discrimination legislation is needed to create a climate in which the rights of people with learning difficulties not to be discriminated against on the grounds of their mental disability are asserted. In particular, a recognition is needed that current unquestioning acceptance of the abortion of 'damaged' foetuses is detrimental to the citizenship of disabled people.
- Above all there is a requirement for a vision that full citizenship for all is possible, and a commitment to creating the conditions to make it possible.

Whatever happens within the debate on citizenship it is imperative that we end the historical segregation and dehumanisation of people with learning difficulties. If we take on their claims along with those who are already competing for recognition, we will indeed be fashioning a pluralistic society which incorporates and values all its members.

References

Abbot, P. (1990) 'Community care for mentally handicapped children in the UK', paper presented to Care in the Community Conference: UK and USSR, Guildford.

Advocacy in Action (1990) Working together: Annual Report June 1989–June 1990, Princes House, Nottingham.

Atkinson, D. and Williams, F. (1990) *Know Me As I Am: an Anthology of Poetry, Prose and Art from People with Learning Difficulties*, Hodder and Stoughton, Sevenoaks.

Barbalet, J. (1988) *Citizenship*, The Open University Press, Milton Keynes.

Barker, D. (1983) 'How to curb the fertility of the unfit: the feeble minded in Edwardian Britain', *Oxford Review of Education*, Vol. 9, No. 3, pp. 197–211.

Barron, D. (1989) 'Locked away: life in an institution', in Brechin, A. and Walmsley, J. (eds) *Making Connections*, Hodder and Stoughton, Sevenoaks.

Bowle, J. (1947) *Western Political Thought from the Origins to Rousseau*, Jonathan Cape, London.

Crawley, B. (1988) *The Growing Voice: a Survey of Self Advocacy Groups in ATCs and Hospitals in Great Britain*, CMH, London.

Dahrendorf, D. (1990) 'Decade of the citizen', *Guardian*, 1 August.

Davis, A. (1987) 'Women with disabilities: abortion and liberation', *Disability, Handicap and Society*, Vol. 2, No. 3, pp. 275–84.

Driedger, D. (1989) *The Last Civil Rights Movement: Disabled Peoples' International*, Hurst, London.

Etherington, A., Hall, K. and Whelan, M. (1988) 'What it's like for us', in Towell, D. (ed.) *An Ordinary Life in Practice*, King's Fund, London.

Finch, J. (1984) 'Community care: developing non sexist alternatives', *Critical Social Policy*, Vol. 9, No. 4, pp. 6–18.

Flynn, M. (1989) *Independent Living for Adults with Mental Handicap: a Place of My Own*, Cassell, London.

Flynn, M. and Saleem, J. (1986) 'Adults who are mentally handicapped and are living with their parents: satisfactions and perceptions regarding their lives and circumstances', *Journal of Mental Deficiency Research*, Vol. 30, pp. 379–87.

Gunn, M. (1986) 'Human rights and people with mental handicaps', *Mental Handicap*, Vol. 14, pp. 116–20.

Harris, D. (1987) *Justifying State Welfare*, Blackwell, Oxford.

Heginbotham, C. (1987) 'Ethical dilemmas of sterilisation', *Social Work Today*, 13 April, p. 14.

Heginbotham, C. (1990) *Return to Community*, Bedford Square Press, London.

Hindess, B. (1987) *Freedom, Equality and the Market: Arguments on Social Policy*, Tavistock, London.
Jahoda, A., Markova, I and Cattermole, M. (1988) 'Towards truly independent living', *The Psychologist*, October, pp. 397–9.
Jenkins, R. (1989) 'Dimensions of adulthood', in Brechin, A. and Walmsley, J. (eds) *Making Connections*, Hodder and Stoughton, Sevenoaks.
Jones, G. (1986) *Social Hygiene in Twentieth Century Britain*, Croom Helm, Beckenham.
Jones, K. (1972) *A History of the Mental Health Services*, Routledge and Kegan Paul, London.
King, D. (1987) *The New Right: Politics, Markets and Citizenship*, Macmillan, London.
Knight, K. (1990) 'State of activity', *New Socialist*, Vol. 69, October/November.
Leach, B. (1989) 'Disabled people and the implementation of local authorities' equal opportunities policies', *Public Administration*, Vol. 67, pp. 65–77.
Lister, R. (1990) 'Women, economic dependency and citizenship', *Journal of Social Policy*, Vol. 19, pp. 445–67.
Lonsdale, S. (1990) *Women and Disability*, Macmillan, London.
Marshall, T.H. (1950) *Citizenship and Social Class*, Cambridge University Press.
Marshall, T.H. (1981) *The Right to Welfare and Other Essays*, Heinemann Educational, London.
Mead, L. (1986) *Beyond Entitlement*, The Free Press, New York.
Oliver, M. (1990) *The Politics of Disablement*, Macmillan, London.
Oliver, M. and Zarb, G. (1989) 'The politics of disability', *Disability, Handicap and Society*, Vol. 4, No. 3, pp. 224–39.
Patten, J. (1988) *Guardian*, 16 September.
Potts, M. and Fido, R. (1990) *A Fit Person to be Removed*, Northcote Press, Plymouth.
Rankin, M. (1989) *Active Citizenship; Myth or Reality?* The Volunteer Centre, Berkhamsted.
Richardson, A. (1989) 'If you love him let him go', in Brechin, A. and Walmsley, J. (eds) *Making Connections*, Hodder and Stoughton, Sevenoaks.
Roche, M. (1990) 'Motherland or motherhood?', *New Socialist*, Vol. 69, pp. 10–12.
Smith, S. (1989) *The Politics of Race and Residence*, Polity Press, Cambridge.
Stone, D. (1985) *The Disabled State*, Macmillan, London.
Turner, B. (1986) *Citizenship and Capitalism*, Allen and Unwin, London.
Walker, A. (1983) 'Care for elderly people: a conflict between women and the state', in Finch, J. and Groves, D. (eds) *A Labour of Love*, Routledge and Kegan Paul, London.
Wallace, C. (1987) 'Between the family and the state: young people in transition', in White, M. (ed.) *The Social World of the Young Unemployed*, Policy Studies Institute, London.
Williams, F. (1990) 'Women with learning difficulties are women too', in Day, L. and Langan, M. (eds) *Women, Oppression and Social Work*, Hyman and Unwin, London.
Williams, F. and Walmsley, J. (1990) *Transitions and Change*, Workbook 3 of K668 *Mental Handicap: Changing Perspectives*, The Open University, Milton Keynes.
Wolfensberger, W. (1975) *The Origin and Nature of our Institutional Models*, Human Policy Press, New York.

5.2

Discrimination, disability and welfare: from needs to rights

Mike Oliver and Colin Barnes

The evidence that disabled people experience severe economic deprivation and social disadvantage is overwhelming and no longer in dispute, whether it be from the government's own commissioned research, from research institutes, academics or disabled people themselves. What is at issue is why this should be so, the role of welfare in compounding or alleviating this situation and what can be done about it. Disabled people have been in the forefront of addressing all of these issues and have identified institutional discrimination as the major problem which has to be dealt with. As a consequence the British Council of Organisations of Disabled People (BCODP) has recently embarked on a major project to ensure that discrimination against disabled people is made illegal.

This paper will not consider the legal and parliamentary issues involved but instead it will attempt to explain why, in late twentieth-century Britain, disabled people are demanding legal protection from discrimination. In order to do this, it is necessary to look at the welfare background and the failure of the welfare state to ensure a decent life for disabled people; to consider the external influences on the demands for anti-discrimination legislation; to reflect on the experiences of disabled people within the context of the restructuring of state welfare in the 1980s; and, finally, to describe the current situation of disabled people and their attempts to explain their unequal economic and social status as the product of institutional discrimination.

The welfare background

It needs to be said at the outset that had the mammoth and imaginative project to establish a welfare state which would provide 'cradle to grave' security for all its members been successful, then the current demands for anti-discrimination legislation would not have materialised. Further, not only has state welfare not ensured the basic human rights of disabled people, through some of its provisions and practices it has infringed and even taken away some

This paper is an edited version of M. Oliver and C. Barnes (1991) 'Discrimination, disability and welfare: from needs to rights', in *Equal Rights for Disabled People*, Institute for Public Policy Research, London.

of these rights. Examples of this include the provision of segregated residential facilities which deny some disabled people the right to live where they choose, and the imposition of assessment procedures which deny some disabled people the right to privacy.

This failure can be traced back almost to the foundations of the welfare state during the Second World War. Although different language might have been used at the time, the philosophy underpinning the Beveridge Report was that of active citizenship within a framework of entitlements. However, in translating this philosophy into practice, the welfare state created passive rather than active citizens (Ignatieff, 1989), and nowhere is this more clearly illustrated than in terms of what happened to disabled people.

Indeed, the first Act of Parliament to treat disabled people as a single group was the Disabled Persons (Employment) Act 1944, which attempted to secure employment rights for disabled people (Topliss, 1983). Further, the Education Act 1944, underpinned by an egalitarian ideology, specified that disabled children should be educated alongside their peers in primary and secondary education (Tomlinson, 1981).

However, it was the concept of need, first introduced in 1946 in the regulations concerning the Education Act which opened the way for the professional domination of welfare provision, and subsequently Section 29 of the National Assistance Act 1948 laid a duty on local authorities to 'arrange services' for people, not to enable them to meet their own needs. It also became clear that implementation of the Disabled Persons (Employment) Act was more concerned with the attitudes of employers than the rights of disabled people seeking employment (Lonsdale, 1986). And the Education Act 1944 became the legal mechanism for the establishment of a huge infrastructure of segregated special education based on 11 medical categories.

The argument could be summed up by saying that the twin ideals of active citizenship and of rights were tentatively incorporated into the initial legislation which was to lay the foundations of the welfare state as we know it. However, everything that has happened since has been a retreat from these ideals, whether it be in the dependency-creating approaches to service provision, the interventionist nature of professional practice or the patronising language used to describe all this.

The very language of welfare provision continues to deny disabled people the right to be treated as fully competent, autonomous individuals. Care in the community, caring for people, providing services through care managers, case managers or even care attendants all structure the welfare discourse in particular ways and imply a particular view of disabled people. As early as 1986 disabled people, in response to the Audit Commission's critical review of community care, were arguing for an abandonment of such patronising and dependency-creating language (British Council of Organisations of Disabled People, 1986). Organisations controlled and run by disabled people, including the BCODP, the Spinal Injuries Association and the newly formed European Network on Independent Living, have already begun to move to a language of entitlement emphasising independent living, social support and the use of personal assistants.

But to return to the argument, this unfortunate retreat from active to passive citizenship and from rights-based to needs-based welfare provision, has been masked since the late 1950s by the rhetoric and policy of community care. Since the late 1950s there has been a concerted attempt by successive governments to reduce the numbers of people living in segregated institutions of one kind or another. The shift towards community-based services took a decisive turn in the early 1960s when the government announced its intention to reduce the number of beds in mental hospitals by half. The rhetoric of community care continued to obscure the reality that, for many previously incarcerated people, living in the community bestowed no more rights other than perhaps to starve, freeze or die alone.

By the late 1960s attempts were being made to rationalise the chaos that was the reality of community care, and as far as disability services were concerned the Chronically Sick and Disabled Persons Act 1970 was to be the vehicle for this rationalisation. This was even heralded at one point by two non-disabled commentators as a 'Charter [of rights] for the disabled' (Topliss and Gould, 1981) but the reality was that it was an extension of the National Assistance Act 1948 (Keeble, 1979) in that the list of services provided under Section 2 was little more than the list of services to be provided under Section 29 of the National Assistance Act.

The only two extra duties to be imposed on local authorities under the 1970 Act were the duty to compile a register and the duty to publicise services. The former produced little information of value (Knight and Warren, 1978) and the latter was widely ignored (Oliver, 1983). The services listed under Section 2 only needed to be provided where it was 'practical and reasonable' to do so, and most local authorities found that it wasn't, so they didn't (Cook and Mitchell, 1982). Hence the 1970 Act gave disabled people no new rights but re-emphasised needs-based provision even if it proved ineffective in meeting needs however defined (Borsay, 1986; Beardshaw, 1988).

This is not to deny that there have been some benefits deriving from needs-based provision in that the majority of disabled people now have more access to relatively more services and, on the whole, are less likely to end up in a segregated institution of one kind or another. On the other hand, the price for those services is usually acceptance of invasions of privacy by a veritable army of professionals and the acceptance of services that the state thinks you should have or can afford rather than those that you know you need.

A further price to pay is often socialisation into dependency because those very services are provided for rather than with disabled people, because the special education system instils passivity and because the voluntary organis-ations continue to promote negative images of disability, accentuated by recent media events such as Telethon and Children in Need (Oliver, 1989, 1990). Hence one study found that disabled young people 'appear to have been conditioned into accepting a devalued role as sick, pitiful and a burden of charity' (Hutchinson and Tennyson, 1986, p. 33).

The 1980s have not seen a reversal of this general trend, despite the rhetoric of integration, community care and rights; neither the Education Act 1981 nor the Disabled Persons (Services, Consultation and Representation) Act 1986 has added substantially to the rights of disabled people or addressed the reality of institutional discrimination which is part of our everyday lives.

External influences

As well as this growing disillusionment with current and proposed welfare provision, it is possible to identify three other key influences on the demands for legislation to outlaw discrimination against disabled people in Britain. While it is possible to treat all these influences as analytically distinct, they are interconnected and have all affected each other and played a significant role in the current demands.

The first of these influences was the Civil Rights Movement in the United States which focused on the struggles of black people in the 1950s to achieve basic rights to vote, to hold elective office and to be tried by a jury of one's peers. As these rights were gradually achieved, the Movement became concerned with social rights generally and had an influence on other groups, such as women and disabled people.

There were two aspects to this influence: a reconceptualisation of the unequal treatment of such groups as a human rights issue and a realisation of the possibilities of achieving social change. As one commentator has put it:

> The Civil Rights Movement has had an effect not only on the securing of certain rights but also on the manner in which those rights have been secured. When traditional legal channels have been exhausted, disabled persons have learned to employ other techniques of social protest, such as demonstrations and sit-ins.
>
> (De Jong, 1983, p. 12)

These techniques of social protest stood disabled Americans in good stead when forcing Section 504 of the Rehabilitation Act 1973 on to the statute books against a backsliding government, and, more recently, played no small part in the passage of the Americans with Disabilities Act 1990, both of which effectively address the issue of institutional discrimination against disabled people in the USA.

A second factor which has influenced the demand for anti-discrimination legislation has been the passage of similar Acts to outlaw discrimination on the grounds of race and gender in this country. Early attempts at legislation in these areas had proved ineffective but both the Sex Discrimination Act 1975 and the Race Relations Act 1976 had an influence on the demands of disabled people for similar legislation. There were two reasons for this: to begin with, the passing of such legislation acknowledged the existence of discrimination and made it clear that it was unacceptable; and in addition, both Acts attempted to deal with indirect as well as direct discrimination. Disabled people, therefore, want similar treatment to other groups before the law and also legal recognition of the fact that discrimination is more than just the intentional acts of prejudiced individuals.

However, the principle of equality for disabled people unlike that for women and black people, has never been enshrined in the law. This is a clear indication of both the lack of acknowledgement of the existence of discrimination against disabled people and the lack of importance attached to notions of equal opportunities. In addition, this lack of acknowledgement of the existence of discrimination against disabled people fails to recognize the way discrimination is compounded for disabled members of the gay community, black people and women with impairments (Campling, 1981; Conference of Indian Organis-ations, 1987; Morris, 1989; Lesbian and Gay Committee, 1990; Lonsdale, 1990).

A third factor which had an influence on the demand for anti-discrimination legislation was the coming together of individual disabled people to form their own organisations (Oliver and Zarb, 1989; Oliver, 1990). This fostered not only a growing collective consciousness among disabled people but also a reformulation of what the problems of disability actually were, shifting the focus squarely away from the functional limitations of impaired individuals and on to contemporary social organisation with its plethora of disabling barriers. This nascent collective organising also saw the start of a developing schism between organisations for the disabled and organisations of disabled people.

This schism is not unrelated to demands for anti-discrimination legislation, for many of the establishment organisations were confidently (and usually confidentially) advising the government of the day that discrimination was not a problem for disabled people and that therefore legislation in this area was unnecessary. This was despite the fact that the Silver Jubilee Access Committee had drawn attention to a number of 'blatant acts of discrimination against disabled people' (Silver Jubilee Access Committee, 1979) and that the official committee which was set up to investigate this discrimination was unequivocal in both its recognition of the fact that discrimination against disabled people was widespread and that anti-discrimination legislation was essential to remedy this unacceptable state of affairs (Committee on Restrictions Against Disabled People, 1982).

The campaign for equal status for disabled people, spearheaded by organisations of disabled people, intensified in the 1980s, and the formation of the Voluntary Organisations for Anti-Discrimination Legislation (VOADL) committee signified the conversion of many of the organisations for the disabled to the point of view articulated by disabled people themselves. Conversion on this issue, however, does not mean that the schism between such organisations has ceased to be of significance.

Nor would it be appropriate to reduce the contribution of the self-organisation of disabled people to that of spearheading the campaign for legal rights, for they have been in the forefront of campaigns for economic, social and political rights as well; they have attacked inappropriate service provision and professional practice and pioneered the demands from disabled people to live independently. Indeed, it was the idea of independent living which gave a focus to the struggles of disabled people to organise themselves, initially in the United States and subsequently elsewhere, including Britain (Pagel, 1988).

The 1980s

In order to harness this growing consciousness of disabled people, to provide a platform to articulate the redefinition of the problem of disability and to give a focus to the campaigns for independent living and against discrimination, the BCODP was formed in 1981 and its success in the subsequent decade is entirely an achievement of disabled people themselves (Hasler, 1991). Its conception and subsequent development have been achieved without extensive financial support from government or from traditional organisations for disabled people.

On the contrary, the BCODP was criticised from the start as being elitist, isolationist, unrepresentative and Marxist by a collection of unrepresentative people with abilities, right- and left-wing academics, isolated and elitist staff and management of traditional organisations and so on (Williams, 1983; Harrison, 1987; Goodall, 1988; Holden, 1990). Yet despite these attacks, the BCODP has gone from strength to strength, now representing over 75 organisations of disabled people and 200,000 disabled individuals.

These initiatives not only established the BCODP as the only representative voice of disabled people in Britain but by its very success it stimulated an ever-growing number of disabled people to adopt a disabled identity. With this growing sense of a collective, political identity has developed the self-confidence not simply to ask for the necessary changes but to demand them and to use a whole range of tactics including direct action and civil disobedience. It is because of this growing collective self-confidence that disabled people are forcing the issue of institutional discrimination on to the political agenda and demanding anti-discrimination legislation to remedy it.

Thus throughout the 1980s there has been a growing campaign to persuade the British government to introduce anti-discrimination legislation to enable disabled people to participate fully in the mainstream economic and social life of society. Since the early 1980s there have been nine attempts to get such legislation on to the statute books (Oliver, 1985; Barnes, 1991). Hitherto successive governments have successfully prevented the passage of these bills, arguing that there is little if any widespread discrimination against disabled people. Indeed the current Minister for Disabled People is still arguing, just as previous ministers have done before him, that discrimination against disabled people is not widespread (quoted in 'Offload', *Community Care*, 18 April 1991).

This constant denial of the reality of discrimination flies in the face of the experiences of disabled people, highlighted recently by the government's own commissioned research published in a series of five reports by the Office of Population Censuses and Surveys at the end of the 1980s.

Describing and explaining discrimination in the 1990s

After over a century of state-provided education disabled children and young people are still not entitled to the same kind of schooling as their able-bodied peers, nor do they leave with equivalent qualifications (Meltzer *et al.*, 1989). The majority of British schools, colleges and universities remain unprepared to accommodate disabled students within a mainstream setting. Thus, many young disabled people have little choice but to accept a particular form of segregated 'special' education which is both educationally and socially divisive, and fails to provide them with the necessary skills for adult living. By producing educationally and socially disabled adults in this way, the special educational system perpetuates the misguided assumption that disabled people are somehow inadequate, and thus legitimates discrimination in all other areas of their lives.

Similarly, since the end of the Second World War at least, disabled people have consistently experienced higher rates of unemployment than the rest of the population, not because they are unable to work but because of the discriminatory behaviour of employers in failing to even attempt to meet their legal obligations under the quota system (Lonsdale, 1986) and the lack of political will to insist upon its enforcement (Oliver, 1985). As a result, currently, disabled people are more likely to be out of work than non-disabled people, they are out of work longer than other unemployed workers, and when they do find work it is more often than not low-paid, low-status work with poor working conditions (Martin *et al.*, 1989). This in turn accelerates the discriminatory spiral in which many disabled people find themselves caught.

The majority of disabled people and their families, therefore, are forced into depending on welfare benefits in order to survive (Martin and White, 1988). Further, the present disability benefit system does not even cover impairment-related costs and effectively discourages many of those who struggle for autonomy and financial independence. Dependence is the inevitable result and this is compounded by the present system of health and welfare services, most of which are dominated by the interests of the professionals who run them (Wolfensberger, 1989; Davis, 1990; Oliver, 1990) and the traditional assumption that disabled people are incapable of running their own lives. Current welfare provision not only denies disabled people the opportunities to live autonomously but also denies them the dignity of independence within interpersonal relationships and the family home.

The evidence that disabled people experience a much poorer quality of life than everyone else is so overwhelming that it is not in dispute, though the precise dimensions of such deprivation and disadvantage may be (Martin *et al.*, 1989; Thompson *et al.*, 1989; Disability Alliance, 1990). There can be only two possible explanations for this: one that disability has such a traumatic physical and psychological effect on individuals that they cannot ensure a reasonable quality of life for themselves by their own efforts; the other that the economic and social barriers that disabled people face are so pervasive that disabled people are prevented from ensuring for themselves a reasonable quality of life by their own efforts.

The former has become known as the individual model of disability and is underpinned by personal tragedy theory. It has been under severe attack in recent years from a variety of sources to the point that it is now generally recognised that it is an inadequate basis for developing a proper understanding of disability. The latter has become known as the social model of disability and has shifted the focus away from impaired individuals and on to restrictive environments and disabling barriers. This has received acceptance to such an extent that it has almost become the new orthodoxy.

Hence it is no longer denied that the systematic deprivation and disadvantage that disabled people experience is caused by restrictive environments and disabling barriers. The point at issue here is what should be done about it. Up to now, successive governments have taken the view that the way to deal with this is through the provision of professional services coupled with a strategy aimed at persuading the rest of society to remove their disabling barriers, and to change their restrictive environments. As the current Minister for Disabled People recently stated: 'Nor would I deny that discrimination exists – of course it does. We have to battle against it, but, rather than legislating, the most constructive and productive way forward is through raising awareness in the community as a whole' (*Hansard*, 1991, p. 1150). As we have already argued, professionalised service provision within a needs-based system of welfare has added to existing forms of discrimination and, in addition, has created new forms of its own, including the provision of stigmatised segregated services, such as day care, and the development of professional assessments and practices based upon invasions of privacy as well as creating a language of paternalism which can only enhance discriminatory attitudes.

On top of that, policies of persuasion have turned out to be bankrupt as the cost of implementing them grows, while at the same time disabled children are still directed into segregated special schools, the numbers of disabled people that are unemployed increases, and the number of disabled people living in poverty continues to expand. That this unacceptable situation is due to disabling barriers rather than personal limitations is now clear; it is also clear that previous attempts to dismantle these barriers have been based on incorrect understandings of the real nature of discrimination. Discrimination does not exist in the prejudiced attitudes of individuals but in the institutionalised practices of society.

This new understanding of the real nature of the problem involves the idea of institutional discrimination, which can be described in the following ways. First, institutional discrimination is evident when the policies and activities of public or private organisations, social groups and all other organisational forms result in unequal treatment or unequal outcomes between disabled and non-disabled people. Second, institutional discrimination is embedded in the work of welfare institutions when they deny disabled people the right to live autonomously, through failure to meet their statutory obligations in terms of service provision, through their differential implementation of legislative and advisory codes, through interference in the privacy of disabled people and through the provision of inappropriate and segregative services.

In terms of what can be done about it, BCODP firmly believes that institutional discrimination can only be addressed by changing organisational, social and individual behaviour, and that such behavioural changes can only be effected by legal prescription. To paraphrase Martin Luther King, legislation may not change what is in people's hearts but it can change what they do about what is in their hearts. Anti-discrimination legislation then becomes the way to address the reality of institutional discrimination, and it would do this in a number of ways.

To begin with, such legislation would send our a clear message to society: namely that any form of discrimination, for whatever reason, was unacceptable. In addition, such legislation would at least accord disabled people equal treatment with other groups who experience discrimination. Further, it would offer disabled people individual and collective redress against those who failed to remove disabling barriers or adapt restrictive environments. Finally, it would force society to cease its current discriminatory welfare provision and move towards forms of provision which are truly enabling.

Conclusions

This paper has argued that discrimination against disabled people is institutionalised throughout society and that welfare provision has compounded rather than alleviated that discrimination. This is unfortunate, for a recent report has reaffirmed the connection between welfare and citizenship.

> The Commission recommends that a floor of adequate social entitlements should be maintained, monitored and improved when possible by central government with the aim of enabling every citizen to live the life of a civilised human being according to the standards prevailing in society.
>
> (HMSO, 1990, p. xix)

Thus spoke the Speaker's Commission on Citizenship. It is patently obvious that the great majority of disabled people are not accorded the entitlements of citizenship listed above and as a consequence it is legitimate to ask the question, how long, therefore, will disabled people continue to accept the obligations and responsibilities of citizenship?

Already some parts of the disability movement have begun to adopt some of the tactics adopted by the civil rights movement two decades earlier, taking direct action to confront the pedestrianisation of some city centres, to insist that transport systems which force a form of apartheid on more than a million people with mobility impairments cannot legitimately claim to be public and to challenge the degrading stereotypes presented by the mass media.

The American disability movement has used such tactics to good effect in the past 20 years to the point where its most recent convert can claim, after signing the Americans with Disabilities Act 1990, which outlawed discrimination: 'Let the shameful walls of exclusion come tumbling down' (Bush, 1990). It would be nice to think that the current Minister for Disabled People will suffer a similar conversion, but his current equivocating does not make this seem likely. 'I am not sure whether blanket anti-discrimination legislation . . . is the appropriate way to proceed' (Nicholas Scott, quoted in *Hansard*, 28 March 1991). Whether or not the politicians are certain that anti-discrimination legislation is the way to proceed, disabled people are, and their ever-increasing self-confidence and political strength makes it inevitable that such legislation will reach the statute books here as well as in the United States. Then the walls of exclusion really will come tumbling down.

References

Barnes, C. (1991) *Discriminating Against Disabled People*, Hurst, London.

Beardshaw, V. (1988) *Last on the List*, King's Fund Institute, London.

Borsay, A. (1986) *Disabled People in the Community: a Study of Housing, Health and Welfare Services*, Bedford Square Press, London.

British Council of Organisations of Disabled People (1986) *Comment on the Report of the Audit Commission*, London, BCODP.

Bush, G. (1990) Quoted in *Worklife: a Publication on Employment and People with Disabilities*, Vol. 3, No. 3.

Campling, J. (1981) *Images of Ourselves*, Routledge and Kegan Paul, London.

Committee on Restrictions Against Disabled People (1982) *Report by the Committee on Restrictions Against Disabled People*, HMSO, London.

Conference of Indian Organisations (1987) *Double Bind: To Be Disabled and Asian*, London Conference of Indian Organisations.

Cook, J. and Mitchell, P. (1982) *Putting Teeth into the Act: a History of Attempts to Enforce the Provisions of Section 2 of the Chronically Sick and Disabled Persons Act 1970*, Royal Association of Disability and Rehabilitation, London.

Davis, K. (1990) 'The denizens of the disability industry', *Coalition*, Greater Manchester Coalition of Disabled People, Manchester.

De Jong, G. (1983) 'Defining and implementing the independent living concept', in Crew, N. and Zola, I. (eds) *Independent Living for Physically Disabled People*, Jossey-Bass, London.

Disability Alliance (1990) *Social Security Bill: Government Proposals for Changes in Benefits for People with Disabilities*, Disability Alliance, London.

Goodall, L. (1988) 'Living options for physically disabled people', *Disability, Handicap and Society*, Vol. 3, No. 2.

Harrison, J. (1987) *Severe Physical Disability: Responses to the Challenge of Care*, Cassell, London.

Hasler, F. (1991) 'The International Year of Disabled People', *Disability Now*, January.

HMSO (1990) *Encouraging Citizenship: Report of the Commission on Citizenship*, London, HMSO.

Holden, G. (1990) 'RADAR's new director; Bert Massie talks to Geraldine Holden', *Disability Now*, April.

Hutchinson, D. and Tennyson, C. (1986) *Transition to Adulthood*, Further Education Unit, London.

Ignatieff, M. (1989) 'Citizenship and moral narcissism', *Political Quarterly*.

Keeble, U. (1979) *Aids and Adaptations*, Bedford Square Press, London.

Knight, R. and Warren, M. (1978) *Physically Handicapped People Living at Home: a Study of Numbers and Needs*, HMSO, London.

Lesbian and Gay Committee (1990) *Disability Review*, Lesbian and Gay Committee, March, p. 12.

Lonsdale, S. (1986) *Work and Inequality*, Longman, London.

Lonsdale, S. (1990) *Women and Disability*, Macmillan, London.

Martin, J. and White, A. (1988) *The Financial Circumstances of Disabled People*, HMSO, London.

Martin, J., White, A. and Meltzer, H. (1989) *Disabled Adults: Services, Transport and Employment*, HMSO, London.

Meltzer, H., Smyth, M. and Robus, N. (1989) *Disabled Children: Services, Transport and Education*, HMSO, London.

Morris, J. (1989) *Able Lives: Women's Experience of Paralysis*, The Women's Press, London.

Oliver, M. (1983) *Social Work with Disabled People*, Macmillan, London.

Oliver, M. (1985) 'Discrimination, disability and social policy', in Brenton, M. and Jones, C. (eds) *The Year Book of Social Policy 1984–5*, Routledge and Kegan Paul, London.

Oliver, M. (1989) 'Disability and dependency: a creation of industrial societies', in Barton, L. (ed.) *Disability and Dependency*, Falmer Press, London.

Oliver, M. (1990) *The Politics of Disablement*, Macmillan, London.

Oliver, M. and Zarb, G. (1989) 'The politics of disability: a new approach', *Disability, Handicap and Society*, Vol. 4, No. 3.

Pagel, M. (1988) *On Our Own Behalf*, Greater Manchester Coalition of Disabled People, Manchester.

Silver Jubilee Access Committee (1979) *Can Disabled People Go Where You Go?* Silver Jubilee Access Committee Report, Department of Health and Social Security, London.

Thompson, P., Buckle, J. and Lavery, M. (1989) *Not the OPCS Survey: Being Disabled Costs More Than They Said*, The Disablement Income Group, London.

Tomlinson, S. (1981) *A Sociology of Special Education*, Routledge and Kegan Paul, London.

Topliss, E. (1983) *Social Responses to Handicap*, Longman, London.

Topliss, E. and Gould, B. (1981) *A Charter for the Disabled*, Blackwell, Oxford.

Williams, G. (1983) 'The movement for independent living: an evaluation and critique', *Social Science and Medicine*, Vol. 17, No. 15.

Wolfensberger, W. (1989) 'Human service policies: the rhetoric versus the reality', in Barton, L. (ed.) *Disability and Dependency*, Falmer Press, London.

5.3
Developments in the disabled people's movement

Frances Hasler

'It will be many years before its impact can be properly assessed . . . the new projects started, new opportunities, new links between people and new attitudes.' This quote is actually from a report on the International Year of Disabled People (IYDP), but it serves equally well when applied to the establishment of a representative disability movement in this country. There are, however, differences in the outcomes of the two.

Like so much of the history of the disability movement, IYDP in the UK represented an official response to disability, rooted in welfarism, led by non-disabled people. It was counterpointed by an unofficial, almost subversive, initiative led by disabled people. Over the decade that followed, the unofficial has developed to a stage where it is the leader, not the follower, in discourse on disability. How did it happen?

International Years are supposed to bring focus to a particular area, and to create new links and opportunities, foster new attitudes. This last aim was very popular at the time, suggesting that disabled people would have far fewer problems if able-bodied attitudes improved. Yet at the end of 1981 the official reporting body in the UK recorded the view of its working party on attitudes that 'disabled people themselves can antagonise others with their demands and isolation'. For most disabled people, if this was a new attitude they could live without it. Such views go a little way to illustrating why, for so many disabled people, IYDP was just a year like any other, and why they turned their backs on the official programme and concentrated on building their own alternative vision.

Where did it come from?

The seeds of the modern disability movement were sown long before 1981. Organisations controlled by disabled people date back to the last century (British Deaf Association, National League of the Blind). However, organisations run by non-disabled people have as venerable a pedigree. A tension between those controlled by disabled people and those run by able-bodied philanthropists arose early, with the National League of the Blind complaining that 'in many charitable agencies only a small proportion of the money subscribed by the public found its way into the pockets of the blind while a substantial percentage went to pay inflated official salaries' (quoted in Pagel, 1988). This split between organisations 'of' disabled people – that is, controlled by them – and organisations 'for' disabled people – where able-bodied people made decisions on disabled people's behalf – has persisted.

In the early years of the welfare state an increasing number of non-representative organisations were set up, some addressing a particular condition (for example the Spastics Society) others a particular perceived need (for example the Leonard Cheshire Foundation). A parallel growth in organisations controlled by disabled people themselves was slower at first. A key event in shaping the modern disability movement was the formation in the 1960s of the Disablement Income Group, set up to lobby against the poverty and consequent deprivation of the majority of disabled people. This was followed in the 1970s by others, some concerned with specific conditions (such as the Spinal Injuries Association), some with particular themes and issues. Perhaps the most influential of this latter group was UPIAS – the Union of the Physically Impaired Against Segregation – a small but intensely active body.

What characterised all these groups was that their leadership was made up of disabled people, and they believed that disabled people should and could develop solutions to the problems they encountered.

1981 and all that

When the International Year was announced, the large non-representative organisations quickly became involved, joining working parties and setting up events. The smaller self-help groups had a different agenda. They wanted to use the year to focus on the real problems of disabled people. The working parties of IYDP centred on the things that organisations for disabled people thought were important. Many of these organisations run residential homes, so there was a working party on residential care. Disabled people in the UK were already exploring the idea of independent living, which provides support in the community, but there was no IYDP working party set up to look at this.

The crucial development in 1981 owed nothing to the official activity of the year; partly fuelled by how irrelevant the IYDP seemed to their own concerns, disabled people were looking at ways of doing something different. It seemed time to combat the effect noted by the League, of public money going to non-representative, ineffective organisations. A group of disabled activists got together to discuss setting up a national body to co-ordinate groups run by disabled people. By November 1981 this had become a solid reality, with the inauguration of the British Council of Organisations of Disabled People (BCODP).

BCODP, the achievement entirely of disabled people, attracted criticism from the start, being characterised as demanding, elitist, isolationist, unrepresentative and Marxist by various commentators from organisations for disabled people. It was not at first a large body – it had 10 member groups originally. Nor was it rich; disabled people tend to be poor, and their own organisations have never accrued the sorts of incomes that the welfarist groups enjoy. However, it was influential. It was able to bring together a range of self-help and campaigning organisations which had already developed, and to foster new ones. It gave a context to their work and provided them with a collective voice.

The big idea

The 'big idea' which set the work in context was the social model of disability. It said something which on the surface sounds like the 'attitudes' idea so popular in IYDP – that the problems disabled people face stem not from their physical or mental limitations but from the inappropriate social response to them. But the social model does not just challenge attitudes; it challenges the very assumption of 'normality'. It suggests that the problems disabled people face constitute a specific oppression, rooted in the systematic exclusion of disabled people from everyday life. This idea, developed within UPIAS, but quickly finding wider currency, made it possible for disabled people to challenge the whole basis on which services for them were arranged. By the end of the 1970s disabled people were actively developing new ways of organising and living.

A key development here was accessible transport. Against a service-provider's attitude – that disabled people did not travel because they did not want to – disabled people advanced a different argument. Being 'housebound' was not an intrinsic part of their condition: the reason they did not travel was simply that they could not get on the bus – or the tube or the train – because all these transport systems were only designed with able-bodied people in mind. Rightly perceiving that any campaign to change bus design would be a very long one, disabled people lobbied to have some specialised accessible transport developed. A Dial-a-Ride scheme was set up in 1980, under the management of a local authority (Islington). After some arguments about whether a council-sponsored service could be used to take people to political meetings, disabled people in London saw the advantage of being in full control of the service, and subsequent Dial-a-Rides in London were constituted as voluntary organisations, managed by committees on which Dial-a-Ride users were in a majority. Although it was, and is, a limited service – demand massively outstrips supply – Dial-a-Ride was important in enabling previously disenfranchised people to become active on their own behalf. What distinguished it from previous mobility campaigns was that it was rooted in a concept of public transport – that disabled people, like the rest of the population, should have access to a bus service.

Another development which used the social model of disability as a philosophical base was the Centre for Independent Living (CIL). Borrowing the terminology (and much of the concept) from the West Coast of America, British pioneers set out to provide a blueprint for living in the community for severely disabled people. Most of the early members of the Independent Living movement in Britain had been in residential care. The social model of disability made it clear that they were 'in care' not because their disabilities made them unable to live in an ordinary house but because existing community services did not meet their needs. Working from first principles, that an accessible flat and workers coming in as and when needed would replace the facilities of 'care', disabled people devised packages of assistance. The mechanism by which ideas about these were shared was the CIL.

A CIL, on the British model, is a clearing-house for ideas, and a source of practical and moral support for disabled people who want to live independently. From the outset, CILs were run by disabled people, using ideas devised by disabled people. They became an important resource for the disability movement, as their success not only helped individuals to lead active lives in their own communities but also provided a source of pride in disabled people's collective skill and creativity.

The beginnings of these initiatives already existed in 1981, although they were being shared by a relatively small group of people. One by-product of the International Year was increased publicity for everything going on in the disability field, including self-help. This enabled more disabled people to find out that there were alternatives. Unfortunately, but predictably, after the IYDP media interest waned, it was left to the disability groups themselves to make contact with disabled individuals, and to promote the cause of the movement.

Language – truth and logic?

A crucial part of the 'big idea' – the social model – was reclaiming language, so that disabled people defined disability in ways which challenged stereotypes. The discussion over which words to use became part of the process by which the movement defined itself. The International Year had originally been one 'for the disabled'. After vigorous lobbying, this was changed to 'of disabled people', to signify, first, that disabled people were at the centre of it, and second, as slogans of the day said, 'the disabled are people'. Some activists took this further, saying that a person is more than a disability, so the term should be 'a person with a disability' or people with disabilities.

The adherents of the social model of disability looked at it differently. They took words used by the World Health Organisation (impairment, disability) and redefined them, saying that disability was not the lack of function – such as the inability to walk – but was the social response to that lack of function – lack of ramps for wheelchair-users, fire regulations which ban wheelchair-users, and so on. The most important thing about this approach is that it locates the problems of disability outside the person – a radical departure from traditional views, which see the lack of function as the problem, and by extension, see the disabled person as the one who needs to 'adapt' to the world. The disabled persons' movement was demanding that the world be adapted to them.

Culture and disability

The terminology debate was important in the early 1980s as a way of exploring the experience of disability. It grew less central by the end of the decade; the term 'disabled people' has become everyday usage. The power of language has not diminished, but the movement had many other concerns to attend to. In the wider context, activists were interested in building strong organisations and having a real influence on the way services are run; language was only a small part of this. The other factor which changed the nature of the debate was the development of an alternative culture – the disability arts scene – which gave people new images of themselves and played an important part in cementing the sense of a 'movement'.

Disability arts includes theatre companies (the best known of which is probably Graeae, which had its roots in student drama), dance companies and visual arts. But it is on the cabaret circuit, songs and comedy, where it has been most closely associated with the politics of disability. Many of the songs and most of the humour are directly political in content. An important part of the movement has been to reclaim humour – to laugh at disabled people not as victims but as role models. In recent years most big gatherings of disabled people have included performers, linking the disability movement with other political movements. Just as CND had Billy Bragg, we have Johnny Creschendo.

New tactics

During the 1980s the consumer movement in disability found new strength. By the end of the decade BCODP had grown from its original 10 member groups to 60. This expansion also led to a debate on the nature of political and social change. Some groups have followed the traditional parliamentary road, lobbying for new laws to extend existing benefits and rights. In this they have made alliances with the non-representative organisations, who take an essentially welfarist approach.

Other people, reasoning that a government committed to public spending cuts did not have the inclination to legislate for rights or welfare, favoured high-profile action. BCODP organised a 'Rights not Charity' demonstration in London in 1989, to protest about changes in social security, and the introduction of a discretionary charitable fund for essential help. The demonstration was supported by thousands of disabled people. The logistics of assembling thousands of disabled people are awesome – transport is a major difficulty – and another group decided that smaller, tightly focused episodes of 'direct action' constituted good tactics. The Campaign for Accessible Transport was born. They have organised mass attempts by wheelchair-users to get on buses, a queue of wheelchair-users stretching right across Westminster Bridge, and 'Stop the Bus' sit-downs in London's Oxford Street.

This has been remarkably effective: there was far more media coverage for 12 people sitting down in Oxford Street than for 3,000 marching to the DHSS. Participants need to be well organised and dedicated – arrests have been made. This high-profile activity is not without its critics from the parliamentary lobby – there is some suggestion that it 'antagonises' those in power. Ironically this echoes the words of the IYDP report, with its implication that disabled people are somehow to blame for the lack of services!

The Campaign for Accessible Transport (CAT) has been linked to a much bigger, wider campaign – that for anti-discrimination legislation (ADL). This campaign has been extremely unifying in the movement, and has made further alliances with non-representative organisations who also support legislation for equality. Both campaigns have borrowed from the American experience (American Disabled for Accessible Public Transport – ADAPT), which used tactics similar to CAT's in support of the Americans with Disabilities Act. (A mixture of direct action and parliamentary lobbying is not new: the National League of the Blind used this method in 1933.

Equal access for all?

A sign of the health of the disability movement is perhaps the number of new groups still emerging, representing particular interest groups. In the late 1980s the Association of Blind Asians and the Asian Disabled People's Alliance were formed in London. People First, run by people with learning difficulties, expanded the franchise of disabled people speaking for themselves. Gemma, a group for disabled lesbians, had been in existence for many years (and was one of the founder members of the BCODP). At the end of the decade it was joined by other, campaigning organisations, such as Languid (Lesbians and Gays United in Disability). In the field of mental health, consumer groups such as Survivors Speak Out were growing. In 1990 a new campaigning voice for black disabled people, the Black and Ethnic Disabled People's Group, was set up.

All of these groups identify with, and make demands on, the disabled people's movement. Although they are disparate in structure, they share one characteristic – they are very under-resourced. For some, this is a matter of choice – not wanting to be registered charities, they remain as small civil rights campaigns. For others, particularly black and ethnic groups, they are simply at the wrong end of the queue for grants – white-dominated voluntary groups got there first. One of the issues for the disability movement in the 1990s is how to spread the available resources more equitably.

In our own hands?

The consumer movement has always been pitifully badly funded compared with the non-representative movement. The complaints made by the League at the beginning of the century are echoed by other groups now. Large disability charities put their money into substantial directorial salaries, not into disabled people's hands. As the movement has grown stronger, disabled people have been challenging this more directly, saying that if an organisation is purporting to speak for them, it must be controlled by them and accountable to them. The most successful challenge of this kind to date has been in London, where disabled activists demanded that the Greater London Association for Disabled People changed its constitution to become the Greater London Association *of* Disabled People (GLAD). The campaign, which began with the resignation of one of GLAD's member groups in 1986 and reached a climax with a sit-in in GLAD's offices in 1988, was successful in 1990, with the appointment of a disabled director and the adoption of a constitution guaranteeing control by disabled people.

The importance of this development lies in its stimulus to other organisations 'for' disabled people. In the face of pressure from disabled members, some of them are discussing similar changes. This poses a number of questions for the disability movement. How can it ensure that change actually does shift power to those people that the organisations represent? Will disabled committee members be accountable to a disabled electorate? If disabled people put their energies into taking over and running the large disability charities what will happen to existing smaller organisations of disabled people?

During the 1980s the disabled people's movement has changed the discourse on disability in Britain. It has done this both by enabling disabled people to be active in public life, and by redefining the meaning of disability. But a new question is emerging. Disabled people may have pride and visibility, but do they have power? The campaign for anti-discrimination legislation has highlighted how far disabled people in this country need to go before they enjoy equality of opportunity. 'Stop the Bus' and similar actions have spread to other UK cities, and disabled people are showing an increasing willingness to sit down and be counted. By the end of the century the movement will look different – some organisations will have merged or closed, new ones will have started. How they address the issue of empowerment is what will shape the disability movement for the future.

Reference

Pagel, M. (1988) *On Our Own Behalf*, Greater Manchester Coalition of Disabled People.

5.4
On the movement

Ken Davis

Measuring up

At the 1991 annual general meeting of the British Council of Organisations of Disabled People (BCODP), in the tenth year of its existence, a campaign was launched for anti-discrimination legislation. It was based on research (Barnes, 1991, p. 227) which confirmed that discrimination against disabled people was 'well entrenched within the core institutions of our society' – a claim echoed by disabled people's organisations world-wide. The strength of this claim is reflected in the rapid growth of bodies like BCODP and its global counterpart, the Disabled Peoples' International (DPI). In 10 years, membership of BCODP has risen to include over 80 member groups, whilst DPI is currently made up of over 70 national assemblies, all run by disabled people. Membership of both is still growing.

By most measures, this world-wide awakening adds up to a bona fide social movement. There's certainly a lot of collective action going on, at local as well as other levels. Structures are evolving and programmes are being formulated. Sacrifices are being made and leaders have emerged. Ideological boundaries are sketched in and histories are being written. Links have been established and pledges of solidarity made for the struggles of other oppressed groups. Over time, as we shall see, the demands and indeed the very character of this collective activity have changed.

These changes can now be argued to locate disabled people's collective activity among those late twentieth-century 'new social movements' which no longer seek change merely through party political systems or along the usual pressure-group lines. Drawing on the work of Touraine, Oliver (1990b, p. 113) sees these movements as: 'culturally innovative in that they are part of the underlying struggles for genuine participatory democracy, social equality and justice, which have arisen out of the crisis in industrial culture'. Within BCODP, this change overlays older, less ambitious objectives. Some BCODP member groups were first formed in the last century, and have interests which differ greatly from the movement's new mood. Whilst this has produced inner tensions, these are balanced, *inter alia*, by an increasingly shared perception of the sheer scale of the social injustice facing the movement as a whole.

Looking back on the gradual and fitful growth of disabled people's collective activity in Britain, it is of passing interest to enquire whether these older groups can be seen as having started the movement in Britain. Any answer in part depends on how a social movement is defined, and such definitions can be a quagmire of imprecision and value judgements. For example, Ralph Turner (1969, p. 391) said that a significant social movement: 'becomes possible when there is a revision in the manner in which a substantial group of people, looking at some misfortune, sees it no longer as a misfortune warranting charitable consideration, but as an injustice which is intolerable to society'. Although the meaning of words like 'substantial', 'manner' and 'misfortune' is a matter of debate, nevertheless it is a statement with a strong ring of truth about it. Accordingly Turner's definition lends itself as a way of looking back on the history of that part of disabled people's collective activity as is reflected in our own organisations. In this article, I have singled out what I see as the main revisions of disabled people's own perceptions of their 'misfortune', which have come in three main stages in over 100 years of self-organisation.

Causes and effects

When disabled people took these steps forward, they were looking pretty much at the same problem area – the same 'misfortune' – but they drew very different conclusions from what they saw. In each case, the roots of their 'misfortune' lay in the rise of capitalism and the free market, and the way these forces were unleashed in the industrial revolution. Finkelstein (1981, pp. 58–63) first pointed out the effect of these forces on the lives of physically impaired people when he said that: 'physically impaired people living in early capitalism were just as crippled by capitalist production using increasingly efficient machinery, as they were by the physical condition of their bodies . . . the Industrial Revolution [gave] the machinery of production the decisive push which removed crippled people from social intercourse and trans-formed them into disabled people.' Those who fell by the wayside were not just discriminated against by changes in the workplace which made it hard for them to compete in the labour market. They were disabled also by the built environment, systems of transport, and by many other developments which were designed to serve able-bodied interests.

The casualties were mopped up by the growing welfare industry, whose job was and is to protect the dominant able-bodied majority by dealing with disabled people on an individual basis: out of private funds in the case of charities or public funds in the case of welfare. Since it is thought not to be in their interests to deal with causes of disability, both private and state charity have merely prolonged the agony. This had produced a further difficult problem area for the movement. The charity–welfare disability organisations are usually run by the able-bodied who speak for disabled people but without any authority from them. On the movement's terms, such bodies are unrepresentative and illegitimate, although they strongly influence disability policy.

In the face of these multiple problems disabled people have, at the end of the day, had little choice but to mobilise a movement for social change. But their marginal social situation has caused almost insurmountable barriers to progress. When, finally, a start was made, it was a moment of great historical importance for all disabled people in Britain.

Making a start

This moment came when disabled individuals first faced up to the fact that they could achieve more for themselves through collective action than they could on their own. This revision of outlook, this shift from personal to collective struggle, happened in the case of the founding members of two organisations which Pagel (1988) describes as: 'the first campaigning organisations controlled by disabled people. The British Deaf Association (formed 1890) and the National League of the Blind (formed as a registered Trade Union in 1899) were founded to give an effective voice to the complaints which blind and deaf people had against the neglect they continued to suffer.'

In taking this step, the founders were much influenced by other events at the time. The use of sign language had been under attack for over 10 years and the report of the 1886 Royal Commission had made public for the first time the widespread poverty and social deprivation endured by people with sensory impairments. The League acknowledged the influence on them of the workers' movement, whose own struggles were gaining ground at that time.

The focus of these early groups was, in the main, centred on the interests of their own members, and this set the tone of the movement for the next 70 years. Most of the groups which followed served disabled people with particular impairments or pursued single issues, and the growth of these accelerated after the Second World War. Examples are the Disabled Drivers Association (1948), the National Federation of the Blind (1949), the Disablement Income Group (1965) and the Disabled Professionals Association (1968).

Such groups proved that disabled people could run their own democratic organisations, and some gave shows of strength on the streets in marches and demonstrations. There was, however, little cohesion between them: some groups embraced charity, others challenged it; some wanted integration, others supported segregation; some were working for greater control by disabled people over their own lives, others were calling for more professional providers and other 'experts' – who had also grown in numbers after the end of the Second World War.

This long early period of development can be seen as a time when social injustice was not viewed as being intolerable to disabled people as a social group, or to society itself – but to the individual disabled person. The remedy was seen basically as being more or better welfare. What the infant social movement needed was a clear shift in this kind of perception: a basis for a group to come together, a vision of unity to help clear the fog of separate identities, single issues, contradictions and general fragmentation.

The turning-point

Events abroad during the 1960s and early 1970s helped to bring about this change of outlook. The Swedish Fokus schemes, Collectivhaus in Denmark, Het Dorp in Holland and Centres for Independent Living (CILs) in the USA contrasted sharply with the building of young chronic sick units here in Britain. The unfulfilled promises of the Chronically Sick and Disabled Persons Act (CSDPA), and DIG's unfruitful campaign for a national disability income led the Union of the Physically Impaired Against Segregation (1974) to sum up the events of this time (Union of the Physically Impaired Against Segregation, 1981, p. 2) as making:

> apparent that hopes had been raised which could not be met by the struggle in hand. DIG had become established, but its spontaneous appeals for State help bore little fruit. The CPDSA won greater advances for professional and specialist services than for physically impaired people themselves . . . It started to become clear, as some of us warned at the time, that 'charters' such as the CSDPA did not herald a new age for disabled people. Rather did it mark the end of an era in which physically impaired people could naively continue to believe that able-bodied people would solve our problems for us.

DIG's lack of headway had caused open disagreements among members. Some had broken away to form UPIAS and others set up a second 'incomes' organisation, the Disability Alliance. For UPIAS, the problem in DIG had been lack of grassroots involvement in increasingly remote and expert leadership proposals. This raised serious questions of principle for the movement and these were debated in a historic meeting between UPIAS and the Alliance in 1975. The Union's view was that split in DIG had led to two opposing tendencies within the movement (Union of the Physically Impaired Against Segregation, 1981, p. 3): 'On the one hand there were people who clung to the elitist, expert, administrative approach of solving our problems for us. On the other, those who advocated a collective, organised struggle by physically impaired people for full social participation.'

The birth of UPIAS signalled the end of the welfare-oriented 'begging-bowl' period, and with it the idea that the 'experts' could administer away disabled people's problems for them. This made the early 1970s the pivotal period in the development of the movement. From this point on, the emphasis was to be less on appeals to able-bodied people's better nature, polite petitions or orderly marches on Parliament Square, but more on the mobilisation of a democratically organised, politically aware movement.

New groups emerged to address new issues: GEMMA raised the concerns of disabled lesbians. The Liberation Network of People with Disabilities focused on the issue of social attitudes, personal growth and awareness raising. Sisters Against Disablement began to address the double oppression of disabled women, and Disabled People Against Apartheid was set up in solidarity with black people in South Africa.

Other groups started to get involved in the design, delivery and control of services. The Grove Road Housing Collective and Project 81 started work on alternatives to segregated institutions. The struggle to gain control was pushed further forward by local Disablement Information and Advice Lines. The influence of many other social movements and trends can be detected in these developments, as De Jong (1979) has noted among the groups involved in the independent living movement in the United States: 'The origins and ideology of the movement for independent living cannot be fully appreciated without noting the contributions of other social movements [which] include: civil rights, consumerism, self-help, demedicalisation/self-care [and] deinstitutionalisation/normalisation/mainstreaming.' Throughout these developments, the Union was working to free disabled people from the way they had been defined and controlled by the experts who manipulate disability policy. They shifted the focus from the individual on to society and paved the way for a social theory with the power to displace the dogma which had for so long portrayed disability as a personal tragedy worthy of sympathy, welfare and charity. The Union's definition (Union of the Physically Impaired Against Segregation, 1976, p. 14) was: 'the disadvantage or restriction of ability caused by a contemporary social organisation which takes little or no account of people who have physical impairments and thus excludes them from participation in the mainstream of social activities. Physical disability is therefore a particular form of social oppression.' It was a statement which had the power to revolutionise disabled people's self-organisation and self-image. It challenged the sense of guilt and denial which follows from the so-called 'medical model' of disability. It offered, in its place, a fresh but unfamiliar outlook whereby disabled people could have pride in themselves as whole beings, impairments, wheelchairs, braces, crutches, warts and all. The Union (Union of the Physically Impaired Against Segregation, 1981, p. 6) encouraged its members to:

> seek pride in ourselves in all aspects of what we are. It is the Union's social definition of disability which has enabled us to cut out much of the nonsense, the shame and confusion from our minds. It has raised the floodgates for a river of discontent to sweep all our oppression before us, and with it to sweep all the flotsam and jetsam of 'expertise', 'professionalism' and 'authority' which have fouled our minds for so long, into the sewers of history.

Above all, the social definition of disability offered an incentive for the growing number of new organisations to come together. The liberating message was that, if disability was socially caused, then it could also be overcome through a struggle for social change. However, this potential for unity carried with it the potential for internal tension, particularly with regard to older groups which had no tradition of radical analysis or action.

In June 1981 the Union took the next step towards realising the unifying potential of their social approach to disability. In a bid to draw together all groups which were known to be controlled by disabled people, representatives of 16 such organisations were invited to consider setting up a National Council. By November this umbrella organisation – now called the British Council of Organisations of Disabled People – had made enough progress to enable three representatives to participate in the First World Congress of DPI in Singapore in December 1981.

Despite all the difficulties, throughout the 1980s the tendency identified and exemplified by the Union – progress through organised, collective action – developed rapidly. The hard fought for unifying influence of the social definition began to bear fruit, as the movement began to coalesce. The decade closed with a widespread acceptance of the radical revision of outlook which had begun in the early 1970s. The social situation of disabled people – the 'misfortune' – was now seen as intolerable, not just to themselves as individuals, but to disabled people as a social group. In 1990 the Union wound itself up. Its members had given more to promoting the development of other organisations than to UPIAS itself.

The new mood

By the arrival of the 1990s, the movement was already gathering itself to take the next major step forward. BCODP's membership was now over 70 groups across the country and a regionalisation programme had become necessary. New trends and currents had emerged, and old tensions remained. Funding, both of BCODP and its member groups, was meagre and uncertain. Communication between member organisations was almost non-existent. Yet, despite these uncertainties and pressures, the movement was holding together.

The energy which had been released into the movement was in need of an outlet. It was being increasingly pushed from the grassroots by its members. A way of moving forward on a broad front was needed, and the chance came with growing pressure for anti-discrimination legislation (ADL). BCODP had lent support to others to introduce such legislation since the start of the 1980s. As each attempt failed, BCODP was pushed nearer to presenting its own case. The attraction was a single campaigning focus for BCODP, which could draw the many loosely connected elements in the movement together in the wake of a major national crusade.

Even as BCDOP was researching its case for ADL, other pressures in the movement were being released. The continued failure of the government to deal with prejudice and discrimination was leading to campaigns of direct action. In 1988 the Campaign for Accessible Transport (CAT) was being planned in London. In 1989 members of the Derbyshire Coalition of Disabled People (DCDP) deliberately broke a pedestrianisation order after a long campaign against it. Later, they said in court (Derbyshire Coalition of Disabled People, 1990) that they normally respected the law, and that they sought:

> neither lenience nor harshness in such judgement as this Court may see fit to make in our case: it is part of our submission that disabled people should accept the same

responsibilities – but also that we should share the same right as our non-disabled fellow citizen . . . We feel we have been unjustly and unnecessarily criminalised by this Order [and that] something as fundamental as access and mobility for disabled people has to be fought for.

With this, the tradition of grinning and bearing unjust laws came to an end. The re-definition of disability as a form of social oppression had, in the last resort, validated the public expression of disabled people's deeply felt anger. Campaigns of direct action escalated between 1990 and 1992 with the arrival of the Campaign to Stop Patronage (CSP), direct action networks at local and national levels, and the setting up of a National Campaign Fund. A vigorous debate ensued about the relationship of these activists to the main body of the disabled people's movement.

This, then, is the most recent stage of the disabled people's movement in Britain. It represents yet another major conscious leap forward. This time the revision of outlook is based on an understanding that the injustice of the multifaceted oppression of disabled people is ultimately as intolerable to society itself as it is to any individual or group within it. When, on 31 January 1992, Alf Morris MP's Civil Rights (Disabled Persons) Bill failed to gain the understanding and support of Parliament at its second reading, it merely confirmed the ongoing nature of the task and the need for the movement to continue growing in strength and unity, and to take a decisive lead in the struggle for social change.

So, what next? Diane Driedger (1989, p. 118) answers that, for DPI, this 'will be told as the future unfolds', and makes the point that the struggle for rights has only just begun. The telling observation on the future of the disabled people's movement, however, comes from Mike Oliver (1990a, p. 93), who sees its ultimate significance in terms of its potential for stimulating a process of ongoing social change and transformation: 'In this process, the disability movement is moving inexorably to the centre of the stage, and its significance lies not in the legacy it will leave behind, but in the new forms of social relations it will be instrumental in creating.'

References

Barnes, C. (1991) *Disabled People in Britain and Discrimination: a Case for Anti-Discrimination Legislation*, Hurst, London.

De Jong, G. (1979) *The Movement for Independent Living: Origins, Ideology and Implications for Disability Research*, University Centre for International Rehabilitation, Michigan State University.

Derbyshire Coalition of Disabled People (1990) *DCDP News*, May.

Driedger, D. (1989) *The Last Civil Rights Movement: Disabled Peoples' International*, Hurst, London.

Finkelstein, V. (1981) 'Disability and the helper–helped relationship: an historical view', in Brechin, A., Liddiard, P. and Swain, J. (eds) *Handicap in a Social World*, Hodder and Stoughton, Sevenoaks/The Open University, Milton Keynes.

Oliver, M. (1990a) 'Book review: *The Last Civil Rights Movement*', *Disability, Handicap and Society*, Vol. 5, No. 1.

Oliver, M. (1990b) *The Politics of Disablement*, Macmillan, London.

Pagel, M. (1988) *On Our Own Behalf: an Introduction to the Self-Organisation of Disabled People*, Greater Manchester Council of Disabled People.

Turner, R.H. (1969) 'The theme of contemporary social movements', *British Journal of Sociology*, December, p. 391.

Union of the Physically Impaired Against Segregation (1976) *Fundamental Principles of Disability*, UPIAS, London.

Union of the Physically Impaired Against Segregation (1981) *Disability Challenge*, No. 1, UPIAS, London.

CONCLUSION

This Reader has presented a collection of papers which focus on the control by disabled people of the services, policies and decision-making which shape and determine their quality of life. Most of the readings are written by disabled people themselves and reflect their own experiences and concerns. The major theme of the Reader has been that disability is not a 'personal tragedy' located within unfortunate individuals, but rather results from the structural and social organisation of society, which presents disabled people with numerous social, structural and economic barriers that deny them the opportunity of full citizenship and equal opportunities. Oppression is a recurrent theme in the analyses of these barriers.

The Reader has shown the many ways in which disabled people have taken the initiative in shaping the meaning of disability and the services and support provided. It is part of a long tradition of literature emanating from the experiences of marginalised groups, including black people and women, as they have struggled for social and political change. We believe that this Reader will make a significant contribution to the growing volume of literature by disabled people as they begin to write their own history, create their own images in literature and art, and develop their own theories of 'disability' which reflect their experiences, interests and concerns. We hope that it will help to shape the attitudes and practices of those who work to help and support disabled people, and to set a framework for future policy and services.

Many issues of central importance to disabled people have been explored and analysed. Alternative models and definitions of disability have been given, concepts such as 'independence' and 'normality' have been subject to critical appraisal, and alternative images of disability have been presented. The psychology of disability, including the pressure to deny its reality, has been addressed, and the benefits of identifying and associating with other disabled people in the struggle for emancipation and equality has been explored. Papers which analyse the marginalised position of black disabled people and the situation of disabled women have also been included, which will help to extend the limited knowledge in these areas.

A major theme of the Reader has been the analysis of barriers which disabled people encounter in terms of education, housing, leisure and employment. Professional practice has been subject to critical analysis and alternative models of support which give disabled people control over their lives have been described. The final section has taken a broad social view of the situation of disabled people. Discrimination, anti-discrimination legislation, citizenship, and the development and achievements of the growing disability movement, as disabled people organise to press for justice and control, are all examined.

Very little is known or documented about the experience of being disabled, indeed the validity of disabled people's experience and lifestyles has only recently been recognised. We believe that this collection of readings will serve as an early but important step on the ladder to discovery. As such it will contribute to the growing collective voice of disabled people in redefining disability, writing their own history and shaping their own future.

Index